John A. Haddock, George Chandler Bragdon

The Thousand Islands of the St. Lawrence River

From Kingston and Cape Vincent to Morristown and Brockville

John A. Haddock, George Chandler Bragdon

The Thousand Islands of the St. Lawrence River
From Kingston and Cape Vincent to Morristown and Brockville

ISBN/EAN: 9783337021566

Printed in Europe, USA, Canada, Australia, Japan

Cover: Foto ©Andreas Hilbeck / pixelio.de

More available books at **www.hansebooks.com**

A SOUVENIR

The Thousand Islands

OF THE

ST. LAWRENCE RIVER

FROM

KINGSTON AND CAPE VINCENT TO MORRISTOWN AND BROCKVILLE

WITH

Their Recorded History from the Earliest Times, their Legends, their Romances, their Fortifications and their Contests

INCLUDING BOTH THE

American and Canadian Channels

PROFUSELY ILLUSTRATED

With Views of Natural Scenery, as well as Pictures of many Summer Villas, Steamers, Fishing Scenes, &c.

Published by

JNO. A. HADDOCK, of Watertown, N. Y.,

A Native of Jefferson County, N. Y.

Under the Patronage of the Thousand Island Club of Alexandria Bay

PRINTED AND BOUND BY THE
WEED-PARSONS PRINTING CO.,
ALBANY, N. Y.

ALEXANDRIA BAY, N. Y.
1895

COMMENDATORY.

OFFICE OF CORNWALL BROS.

ALEXANDRIA BAY, N. Y., October 31, 1894.

Mr. JOHN A. HADDOCK:

Dear Sir — I have heard that you are about preparing an elaborate and highly illustrated history of our river, to be sold as a more worthy Souvenir of our river and islands than has yet appeared. I have for some years felt the want of such a book, many copies of which my sons could sell over their counter here if it could have been procured. Having known you personally many years, I have full faith in your ability and zeal for the preparation of such a work, and I wish you much success and encouragement in your labor, which will, I hope, be remunerative.

Your friend,

ANDREW CORNWALL,

One of the original owners of all the American islands from Round Island to Morristown.

LAW OFFICES OF JAMES C. SPENCER, 280 BROADWAY, NEW YORK.

Mr. JOHN A. HADDOCK, WATERTOWN, N. Y.:

My Dear Sir — Having heard you express your ideas as to a needed book which should suitably illustrate the natural beauties of the Thousand Island Archipelago of the St. Lawrence, with views of leading cottages and sketches of the individuals occupying them, I take pleasure in approving your plan, and do not hesitate, from my knowledge of you personally, to fully believe you will carry out all you undertake in making a book which will be a Souvenir to be treasured by all who can appreciate the grandest river and the most beautiful islands upon the globe. Wishing you great success, I remain,

Very truly yours,

Summer residence,   JAMES C. SPENCER,
MANHATTAN ISLAND,   *Vice-President Thousand Island Club.*
ALEXANDRIA BAY, N. Y.

INTRODUCTORY.

There have been many attempts to depict the Thousand Islands, with their ever-varying, changeful scenery, and the opulence of their later adornment. Some of these efforts have been honest but inefficient, some sporadic and fitful, others resulting only in a poor attempt to make money out of a subject...

COPYRIGHTED, 1895.
ALL RIGHTS RESERVED.

a fair illustration of the progress made up to 1894 in the art of typography and artistic decoration.

In this spirit, then, this Book is issued, in the full belief that it will fill a want which has been felt for the past three years among the intelligent and appreciative class who come annually to this section, the importance of which appears now to be permanently established.

JNO. A. HADDOCK,
WATERTOWN, N. Y.

Address on the River,
"CARE OF CORNWALL BROS.,"
ALEXANDRIA BAY, N. Y.

THE HAPPY ISLANDS.

By George C. Bragdon.

There, where a Thousand Islands sleep,
Come pulsing from Niagara's leap
The blended lakes with tireless sweep —
Vast lakes, which float the grain and ore
Of mighty States from shore to shore,
A thousand billowy miles and more.

'Tis there the centering waters meet
In rush sublime and beauty sweet,
Which we with happy thrills shall greet
We who in fevered towns have sighed
For green and watery spaces wide,
And Nature's murmuring love beside.

Ah, here they are! The river here,
Swift, slow, tumultuous, crystal-clear,
Lapping the islands which uprear
Their rocky heads with crests of trees,
Has sure enchantments to release
The heart, and change its pain to peace.

Hail! River of the Thousand Isles!
Which so enchants and so beguiles
With countless charms and countless wiles
Flow on unpent, forever free
And pauseless to the ocean-sea
Which belts the globe's immensity.

Not there our goal. Here, here we stay
Amid the islands green and gray,
Nor strive, but idly float and play
Along the river's glints and gleams,
And yield to reveries and dreams
With which the quickened fancy teems.

Here where the airs are always pure,
And wave and earth and sky allure,
And whisper, " Let the best endure,"
The wiser thoughts and instincts grow,
Hearts truer feel and surer know,
And kindle to a tenderer glow.

St. Lawrence River, here we rest,
And here we end our wandering quest
To reach the Islands of the Blest,
Where Nature's sweetest sweets abound
Are sacred waters, sacred ground —
The Earthly Paradise is found!

THE THOUSAND ISLANDS.

INTRODUCTORY AND DESCRIPTIVE.

THERE is in North America a mighty river, having its head in remote lakes, which though many in number, are yet so great that one of them is known as the largest body of fresh water on the globe — with a flow as placid and pulseless as the great Pacific itself, yet as swift in places as the average speed of a railway train. Its waters are pure and azure-hued, no matter how many turbid streams attempt to defile them. It is a river that has no freshets nor scarcely any drying up, no matter how great the rain or snow-fall or how severe the drouth on all its thousand miles of drainage or of flow — so grand and yet so lovingly beautiful as to enthral every appreciative soul.

It rises in the great fresh-water sea, and ends in the great Atlantic — some places ten miles wide, at others less than a mile. This great river has never as yet had a respectable history, nor more than an occasional artist to delineate its beauties. It runs for very many miles between two great nations, yet neglected by both, though neither could be as great without it — a river as grand as the La Plata, as picturesque as the Rhine, as pure as the Lakes of Switzerland. Need we say that this wonderful stream is the St. Lawrence, the noblest, purest, most enchanting river of all God's beautiful earth?

This noble stream drains nearly the whole of that vast region lying between the 41st and 49th degrees of north latitude, and the 60th and 93rd parallels of longitude — a region perhaps not as extensive nor as productive as that drained by the mighty Mississippi, yet the flow of water in the St. Lawrence must exceed that in the Mississippi, for the current in the former is rapid, while the latter, except in great freshets, is contented with a medium flow. Rising in $49°$ north latitude, the waters of the St. Lawrence flow down through their many lakes to near the 41st parallel, whence they are impinged towards the north, and at Cape Vincent take an almost northeast course, following that general direction until they reach the great sea — entering it on almost the same meridian of longitude that crosses its remote source in British North America. Why its history has so long remained unwritten, and why this noble river is not more generally known, is perhaps accounted for in part by the fact that the St. Lawrence traverses a region of country remote from the great thoroughfares of the world's commerce or trade. It lies along the boundary line of business. Its banks, to be sure, are dotted here and there with thriving towns and cities, several of considerable importance in the world's traffic, but its grand use is in connecting the great lakes with the ocean. The region through which it passes is one of great interest. The geological formation attracts the attention of the student and the artist. It bears on its face the unmistakable traces of a primeval condition, found nowhere else on our continent, and probably not in more striking beauty anywhere on the face of the globe. Its picturesque windings, pure water, wonderful atmosphere, and great and varied beauty of scenery, are witnessed in such wonderful and lavish profusion nowhere else.

The air is an element of more worth than weight, and exceeds all others in its ability to impart pleasure and comfort, as well as to pain and annoy. Every pleasure or pain is affected by the quality of the air we breathe. The atmosphere has not only to do with our temporal happiness and comfort, but it has very much to do with making character. It has been observed that the inhabitants of high, rugged countries, who breathe the clear, pure air of heaven, are those who come nearest to living the lives of noble freemen. The spirit of liberty and honor is said to inhabit the mountains, while the spirit of dependence, sloth and venality is found in the humid, luxurious low countries; and as man, so nature partakes of that spirit and element which build up and beautify. The air of the St. Lawrence region is one of its greatest attractions. It is pure, clear and invigorating. The early dawn and the evening twilight there are among the loveliest on the globe.

Next to air in importance comes water, the eldest daughter of creation. It was upon the water that the spirit of creation first moved. It is coupled with water that the greatest beauty in nature is found. It is the element that God commanded to bring forth living creatures abundantly; the element without which all creatures on land, as well as those within its folds, must perish. Moses gives it the first place, and justly so, because out of it all things came. Nowhere is there a stream which resembles the St. Lawrence in the particular feature of its purity and the rarefying influences of the atmosphere. Throughout its entire length this great stream has the clearness and purity of a mountain spring, and the water and air combine to make more beautiful and enjoyable those natural attractions in scenery for which it is fast becoming known to the traveler and the world in general. Yet its wonderful breadth of attractiveness, in all its wide range, is even more imperfectly understood.

If the waters of the St. Lawrence are attractive and full of enjoyment and recreation for the pleasure-seeker, its thousands of beautiful islands present pictures grand and sublime — pictures of which the poet-painters have only dreamed. Its romantic and unwritten history is only an attractive field in which facts assume the air of fiction. The romance of American history is an interesting and important harvest, which is fast passing away, and soon will be lost forever, unless garnered into the great treasure-house of the printed page, where it can be preserved for the coming ages. No section of the continent is the scene of events more important and numerous, in our unwritten history, than that through which this great river flows. For it has been the principal artery along which the pulse of civilization throbbed for ages in its struggles to penetrate the unknown region of the inland seas of the far West.

Its civilization is older than that of any other section of the continent. The scenes and struggles on its banks have been nobler, grander and more persistent than those of any other section. Nowhere else can be found such determined and Herculean efforts. Coupled with this, in turn, have come some of the sublimest and grandest examples of Christian faith and forbearance to be found anywhere, for the civilization and conversion of the native North American and the possession of this continent. Almost every village and hamlet — especially of the lower portion of the river—has a history full of stirring records, important in the first settlement of this continent, while the upper St. Lawrence is closely identified with all the leading events of the early history of our own country; and, in addition to this, has an interesting local history, illustrative of the events and trials undergone by a struggling pioneer people for the enjoyment of the priceless boon of Liberty.

To reach back down the line of years past, and gather up the forgotten and almost lost scenes and incidents, and weave about these newly-discovered sources of beauty and popular resources of pleasure the history of early days and discoveries, and preserve it all, embellished by the hand of the artist, for future ages, is not a work of ease, though we have found it a work of pleasure. History will take us back more than fifteen hundred years, and

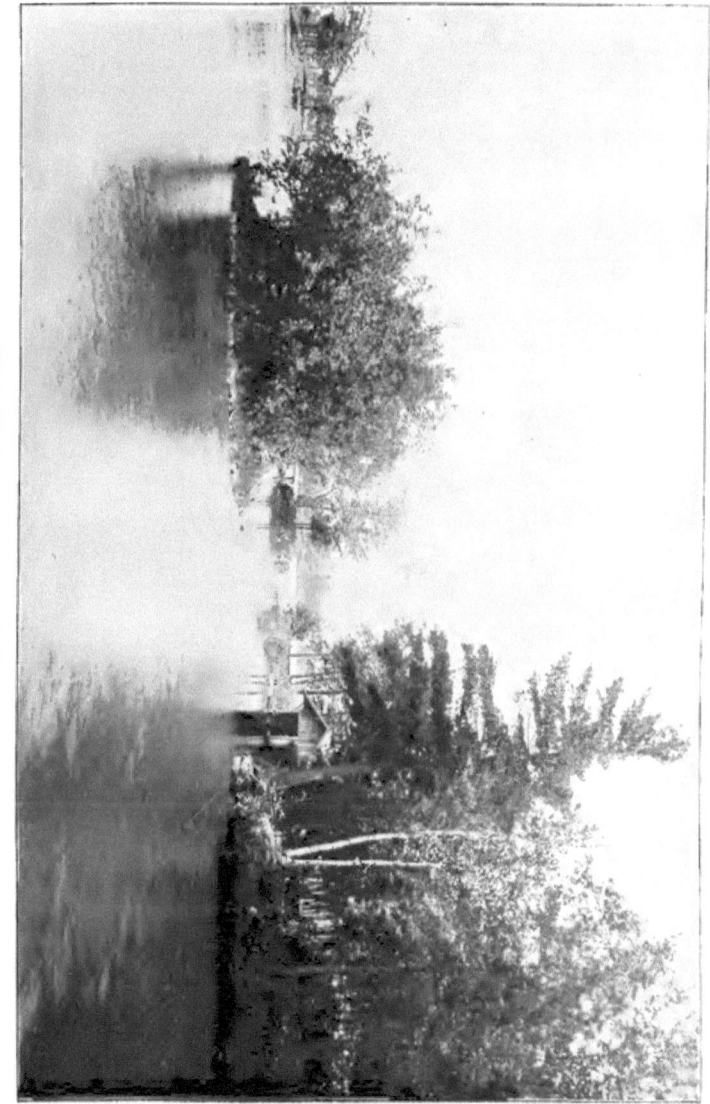

VIEW IN SIVAS FROM PROPERTY OF GEN. BRADLEY WINSLOW.

we find that there are few martyrs in the Church of Rome whose name or fame rests upon a more lasting or better foundation than that of St. Lawrence. And yet in the New World it has found a fame and foundation that shall be admired long ages after the story of his deeds and even the holy church which canonized his bones may have been forgotten. It is gratifying to know that the object of our adoration is so honorably and worthily christened, although in learning this we are reminded of the ceaseless spirit of change written upon all things. St. Lawrence the martyr has become St. Lawrence the river.

The stereotyped falsities of history are very many in America, and they creep upon us with our eyes wide open. They come because legend has taken the place of fact. The writer who would dare seriously to dispute the claim of Columbus to the honor accorded him for nearly three hundred years, would be bold indeed; and yet the position that he was not the discoverer of America has been attempted to be maintained. The Pilgrims landed at Plymouth Rock, and came to found a government where they could enjoy religious freedom and liberty, and open an asylum for the oppressed of all other countries. But long before them there came a colony whose sole purpose was to fish; and the nation they founded has vied with the others, and grown mighty and formidable in wealth and greatness. It seems not altogether unlikely that the American nation may develop characteristics which will be better evidence of its origin and the original purpose of its founders than can be found in the piety or exalted purpose of the Pilgrims. So, everywhere, the great incentive to explore and extend government bounds and influence has been that gain might follow.

As early as 1500, great fleets of British and Norman sailors visited Newfoundland, whose cod-fisheries were even then known throughout the Old World. The coasts of Newfoundland and Labrador were visited many times by these great fleets before any attempt was made at exploring the Gulf of St. Lawrence or the river, even at its mouth. The Spaniards had then begun to seek for treasure on the south west coast of America. Faint glimpses of the great father of waters had gone out to the world, and strange stories came from the Indians of its source and the great lakes beyond. Jesuit missionaries, little by little, dared to penetrate the great unknown, and suffer the cruelties and hardships of life in a wilderness teeming with savage men and beasts. Spain was pushing her researches, and the Old World was filled with reports of strange people and of a strange land. Of course, fiction and romance are never idle, and they clothed the whole in wonderful beauty and decked the New World with gold, precious stones and gems of rarest worth and excellence.

It was under these circumstances that Jacques Cartier, a French sea captain, in 1534, came with two vessels to explore the great river that empties through the Gulf into the Atlantic, which had been known by the Labrador and Newfoundland fishermen for nearly a hundred years. He landed at the mouth of the river in the Spring, and had not proceeded far — in fact, had not entered the river at all — before he became satisfied that the Spaniards had been there before him; and as he progressed further, he found unmistakable evidence that these restless, undaunted explorers had several times visited those shores in search of mines. They had ascended the river some distance, but abandoned the search after amusing themselves by cruel treatment of the innocent natives. It is claimed by some that the name of Canada comes from a corruption of their expression of disgust and disappointment —"Aca-Nada" (here is nothing), which the natives picked up and held on to, without knowing its meaning, for the purpose of designating the place and associating with it the strangers who came. Whatever may be the merit or truth of this story, it has the authority of the oldest and best historian of Canada (Heriot).

Cartier returned to France during the Summer, having accomplished little or nothing by his journeying. The next year he made another voyage to the Gulf, which was almost as barren of results as his first one. He effected a landing on the north entrance of the great river, and called the place St. Nicholas, which name it still bears. He also named a bay on the same coast St. Laurence, for the reason that he entered the bay on the 10th of August — St. Laurence's fast-day. Thence the name has spread the entire length of the river. The Spaniards were the first to explore the river, but by a strange coincidence, a Frenchman names it after a saint of Spanish birth and education.

Cartier passed up the river on this voyage as far as where Montreal is now situated, and there he remained during the Winter, becoming acquainted with the natives, trading with them and studying their habits, customs and language. This point was at that time something of an Indian village, under the name of "Hochelaga." In the Spring he returned to France, and for four years the wars and internal troubles of his own country prevented any further visits or explorations.

About 1542 King Francis First issued letters to Francis de la Roque, Seigneur de Robervale, giving him power of the King over "Canada, Hochelaga, Saguenay, Terre Neuva, Labrador," and other countries or "cities" of the New World. The commission was almost equal to the command to go forth and possess the earth. Six ships embarked in this expedition, Cartier accompanying it as chief captain. A portion of the party settled at Quebec, but the most of those who remained settled at Montreal — Cartier among the number. The vessels returned to France laden with furs which were gathered during the Winter. The next year they came again, and found the little colony in good condition. Cartier then explored the river to the mouth of the Saguenay, and the new scenes could hardly be believed even by those who were in the midst, much less by those who listened to the report of them. This feeling is still shared in a pleasurable degree by those who behold for the first time the scenery of the lower St. Lawrence and its tributaries. A third expedition to Canada was undertaken two years after, under Roberval, but it proved a failure — all the ships being lost, and no survivor was left to tell the story.

The growth of the French colony was very slow, and its history is one of great hardships and privations. The rigorous climate, the bloodthirsty and hostile natives, the great number of wild beasts, all combined to neutralize and circumscribe every effort at happiness, and even a tolerable existence was hardly attainable. Then follow the expeditions of Champlain, who traversed the discoveries of Cartier, and penetrated still farther west, and reached out to the north and south through the tributaries of the great river; and for the first time the exploration of the country was begun in earnest. Companies were formed, and aid and assistance obtained from the French government, and large investments were made by capitalists and speculators. The Indian wars and massacres which followed have scarcely parallels in American history. The great tribes of Algonquins, Hurons and Iroquois roamed at will from the upper Mississippi to the Gulf of St. Lawrence, and began to look with jealous eyes upon the incursions of the white man. The fur-trade began to be the great business of the colonists, and the St. Lawrence river was the thoroughfare by which the tribes from the lake country were enabled to reach Montreal, where they disposed of their stock of skins. It was by this trade that the river was really opened up to the adventurous white man.

The events of these years, and the progress of civilization are interesting; they are the very romance of American history, and pertain to that which is fast becoming the most enjoyable and pleasing portion of our continent in Summer. From the foot of Lake Ontario to Prescott is a continued stream of romance and beauty, which our artist will portray by his camera. Surely the region in Summer is one calculated to make us ask, as we move amid the delights,

"Was it not dropt from heaven?"

Not a breath but bears enchantment; not a cliff but flings on the clear wave some image of delight. Every turn and motion of the boat brings new views, new scenes, new life: scenes that fascinate the eye, and pictures

VIEW IN SEVEN ISLDS., PROPERTY OF GEN. BRADY WINSLOW.

that draw the soul in wondering admiration to the great Artist Divine. Be it ours to muse on such scenes ; ours to glide through them from daybreak till the beautiful night creeps on and broods in solemn stillness over all. Through all the years of life the memory of such scenes last ; they come in dreams, and we revisit them in memory's treasure-house. They draw us nearer the really good and beautiful which we all some day hope to enjoy.

The work in hand is one of importance to Canada and the United States, and is of especial interest to persons who live within the section of country covered by it, as well as to all admirers of American scenery. The scope and design is sufficiently broad to comprehend everything of interest. The picturesque portions are within the limits named, and they are artistic. Views of scenery and of villas alone will make the work of great value. The scenes will not only be new, never before having been presented to the public in this complete form — but the enjoyment and improvement of them by the pleasure-seekers who make the islands their permanent Summer homes, is also a new feature in American Summer-life, and adds very much to the natural beauty. These islands are petty kingdoms, lying in close and friendly proximity to each other — ruled by no power except the wishes, comfort and happiness of those who call them "Home." In the upper St. Lawrence there are over fifteen hundred of these islands. A large portion of them are owned by wealthy persons, many of whom have built upon them fine residences, and laid out tasteful grounds. Within the past few years the improvements in this direction have been very great. One immense camp-meeting enterprise has called into existence hundreds of fine cottages on the largest island, and many desirable residences on the lower end of the same, while every island, during the summer months, seems to bear its portion, if not of permanent Summer-homes, of transient tenting or camping parties. Skiffs and steam yachts being the only means of getting from island to island, or from an island to the main shore, they are of necessity numerous, and handsome and expensive ones are plenty. They move silently about, with fishing or visiting parties, in the day-time ; and when the soft evening air, so peculiar to this region, has settled down, and the beautiful sunset faded out, the different islands will become illuminated ; boats loaded with happy pleasure-seekers glide about among them ; then it is that the search-light expedition gets in its weird work ; the music of bands and of voices floats out upon the pure, clear air, over the placid waters — and the heart cannot but respond in its fullest gladness. Nowhere on earth, away from the silent Adriatic, has the poet's dream of Venice been so fully, rapturously realized. For fully forty miles in the upper St. Lawrence (between Kingston, Cape Vincent and Brockville), where these islands are thickest, the scenery by day is grand and inspiring, while the illuminations, the music, the flashing boats and the festivities make the evenings enchanting.

THE CHAIN OF TITLE.

THE importance of these islands, which form the northwestern boundary of Jefferson county, demands historical consideration distinct and separate from the towns in which they are situated. Cape Vincent, Clayton, Orleans and Alexandria each claim a part of the islands, since they are mapped and described as belonging to the towns which front upon the river opposite. The islands proper really begin at Cape Vincent and Kingston, and extend to Morristown and Brockville, about thirty-eight miles below, and are about 1,500 in number.

The author has been sometimes puzzled what to believe as he listens to diverse statements of the same general facts as related by different individuals. To understand the errors of many such statements, at once demonstrates the unreliability of oral testimony, and shows the importance of serious investigation before making a record for the printed page. It was once believed by many that Wellsley Island was for a time held half-and-half by both Canada and the United States. The inconsistency of such a location of the dividing line between two governments will be apparent to the most casual observer. But under such misinformation there were numerous settlements by Canadians upon that important island, claiming that they were within the limits of their own country. The truth is that in the treaty division of these islands there was no attempt to divide any island. The treaty called for a line running up the "main channel of the St. Lawrence," but when the commissioners came on to locate the line, they found two main channels, both navigable, though the southeast (the American) channel was by far the straightest, and is undoubtedly the main channel of the river at that point; and so the commissioners "gave and took" islands under the treaty, Wellsley Island falling to the United States because so near its main shore, and Wolfe Island going to the Canadians for a similar reason.

The place which this beautiful region holds in American history is second only to that occupied by New England and Plymouth Rock, while the memories and traditions which cluster around it are as thrilling and romantic as are to be found in the new world. Wars, piracy, tragedy and mystery have contributed to its lore. The people of the United States should ever bear in mind that this river was discovered by the Spanish, conquered by the French, again conquered by the English, whose footprints have become indelible. That nation yet controls the whole river for long distances, and is half owner for yet other long distances. It is the grand highway for both Canada, England and America. May it ever remain such.

The St. Lawrence was discovered by Jacques Cartier, the French explorer, in 1535, but he did not proceed further up the stream than to explore the St. Louis rapids above Montreal. There is much uncertainty as to the identity of the white man who first gazed upon the beautiful scene presented by the Thousand Islands. The early discoverers were less interested in scenery than in the practical things which pertained to navigation, trade and travel, and the spreading of Christianity. Champlain, in 1615, beginning at the western end of Lake Ontario, explored that lake and the St. Lawrence to Sorel river, thus passing through the Thousand Island region on to Lake Ontario and the Bay of Quinte.

How or when or by whom the world's attention was first called to this archipelago is certainly a matter of doubt, but certainly at an early date it had impressed itself upon the lover of the grand and beautiful, for at least two centuries ago the French christened it "Les Mille Isles"—"The Thousand Isles." The later and more completely descriptive English name for it is "The Lake of a Thousand Islands." The St. Lawrence has marked the line of separation, and the Thousand Islands have been the scene of some of the important campaigns in four great conflicts between nations. The first was the Indian war between the Algonquins and the Iroquois, which continued many years, with occasional intermissions. The second struggle was between the French and English, and some of its hostile meetings and victories and defeats took place among the islands and on the neighboring shores. In the American Revolutionary war with England, and that between the same forces in 1812, the defense of this locality was of decided importance, but its joint occupancy was settled by the wise men of both countries.

Some of the most exciting incidents of that disgraceful military adventure known as the Patriot War, with its intermittent outbreaks from 1837 to 1839, took place on this part of the river, notably the burning of the Canadian steamer Sir Robert Peel, on Wellsley Island, on the night of May, 29, 1838, and the battle of the Windmill, near Prescott, Ont., November 13, of the same year.

The development and wonderful increase in the value of these islands have been more especially due to influences which have originated at Alexandria Bay. The islands were transferred to the State of New York through the several treaties with the aboriginies, following the same chain of title by which the main shore, from the Hudson to the St. Lawrence, came under the proprietary and governing control of the State. The dividing line between the United States and Canada passes somewhat arbitrarily among the islands, varying in size from a small pile of rocks covered by a few stunted trees, to others quite large — one of them (Wellsley Island) containing nearly 10,000 acres of arable land. This valuable island was conceded to the United States under the treaty with England, negotiated at the close of the war for independence. The State of New York, by patent under its great seal, conveyed the islands to Colonel Elisha Camp, a distinguished citizen of Sackets Harbor, N. Y. In 1845 Azariah Walton and Chesterfield Parsons purchased (not from Col. Camp, but from Yates & McIntyre, of lottery fame, whose title came from Camp), the northwest half of Wellsley Island and "all the islands in the American waters of the river St. Lawrence from the foot of Round Island (near Clayton) to Morristown," a distance of some thirty-five miles. The consideration was $3,000. Eventually the Parsons interest was purchased by Walton, who became sole owner, and continued as such until the firm of Cornwall & Walton was established in 1853, when they purchased nearly the whole of the remaining half of Wellsley Island, and then that firm became sole owner of all these islands, having vested in them all the rights and title originally granted Colonel Camp by the State of New York. To Hon. Andrew Cornwall, for nearly fifty years at Alexandria Bay, and always its devoted friend and advocate, is due the greatest credit for the movement which has developed the Thousand Islands, and he is yet spared to greet each season the great company who come year by year to enjoy the grand river. A brief sketch of his life, as well as his portrait will be appreciated. He is the patriarch of the American side of the upper St. Lawrence.

The value of the islands was quite nominal until they fell under the new firm's control, and even for several years afterward. Eventually there grew up a demand for them, and they were sold low, but with a clause in the conveyance requiring a cottage to be erected within three years. Col. Staples obtained as a free gift the grounds upon which he erected the Thousand Island House. As an indication of the present value of at least one of these islands, it is now made public that $10,000 was offered and refused for an island sold by Cornwall & Walton for $100. The Canadian islands were not, of course, included in the grant to Camp, Yates & McIntyre, or to Cornwall & Walton. A considerable number of these Canadian islands were lately sold by that Government.

A RAINY DAY AT THE ISLANDS.

SUNSHINE and daylight are at their best among these islands. But even a rainy day has its compensations. Then the men stay around the hotels, and devote themselves to the ladies, who are not so much given to fishing as are their escorts. The book that was but lately cast aside for something promising greater zest, is now resumed at the turned-down page, and the promised letter is thought of and leisurely written. The ladies gather upon the verandas of the hotels, and with crocheting and talk and exchange of experiences, pass away the time. Many predictions are made as to the duration of the rain, and with friendly chat, not disguising an occasional yawn, the hour for an early dinner soon arrives, and after that comes the afternoon nap, the early tea and then the pleasures of the evening. Some dance, the young brides and the other bright ones who are very willing to become brides and share in the happiness they watch so intently, these steal away to the darker corners of the verandas, where confidences and an occasional pressure of the hand (possibly a kiss) may be indulged in without too much publicity. So, almost unflaggingly, the day passes away, and John, the oarsman, promising fair weather to-morrow, stillness and sleep creep over the happy company, who are willing to declare that even a rainy day is enjoyable among the Thousand Islands, where the soft outlines of the ever-varying shore are half hidden, half revealed through the rainy mist, as if waiting for the sun's enchanting power to develop their hidden mysteries and reveal their entrancing, restful beauties. This is indeed that "Port of Peace," into which, when once you have sailed your boat, you are glad to stay, and you leave the spot with sad regrets, to be remembered always as the place where the soul is lifted up to God in glad thankfulness that He ever made such a resting spot for His weary children, who, through many pilgrimages in many lands, at last find here a spot that fills the hungry soul with satisfaction.

Now, as to Health.

All who have ever remained here for a week are conscious that after the third or fourth day there is a peculiar change in the system. If you have been troubled with insomnia, it begins to leave you, and natural, restful sleep asserts its sway. You like to sit and rest, your legs become lazy, and you are not at all anxious for long walks. The hotel's shady settees have become matters for consideration; you conclude, after much argument, which is the easiest one, and best protected from the sun. You yawn often, and wonder what has come over you. You can lay down and take a nap at almost any hour after 10 A. M. You languidly push aside the newspaper whose leaders only last week were read with the most intense interest. The spirit of Rest creeps upon you almost unawares, for your system is being fed upon the ozone of this health-giving spot. The very air becomes an active ally in behalf of your overworked nerves, and before you are aware of it, you begin to fill up with reserve force, that shall stand you in good stead in the city's heat and push.

These beneficial influences are within the reach of all. There are now hotels and boarding-houses at Alexandria Bay, Thousand Island Park, Clayton, Cape Vincent, Westminster Park, Round Island, and at many other resorts, where the poor man can find entertainment within his means, and the rich man, too (much as he is criticised), may also find comforts adapted to his desires. In former times there were only the more expensive resorts, and that kept away the middle-class of summer tourists. That is all changed now, and every condition except the chronically poor can find boarding houses within their means. It will not be long before this great national Vacation Park, 38 miles long, will be eagerly sought by all conditions of society, from the skilled mechanic to the millionaire.

The Value of Rest.

Many people make the mistake of supposing that a summer vacation is not complete unless devoted to various sorts of physical exercise. It seems to be taken for granted that the energies of body and mind cannot be recuperated except by trips and diversions that call for muscular effort. Summer resorts that do not offer such opportunities are often thought to be wanting in proper attractions. There is another class of people, such as artists, teachers and clergymen, who seek places where they may pursue their usual work amid new surroundings. Under suitable restrictions perhaps no harm comes from this. Change of air and of diet are beneficial, and new faces and new scenery tend to break up the monotony of all toil and care. There are not enough people, however, who appreciate the value of a period of absolute rest, an entire cessation from activity. Just as land is better for being allowed to lie fallow, the physical and mental energies of man are better for being allowed to repose for a time. Nothing is lost by permitting mind and body each year to indulge thus in a few days' slumber. A short season spent in lounging about the Thousand Islands, watching the shifting water, or in idling in the woods and fields, with their fresh odors and changing views of hill and dale, light and shade, island and shore, as they intermingle and then separate, will often fill the frame with new vigor

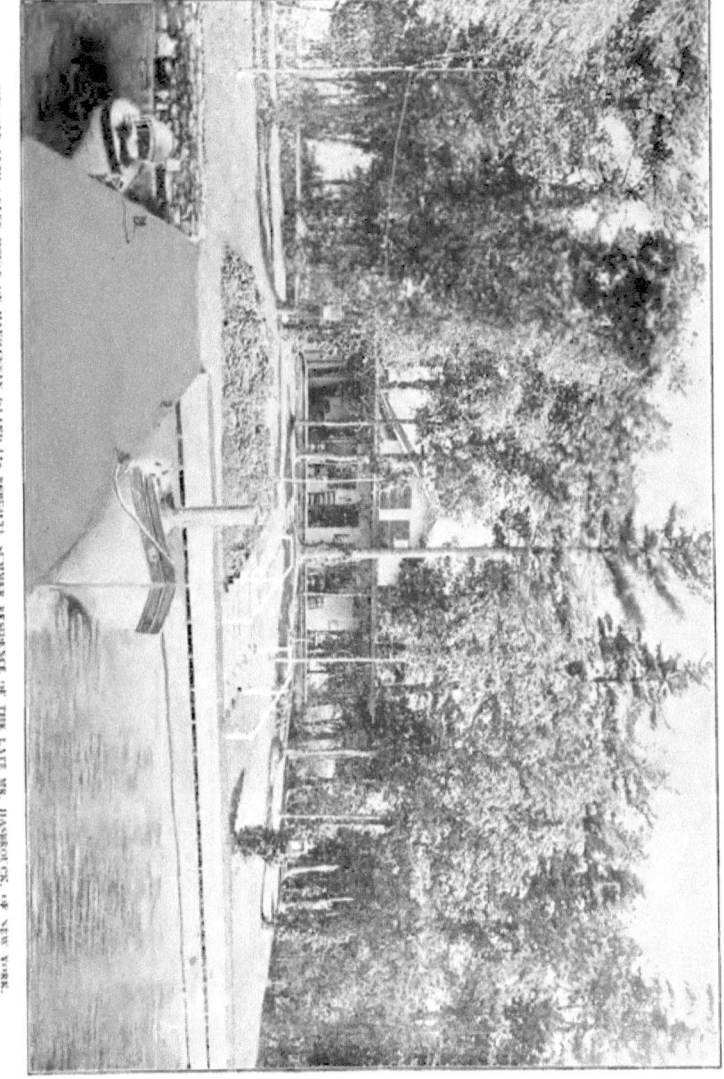

THE OLD SETH GREEN HOUSE ON MANHATTAN ISLAND (AS REPAIRED), SUMMER RESIDENCE OF THE LATE MR. HASBROUCK, OF NEW YORK.

HON. ELDRIDGE G. MERICK, OF CLAYTON,
ONE OF THE PIONEERS OF THAT TOWN, AND ONCE THE LARGEST VESSEL OWNER
ON THE UPPER RIVER.

and the mind with new impressions. Particularly is such a change beneficial when the thermometer is up among the nineties. Then, if ever, the energies should be carefully husbanded. The English philosopher who asserted that Americans work too hard and take too little leisure, stated a truth which intelligent foreign visitors have frequently noted. This warning has a special timeliness just at present, and the seeker after a spot where the very soul may rest will find his El Dorado among the Thousand Islands.

HON. ELDRIDGE G. MERICK.

It is fortunate for our history that we are able to present to our readers, from an entirely reliable source, a very circumstantial and accurate record of the life of one of the great river's most widely known, distinguished and able denizens, who rose from small beginnings to the very first rank in business and in citizenship. Indeed, the writer remembers no man in Jefferson county who was superior to Mr. Merick. There were two or three, Hon. Orville Hungerford, Hon. C. B. Hoard, and perhaps Gen. Wm H. Angel, who stood as high in probity and faithfulness to friends and to society, and were as patriotic and high minded as Mr. Merick, but he had no " superior " in his adopted county, nor in Northern New York, nor on the river.

He was the fifth child in a family of nine children, six boys and three girls, and was born March 6, 1802, in Colchester, Delaware county, N. Y., from which place he moved with the family to Sherburne, Chenango county, at the age of about four years. The section to which the family removed was almost an unbroken wilderness, with few inhabitants and no schools or opportunity for obtaining an education. The principal amusement for a boy of his age was picking up the brush and burning it, preparing the land for crops. The first school he attended was at the age of nine. The school held for only four months. At the end of the four months he was able to read a newspaper fairly well. He continued at home, himself and brother carrying on the farm, until eleven, at which time he went to live with a man named Clark. That family had no children, and Eldridge was treated as their own child. Mr. Clark had a small farm on the Chenango river, which this boy carried on principally, with occasionally a little help from the owner. His business, after getting through with the work of the farm in the fall, was to chop and put up ten cords of wood before going to school the first year, increasing it five cords each year until he got twenty-five cords, which was all that was needed for the family. Eldridge attended the country school from three to four months each winter, until seventeen years of age, and then he commenced teaching. When Mr. Clark went to St. Lawrence county in 1820, young Merick went with him, remaining there until twenty-one years of age.

Arriving at majority, the people with whom he lived not being in a situation to do anything for him, he found it necessary to shift for himself. His first effort was a contract for building a stone wall at Russell, St. Lawrence county, after which he went to Watertown, Jefferson county, working there for several months, and delivered the material for the old stone Presbyterian church; thence to Sackets Harbor, to work for Festus Clark, a brother of his former employer, as clerk in a small store. Remaining there for a short time, he went to Depauville, in the same capacity, with Stephen Johnson, who had a country store, and was also engaged in the lumber business for the Quebec market.

He remained with Mr. Johnson two years, superintending his lumber business largely, and while there became acquainted with Mr. Jesse Smith, who had been furnishing Mr. Johnson with means to carry on his lumber business. Mr. Johnson was unfortunate in business and failed at the end of two years, and was sold out by the sheriff, which sale was attended by Mr. Smith as a creditor, and knowing it threw young Merick out of employment, he offered him a situation, which was gladly accepted. This was about 1826. Mr. Smith was doing a very large mercantile and manufacturing business for those times. After being with him for a little over a year, he sent Mr. Merick with a stock of goods to Perch River, and the following Summer sent him to Quebec to look after his lumbering interests, and in the Fall of the same year offered him a partnership and an interest in the business, which was accepted, and so young Merick became the manager. The business developed into a pretty large one, devoted principally to lumber designed for the Quebec market, and also the building and running of vessels. The timber and staves, which were the principal business, were obtained about the head of Lake Ontario and Lake Erie, extending into Lake Huron, and were transported by vessels across the lakes to Clayton, on the St. Lawrence, and there made into rafts for transportation to Quebec. Of these rafts there were several made up every year, amounting (according to their size) to $40,000 or $50,000 each. These rafts had to be made very strong to run the rapids of the river, seven or eight in number. Each stick of oak timber was tied up with large oak wisps, forming what was called a dram, and from ten to twenty or thirty drams in a raft. The rafts were propelled by a number of small sails, but usually went but little faster than the current. At the rapids a pilot and extra men were taken to conduct the raft through the rapids ; a pilot for each dram or section, the raft being divided into several sections for running the rapids. Sometimes a large raft required from 200 to 300 men. Frequently they would get broken up in the rapids and run ashore, attended with considerable loss and expense in saving the pieces. Arriving at Quebec, they were usually sold on from two to six months' time, but the percentage of loss by bad debts was very small. Better facilities were needed for transporting this square oak timber, and a ship yard was established at Clayton. After Mr. Smith removed to Ohio, Mr. Merick continued the timber trade, adding forwarding and grain business, associating with Messrs. Fowler and Esselstyn.

The business in the winter was arranging and superintending the shipments, selecting the timber in the country, and getting it forwarded for shipping, and in building vessels, of which the firm generally had one or more on the stocks. They built, with one or two exceptions, all the steamboats forming the justly celebrated line on Lake Ontario and the River St. Lawrence, on the American side.

The "Reindeer" fleet, which at one time numbered fourteen vessels, were built at his Clayton yard ; also three steamers of the Ontario Navigation Company, all of them having his careful supervision.

With D. N. Barney & Co., he built, about 1844, the steamer Empire, to run between Buffalo and Chicago. Her increased tonnage and decks attracted much attention, with many prophecies of failure, but she proved a success and was the vanguard of the fine fleet of lake transports.

When the Grand Trunk Railroad was built, however, following up the St. Lawrence and Lake Ontario, the competition ruined the business of these passenger steamers. The line ceased to be remunerative, and the boats were sold, some to go to Montreal ; one went to Charlestown, S. C., and afterwards was engaged in the rebel service in the war of the rebellion.

He had previously established a house in Cleveland, one in Oswego and one in Buffalo, the object being to furnish business for the vessels on the lakes. Each additional facility only showed the necessity of still further facilities. The firm decided to build a large flouring mill in Oswego, which had the largest capacity of any mill in the country at that time, turning out from 1,000 to 1,200 barrels a day, and having thirteen runs of stone.

He was interested in railroad building in Ohio, but it was before the days of floating bonds and watering stocks, but not of incompetent, reckless superintendents. The enterprise was a failure. But through their railroad enterprise the firm was enabled not only to control the wheat over the road and to market by vessels, but for the mill at Oswego. During the war, or at the close, the mill was making very large profits, from $1 to $2 a barrel, but unfortunately it took fire and burned down, with a large stock of grain and flour on hand. The loss was pretty well protected by insurance, but the profit which they would have made if the mill had not burned down, could not have been provided for. The actual loss was nearly $150,000.

Perhaps his first and greatest financial loss was through the failure of a large commission house (Suydam, Sage & Co.) in New York, in 1850. But that loss brought generous and prompt proffers of aid from business men in Watertown, Kingston and Quebec, which were long after most gratefully remembered. The great financial disasters of 1857 and 1873 also brought misfortune to him, as well as to many others. He was greatly helped in all these reverses by the confidence that his creditors had in his ability and strict integrity, steadily refusing compromises when offered. He paid dollar for dollar, though often at great sacrifice of property. For many years Mr. Merick was president of the Sackets Harbor Bank, relinquishing the position on leaving Jefferson county.

For many years he found Clayton was too much at one side for the prompt and successful management and oversight of his varied interests. He was strongly attached to the people of Jefferson county and the beautiful St. Lawrence, and it was with many regrets that he left his old friends and pleasant home, with all the associations of youth and manhood, to make a home, in 1859, at the more central point, Detroit. Here he took an honored position among the business men of the city, many of whom sought advice from him, glad to profit by his large experience. In addition to other business, he bought an interest in the Detroit Dry Dock Company for the firm of Merick, Esselstyn & Co. John Owen, Gordon Campbell and Merick, Fowler & Esselstyn each owned one-third of the Dry Dock stock—the total stock being $300,000.

Mr. John Fowler, a partner of the firm of Merick, Fowler & Esselstyn, died in May, 1879. The surviving partners purchased his interest in the business, and continued under the name of Merick, Esselstyn & Co.

After the failure of 1873, Mr. Merick was too old a man to again do business with his former confidence and success.

In 1829 Mr. Merick married Miss Jane C. Fowler. She died in 1881, leaving four surviving children — all of whom have proven useful and honored members of society.

Mrs. Cyrus McCormick, who was Mr. Merick's niece, was the daughter of Melzar Fowler, born at Brownville, N. Y., and survives her distinguished husband, who was that C. H. McCormick, so long the leader in manufacturing reapers for the harvest field, whose machines have gone into all lands. He was the one to introduce that inestimably valuable machine into England, as is so well spoken of in Haddock's History.

Mr. Merick was very early interested in the temperance movement. It had been the custom to put whisky among the necessary stores for every raft and vessel. He very soon realized the injury it was doing, made liquor a contraband article, supplied tea and coffee instead, and made it his personal duty to visit cabin and forecastle, to confiscate and throw overboard any spirits smuggled on board.

The sailors who manned his vessels came from the adjacent farms and villages. Young men, beginning as cabin boys, or before the mast, were frequently advanced as they proved worthy and capable to be mates, captains and shareholders, and all looked up to him as to a personal friend and father.

One who had sailed for him thirty-five years wrote: "The accounts for these years aggregated more than half a million of dollars, but never an error to the value of a cent in his books, never a sour look or unkind word. I was always treated more as an equal than as a servant." Another who served him forty years said: "I have received from him nothing but kindness. When in need of aid or counsel his generous heart always responded to my wants. In prosperity and adversity, sunshine and storm, he was always true to principle, and true to himself as a man, ever following the Golden Rule."

Mr. Merick had no political aspirations, beyond wishing to do the best possible for his own township, of which he was several times supervisor. He was a strong Whig, and gave money, time and influence to promote the interests of that party. Twice he was nominated for Congress, and ran ahead of his ticket; once both parties wished to unite upon him as their candidate, but his business interests would not permit him to accept the nomination. He was also one of the Electoral College, voting for President William H. Harrison.

The title of judge was given him when he was appointed associate judge of Jefferson county, but he felt that it rightfully belonged only to a man of legal training and ability.

The Patriot War of 1837-38 caused much trouble and anxiety all along the border, and brought together many of the best men of Northern New York and Canada to council together and take such measures as would insure peace.

One of the Canadian members of that committee of arbitration wrote: "How much the high character and the confidence inspired by your father in Canada, assisted in allaying the irritation which existed on both sides of the line. To him many misguided men owe their deliverance from extreme peril. I well remember the effect upon my own mind, not a little exasperated at the time, by his explanations as to the sincere, but mistaken views which induced many good and worthy people to engage in or extend aid to what they suppose to be a movement in assisting the oppressed."

Mr. Merick, deploring his own inability to obtain a collegiate education, was ready to aid young men with such aspirations. The success of many business men was owing to the counsel and substantial aid he gave. Academies, colleges, churches, public and private charities were cheerfully aided by him as "the Lord prospered him."

His noble, courtly bearing, his unassuming manner, his thoughtfulness, tenderness and benevolence, his faithfulness and integrity make a rich legacy to children and children's children.

It had always been his thought that a business man should keep at work till the end of life. In the winter of 1887-88, realizing from his advanced years that his strength was fast failing, he decided to sell the remaining vessels of the fleet. Friday, February 10, 1888, the contract was made for selling the last one. Saturday, February 11, the papers were to be signed. He tarried a little in the morning, perhaps not quite as well as usual, after a somewhat restless night — his mind no doubt busy with reminiscences of the past, and saddened by the change of affairs. The mail brought news from absent loved ones. While talking with his daughter, sitting beside him, of the good tidings received, his head dropped, one sigh was given, "the silver cord was loosed," "the golden bowl was broken,"— he had gone from his work to his rest and his reward.

Thus passed away, after an honorable and a useful life, one of the most widely-known and justly-honored of the river men, who came to man's estate in Jefferson county, and spent the flower of his life there. His death occurred at Detroit, February 11, 1888, in his 86th year.

Mr. Merick and wife reared a family of four children. They were:

MARIA D., wife of Isaac L. Lyon, a native of Ogdensburg, N. Y. They reside at Redlands, Cal.

ERMINA G. MERICK, wife of E. J. Carrington, of Fulton, N. Y. They reside at Detroit, Mich.

MELZAR F. MERICK, died March 28, 1893. His wife was Mary Whittlesey, of Danbury, Conn.

JEANNIE C., wife of G. N. Chaffee, of Detroit, Mich., which is their home.

Mr. Merick was in many respects a peculiarly able man, and should be spoken of apart from his many business enterprises. Judgment was the leading quality of his mind. To strangers he appeared reserved, the result of his native modesty, and not the outgrowth of any feeling of superiority or of self-elation.

PIAZZA OF JUDGE SPENCER'S HOUSE, OVERLOOKING THE RIVER.

His soul was too great and his judgment too solid for any such folly as that. He was eminently democratic, simple in his manners and his tastes, as have been all the really great men the writer has encountered. Mr. Merick was not a sharer in the command of armies, nor is it probable that he ever knew what it was to be thrilled by a bugle call or beat of drum; yet he intensely appreciated the struggle endured by the Union armies, whose perils he would surely have shared had he been of suitable age. He was a patriot in the highest sense of that term. Amidst all the duties of his exacting business, he was a consistent Christian; the traveling Methodist minister always found a welcome at his fireside, both from him and his amiable wife, a fact the writer has heard the late Rev. Gardner Baker speak of with grateful tears. Mr. Merick's unostentatious and democratic ways made him life-long friends, for his manner invited confidence, and confidence in him meant safety. Children and animals never shunned his society, for they intuitively perceived his gentleness under his greatness. Viewed in any light, as a man of affairs, the possessor and dispenser of large wealth, as the unostentatious but ever vigilant citizen of a free country, or as the sincere Christian, he possessed so many excellencies that he fell but little short of earthly perfection. He left a memory in Jefferson county that remains peculiarly sweet, and entirely untarnished. And it is fitting to hold up such a character to the admiration of the youth who come after him, as an evidence that the age in which he lived was not altogether one of greed and money-getting, but was adorned now and then by souls as grand as can be found in the records of any people. And so Eldridge G. Merick passes into history as one of the very ablest and best of his time.

HON. ANDREW CORNWALL.

ANDREW CORNWALL, the ancestor of Andrew Cornwall of Alexandria Bay, emigrated to this country from England with his family, somewhere about 1710, and settled in Old Chatham, Conn. (now Portland), where three generations of the same name lived and died. The third Andrew Cornwall, grandfather of our subject, was a soldier in the Revolutionary War, and died after the close of the war, from a wound received at Bennington.

Andrew Cornwall, the father of our subject, with two brothers, William and Ancil, left Connecticut about 1800, and came to what at that time was called the Far West, or Genesee country. Their first stop was at what is now the city of Rochester, where there was a small settlement; but thinking it was not a good place to locate, they went to what is now Pultneyville, Wayne county, N. Y., where there was another small settlement with a saw mill and grist mill. Here they located and married, and here our subject was born March 25, 1814. After attending the district school winters, and working on the farm summers, until thirteen years old, he entered the country store of John Reynolds, and continued in his employ for thirteen years as clerk and book-keeper. His health failing him from a too close application to business, he purchased a small vessel and went on the lakes as a sailor. After three years of this business, his health being fully restored, he sold his vessel and left the water. In January, 1843, he was married to Mary C. Calhoon. She was a daughter of Capt. Calhoon, of Williamson, Wayne county, who was a pensioner of the War of the Revolution, and a captain in the war of 1812.

In July, 1844, he moved to Redwood, N. Y., and entered the employ of DeZeng & Burlingame, manufacturers of glass. He was in charge of their store for two and a half years. In November 1846, at the solicitation of Azariah Walton, he moved to Alexandria Bay, and took an interest in the firm of L. A. Walton & Co., which continued until 1853, when L. A. Walton died. A new firm was then organized, under the name of Cornwall & Walton (John F. Walton being the junior partner), which partnership continued until April 1, 1877, when both Cornwall and Walton retired from business, and the firm of Cornwall Brothers was established, consisting of the four sons of Andrew Cornwall, viz.: Andrew C., Charles W., John L., and Harvey A. This firm is still in business, and very popular, dealing in everything required in a country store.

Andrew Cornwall was supervisor from 1852 to 1856, and again from 1861 to 1865. Being a war Democrat, he was made a member of the war committee of the county, though the board was largely Republican. He served the committee faithfully in recruiting and filling the quotas of his own town and the county. In 1867 he was nominated by his party for member of Assembly, and although his competitor was elected the year previous by a large majority, Mr. Cornwall was successful. While in the Legislature of 1868 he was a member of the Committees of Ways and Means, of the Manufacture of Salt, and of the Sub-committee of the Whole. In 1868 he was a candidate for Congress against Hon. A. H. Laflin; his party being largely in the minority he was defeated by a very small majority, though he could have been elected if his friends had had ten more days for work.

In 1845 Azariah Walton bought of Henry Yates, of the well-known firm of Yates & McIntyre, of New York city, the north half of Wellsley Island, and all the small islands in the river St. Lawrence in American waters, from Round Island, in Clayton, to the village of Morristown, St. Lawrence county. At his death, the firm of Cornwall & Walton bought them from his estate, for the timber, and for many years they cut steamboat wood from them, some years getting as high as 16,000 cords. After the wood was mostly cut off, the larger ones were sold for farms. In 1860 wood began to give way to coal, and they determined to sell their lands at a nominal price to induce people to build summer homes, and thus make the St. Lawrence river a famous watering place, in which plan they succeeded to a remarkable extent, as is apparent to-day.

Mr. Cornwall commenced his business career with very limited means, but with a determination to succeed. With close attention to every detail, and a constant care that no debt should be made that could not be met when due, and no unnecessary expense incurred, he has succeeded in his determination to attain a reasonable competency.

He has never been an ostentatious man, though in business matters he has always been energetic and prompt, exacting from others only what he would himself do if in their place. The example of such a life is a benefit to any community.

Mrs. Cornwall died August 13, 1890, after she had seen her four sons located in business at her home for thirteen years, and enjoyed her grandchildren playing about her knees, and their father the most useful man on the river.

HON. JAMES C. SPENCER,

Ex-Judge New York City Superior Court, is another of the men who have done much to embellish nature. An extended account of his lovely property, "Manhattan," may be found elsewhere. He is a native of Fort Covington, Franklin county, N. Y. His father, the late Judge James B. Spencer, was one of the early settlers of Franklin county, and was a prominent and respected citizen and recognized political leader in the northern part of the State, having held many important positions, including that of Judge and Representative in the State and National Legislatures. He also distinguished himself in the War of 1812, participating actively in the important engagements of that contest, including the battle of Plattsburg. In politics he was a Democrat of the Jefferson, Madison, and Jackson school. He was the personal friend and colleague of Silas Wright, and was recognized and appreciated by that great man and other prominent Democrats of the State of New York, as an intelligent and reliable political coadjutor, in the struggles of more than

a quarter of a century to secure and perpetuate Democratic ascendancy in the State. He also enjoyed the confidence and esteem of all his fellow-citizens who knew him, without regard to political differences. He died in the year 1848, at the age of sixty-eight.

This branch of the Spencer family and that represented by the late Chief Justice Ambrose Spencer, and his son, Honorable John C. Spencer, were kindred, and claim a common ancestry. The family emigrated to New York from Connecticut, their original place of settlement in the New World, springing from an English ancestor, William Spencer, who came to Cambridge, Mass., before or early in the year 1631.

It appears that he returned to or visited England afterwards, for he married his wife, Alice, in that country about the year 1633. He was again a resident and a prominent man in Cambridge in 1634-5, and was afterwards one of the first settlers in Hartford, Conn. He was the eldest of three brothers, all of whom were among the early settlers of Hartford.

The family of the present Judge Spencer, on the maternal side, were purely Irish. His grandfather emigrated to this country from Ireland prior to the American Revolution, and served his adopted country as a soldier during the War of Independence.

Judge Spencer, before he had fully attained manhood, was thrown upon his own resources, and acquired his education and profession mainly by his own exertions. He commenced the practice of law in 1850, in his native county, and soon became popular and respected in his profession.

In 1854, he removed to Ogdensburg, St. Lawrence county, and, with judge William C. Brown, formed the legal firm of Brown & Spencer, which for many years enjoyed a successful and profitable practice in the courts of Northern New York. In 1857 he was appointed United States District Attorney for the Northern District of New York.

The performance of the duties of that office extended his professional acquaintance into nearly every county of the State. After the expiration of his term of office, he removed to the city of New York and entered upon the practice of his profession in that city. His energy and industry, added to his former professional reputation in the State, soon brought him clients and a very successful business.

In 1867, he entered into partnership with Hon. Charles A. Rapallo and other legal gentlemen, under the firm name of Rapallo & Spencer, which became familiar to the public and in the courts as associated with some of the most important causes of the day, including the famous Erie controversy and other equally important litigations connected with railroad and steamship companies. The existence of that firm terminated with the election of its senior members to the bench — Mr. Rapallo to the Court of Appeals, and Mr. Spencer to the Superior Court of New York. He was a candidate at a later day for reëlection as judge, but was defeated by a small majority.

On his retirement from the bench and return to the active practice of his profession in New York city, the Judge was heartily welcomed, and his old clients renewed their allegiance. As years have worn away he has become more attached to his Manhattan Island (see description elsewhere), and there he spends much of each summer, a practice dating back for twenty years. He has improved and beautified every thing he has touched, and is known as a liberal, progressive gentleman, taking a deep and healthy interest in all that relates to the St. Lawrence and the improvement of its Islands. Such men become, in a sense, public benefactors, and their memory should not die for want of proper recognition, nor their example be lost upon posterity.

CANADA'S WEST POINT.

[SEE VIEW OF KINGSTON HEREWITH]

THE ROYAL MILITARY COLLEGE AT KINGSTON.

BY J. JONES BELL, M. A.

WITH a frontier extending across a continent, bordering on a nation from which several hostile raids on behalf of "Irish independence" have taken place, and with a half-breed and Indian population in her own north-west, which has on two occasions broken out into open rebellion, Canada finds it necessary to maintain the nucleus of a military force, which shall be available on short notice to defend her frontier or to put down rebellion. She cannot afford to maintain a standing army, but she has three batteries of artillery on permanent service and a cavalry school, four infantry schools and one mounted-infantry school, at which the officers and non-commissioned officers of the Volunteer Militia may receive such a training as will fit them to take command and give instruction to the volunteers, who, taken from the field or workshop, would otherwise be wholly untrained and undisciplined.

But while her volunteers have given a good account of themselves when occasion called them into active service, and while her schools of military instruction have been the means of placing good officers at their head, it was felt that something more was needed to complete the system, and accordingly the Parliament of Canada, in 1874, passed an act authorizing the establishment of a Royal Military College "for the purpose," as the act states, "of imparting a complete education in all branches of military tactics, fortification, engineering and general scientific knowledge in subjects connected with and necessary to a thorough knowledge of the military profession, and for qualifying officers for command and for staff appointments."

In selecting a site for the college the government naturally turned its eyes to three places which were specially adapted for the purpose by virtue of their historical associations and the possession of extensive fortifications which might be utilized for technical training. These were Halifax, Quebec and Kingston. The latter was ultimately chosen, for, in addition to being the most central, it possessed certain buildings which could be utilized.

After the conquest of Canada, Kingston, the site of Fort Frontenac, built in 1673 by the French commander after whom it was named, became a military post of great importance. During the war of 1812 it was the British naval station for the lakes. A dockyard was established on a low promontory which juts out between the Cataraqui river and a small inlet of the St. Lawrence called Navy Bay. At this dockyard Sir James Yeo built his fleet for Lake Ontario. After the war the dockyard was dismantled, but a large three-story stone building remained, known as the Stone Frigate, which had been occupied by the marines. This, with a large blacksmith shop close by, was utilized for the college. [See building at left center of picture.]

In 1876 the first classes were opened, eighteen cadets being admitted. The staff consisted of a commandant, a captain and three professors. As the classes grew, more accom-

BULL NEVIS'S RESIDENCE, HARLEM, 126TH AVENUE OF MANHATTAN.

modation was required, and a large building, of the grey limestone for which Kingston is famous, was added. It contains offices, reading and mess rooms, library, class rooms, laboratory, hospital and kitchen. The Stone Frigate became a dormitory, and the blacksmith shop was converted into a well-equipped gymnasium.

The main building faces a spacious parade ground, with tennis lawn and cricket ground, and opposite, on the point, is Fort Frederick, a battery which guards the entrance to the harbor, with a martello tower at its apex.

Though modeled after Woolwich, the college is intended to give the cadets a training which will fit them for civil as well as military life. The course, which is four years, though provision is made for a two years' course in certain subjects, embraces English, French, drawing, mathematics and mechanics, engineering, surveying, fortification, architecture, astronomy, chemistry, geology, mineralogy, physics, electricity, tactics and strategy, signaling, military law and administration, military drill, gymnastics, fencing, swimming and riding. A few of these subjects are voluntary, but most of them are obligatory. A rigorous examination has to be passed by candidates for entrance, and if more reach the minimum than can be admitted — two from each of the twelve military districts into which Canada is divided — those who make the highest number of marks are given the preference. The age of admission is from fifteen to nineteen.

The military staff consists of a commandant, staff adjutant and seven professors and instructors, four of whom are graduates of the college, and two of the latter hold commissions in the regular army. Five of the staff are officers of the active list of the imperial army, lent to the college for a five years' term, at the close of which they are required to rejoin their command. Two are officers of the retired list. There is a civil staff of five, holding permanent appointments from the government. The presence of imperial officers gives a standing to the institution which it would not otherwise possess, and helps the proper training of those of the cadets who are destined for commissions in the regular army. The government was fortunate in the choice of the first commandant, Col. Hewitt of the Royal Engineers, who, in addition to being an accomplished scholar and a good soldier, was possessed of great tact and energy, and knew Canada from former service. To his skill is due in large measure the success which attended the college from its very outset, and his guiding hand directed it through the difficulties which invariably attend the early career of a new institution, which, in this case, was to a large extent an experiment. Having completed his term he returned in 1886 to Plymouth, and was succeeded by Col. Oliver of the Royal Artillery, who had been professor of surveying and astronomy from the beginning, and who proved himself to be a worthy successor. The present head of the institution is Maj.-Gen. Cameron, late of the Royal Artillery.

Sir Frederick Middleton, now retired from the command of the Canadian forces, took a deep interest, officially and personally, in the college, and during its early days helped it with counsel and advice, which his experience at Sandhurst well qualified him to give. The general officer commanding the militia is ex-officio president of the college.

The entrance examinations are held in June at the headquarters of each military district, and the twenty-four successful candidates report themselves at the opening of the term the following September. The first week is spent in being uniformed and drilled into some kind of form. The second week the old cadets return, and the garrison settles down to hard work. The daily routine embraces drill and class parades, study and other duties. From reveille to tattoo, with the exception of two hours — from four to six, during which he is free — the cadet is under the eye of authority in the class or lecture room or on parade. There is none of that loitering which so often takes place at civil colleges, none of that individual liberty which often means license. The cadet has, however, two half holidays, on Wednesday and Saturday, when he may go out on pass till eleven o'clock, or with extra leave till one. Balls and parties in Kingston are timed for these days, for the cadet, with his gay scarlet uniform, is an important factor in the social world. While attending the college the cadets are of course subject to the Queen's Regulations, the Army Act, the Militia Act, and such other rules and regulations as Her Majesty's troops are subject to.

The physical training is excellent. SERGT.- MAJOR MORGAN, of the Scots Guards, presides over this department, and well qualified he is to fill the position. Cadets who pass four years under his instruction come out with deep chests and erect figures, and show what a thorough physical training can accomplish.

One of the rewards of good conduct is promotion to the rank of non-commissioned officer, the commandant having authority to appoint such from among those best qualified. Proud is he who is invested with the chevrons, or given the right to wear the sergeant's sash.

But while subject to strict discipline the cadets have opportunities to cultivate their social qualities. One of the events of the season is the annual sports, which take place in September. The campus is alive with carriages and pedestrians, while pretty girls, with their chaperons, form the center of groups engaged in animated conversation, or watching with interest the various competitions of speed and skill. Races, jumping competitions and steeplechases follow each other in quick succession, while the tug of war between the right and left wings creates almost as such interest as the struggle on the Isis between the college eights. The games over, all adjourn to the gymnasium, where the prizes, more substantial than the crown of ivy at the Olympic games, are distributed to the victors. Tea and an impromptu dance follow in the college halls.

A ball is given at Christmas by the staff and cadets, and a yet more elaborate entertainment of similar character at the close of the college year in June. On closing day a series of field manœuvers takes place, with blowing up of imaginary fortifications and fleets, and an exhibition of drill and bayonet exercise, after which the results of the examinations are announced, the prizes distributed, and the session brought to a termination. The governor-general, the minister of militia, or someone else high in authority, is secured, if possible, to distribute the prizes and make a speech. Four commissions, one each in the engineers. artillery, cavalry and infantry branches of the imperial service, are available, the cadets who stand highest on the honor roll, if otherwise eligible, being entitled to them in the order named. The first two are eagerly sought, the third generally goes a-begging. as there are few Canadian youths with sufficient means to keep up a position in such an expensive branch of the service, in which case an additional commission in the infantry is generally substituted. All who have taken the full four years' course, and qualified in all the obligatory subjects, are entitled to receive a diploma of graduation, those who have specially distinguished themselves also receiving honors. Those who leave at the end of two years, and pass the subjects required, receive a certificate of military qualification only.

After the official proceedings are over on the closing day the cadets have a parade of their own, when the members of the graduating class have to undergo an ordeal of hand-shaking and leave-taking in true college form. A valedictory dinner in the evening follows, and then steamer and car bear the cadets off, and the halls are deserted for three months.

Some of the passed cadets of the college have already won fame for themselves. The name of STAIRS, who accompanied STANLEY in his march through darkest Africa, is well known the world over. LIEUT. HEWITT served in the Soudan and bears a medal won on the banks of the Nile, and LIEUT. DOBELL has distinguished himself for bravery in Burmah.

Occasion has not yet arisen to call into full play the energies of the rapidly-growing members of the graduates of the Royal Military College, and it is therefore too early to judge of its full benefit to Canada. But the opinion

however, two half holidays, on Wednesday and Saturday, when he may go out on pass till eleven o'clock, or with extra leave till one. Balls and parties in Kingston are timed for these days, for the cadet, with his gay scarlet uniform, is an important factor in the social world. While attending the college the cadets are of course subject to the Queen's Regulations, the Army Act, the Militia Act, and such other rules and regulations as Her Majesty's troops are subject to.

The physical training is excellent. SERGT.-MAJOR MORGAN, of the Scots Guards, presides over this department, and well qualified he is to fill the position. Cadets who pass four years under his instruction come out with deep chests and erect figures, and show what a thorough physical training can accomplish.

One of the rewards of good conduct is promotion to the rank of non-commissioned officer, the commandant having authority to appoint such from among those best qualified. Proud is he who is invested with the chevrons, or given the right to wear the sergeant's sash.

But while subject to strict discipline the cadets have opportunities to cultivate their social qualities. One of the events of the season is the annual sports, which take place in September. The campus is alive with carriages and pedestrians, while pretty girls, with their chaperons, form the center of groups engaged in animated conversation, or watching with interest the various competitions of speed and skill. Races, jumping competitions and steeplechases follow each other in quick succession, while the tug of war between the right and left wings creates almost as such interest as the struggle on the Isis between the college eights. The games over, all adjourn to the gymnasium, where the prizes, more substantial than the crown of ivy at the Olympic games, are distributed to the victors. Tea and an impromptu dance follow in the college halls.

A ball is given at Christmas by the staff and cadets, and a yet more elaborate entertainment of similar character at the close of the college year in June. On closing day a series of field manœuvers takes place, with blowing up of imaginary fortifications and fleets, and an exhibition of drill and bayonet exercise, after which the results of the examinations are announced, the prizes distributed, and the session brought to a termination. The governor-general, the minister of militia, or someone else high in authority, is secured, if possible, to distribute the prizes and make a speech. Four commissions, one each in the engineers, artillery, cavalry and infantry branches of the imperial service, are available, the cadets who stand highest on the honor roll, if otherwise eligible, being entitled to them in the order named. The first two are eagerly sought, the third generally goes a-begging, as there are few Canadian youths with sufficient means to keep up a position in such an expensive branch of the service, in which case an additional commission in the infantry is generally substituted. All who have taken the full four years' course, and qualified in all the obligatory subjects, are entitled to receive a diploma of graduation, those who have specially distinguished themselves also receiving honors. Those who leave at the end of two years, and pass the subjects required, receive a certificate of military qualification only.

After the official proceedings are over on the closing day the cadets have a parade of their own, when the members of the graduating class have to undergo an ordeal of handshaking and leave-taking in true college form. A valedictory dinner in the evening follows, and then steamer and car bear the cadets off, and the halls are deserted for three months.

Some of the passed cadets of the college have already won fame for themselves. The name of STAIRS, who accompanied STANLEY in his march through darkest Africa, is well known the world over. LIEUT. HEWITT served in the Soudan and bears a medal won on the banks of the Nile, and LIEUT. DOBELL has distinguished himself for bravery in Burmah.

Occasion has not yet arisen to call into full play the energies of the rapidly-growing members of the graduates of the Royal Military College, and it is therefore too early to judge of its full benefit to Canada. But the opinion

KINGSTON HARBOR AND FORTIFICATIONS

however, t
Saturday,
eleven o'c
Balls and
these days
uniform, i
world. W
are of cou
tions, the
other rules
troops are
 The phy
Major M
sides over
he is to
four year
with deep
what a th
plish.
 One of
motion t
officer, th
appoint so
Proud is h
or given t
 But wh
cadets ha
social qua
season is
in Septem
riages and
their chap
engaged i
ing with i
speed and
and steepl
succession
right and
interest a
the colleg
journ to
more subs
Olympic
Tea and
college ha
 A ball i
cadets, an
of similar
year in Ju

of LORD LANSDOWNE, expressed when governor-general, is worth quoting. These are his words:

"There is no Canadian institution of which Canada should be prouder or which will do better service to the country and to the empire. It forms an interesting and distinctive feature in the military system of the Dominion. That system, as I understand it, is based upon the recognition of the fact that Canada cannot afford in her own interests, or in those of the empire, to disregard those precautions which every civilized community takes in order to ensure its own safety from internal commotion or external attack. Upon the other hand it is a system entirely opposed to the establishment of a numerous standing army or to the withdrawal of a large body of citizens from the peaceful pursuits which are essential to the progress and development of the country.

"That being so, it is clear that in case of a national emergency the Dominion would have to trust largely to the spontaneous efforts of its own people, to the expansion of its existing organization, and the rapid development of the resources already at our command.

"But, gentlemen, it is needless for me to point out to you that there is one thing which it is impossible to produce on the spur of the moment, and that is a body of trained officers, competent to take charge of new levies or to supervise operations necessary for the defense of the national territory, and therefore it appears to me that we cannot overrate the value of an institution which year by year is turning out men who have received within its wall a soldier's education in the best sense of the word and who, whatever their primary destination, will, I do not doubt, be found available whenever their services are required by the country."

The cost of education at the Military College is not unreasonable. Each cadet is required to deposit annually $200 to cover the cost of messing and quarters, and in addition $200 the first year and $150 each year afterwards for uniform, books and instruments. The messman receives forty-six cents per day for each cadet present. Extras are obtainable at fixed prices. No cadet is allowed to spend more than $2 per month, non-commissioned officers more than $4, for extras, which they pay out of their pocket money.

In addition to the full course of four years and the military course of two years, provision has been made at the college for officers of the militia, who require higher instruction than the military schools afford, to take a three months' course, one class being instructed each year. By this means a number of officers have been enabled to qualify for important positions in the service.

Taken all in all, Canada's West Point has been an unqualified success.

THE view of the grand old city of Kingston, presented in photo-gravure at the beginning of this article upon "Canada's West Point," shows the Military College buildings at left center—the building with so many windows being the main edifice, and the smaller buildings near by are the gymnasium and other necessary adjuncts to so large an institution, of which Ontario may well be proud.

GENERAL DESCRIPTION,

Historical and Otherwise, with some Opinions of Travellers.

THE route of the St. Lawrence has long been noted for the variety and beauty of its scenery. The traveller coming up from the sea, should he turn aside to explore the chasm of the Saguenay, would witness a scene of grandeur scarcely equaled by any other of its kind in any part of the world. Further up, the Rapids of the St. Lawrence present in succession displays of majestic power and volume that command admiration, and on finally reaching the level or navigable waters above, the approach to the first of the Great Lakes leads throught a labyrinth of islands, which, for variety of scenery and quiet beauty, have seldom failed to awaken the enthusiasm of the traveller.

To this group of islands, with their historical associations, and the impressions which their scenery has inspired, the greater part of this volume is devoted.

In arranging the materials of this work, the editor has been engaged in no small degree in presenting the thoughts of others; but, believing that the enjoyment of this scenery would be enhanced by learning the manner in which it has impressed those who have witnessed it in the years that are past, he has sought to present as wide a range of these impressions as opportunities allowed, yet not failing to present much that is original and never before published.

No one will doubt that places acquire extraordinary interest when associated with great events, or even when linked with the ideal incidents of poetry and romance. In allusion to the interest which these associations impart to so many places in the Old World, while there are comparatively few in the New, the naturalist Wilson, in whom were united a keen perception of the beauties of nature and a highly poetic temperament, in the opening part of his Foresters, says:

"Yet Nature's charms, that bloom so lovely here,
Unhailed arrive, unheeded disappear;
While bare, bleak heaths, and brooks of half a mile
Can rouse the thousand bards of Britain's Isle.
There, scarce a stream creeps down its narrow bed,
There, scarce a hillock lifts its little head,
Or humble hamlet peeps their glades among,
But lives and murmurs in immortal song.
Our western world, with all its matchless floods,
Our vast transparent lakes and boundless woods,
Stamped with the traits of majesty sublime,
Unhonored weep the silent lapse of time;
Spread their wild grandeur to the unconscious sky,
In sweetest seasons pass unheeded by;
While scarce one Muse returns the song they gave,
Or seeks to snatch their glories from the grave."

In some of the prose descriptions that follow, the reader will find a poetry of sentiment and imagery of thought that cannot fail to engage the attention. In others, there are incidents and events described that may add new interest to this region, especially those relating to the accounts of travel in the olden time, with the humble accomodations and the discomforts of the period, that afford a striking contrast with the exact appointments and the ample luxuries of the present day.

EARLY INDIAN HISTORY.

"In the beginning," so far as history or tradition extends back into the past, this region

VIEW FROM JUDGE SPENCER'S TOWER, SHOWING ALEXANDRIA BAY IN THE DISTANCE.

was the border-land of the Algonquin and the Iroquois,—the former dwelling for the most part to the northward and eastward, while the latter, at least in the later period, had their principal homes along the lakes and rivers of Central and Western New York.

The early historians of Canada record the fact that a bloody war was going on between the Adirondacks or Algonquins on the St. Lawrence, and the Iroquois or Five Nations of the region now included in Central and Western New York, when the country was first visited by the French. Champlain took part in this war on the part of the former, and by the use of fire-arms, hitherto unknown in Indian warfare, turned the tide of success for a time in favor of his allies — but gained thereby the lasting hatred of their enemies towards the French. The origin of this warfare is traced by tradition to a long time before the first appearance of the white man, and although not measured by moons or seasons, it still appeared to be consistent, and probable,— and according to the little that could be gathered, was as follows :

The Algonquins and the Iroquois had lived for a long time in harmony, the former being the stronger, and chiefly subsisting by the chase, while the latter were more inclined to fishing and agriculture. Now and then the young men of the two races would go out on their hunting expeditions together, but in these the superiority of the man who killed the game, over him who skinned and dressed it, was always insisted upon, and when the party saw an opportunity, it was the business of the one to pursue and slay, and of the other to stand by and see it done.

At one time, half a dozen of each class were out in the winter on a hunting excursion together. They saw some elk and immediately pursued them, but the Algonquins, presuming on their superiority, would not suffer the young Iroquois to take part, at the same time giving them to understand that they would soon have business enough on hand in taking care of the game they were about to kill. Three days were spent in vain pursuit, for although they saw there was an abundance of game, ill-luck followed them at every step.

At length the Iroquois offered to go out themselves, and the former, not doubting but that a like failure would soon put an end to their unwelcome comments upon their own efforts, consented. The tide of success turned in their favor, and the Iroquois soon returned with an abundance of game. Mortified at this result, the jealous Algonquins the next night killed all of their successful rivals as they lay sleeping. The crime, although concealed and denied, was soon discovered, and the Iroquois at first made their complaints with moderation — simply asking that justice should be done to the murderers.

No attention was paid to these complaints, and the injured party took justice into their own hands, solemnly vowing to exterminate the haughty race or perish in the attempt. Long series of retaliatory inroads were from this time made by each into the territories of the other, which finally ended greatly to the advantage of the Iroquois, and in the almost total annihilation of their enemies. The St. Francis Indians are a remnant of this once powerful tribe.

HIAWATHA.

The legend of Hiawatha has been rendered familiar to most readers of American poetry by the metrical version of Longfellow, and the prose of Clark. Schoolcraft and others, and much controversy has been had with respect to the author of the legend as it first appeared in English. We accept, as fully reliable, the statement made by the late Hon. J. V. H. Clark, of Manlius, author of the History of Onondaga County, in a letter to the New York Tribune, in January, 1856, in which the claims of various writers and the dates of their publications are precisely stated.

The legend relates to the origin of the League of the Iroquois, at a time which no record fixes by date, and no circumstance acceptable to the historian would lead him to locate otherwise than somewhere in that period clouded in the uncertainties of the forgotten past. We cannot present its beginning, which was in this region, more appropriately than in the original language of Mr. Clark:

"Hundreds of years ago, Ta-oun-ya-wat-ha, the Deity who presides over fisheries and streams, came down from his dwelling place in the clouds to visit the inhabitants of the earth. He had been deputed by the Great and Good Spirit, Ha-wa-ne-u, to visit streams and clear the channels from all obstructions, to seek out the good things of the country through which he intended to pass, that they might be more generally disseminated among all the good people of the earth — especially to point out to them the most excellent fishing grounds, and to bestow upon them other acceptable gifts. About this time, two young men of the Onondaga Nation were listlessly gazing over the calm blue waters of the Lake of a Thousand Isles. During their reverie they espied, as they thought, far in the distance, a single white speck, beautifully dancing over the bright blue waters, and while they watched the object with the most intense anxiety, it seemed to increase in magnitude, and moved as if approaching the place where they were concealed, most anxiously awaiting the event of the visitation of so singular an object — for at this time no canoes had ever made their appearance in the direction whence this was approaching. As the object neared the shore, it proved in semblance to be a venerable looking man, calmly seated in a canoe of pure white, very curiously constructed and much more ingeniously wrought than those in use among the tribes of the country. Like a cygnet upon the wide blue sea, so sat the canoe of To-oun-ya-wat-ha upon the Lake of a Thousand Isles.

"As a frail branch drifts towards the rushing cataract, so coursed the white canoe over the rippling waters, propelled by the strong arm of the god of the river. Deep thought sat on the brow of the gray-headed mariner; penetration marked his eye, and deep, dark mystery pervaded his countenance. With a single oar he silently paddled his light-trimmed bark along the shore, as if seeking a commodious haven of rest. He soon turned the prow of his fragile vessel into the estuary of the 'double river,' and made fast to the western shore. He majestically ascended the steep bank, nor stopped till he had gained the loftiest summit of the western hill. Then silently gazing around as if to examine the country, he became enchanted with the view, and drawing his stately form to its utmost height, he exclaimed in accents of the wildest enthusiasm, Osh-wah-kee, Osh-wah-kee."

He approached the two young hunters, gained their confidence, and having drawn from them a knowledge of the difficulties under which they labored, disclosed to them the spirituality of his character, and the object of his mission. He invited them to attend him in his passage up the river, and they witnessed many things which could only be accounted for as miracles, or be described but in the wonders of Indian mythology. He ascended to the lesser lakes, placed all things in proper order for the comfort and sustenance of man, taught them how to cultivate corn and beans, which had not before been grown by them, made the fishing ground free, and opened to all the uninterrupted pursuit of game. He distributed among mankind the fruits of the earth, and removed all obstructions from the navigable streams. Being pleased with his success, he assumed the character and habits of a man, and received the name Hi-a-wat-ha, (signifying "very wise man,") and fixed his residence on the beautiful shores of Cross Lake. After a time, the country became alarmed by a hostile invasion, when he called a council of all the tribes from the east and the west, and in a long harangue urged upon them the importance of uniting themselves in a league for their common defense and mutual happiness. They deliberated upon his advice, and the next day adopted and ratified the League of Union which he recommended. As Lycurgus gave law to the Spartans, and swore them to faithfully observe its precepts until his return from a journey, and then departed to return no more, so Hi-a-wat-ha, having brought the council to a close, and as the assembled tribes were about to separate on their return home, arose in a dignified manner, and thus addressed them:

"Friends and Brothers: — I have now fulfilled my mission upon earth; I have done everything which can be done at present for the good of this great people. Age, infirmity and distress sit heavily upon me. During my sojourn among you I have removed all obstructions from your streams. Canoes can now pass everywhere. I have given you good fishing waters and good hunting grounds; I have taught you how to cultivate corn and beans, and have learned you the art of making cabins. Many other blessings I have liberally bestowed upon you.

"Lastly, I have now assisted you to form an ever-lasting league and covenant of strength and friendship, for your future safety and protection. If you preserve it without the admission of other people,

THE HASBROUCK HOUSE AND DUFFY'S HOUSE, MANHATTAN ISLAND.

you will always be free, numerous and mighty. If other nations are admitted to your councils, they will sow jealousies among you, and you will become enslaved, few and feeble. Remember these words: they are the last you will hear from the lips of Hi-a-wat-ha. Listen, my friends; the Great-Master-of-Breath calls me to go. I have patiently waited his summons. I am ready: Farewell."

As the wise man closed his speech, there burst upon the ears of the assembled multitude the cheerful sounds of the most delightful singing voices. The whole sky seemed filled with the sweetest melody of celestial music; and heaven's high arch echoed and re-echoed the touching strains till the whole vast assembly was completely absorbed in rapturous ecstacy. Amidst the general confusion which now prevailed, and while all eyes were turned towards the etherial regions, Hi-a-wat-ha was seen majestically seated in his canoe, gracefully rising higher and higher above their heads through the air until he became entirely lost from the view of the assembled throng, who witnessed his wonderful ascent in mute and admiring astonishment — while the fascinating music gradually became more plaintive and low, and finally sweetly expired in the softest tones upon their ears, as the wise man Hi-a-wat-ha, the godlike Ta-oun-ya-wat-ha, retired from their sight, as mysteriously as he first appeared from The Lake of a Thousand Isles, and quietly entered the regions inhabited only by the favorites of the great and good spirit Ha-wah-ne-u.

In the legend, as rendered by Longfellow, no allusion to this region is specifically made, and the scene of events is located in the west, on the south shore of Lake Superior, in the region beyond the Pictured Rocks and the Grand Sable.

CREATION OF THE INDIAN RACE.

Among the traditions of various Indian tribes we find a legend of their creation, which, although differing more or less in details, agrees in ascribing their origin to a people who came out of the ground. Of this mythological belief we have an interesting example in this part of the world, as given by M. Pouchet, a French writer of acknowledged merit, who recorded what he saw and heard. This writer was an officer in the French service, and commanded Fort Levis, on the Oraconenton Isle, a short distance below Ogdensburg, when this last stronghold of the French was captured by Lord Amhurst in 1760.

He subsequently prepared a history of the events in which he had himself borne an important part, which was published some years after his death, and in this he gives much information concerning the Indians who then inhabited this region. In describing the shores of Lake Ontario, he speaks of a great arc of sand hills along the eastern end of the lake, behind which are marshy meadows, through which the rivers wind. This description clearly identifies these streams with those now known as the North and South Branches of Sandy Creek, in the town of Ellisburgh, Jefferson county, which unite just above the point where they enter the lake. They are remarkable in this, that at the head of the South Branch is the place where the traditions of the Iroquois fix the spot "where they issued from the ground, or rather, according to their traditions, where they were born."

TRACES OF INDIAN RECORDS ON THE ST. LAWRENCE.

Opposite the village of Oak Point, in Elizabeth Township, Canada, there existed in 1850, and perhaps does still, a rude representation of a canoe with thirty-five men, and near it a cross. On the rocks below Rockville there were two similar paintings, each being a canoe with six men. A deer rudely painted on the rocks was found on the shore of Black Lake, a few miles inland from Morristown, and doubtless other rude sketches of the kind may be found. These are probably of comparatively modern origin, or at most not earlier than the time of European settlement. They may have been significant of some event at the time when made, but whatever the objects may have been, they have passed into oblivion with the memory of those who made them.

Expeditions of De Courcelle and De Tracy.

In the papers relating to De Courcelle's and De Tracy's expeditions against the Mohawk Indians (1665-6), in describing the routes leading into the Iroquois country, the navigation of the St. Lawrence is mentioned as exceedingly difficult until the rapids are passed.

"But when the mouth of the Great Lake is reached, the navigation is easy, when the waters are tranquil, becoming insensibly wider at first, then about two-thirds, next one-half, and finally out of sight of land; especially after one has passed an infinity of little islands which are at the entrance of the lake in such great numbers, and in such a variety, that the most experienced Iroquois pilots sometimes lose themselves there, and have considerable difficulty in distinguishing the course to be steered in the confusion, and, as it were, in the labyrinth formed by the islands. Some of these are only huge rocks rising out of the water, covered merely by moss or a few spruce or other stunted wood, whose roots spring from the clefts of the rocks which can supply no other aliment or moisture to these barren trees than what the rains furnish them. After leaving this abode the lake is discovered, appearing like unto a sea without islands or bounds, where barks and ships can sail in all safety so that the communications would be easy between all the French colonies that could be established on the borders of this great lake which is more than a hundred leagues long, by thirty or forty wide."

French Missionaries.

Among the pioneers of discovery were the missionaries who were sent out to gain the friendship and secure the conversion of the Indian tribes of the interior. These zealous men allowed no obstacles or dangers to interrupt their efforts or dampen their ardor, but with an energy and perseverance that cannot fail to excite our admiration, they pursued their way to the remotest parts of the interior, where some lived many years among the savages amid all the privations of a wilderness, and others were murdered, or miserably perished in the solitudes of the forest. We can here mention but a few of these pioneers and discoverers:

François de Salignac de Fenelon, half brother of the illustrious French writer, the Archbishop of Cambray, came to Canada in 1667, and was for some time engaged in the Indian missions at Toronto and elsewhere.

The Abbe Fenelon accompanied the Count de Frontenac to Lake Ontario in 1673.

Louis Hennepin, a Franciscan, came to Canada in 1675, and was stationed the next year at Frontenac, Kingston. He was afterwards sent by La Salle to explore the country, and was the first European who saw the Mississippi river. In 1697 he published an account of remote regions that he pretended to have visited, but which is now regarded in part at least as a fiction. Father Marquette also made extensive journeys in the west, and died at Mackinaw, May 14, 1675. Ménard, Allouez and many others passed this way on their journeys to distant points, but these men were, as a rule, little given to romantic descriptions, and their "relations" pertain more to the proper object of their missions, than to the scenery that they passed.

Father Emmanuel Crespel, in a little work published in 1742, describes some incidents of a journey into the Indian country on the Upper Lakes. He was fifteen days going from Montreal to Frontenac, and was there detained some time in waiting for a vessel to Niagara. This was of about eighty tons burthen, and apparently the only one then on the lake. The passage was made in less than thirty-six hours. The lake was very calm and he sounded with a line of a hundred fathoms without finding bottom.

On his return he remained two years at Frontenac, when he was recalled to Montreal, and soon afterwards was sent to La Pointe de la Chevelure on the east side of Lake Champlain, in the present State of Vermont, and opposite the French post at Crown Point.

First Military Establishment Upon Lake Ontario—Fort Frontenac.—(1673.)

In order to protect the French interests, the Count de Frontenac resolved to establish a military post at the outlet of the Lake, and with the view of impressing the natives with the power of the French, he resolved to take two flat bottomed canoes up the rapids, and even to mount them with cannon, to inspire them with awe. The boats were built after a particular model, painted unlike anything ever seen before, and were each manned by sixteen men. With these and about one hundred and twenty bark canoes he left Montreal on the 16th of June, and in about three weeks reached the beginning of smooth-water navigation. Hearing that the Indians had assembled in great numbers, and were uneasy about the object of his expedition, he resolved to proceed with caution, in one body, and in closer column than before. The weather was so serene, and the navigation so smooth, that they made more than ten leagues the first day, and went into camp at a cove about a league and a half from Grenadier Island, where the eel-fishing begins. In his Journal he says:

"We had the pleasure on the way to catch a small loon, a bird about as large as a European Outarde, of the most beautiful plumage, but very difficult to be caught alive, as it dives constantly under, so that it is no small rarity to be able to take one. A cage was made for it, and orders were given to endeavor to raise it, in order to send it to the King. On the 11th [of July], the weather continuing fine, a good day's journey was made, having passed all that vast group of islands with which the river is spangled, and camped at a point above the river called Gananoque, up which many of them go hunting. It has a very considerable channel. Two more loons were caught alive, and a kind of deer, but the head and antlers are handsomer than the deer of France."

The narrative continues with an account of the regal manner with which the Count de Frontenac entered the lake, and the interviews he had with the Indians. In short, nothing which pomp and ceremony—the waving of banners, martial music, and the discharge of cannon could do, was omitted, to impress the wondering natives with an overwhelming idea of the omnipotence of the French. The speeches and proceedings of the occasion are all found fully recorded. The outline of a fort was at once traced out, and its construction commenced. Beginning work by daylight on the 14th, the ground was cleared before night. The Indians were astonished to see the large clearance made in a day—some squaring timber in one place; others fetching pickets; and others cutting trenches, all at the same time, and with the greatest dispatch and order.

EXPEDITION OF DE LA BARRE.—(1684.)

De La Barre, Governor of Canada from 1682 to 1685, had distinguished himself in the West Indies, where he had taken Antigua and Montserat from the English. In 1684, he repaired to Fort Frontenac, and ordered three vessels which the French had built upon the lake to be repaired, with the design of crossing to the country of the Iroquois, and frightening the people into his own terms of peace. His army consisted of 600 soldiers, 400 Indians, and 400 men for carrying provisions, besides 300 men left in the fort.

The Governor tarried six weeks at Frontenac, his encampment being near a pestilential marsh, causing so great sickness and mortality that he found himself unable to accomplish his object by force of arms. He accordingly resolved to effect what he could by treaty, and having vainly hoped to obtain the co-operation of Gov. Dongan, he sent agents to invite the Five Nations to a council. The Governor of New York, although in sympathy with the religious influences so actively employed by the French, did not consent to any concurrence, but secretly put every obstacle in the way; and in this he so far succeeded, that the Mohawks and Senecas remained at home. The other tribes, who were more under the influence of the French missionaries, sent representatives to meet him, consisting of Garangula and thirty warriors. The place of meeting was at the mouth of Salmon river, at the eastern end of Lake Ontario, about forty miles from Onondaga castle.

After remaining two days in the French camp, the Governor proceeded to address the Indians, a circle being formed by the French officers on one side, and Garangula and his warriors on the other.

We have not space to print the speeches made upon each side by the "high contracting parties," but De la Barre entirely failed in placating or overawing the Indians, who became insolent, and at last openly defied that officer, who was soon compelled to retreat, and his command reached Frontenac (Kingston) at last much demoralized. The expedition was so much of a failure as to be almost stigmatized as puerile.

EXPEDITION OF DE NONVILLE.—(1685.)

In 1685, the Marquis De Nonville made an expedition into the Genesee country, but left no record of local interest concerning the islands.

THE AVENGING INROAD OF THE IROQUOIS UPON THE FRENCH—(1688.)

Early in July, 1688, an act of perfidy on the part of the French brought down upon their settlements the terrible vengeance of the Iroquois. Passing down the St. Lawrence, they landed at Lachine on the 26th of July, and fell upon the unsuspecting inhabitants, burning, plundering and massacreing in all directions, and almost up to the defenses of Montreal. They lingered weeks in the country, laid waste the settlements far and wide, and returned with the loss of only three men. The French lost about a thousand persons by this inroad, and many prisoners were carried off for a fate worse than sudden death.

The French at Fort Frontenac were obliged to burn the two vessels they had on the lake, and abandon the fort, first setting a slow match to the powder magazine. The fire happened to go out before the powder was reached, and the place was soon plundered by the Indians. The garrison set out in seven bark canoes, travelling only by night, and hiding by day, and after much difficulty reached Montreal with the loss of one canoe and all on board.

De Nonville witnessed the devastation of his colony without daring to resist the enemy while engaged in their work of ruin, nor on their return. He was succeeded the next year by Frontenac.

ONONDAGA EXPEDITION OF THE COUNT DE FRONTENAC.

In 1696 the Count de Frontenac made an incursion into the country of the Onondagas, but the only mention that he makes of this region is his encampment for a night upon what is now known as Carleton island.

SUBSEQUENT OPERATIONS OF THE FRENCH ON LAKE ONTARIO.

During the next fifty years, the French were steadily extending their trade, and endeavoring to attach the remote Indian tribes to their interests. In 1687, they established a fort at Niagara, and in 1722 the English built a trading house, and in 1727 a fort at Oswego. Although England and France were during much of this time at peace, and the Governors of their colonies on terms of correspondence, there was probably no period down to the conquest of 1760 during which each of the two powers was not busy, through its agents, in endeavoring to monopolize the Indian trade, and in extending this influence with the native tribes.

INDIAN MISSION AT OSWEGATCHIE; LA PRESENTATION.—(1749.)

A considerable number of Iroquois, chiefly Onondagas, having been induced to settle on the St. Lawrence, a mission was established in 1749, at the mouth of the Oswegatchie, on the site of the present city of Ogdensburg. This mission was named La Presentation, and its founder was Francis Picquet, a Sulpician. During the first season he built a storehouse and a small fort, but before the end of the year his settlement was attacked by a band of Mohawks, who burned two vessels loaded with hay, and the palisades of the fort. After this, some soldiers were stationed here for protection. The station progressed rapidly, and in 1751 a saw mill was begun.

The English who had built a trading house and a fort at Oswego many years before, naturally looked with jealousy upon this establishment by the French. Word was brought to them by the Indians, concerning their posts lately erected on the Ohio, and the informant said "he heard a bird sing that a great many Indians from his castle, and others from the Five Nations, were gone to Swegage."

In June, 1754, the celebrated Congress of

ISLAND KATE, SUMMER HOME OF THE LATE MRS. P. C. TOMLINSON.

Representatives from the English Colonies, met at Albany, to consider a Plan of Union for their common defense, and on this occasion these encroachments were fully discussed.

In the war which followed, La Presentation became a point of outfit and rendezvous for many of the war parties that laid waste the frontier settlements of the English, from which they usually returned bringing prisoners and scalps. Many of these expeditions were led by Picquet himself. Thomas Mante, in his history of the French war, says:

"As to the Abbé Picquet, who distinguished himself so much by his brutal zeal, as he did not expose himself to any danger, he received no injury; and he yet lives, justly despised to such a degree by every one who knows anything of his past conduct in America, that scarce any officer will admit him to his table. However repugnant it must be to every idea of honor and humanity, not to give quarter to an enemy, when subdued, it must be infinitely more so not to spare women and children. Yet such had often been the objects of the Abbé Picquet's cruel advice, enforced by the most barbarous examples, especially in the English settlements on the back of Virginia and Pennsylvania."

He returned to France, where he died July 15, 1781. He was succeeded at La Presentation (Ogdensburg) by La Garde, a Sulpician, and the mission was continued until broken up in 1760. The Oswegatchies continued to live on the south shore and on the islands at the head of the Rapids until 1806, when the proprietor of the lands caused their removal, a part going to St. Regis, and others returning to Onondaga. Some years since, the corner-stone of a building erected near the site of the present light-house, at the entrance of the harbor at Ogdensburg, was found in taking down the building. It may now be seen over the door of a building erected for a State arsenal in that city, and bears the following inscription:

In nomine ✠ Dei Omnipotentis
Huic habitationi initia dedit
Frans Picquet. 1749.

These premises remained standing when settlement began under title from the State, in 1796, and until long afterwards. They were fitted up for a store and for dwellings until better could be built, and the site of the foundations may still be traced.

OPERATIONS IN 1755-6: CAPTURE OF OSWEGO.

The war, which ended in the conquest of Canada, is without incident so far as relates to the Thousand Islands; but many events occurred upon this frontier, which became the thoroughfare of large armies, the only communication then known being by the river, between the settled parts of Canada and the upper lakes.

In the summer of 1755 the French were engaged in strengthening the post at Frontenac, and later in the season at Niagara. The first detachment in going up was met by a party of Indians among the Islands on the 1st of August. They had a number of scalps, and gave the first intimation received in Canada of the defeat of Braddock's army near Fort DuQuesne a fortnight before. This success of the French determined many of the Indians to take up arms against the English, and many of the cannon captured on that occasion were used by the French at Niagara and elsewhere on the northern border during the following year.

In 1756, considerable bodies of troops were sent from France, and in May, the Marquis de Montcalm, Gen. Bourlamaque, two engineers, and an army of 1,350 regulars, 1,500 Canadians and 250 Indians, ascended the river to Fort Frontenac, and M. de Villers, with 500 men, established a post of observation on Six-town Point, in the present town of Henderson, Jefferson county, the outlines of which may still be plainly traced. It was square, built of upright timbers, with bastions at the corners, and was surrounded by a ditch, and at the time hidden from view by surrounding trees and bushes. This officer, who was captain of the marine, was brave and prudent, and had greatly annoyed the English by pillaging their munitions, and obliging them to take great precautions in sending provisions to their troops at Oswego.

Montcalm left Fort Frontenac for Point Peninsula on the 5th of August, and on the 7th the French appeared before Oswego. There were at this time two forts at this place

— Fort Ontario on the east side, and Fort Pepperell on the west. The latter, then newly erected, was 120 feet square, a rampart of earth and stone, 20 feet thick, and 12 feet high, besides the parapet.

The French began their approaches on the 12th, and on the next day the English, having spiked their guns and destroyed their provisions and ammunition, withdrew to the old fort on the eastern bank. This Col. Mercer was also obliged to surrender on the 17th. The English force consisted of 2,400 men, who yielded upon terms dictated by Montcalm, with all their effects, munitions, arms and military stores.

It is stated by English historians that, notwithstanding the pledges of Montcalm, twenty of the garrison were given up to the Indians, by way of atonement for the loss of friends, and that all the sick in the hospital were scalped. At least one hundred men are said to have fallen victims to Indian ferocity after the surrender, the remainder being taken down to Montreal, where they were mostly exchanged. The French did not attempt to hold this post after surrender, but most of the provisions were sent to Niagara and the artillery to Frontenac and Montreal. According to Pouchot, the government got small returns of the booty, as it was mostly stolen or converted to private use by the commissaries, stewards and other agents of the service, who lost no opportunity of enriching themselves at the king's expense. Some of the very articles captured were sold back to the government through contractors. Two sloops were set on fire by the French and cast adrift upon the lake. The greater part of the French army returned a week afterwards to Montreal, and appeared later the same season upon Lake Champlain.

DESTRUCTION OF FORT FRONTENAC, (1758).

In August, 1758, Colonel John Bradstreet arrived at Oswego with an army of 3,340 men and crossed the lake to Fort Frontenac, which he captured with a trifling loss. After destroying the fort and securing what he could of the immense military stores there deposited, he returned without accident to Oswego. He repaired the works on the east side of the river at that place, which remained in British possession until surrendered to the United States under treaty in June, 1796.

EXPEDITION OF LORD AMHERST, (1760).

The war between the French and English in North America, which begun in 1755, had led, by the end of 1759, to the reduction of Niagara, Ticonderoga, Crown Point and Quebec. To complete the conquest, three expeditions were planned for 1760 : one from Quebec, another by way of Lake Champlain, and a third by way of Oswego and the St. Lawrence river. The latter was placed under General Jeffrey Amherst, and the forces assembled at Oswego were reported on the 5th of August as consisting of the 1st and 2d battalion of Royal Highlanders, the 44th, 46th and 55th regiments, the 4th battalion of the 60th, eight companies of the 77th, five of the 80th, 597 grenadiers, an equal number of light infantry, 146 rangers, three battalions of the New York regiment, the New Jersey regiment, four battalions of the Connecticut regiment, and 157 of the Royal Artillery — amounting in all to 10,142 effective men, officers included. There were besides 706 Indian warriors under Sir William Johnson.

The first detachment of troops sailed in two vessels, the Mohawk and the Onondaga, on the 7th, to take post at the entrance of the St. Lawrence. On the 13th all had embarked, and on the evening of that day they encamped at the head of the St. Lawrence. Captain Loring, with the two vessels, who had been the first to leave Oswego, lost his way among the islands, and while endeavoring to extricate himself, the main army passed him. They, however, arrived a day or two after at Point au Baril, near the present village of Maitland, where the French the year before had built a dock, and established a fortified ship-yard. The grenadiers and row-galleys had, in the meantime, taken an advanced position at Oswegatchie, preparatory to an attack upon Fort Lévis.

This fort stood upon an island called Oraconenton by the Indians, and Ile Royale by the French,—about three miles below the mouth of the Oswegatchie, and near the middle of the channel, which it completely commanded. In modern times it is known as Chimney island, from the ruins of the French works still visible upon it. (In Canada.)

The works upon this island were begun under the direction of the Chevalier de Lévis in the summer of 1759, and finished in 1760 by Pouchot. A map given by Mante shows that the border of the island was set with the trunks of trees having their tops still on, and firmly set in the ground, so as to present an impenetrable abatis of brush on every side but the landing at the lower end. Within this was a breastwork of earth, and behind this a deep ditch filled with water, through the middle of which there ran a stockade of strong, sharpened pickets, closely set and sloping outwards. Inside of the ditch stood the Fort proper, consisting of a timber parapet filled with earth, with a line of strong, sharpened pickets sloping out over the ditch, and platforms for cannon, and in the center of the works the magazines and quarters. The lower point of the island was not included within the ditch and parapet, but had defensive works sufficient to prevent the landing of boats.

A small church stood near the head of Gallop island, a short distance below the fort, at the time when this post was taken. The English, finding a scalp displayed in the building, burned it to the ground. The outline of the foundations of this church can still be traced.

The events attending the reduction of this fort — the last that offered any resistance in Canada, may be learned from two accounts: one by Mante, an English historian of approved credit, and the other by Pouchot, the French officer who defended the fort, and afterwards wrote a history of the war, that was published after his death.

The loss of the English was twenty-one killed and nineteen wounded. The first shot from the English battery killed the French officer of artillery. Eleven more were killed afterwards, and about forty wounded. The garrison, except the pilots, for the sake of whom chiefly the place had been attacked, were sent to New York; and the general named the fort FORT WILLIAM AUGUSTUS.

OSWEGATCHIE UNDER THE ENGLISH.

The English continued to occupy Oswegatchie as a trading post until 1796, and during the Revolution it was a point of some importance as a place for the storage of supplies, and the transfer of freight from boats to vessels. Although the St. Lawrence river had been declared the boundary by the Treaty of 1783, the British held possession of the whole line of posts on the northern frontier to secure, as they claimed, the rights of certain British subjects. In the absence of authority to prevent it, the owners of land under purchase from the State suffered great damages from timber thieves, who operated extensively and without the least restraint. A mill on the Oswegatchie owned by one Verne Francis Lorimer, a half-pay captain, did an extensive business in this line, but the remonstrances of proprietors obtained no relief. The usual plea when these complaints were brought to the attention of officials was that they had no jurisdiction in the matter, and that relief should be sought in some higher authority.

According to the terms of "Jay's Treaty," all the posts within the United States were to be given up on or before June 1, 1796. Mr. Nathan Ford, agent of Samuel Ogden the proprietor, took possession, and at once began improvements with an energy that could not fail of success. During his absence the first winter the Canadians came over, held a town meeting, elected civil and military officers and opened a land office for selling and settling his lands; but he made short work with these squatters and their title, and the settlement grew rapidly until its prosperity was checked for a time by the embargo of 1812 and the war.

CARLTON ISLAND IN THE REVOLUTION.

FOR more than eighty years the traveller on the river St. Lawrence by way of the American channel, could scarcely have failed to notice a group of stone chimneys standing on the bluff at the head of Carlton Island. Inquiry or examination disclosed the fact that these old chimney stacks stood within an elaborately fortified enclosure of which the outlines are not only distinct, but in a degree quite perfect, so that the plan is readily determined, the system identified, its armament approximately adjudged, its magazines and barracks located, and, in short, its whole scope, object and intent made reasonably plain.

It will be remembered that the head of Carlton Island consists of a comparatively low peninsula, connected by a neck of land with the main island. On each side of this neck or isthmus is a bay, one arm of which is called South bay and the other North bay. Back of the two bays the island rises abruptly in a steep bluff to a height of about sixty feet above the water, and upon this bluff the fort was constructed.

The work occupied three-eighths of an octagon, extending from edge to edge of the cliff on which it was built, which faces to the southwest. The rear, or landward side, was protected by a strong earth-work, a ditch, an out-work and glacis of stone and a strong abatis. The ditch was cut in the limestone rock. In the center of each face of the ramparts, and midway between the salients, was a strong bastion, constructed for four guns, two of which in each bastion could enfilade corresponding angles of the ditch, which was cut to a depth of nearly five feet, with an average width of twenty-four feet. The scarp was vertical and protected by a cheveaux-de-frise of cedar logs, sharpened at the outer ends, and extending beyond the berme ; these were held in place by the earth of the parapet. The counterscarp was also vertical, and beyond it extended a couvert way of about the same average width as the ditch. There were also bomb-proof magazines and barracks erected, and a well sunk to a level of or below the water in North bay. On the 10th of June, 1793, there still remained in the fort ten eighteen-pounders, five twelve-pounders, two nine-pounders and two six-pounders. In 1783, ten years previous, six eighteens and

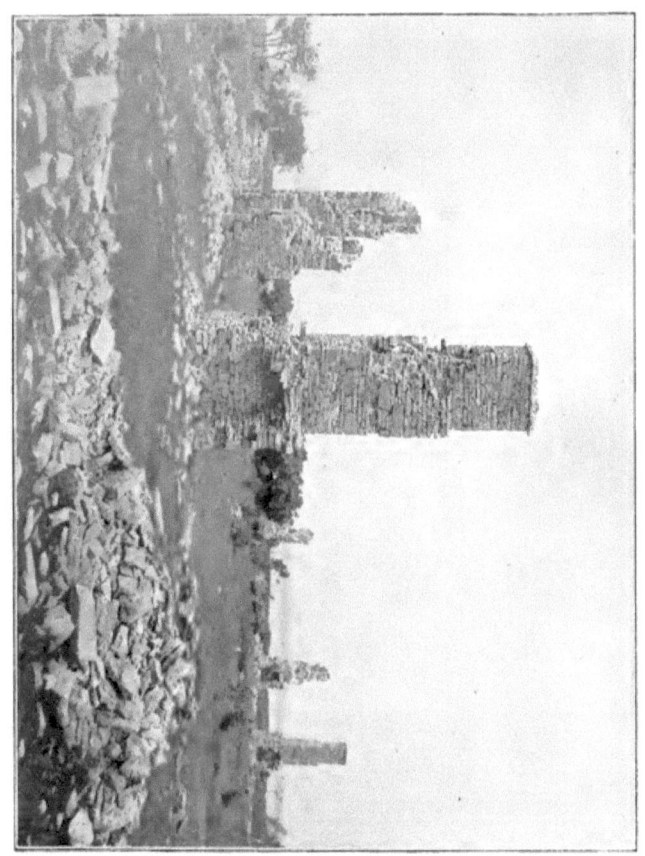

RUINS OF FORT MALDONADO, CARLTON ISLAND.

five twelves had been taken from the armament of the fort and placed upon vessels; so that the complete armament must have been sixteen eighteens, ten twelves, two nines and two sixes; in all, thirty guns.

As early as 1774, Carlton Island, then known as Buck, or Deer Island, became a trading post of much importance for Quebec merchants who were dealing with the Indian tribes. In 1775-6 the British government had located a military and naval supply department on the island, but it was not until August, 1778, that any attempt at fortifying it was made. The reasons for so doing may be very briefly stated. At the breaking out of the War of the Revolution, the British held Niagara, Oswego, Fort Frontenac (now Kingston), and undisputed sway of the lakes and of the river St. Lawrence. Sir Guy Carlton was governor of the Canadas, and commander-in-chief of his Majesty's forces therein. A campaign against the colonies was planned early in the war, and its management entrusted to Gen. John Burgoyne, instead of Sir Guy Carlton. The plan was well laid. Burgoyne was to move on Albany by way of Lake Champlain; Col. Barry St. Leger was to proceed up the St. Lawrence to Oswego and thence to Fort Stanwix (Rome), and, reducing that, reach Albany by way of the Mohawk, and form a junction with Burgoyne; while Sir Henry Clinton was to move up the Hudson River to the same point. But Burgoyne was defeated at Saratoga, St. Leger was forced to raise the siege of Fort Stanwix, and Clinton failed to reach Albany — so the well-laid plan was defeated. Thinking himself aggrieved by the appointment of Burgoyne, Sir Guy Carlton resigned his position and returned to England; and Sir Frederick Haldimand was appointed to his place.

In July, 1778, Gen. Haldimand issued an order to Lieut. William Twiss of the Engineers, Lieut. Schank of the Navy, and Capt. Aubrey of the 47th Regiment, to proceed to the upper St. Lawrence and there select such a place as in their judgment was best suited to establish a ship-yard and all its necessary requirements. After a careful examination of several points they pitched on Deer Island. Capt. Schank had a force of artificers, and Capt. Aubrey his own company and a detachment of Sir John Johnson's "Royal Greens." Lieut. Twiss drew the plans for the fort, and named it Fort Haldimand, in honor of the new commander, and the three officers changed the name of the island from "Deer" to "Carlton," in honor of their former commander, Sir Guy Carlton. The fort was never fully completed, work being discontinued by order of Gen. Haldimand in 1783.

During the War of the Revolution, Carlton Island was the most important post above Montreal. Many vessels of war and gunboats were built in the North Bay, and the place was the great depot of military and naval supplies for the Northwest. It was the place of refuge for the Tories of New York, Pennsylvania and New Jersey. Thayendanagea, the great chief of the Six Nations, made this his headquarters. Large numbers of those tribes encamped on Carlton and Wolfe islands. The bloody massacres of the Cedars, Wyoming, Cherry Valley, and Stony Arabia, were planned here, and executed by forces which went from here.

What a contrast between the Carlton Island of 117 years ago, and now. Then all was bustle. Vessels of war were building, a fort in construction; the drums beat the reveille, and the roar of the evening gun startled the echoes amid the dense forests on island and mainland. The notes of the bugle rang shrill and clear across the crystal waters of the St. Lawrence, while the war-whoop of the painted Iroquois boded death and disaster to the frontier settler. To-day, all is quiet. Where the artificers of the Revolution built their vessels of war, the artificers of to-day are completing the finest cottage on the St. Lawrence river. The land earned by his service in the Continental army, and granted to a soldier of the Revolution, now belongs to a gallant soldier of a later Revolution, which established as a permanent fact that which the first Revolution only inaugurated as an experiment — "The Union, one and inseparable."

HON. THOMAS G. ALVORD'S FISHING EXPERIENCES

UPON THE RIVER, EARLY IN THE FORTIES.

WHEN I first resolved to proceed with the preparation of this Souvenir, my mind conceived the idea of asking some one of the early frequenters of the Great River to write up his early experiences. I knew that Silas Wright, and Preston King, and Martin Van Buren and his son Prince John, and Dr. Bethune, and Dr. Holland, as well as the hundreds of later men of equal ability, including Grant and Sherman and Sheridan, had all passed away — their names now only a memory — their presence never more to be recognized by the great nation that delighted to honor them when living. Casting about for some aged one, yet spared, we thought of Lieut. Gov. Thomas G. Alvord, of Syracuse, and he has graciously complied with our request. Without further introduction we give his admirable letter; preceding it, however, by saying that he was for many years the owner and occupant of what is known as "Governor's Island," now the property of Mr. Emery. It is the first island above the one upon which Mr. C. G. Emery built a beautiful villa, which he has lately enlarged and greatly improved. Mr. Alvord's long connection with the political history of the State has made his name most familiar to our people under the cognomen of "Old Salt," a name earned in the Legislature by his persistent adherence to the fortunes of Syracuse where the well-known Onondaga Salt Springs have been so long a source of profit to the State, as well as the source of very much of the earlier wealth and importance of that city.

SYRACUSE, February 25, 1895.
JNO. A. HADDOCK, ESQ.:

MY DEAR SIR,—I am in receipt of your pleasant letter of request that I dot down something of a history of my early experiences as an amateur fisherman on the glorious and lordly St. Lawrence. To this request I cheerfully accede, and leave to you the decision and final judgment whether or not it shall find its way into your contemplated history of the St. Lawrence and its 1,000 islands.

I first began my piscatorial career in the waters of the Hudson river, nine miles above Albany, when I was young enough to be without discretion, but old enough to hook a sunfish, and consequently came near, on one occasion, being drowned by falling from the dock into the river. My love for the sport followed me into my college life, and as often as possible I explored the waters of Long Island Sound for its black-fish, porgies, etc. I carried the taste with me to the Berkshire Hills, and in a sojourn of two years explored all the trout streams and pickerel and bass ponds within reach of a day's journey from Pittsfield, Massachusetts. I divided my time for two years between Blackstone and my trout-rod, on the edge and over the line between wilderness and semi-civilization at Keeseville in Clinton county, and, when a full-fledged lawyer in Salt Point, I had a right to stick out my sign as "Atty. at Law," there was quite often added at the bottom a temporary postscript, "P. S. Gone fishing."

From time to time I would hear about the beauties of the St. Lawrence and its many islands in conjunction with its unequalled excellence as a hunting ground for ducks, and its great abundance of the gamiest fish to be found in fresh waters. I had a long-time acquaintance with a Mr. Dutton, a noted music dealer of Utica, who as early as in the later forties, was in the habit of spending a portion of the year with his sons fishing on the river; so finally, in 1852, I proposed to a brother-in-law visiting me from Indiana, an excursion to Alexandria Bay via Oswego. Accordingly, one September morning we landed there from the old "Cataract," whose bones have but

GOVERNOR ALVORD,
Author of Two Interesting Articles in this Souvenir.

NAPTHA LAUNCH, OWNED BY PROF. BLANDER, AT WESTMINSTER PARK.

very lately disappeared from the waters of the lower bay at Clayton, where she had enjoyed a rest for many years after she ceased to be a floating passenger transport. At that time Alexandria Bay was the Mecca of fishermen, and Clayton the headquarters of square-timber cutting, and no boatman for fisher-folk hailed from there until some years thereafter. Old man Crossmon kept the only caravansarie at Alexandria Bay, and his then small establishment on the rocks was hardly ever found unable to accommodate all comers. The enormous charge of $1.00 per day also included sufficient lunch for the noon-day meal of both sportsman and guide, taken "al fresco," on some opportune island; the food furnished was well prepared, and the more delicate accessions, now considered almost necessities, were provided under the careful watch of the hostess. It was always neat, abundant and palatable.

The boats of that day were but the crude prototypes of the present exquisite ones, which have no superiors on the globe in form, finish or perfect adaptability, with their well-matched oars, center boards, cushioned chairs, and other requisites, superior in all respects for the uses to which they are put. Then, under the command of Commodore Ned Patterson, still living and still a guide (octogenarian sure, if not centenarian), I embarked on my first fishing excursion in a boat made of pine (not piano finished), sharp at each end, not more than 14 feet long, low-sided, with naked wooden boards, without back-rests for seats. Loaded down almost invariably on the return from a day's fishing with their human cargo and catch of fish, the gunwales would be perilously near the level of the water of the river. The remembered oarsmen or guides of that day were old man Griffin, Ned Patterson, Alph and Tom Comstock, the last named being my favorite, and after my first visit invariably my guide until some time after Alexandria Bay was abandoned for Clayton as the nearer point for the more desirable fishing grounds. Not knowing the outfit best adapted to the river in the matter of fishing-tackle, and being advised that the boatman furnished all that was necessary in that regard, we took none with us, but used the native tools. These were crude in very deed, the poles were home-made; the lines were rough and the spoon for trolling was literally the bowl of an iron or pewter spoon with a single big coarse hook, brazed on the lower end, and attached to the line without swivel, and did not rotate but simply wobbled in the water; live bait for bass was not then thought of, but a supply of worms accompanied each boat. The Duttons were there with their more artistic appliances, consisting of spoons with swivels, and of various colors, and fairly smooth laid-lines and jointed bamboo rods; but with all their fancy rigs they very seldom succeeded in beating our catch with the homelier tools. Rev. Dr. Bethune was there; he was the donor of the Stone Church in the village, in which, much to the gratification of the natives and visitors, he always officiated on Sundays when in town. He was a bass fisherman and used a fly as a lure. After leaving Utica for New York he still occasionally was to be met in the season at his favorite resort luring the bass with the delusive fly during the week, and tempting men and women on Sundays, by his powerful pulpit eloquence, to a better and purer life. There and then I first met Seth Green, and then commenced a warm friendship which ended only with his death. He never failed for years to supply me, "unsolicited on my part," with an abundance of his own-make of flies, both single and in gang, and whenever we met he always gave me a learned lecture on the progress in piscatorial science and art. He was at that time and for many years thereafter the only fisher dweller on any of the beautiful islands of the St. Lawrence Archipelago, making the now renowned Manhattan Island his home where his house may still be seen, though remodeled [see frontispiece]. His memory will be " Green "in the recollection of many to whom his example and teachings have imparted a love for a sport and pastime compelling them to commune with nature where dressed in her most enticing garb and to drink in the pure air of heaven, bearing to them a healthful cure — restoring body and soul to a perfect health and vigor, and sending one back to battle with the world with not only renewed and restored bodily strength but with a mind attuned to a higher and purer conception of duty to themselves and others.

The recital of the surroundings of my first visit to the St. Lawrence would be incomplete if I did not dot down my impressions of the natural beauties of the scene afforded by the river and its many island gems. I am a natural fisherman; given intensely, whenever opportunity permits, to entice and ensnare the cunning water dwellers. I have been a visitor to the St. Lawrence, with but two exceptions, each returning season, for over forty years; and during that period I have again and again traversed in its widest extent every nook and corner, islet and island, and mainland as well, every shoal and deep of the St. Lawrence, from Chippewa on the north to the deep indentation at the head of Long or Wolfe Island, stretching up into Lake Ontario, called Reed's Bay. I have never been any day upon the water, when my line has not been neglected for hours in order to drink in the invigorating and health-laden air and the wondrous, indescribable beauty and (may I say it?) sublimity of diversified island and encircling water.

I am not going to prolong this screed by a recital of my wonderful exploits as a fisherman. I leave that task to time, and, perhaps, in the distant future I may be deified as the great "American Fisherman," and my reported deeds almost match with those wonderful tales rehearsed at camp fire, or where'er the jolly fishermen congregate.

Suffice it to say that I generally captured all the fish I was entitled to, but, what was far better, I took in annually a load of health which has prolonged my life and made me retain the feelings of youth in spite of the increasing number of years added to my roll-call.

An article on the 1,000 islands of the St. Lawrence would be incomplete unless a full description of one of their noted features, "The Boatman, or Guide," was given. Both by an experience and observation of 40 years I have carefully noted and studied them, and can safely claim for them a deservedly proud position; in the main, browned by their constant exposure and wearing the rough habiliments necessary for their calling, they are, with rare exception, Gentlemen in the truest acceptation of the word; accomplished oarsmen and sailors. Though not learned in books, they read the weather more correctly than do the trained signal-service men of the Government; they are perfect masters in the knowledge of the ways of the errant fishes; under their care, gentle woman and careless child are safe from all harm or danger. They are enthusiastic sportsmen, they never strike for an eight-hour day, but urge the lazy fisherman to an early breakfast and sunrise-start; and, oftener than their employer, insist upon one more circle or cast, so as to add another to the well-filled fish box, even if the shades of night are deepening around them. In all the time I have known the river I have never heard of the loss of the life of a fisherman or visitor by the carelessness of the Guide. Without apparent fatigue, they ply the oar for more than twenty miles, to be repeated each recurring day. They teach the tyro the gentle art, they cook you a noon-day meal the gods might envy; never sulking, always anxious to do all they can for your comfort and success. The Boatman of the 1,000 islands is easily the peer of that great army who contribute to the innocent enjoyment of others.

THOMAS G. ALVORD.

Syracuse, February, 1895.

THE FIDLER'S ELBOW, CANADIAN CHANNEL.

THE FRENCH OWNERS OF THE THOUSAND ISLANDS.

IT may interest the reader to know who, next to the Aborigines, were the first owners of what where known to the French as "Les Milles Isles," and to their British conquerors, and to us, as "The Thousand Islands." In the abstracts of "the Fealty Rolls" (Actes de foy et Hommage), to be found in Vol. IV of the Canadian Archives at Ottawa, is a record of the original title to these islands, which then constituted a single grant or "fief." The entire body of islands was first granted to Sieurs Piot de Langloisierie and Petit, in 1714; and, with some enlargements, was regranted to the same parties in 1752. After the death of the original grantees, one-half of the original fief, that is to say, one-half of the entire body of islands, was granted to Louis Hertel and Sieur Lamarque; both of whom took the oath of fealty, the former as the widower of Marie Hippolyte Celeron, and husband of Susanne Piot de Langloisierie; and the latter, as the husband of Marie Anne Theresa Celoron de Blainville, who was the daughter, as was Marie Hippolyte Celeron, of Sieur Celeron de Blainville, M'd'lle Piot de Langloisiere, daughter of the first owner.

The other half of the fief, with its enlargement, was granted to Eustache Louis Lambert Dumont, who had acquired the right of his brothers and sisters, all being children of Eustache Lambert Dumont and his wife Charlotte, also a daughter of the first owner. Later on, one-fourth of the fief was transferred to Catherine Claus, widow of William Claus, John Johnson Claus and Warren Claus, sons of William Claus; and Catherine Anne Claus and a widow Geale, a married daughter of William Claus, and also her children by marriage, took the oath in relation to William Claus' part of the fief, which he had purchased from one Jacob Jordan, and he from Simon Fraser, who purchased from Louis Hertel de Chambly, who took the oath for half the fief in 1781. Another fourth of the fief was held at this time by Jouvier Dontail Lacroix, as heir to his father, Hubert Lacroix; and by the purchase of the rights of his brothers and sisters. Hubert Lacroix had received this part of the fief as a gift from Marie Anne Theresa Celeron, the widow of Sieur Lamarque.

The William Claus above mentioned was the son of Col. Daniel Claus, who was a prominent officer in the War of the Revolution. He was the deputy superintendent of Indian affairs, and at one time was deputy quartermaster-general under Col. Barry St. Leger, on the expedition to Fort Stanwix. Col. Claus spent a great portion of his time during the war at Montreal, but was a frequent visitor at Carlton Island, and other posts on lake Ontario. He was born in the Mohawk valley, and having an intimate knowledge of the Iroquois language, he was appointed interpreter for Sir William Johnson, and accompanied him on the expedition against Dieskau, as a lieutenant of rangers. He married a daughter of Sir William Johnson. He became a captain in 1761, and in 1776 visited England, and returned as deputy superintendent of Indians, with the rank of colonel. He died in Cardiff, Wales, in 1787. His wife died in Canada in 1801. It was he who translated the book of Common Prayer into the Indian tongue.

How these grants were finally disposed of, the writer is unable to say; but at all events, one-half of the original fief passed into the hands of the United States after the War of the Revolution, and were by them sold to Alexander Macomb. Whether the owners were reimbursed by the British government, does not appear, nor does it appear in what way the St. Regis Indians have a claim upon that part of the Thousand Islands which lie in Canadian waters. One thing, however, is certain; if those old proprietors could be favored to-day with a bird's-eye view of their former possessions, they would be somewhat astonished at their appearance, especially with the Yankee half of the original fief; and, but for a peculiar sentimentalism which for years has pervaded the country press of Canada, the whole fief would be to-day the wealthiest and most attractive summer resort in the world, and equally as beneficial to Canada as to the United States. Now that the sale of many of the islands in Canadian waters has been made, let us look for such improvements as will correspond with their natural beauties and splendid situation, and commensurate with the magnitude of the grand Canadian province in which they are located, and with the energy and patriotism of her refined and cultivated people.

SHOOTING THE RAPIDS.

THOUSAND ISLAND PARK.

THIS park seems to have been an outgrowth of that wave of religious sentiment which swept over the country about 1874 — the result, perhaps, of the reaction in men's minds which usually follows great financial depression. Its contemporary developments are visible at Asbury Park and Ocean Grove, two grand summer resorts upon the seaboard of New Jersey, and the latter manifestation of the same sentiment at Chautauqua, in Western New York. All of these movements towards summer residences bore a distinctly religious character, and were the outgrowth of a sincere desire to glorify God, and yet, in doing so, to make summer homes where families could receive the benefit of change of scene and of air and perhaps in their manner of living.

The manifestation of this impulse at Thousand Island Park is due to the efforts of Rev. J. F. Dayan, a well-known Methodist minister, now on the retired list. He conceived the idea that the Methodist denomination would gladly support such a resort, and he selected the southwesterly end of Wellsley Island as the most eligible spot. The selection was judicious, and his efforts were soon appreciated. The needed lands were mainly purchased (1,000 acres) from Capt. Throop, whose title was only the third remove from the State itself. Success crowned the Association's efforts, $22,000 worth of lots having been sold in a single day. Men struggled to secure the most desirable sites. It was unfortunate for the young town, however, that the extreme religious element so far prevailed that illy-considered restrictions were imposed as to entrance fee, etc., but in time these peculiar views have given way to more liberal ideas. To this day, however, no steamer is allowed to land at their dock on the Sabbath, the present management adhering to the original plan that the Sabbath should be not only a day of rest but of religious observance. The Thousand Island Park is now, as it was at the beginning, a place where a man can leave his wife and children and feel sure that they will not be exposed to any harmful influence of any nature — a place where "the assassins of society" would have no inducement whatever to come.

The situation of the park is superior. Back from the river-front plateau rises a rocky mound, nearly 200 feet in height, which afforded a permanent and accessible locality for a water reservoir with pressure enough to flood the highest buildings. The soil is productive, resting upon the moraine of this region, the result of glacial action. The second-growth of timber is mainly oak and elm, remarkably straight and vigorous, and the lot-owners are only called upon to decide what tree should be felled, and not what they should plant. It is difficult to conceive of a finer location. With man's intelligent supervision the place may be made the most delightful in America. Other resorts have the ocean, with its drifting sands, its fogs, its storms — this park has the great St. Lawrence, whose waters come sweeping down from the far Northwest, pure as the melting snow can make them, fresh as the breath of spring, placid as Nature itself. To live in such a spot is a benediction for man; there he forgets his cares, and grows into a life of contentment and thankfulness.

At the Thousand Islands there is a perceptible odor of ozone in the atmosphere. By some it is called a "sulphurous," by others a fishy smell. But there is a difference. Ozone is of itself an energetic chemical agent. It is a preservative, not a putrifying influence. In this it differs widely from oxygen, the principle in the air which assists in decay. There seems to be a reason for the belief that the beneficial effects produced upon many invalids from a residence among the Thousand Islands

The original trustees were: Chancellor E. D. Haven, D. D., President; Willard Ives, Vice-President; Col. Albert D. Shaw, John F. Moffett, J. F. Dayan, E. C. Curtis, E. Remington, Hon. James Johnson, M. D. Kinney.

Mr. Dayan continued a member of the board and as secretary and general manager until 1881. Chancellor Haven resigned in 1881, having been made one of the Bishops of the church at the preceding General Con-

THE COLUMBIA HOTEL AT THOUSAND ISLAND PARK.

or upon the sea-shore, is due largely to the ozone discernible in those localities.

An indication of the progressive spirit of the park is the Thousand Island *Herald*, a weekly newspaper published there, ably conducted, of which E. F. Otis is editor, and Rev. William Searle, manager.

The original capital of the Association was fixed at $15,000, of which $7,100 was paid in cash. On January 11th, 1876, the indebtedness of the Association was $24,647.81 and the assets $57,300.94. The capital was afterwards increased to $50,000.

ference. He was succeeded by Rev. I. S. Bingham, D. D., who, in 1883, gave place to Rev. M. D. Kinney, A. M., who had been a member of the board of trustees from the first. Under his energetic management many improvements were perfected, and there came a period of decided growth. He continued as President for seven years, and the Park owes much to his management, and to the fact that he has been of financial aid at many times.

The present trustees are: George P. Folts, President; George C. Sawyer, Vice-President; Dr. A. W. Goodale, Treasurer; Walter Brown, Assistant Treasurer; W. R. Fitch, Secretary. Trustees: George P. Folts, F. G. Weeks, George C. Sawyer, W. R. Fitch, Walter Brown, Dr. A. W. Goodale, James P. Lewis, M. R. LeFevre, A. Gurnee. Rev. celebrated preachers in the United States and Canada, and the reputation of the Park in this respect has been admirably sustained. Rev. Dr. J. E. C. Sawyer, editor of the Northern Christian Advocate, delivered two sermons there on July 22, 1894, that were the

THE LATE CHARLES CROSSMON,
The First Summer Hotel-keeper upon the St. Lawrence.

Wm. Searles, D. D., is director of the Tabernacle services.

From the very first the design of the Association has been to secure the best native talent for religious services, and also bringing from abroad men of established reputation and ability. In this way the noble Tabernacle has had under its roof some of the most finished and stirring the writer has ever listened to. The influences that have gone out from that Tabernacle have been peculiarly inspiring and noble, and its services have done much to popularize the Park. The auditorium has a natural slope, the acoustics are admirable, and the sight most unique and interesting when the vast place is filled with the sea of upturned faces confronting the speaker. Situated in a fine growth of oak, with great curtains at the sides, which can be raised or lowered as desired, the people are brought face to face with nature, whence they are inspired to look up to nature's God.

It should not be forgotten that the Park as well as the Islands partake of an international character to a great extent, and the Union Jack floats in close proximity to our own beloved Stars and Stripes, and that prayers ascend for the noble Queen from the same desk as the petition for our honored President.

The population of Thousand Island Park is somewhat of a floating one, as regards its permanence, but there can be no doubt as to its pre-eminent respectability. It numbers 800 to 6,000 souls. Indeed the only occasion for fear in these established popular resorts is that they may become exclusively the summer abodes of the rich alone. At this place, however, there are ample accommodations for people of every class in point of material wealth, the hotel charges being $3.00 per day for the best, $1.00 per day for a cheaper but really comfortable place, and board in private cottages at even less rates. It is pre-eminently a democratic place, and friendliness is cultivated as not an altogether obsolete sentiment. The trustees and officers are capable men, composed of persons who have made their way from small beginnings and have always been in sympathy with plain and home-like methods. The cottages are numerous, all of them attractive, some beautiful. We give views of the new hotel which replaces the one burned in 1891, and some of the more elegant structures. A traveler upon any of the steamers which thread their way among the islands will observe that more people get on and off at Thousand Island Park than all the other resorts put together. The plotted ground for cottages occupies about 100 acres. The Association has sold off 200 acres for farming, and about 700 acres are left, devoted to dairying.

The pumping engines of the Association, their system of sewerage, water supply and electric lights are superior and unexcelled. Their dynamo plant and the beautiful machinery there (of the Watertown Steam Engine Company) are models of mechanical skill.

J. A. H.

STREET VIEW OF THE CROSSMON, ALEXANDRIA BAY.

THE CROSSMON HOUSE AND ITS FOUNDER.

IN speaking of Mr. CHARLES CROSSMON, whose portrait is shown on page 65, necessitates an extended notice of his house, now one of the finest on the river, and ably managed by his son, though Mrs. CROSSMON, SR., is yet able to be about and to give general supervision of much of the inner workings of the establishment.

"THE CROSSMON IN 1848."

CHARLES CROSSMON came to Alexandria Bay in 1846, and none of the energetic men who have become so prominent in that locality has done more (and very few as much) to bring into prominence that most deserving and popular summer resort than Mr. CROSSMON. Without any special influence to aid him, and without any capital save his own right hand and the clear head to govern it, aided by one of the most capable and industrious wives the country has ever known, he grew into a great success as a hotel-keeper, and left an indelible impress upon the Bay that will not be soon forgotten, and can never be altogether effaced. He was born in Watertown, N. Y., and had but few advantages in his youth, his education having been confined to the common school. Unluckily for him, and certainly an unpromising beginning of a business life which has proven so successful, he was one of the youngsters who were seduced into that "Patriot" army that undertook, in 1837, to invade Canada and redress the "wrongs" which a few Canadian malcontents had glowingly depicted in "Hunter" lodges and elsewhere. CROSSMON was one of those who were "cooped up" in the old windmill below Prescott, and who courageously refused to desert Von Schoultz, their leader, when Preston King came at night with the "Paul Pry" and offered to carry them away to the American shore. He was about twenty years of age at that time, and on account of his youth was finally pardoned by the British authorities, and released after an anxious and somewhat protracted imprisonment in Fort Henry at Kingston, from which several of these "patriots" were marched to a felon's death upon the scaffold.

He commenced hotel-keeping in an humble way at the Bay in 1848, succeeding his father-in-law in a small country tavern adapted to the wants of that early day. There were, however, even then some visitors to the islands and river in pursuit of fish and rest. Among the distinguished men who made the old "Crossmon" famous were William H. Seward, William L. Marcy, Martin Van Buren and his son John, Silas Wright, Frank Blair, Preston King, Rev. Dr. Bethune, General Dick Taylor, the Breckenridges, and many others equally distinguished.

As the tide of pleasure travel set in toward the St. Lawrence and its islands, "The Crossmon" was, from time to time, enlarged, and finally the present magnificent hotel was built on the site of its earliest predecessor. In the new structure everything that is desirable in a first-class hotel has been provided for, and in its management every facility is furnished, and the fullest attention given to the wishes and requirements of its guests. Its rooms are all pleasantly situated, affording charming views of the neighboring scenery. There are suites for families, with private bath-rooms and all conveniences, besides single and connecting rooms in every part of the house, all handsomely furnished. The elevator is in operation constantly, and the stairways are broad and easy. There are spacious and elegantly furnished drawing-rooms, wide corridors and broad verandas, and, from the latter, one of the most delightful views to be found in this entire region may be had. The main diningroom is on the river side of the house. Its tables are furnished with costly china, silver and cut glass and the finest linen, and supplied with the rarest fruits and delicacies. Its service is unexcelled. A pleasant dining-room is provided for children in charge of nurses. The importance of providing special comforts and amusements for the children is recognized in and about this establishment. There are accommodations for nurses in their care of the little ones, and opportunities for wholesome sports are at hand.

"The Crossmon's" surroundings are attractive. Every crevice of the immense rock upon which its river side rests is adorned with a bed of flowers or a small shrub. On the street side are graveled walks and drives, and a circular plat for out-door games, with easy benches protected by a canopy. Stretching eastward from the hotel is Crossmon's Point, with its broad, level lawn, bordered by the docks and landings for steamboats and skiffs. The dockage here is the most complete and extensive of any on the river. The smooth, new planking invites the guests for a promenade.

At night "The Crossmon," in doors and out, presents a scene of brilliancy. Rows of colored lights illumine the verandas, and shine from its many towers, shedding a wealth of color upon the water. The drawing-rooms are filled with guests engaged in social pastimes, and all about the place there is light and life and gayety. The arrival of the steamers at evening is celebrated by a display of fireworks in front of the hotel and on the neighboring islands, making a picture indescribably beautiful.

In speaking thus extendedly of "The Crossmon," we have really been illustrating the successful efforts of Mr. CROSSMON himself, for his hotel was his life, and upon it he lavished all his energy, and it rewarded his honest faith. No trouble was too great for a guest; the sick had all the care possible if by chance they fell ill there, and the result was that every guest became a personal friend. In that way "The Crossmon" has enjoyed a steady return of its old patrons year by year. Indeed one patron has spent thirty-eight consecutively recurring summers there.

Personally Mr. CROSSMON was unassuming, earnest in his friendships, steadfast in his purposes, and loyal to all those who aided to develop Alexandria Bay. In the midst of his complete success he was called away to another country, leaving a name unblemished, and a memory sweet and grateful.

The elder CROSSMON having died in 1892, Mr. CHARLES W. CROSSMON succeeds the firm of Crossmon & Son, whose management has made this hotel noted throughout the world, and the favorite headquarters in later days of such men as President Arthur, Gen. Sheridan, Cardinal McClosky, Herbert Spencer, Charles Dudley Warner, B. F. Reinhart, Will Carleton, and other notables, whose spoken and written praises have added greatly to the popularity of the islands and this fine hotel, which keeps pace with progress.

THE PROMENADE, WITH STEAMER ST. LAWRENCE MAKING A LANDING.

DR. ADDISON WIGHT GOODALE.

SOME BIOGRAPHICAL SKETCHES.

DR. ADDISON WIGHT GOODALE,
Financial Agent of the Thousand Island Park Association.

AS the son of Ruggles and Betsey Wight Goodale, who settled at an early day in Fowler, St. Lawrence County, N. Y., where the subject of our sketch was born, August 17, 1831. His early education was in the common schools of that primitive period, until 1851. He afterwards attended the Gouverneur Wesleyan Seminary for two years. In 1855 he began to study medicine with Dr. Abell, at Antwerp, afterwards graduating at the Albany Medical College as an M. D. This was in 1858, and in that year he married Miss Helen Jane Fowler, daughter of Lester and Dollie Fowler, of Antwerp. In 1858, he began the practice of medicine in the town of Rutland, following those older men, Drs.

Munson, Smith and Spencer. He was in practice there when the Rebellion showed its horrid front, and when the 10th Heavy Artillery was recruited, he joined it as assistant surgeon. He served with that fine body of troops until their final muster-out in July, 1865, proving himself an able, industrious, and conscientious officer. [For muster-out rolls of the officers of this large and gallant regiment, see p. 75 of Haddock's History of Jefferson County.]

His protracted absence in the army had largely depleted his practice, and when he was mustered out he removed his family to Watertown, where he remained until 1867, and then accepted a position in the medical department of the Phœnix Mutual Life Insurance Co., at Hartford, Conn. The Doctor became a trusted and important officer in that company, particularly in settling claims. This relation with that leading company continued until 1885, when he returned to Watertown. He has since been engaged in banking in South Dakota, now being president of a bank there. He is a large land-owner in the West and in Jefferson county. Though educated as a physician, he may appropriately be classed as a farmer. But the only thing the writer has ever heard him allude to in any spirit of pride or emulation was in connection with his service as a school teacher, he having taught eight seasons, and there are hundreds of men and women now in active life who can look back to Dr. Goodale's advice and instruction for the starting point in their endeavors to live useful lives.

In 1885, Dr. Goodale was elected one of the directors of the Thousand Island Park Association, and is now the treasurer and chief financial officer of that important organization, which is spoken of elsewhere in this History. The exacting duties of this position, together with his own private business, now take up all his time, leaving him no leisure for the practice of his profession.

The Doctor is a large man, nearly six feet tall, of pleasant face and agreeable speech — companionable and friendly — inviting confidence by his open countenance and pleasant ways. Springing from "the plain people," he is pre-eminently democratic, easily approached, an honored citizen, because an honorable one. He is yet in the prime of life, although he is one of those who passed through our great war after he had come fully to man's estate. His excellent wife shares his prosperity, and it is a pleasure to see them together.

REV. JOHN FERDINAND DAYAN,

WELL known as a distinguished minister in the Methodist Episcopal church, was born in the town of Lyme, Jefferson county, N. Y., January 23, 1819. His father was Dr. John Dayan, a distinguished physician, who came from Lowville, where he was educated and studied medicine with Dr. Perry, also a distinguished surgeon in his day. Soon after obtaining his degree, Dr. John Dayan married Polly Henry, of Lowville, N. Y., whose father was a captain in the Revolutionary army, and among the earliest settlers of Lewis county. The doctor emigrated to the town of Lyme, where he commenced the practice of his profession, and continued it until his death by accidental drowning in July, 1835, in his 42nd year.

The Dayan family trace their descent from a prominent Austrian family, in which were three celebrated military generals, the last of whom was that field marshal who was commander-in-chief of all the armies under Maria Theresa, in her seven years' war against Frederick the Great. The family was originally of German origin — a town bearing the name of Daun still existing in that country. About a hundred years ago the name was Americanized by changing the spelling from Daun to Dayan. On leaving college, the paternal grandfather of Mr. Dayan came to America during the Revolutionary war. He landed in New York in 1780, and died in Amsterdam, N. Y., in 1893.

After the death of his father, the subject of this sketch went to live with his uncle, Judge Charles Dayan, of Lowville, N. Y. There he entered the Lowville Academy. After completing his academic course, he studied law. Just previous to his being admitted to the bar, he became interested in the study of the Bible as a law book, which led to his conversion and connection with the Methodist Episcopal church in the Spring of 1842. Under the pastoral guidance of Rev. James Erwin, he united with the Black River Conference in 1844, and entered upon the work of the ministry, in which he continued until 1867, when his failing health necessitated his giving it up.

In 1845 he was united in marriage to Miss Clarissa Julia Chase, eldest daughter of Rev. Squire Chase, one of the earliest missionaries to darkest Africa. The writer remembers him as a man of extraordinary force and capacity. He was one of the best organizers the Methodist heirarchy could command at that time. Of stalwart frame, his presence was commanding. He possessed a voice of great volume, and it reached to the uttermost parts of the largest church. He was regarded as the ablest preacher in the old Black River Conference.

Rev. Mr. Dayan served the following charges: LeRay, Adams, Clayton, Syracuse,

REV. JOHN FERDINAND DAYAN.

Fairfield, Lowville, Theresa, Cape Vincent, Ilion, Carthage.

At Theresa the writer and his family sat under his preaching. His manner was persuasive, his diction classical, his sermons more than interesting — they touched the heart. The largest revival remembered in Theresa was during his pastorate, and when he left that charge he carried with him the affectionate remembrance of every member of the church and congregation.

In 1866 he was made Presiding Elder of the Watertown district, a position calling for a robust constitution and endless industry. His labors in that position impaired his health, and he relinquished with many regrets his cherished life-work.

Mr. Dayan was in every respect a progressive man, and in 1872-3 he had given much thought to the project of opening a Christian summer resort among the Thousand Islands. To him, more than to any other one man, is due, not only the inception of the plan, but its reduction to a practical basis. Not that his plan met with disfavor or that some capitalist could not be found who would invest money enough to try the experiment. But the details were enormous; the amount of tact required was surprising, for local jealousies had to be placated, the enthusiasm of the Methodists aroused, and the organization so poised as to be distinctly religious, yet not repelling those who were not church members nor church goers. In all these intricate manipulations Mr. Dayan showed himself an adept — manifesting a business capacity that surprised his friends. His plans found ample fruition, and the Thousand Island Park stands to-day his ablest advocate. For six years Mr. Dayan was the manager of that Association, and, up to the time he resigned from its board of control, it owed to his forethought, perseverance and zeal all that it was.

Thenceforward his life has merged gradually into the "sere and yellow leaf." With health much impaired he waits patiently for that passing hence which will reveal to him the blessedness of those who, through evil and good report, in hours of deepest despondency, even when tormented by doubts and uncertainties, have yet steadily stood for Christ and his glorious cause; and who, having been faithful over a few things, shall surely be called to the command of higher things, and even reign with Him whose faithful servant he has been for nearly sixty years.   J. A. H.

THE MEN I HAVE MET UPON THE GREAT RIVER.

BY THOS. G. ALVORD, EX-LIEUT.-GOV. OF NEW YORK.

A FRIEND has suggested that I could write a very interesting human history of the river's rapid growth as a sportsman's paradise, a health-bearing, exhilarating, joy-inspiring refuge for tired and invalid humanity. It will be readily conceded that in the performance of my task I must omit mention of many — for the many I have met are legion in number. And again, looking back over a period of more than forty years, I must unavoidably fail to recall many, the mention of whose names would be of great interest. In order to do justice to my own city and to scores of other cities and towns, I would need but strike a few names from their annual directories, and then append the corrected lists to this article, to enumerate "The Men I Have Met upon the Great River." But to accomplish the undertaking in some acceptable way and within reasonable limits, I must cease apology and explanations, and proceed with my projected work, or I shall never finish it.

I have already, in another chapter in this Souvenir, had something to say of my first experience on the noble river, and I beg again to introduce to your notice the REV. DR. BETHUNE, the original fly-caster of the St. Lawrence. Need I say that his profound learning, his acknowledged preëminence as a pulpit orator, and withal his kindly, open-hearted, Christian benevolence will remain a pleasant remembrance so long as the waters of his beloved river flow from the lakes to the sea.

The DUTTONS, father and sons, who gave us the silken line and the polished rotating spoon, will be remembered as giving as much of music and harmony to their beloved pastime as did their unequaled collection of drum and fife, cymbal and hautboy, fiddle and flute to their music-loving neighbors in "the pent up city," where their memory is ever green.

Is it necessary to make aught of explanation in bringing SETH GREEN to your notice? Not learned in schools, but an untiring, bright student of nature, he read as from an open book all the secrets of the finny tribe, over whom, by the consent of fishes and men, he was the sole and undisputed ruler. Educated in the school of Nature, he was Nature's nobleman, with a heart beating kindly toward all things animate.

Another noted individual is mixed in with my earliest recollections of the river. It is true I had never met him there, for he had visited the bay for the first and only time the year before my first arrival, but every time (and that was often) I tried the then super-excellent fishing-ground near the foot of Grenadier, I was very emphatically told where he had lunched when fishing, and he had lunched there so often that the natives, taking advantage of the fact that the much-lunched island lacked a name, solemnly decreed that from that time and forever thereafter it should be known as "VAN BUREN'S Island." It may be that the man is forgotten, but I believe that it is a matter of history that he was in the cloudy and distant past once President of the United States; but, not being reëlected, he went—fishing. But once I did come near to fishing in his company. Having given up his "job" at Washington and retired to the Lindenwold shades of sleepy Kinderhook he, after "cradeling his buckwheat," would hie to the lovely Hudson, a short two miles away, to fish. I happened one day to be the guest of a gentleman who lived on the bay where "Matty" was wont to fish; and on that day, he at one end and I at the other of the bay—both "Matty and myself—bobbed for white perch; each, I am happy to say, with great success.

In the later days of my periodical sojourn with old man Crossman, there came thither two of our country's most distinguished men on their way to the haunts of the princely salmon of the Saugeunay, pausing here for a few days to tempt the springy, cunning, sport-creating bass of the St. Lawrence. Theirs was a friendship at that time (somewhat clouded in later years) like that of Damon and Pythias. Utterly unlike in temperament, manners and action, they were both, I sincerely believe, a unit in their unselfish, powerful devotion to the best interests of their country in her hour of sorest trial and direst need. If in ROSCOE CONKLING, that stubborn, self-will, uncontrollable temper, never-dying enmity to all who dared oppose his will, had been tempered and softened by the suave, courtly and conciliatory manners and tact of CHESTER A. ARTHUR—in fine, if the better qualities of each had been used to neutralize the failings of both, it would have added increased weight to their great deeds patriotically done to save the Nation's life. Humanity is frail, never perfect; but in the world's picture of great men the heads of CONKLING and ARTHUR will loom up as did that of Saul among the prophets.

In the last year of my annually recurring stay at Alexandria Bay I met and fraternized with WILLIAM J. SKINNER, GEN. BENJAMIN F. BRUCE and FRANKLIN A. ALBERGER, the three Canal Commissioners of the State, and in their company NATHANIEL S. BENTON, then and for twelve years Auditor of the Canal Department, who had also during his long and busy life well and worthily discharged the duties of Surrogate, State Senator, United States Attorney for ten years, County Judge and Secretary of State. While they were ostensibly fishing, they were really weighing and measuring the probabilities of the success of an attempt of the mighty river to deflect to its own channel on its way to the ocean, the rapidly growing tonnage of the boundless

West, and to steal it away from our canals — those magnificent artificial waterways, alike the glory of the State and the wonder of the world, then under their official care. SKINNER proposed that above where the Great River took its primal leap in its heedless flight o'er rocky barrier and through mountain gorge in its mad haste to meet the sea, to swerve the mighty flow of its great body of waters to the valley of that other Great River the incomparable Hudson; but BRUCE and ALBERGER, with the potent aid of BENTON, rolled the mighty cloud-piercing peaks of the Adirondacks in his pathway, and sadly and reluctantly SKINNER abandoned the attempt. They finally departed with the satisfying belief that Nature had reared insurmountable barriers to the accomplishment of the river's dream of victory. Charon's boat has long since ferried them all across the dark stream, all too soon for them to know that men of their own blood pull down mountains and fill up seas with nature's forces tamed to their bidding. Already that growing city standing at the head of the greatest body of inland waters known to the world, demands and will have an unbroken waterway to the earth-encircling oceans. PROCTOR KNOTT, with burning eloquence, intentionally sarcastic, but truly prophetic, has made enduring fame for Duluth, its own great opportunities, coupled with its determined push and energy, compliment — aye, accentuate his unintentioned prediction. Our blood cousins and friendly rivals over the border, unstintedly aided from the overflowing coffers of the grand old Mother across the sea, are already deeping and widening the channel and curling the rush of the mighty river, building with its own stone and filling with its own water the gigantic steps overcoming the elevation from the Atlantic to the Great Lakes, and soon shall we view floating easily past our shores the mammonth freight-bearing ships of the world, laden with cargoes at the elevator-docks of Duluth, 2,000 miles inland from the western shore of the Atlantic, to be discharged unbroken at the distant ports of Europe, another 3,000 miles away from where inland flow and ocean tide meet to greet its coming.

In company with the Commissioners, and often thereafter, we joyfully welcomed the pleasant companion, skilled angler and accomplished clerk of Mr. SKINNER, Mr. HOPKINS, of Little Falls, occasionally accompanied by his worthy brothers in unity, BIRCH and LADUE, whose names and merited fame in those olden days scorned to be bound by the narrow valley of the bloody Mohawk. WRIGHT, the story teller of Geneva, the Jefferson county wit, and WALRATH, the terrible joker of Oneida, both good men and true, sometime Division Commanders on the Erie, have been met sounding the depth and measuring the breadth of its giant rival, the St. Lawrence.

In 1866 I changed my base, for at this time the habitat of the desirable game-fish seemed to have moved up stream, so that the boys of the Burg had to pull against the current of Wellesly Island in order to successfully compete with their Clayton rivals; at Clayton there were then two notable caravanseries, the Hubbard and the Walton, and without premeditation I dropped into the Hubbard, where for eleven years I was a summer fixture. Permit me to say here that both houses had good and well-deserved reputations, enhanced by the fact that the genial hosts were friends not rivals, and in its best sense friends of the guests of both; a favor (often offered) asked by the guest of one at the hands of the other, was met and granted promptly and cordially. I but voice the sincerely deep regret of their army of friends at their untimely taking off, and bespeak for their brave widows the kindly and bounteous support of all those who knew and esteemed their departed husbands. Mrs. JOHNSON is yet actively engaged in the care of the Walton, the grand property left her by her husband; and one who has seen her and recalls the fact that she was a neice of General WILLIAM H. ANGEL, the broadest man Clayton ever knew, will not fail to gladly come within the charmed circle of her kindly care and elegant personality.

About this period began the idea of island ownership and summer cottage; among the first to adventure was a broker from New York, EUGENE A. ROBINSON, who expended money

STEAMER ISLANDER, AT WESTMINSTER PARK DOCK.

freely on his island in grading and docking and the erection of a commodious and roomy mansion. He flourished for a time, an erratic meteor athwart the island sky, but at last the gravitation of his own errors brought him, burnt out and exhausted, down to earth.

One of my esteemed colleagues in the halls of legislation, and later, an honored representative of his district in Congress, E. KIRK HART, of Orleans, built himself at an early day, an imposing mansion facing Alexandria.

I have sailed and angled on the water and often lunched on the green-sward of an island in the company of the world-renowned sculptor, R. H. PARK. His more recently reported social standing, if true, leaves his artist fame his only claim for recollection.

I must occasionally bunch the men I have met on the river, and generalize their good points, else I will be unable to enumerate a tithe of the most worthy; so permit me to say that at Albany "as colleagues," and on the noble stream that marks the northwestern bounds of their county "as friends" I have met Hon. WILLIAM DEWEY, Hon. WILLIAM BUTTERFIELD, JAMES JOHNSTON, Col. W. W. ENOS, Hon. GEORGE E. YOST, HON. CHAS. R. SKINNER, Hon. HENRY SPICER, Hon. WILLIAM M. THOMSON and Hon. JOHN D. ELLIS, representatives of the County of Jefferson. In the rôle of law-makers of the State, I pronounce them all to have been faithful, capable and honest in the discharge of their official duties. We always meet with smiles of welcome and with hearty handshake. Some of them have been called, and have not been found wanting in the faithful and worthy discharge of other public duties.

It would seem proper in this connection to mention others of my fellow-legislators who renewed and strengthened the friendship begun at Albany by kindly greeting and mingled pleasures on the peaceful islands of the St. Lawrence; VAN HORN, VAN VALKENBURGH and LOW followed down, from Niagara's colossal leap, her angry waters, until, peaceful and quiet, they gently laved the shores of the many island-gems of the Great River; BURNS and DUGUID, of Onondaga, the "TWO CHARLIES," BAKER, of Monroe, and CHICKERING, of Lewis; WARNER MILLER, of Herkimer; CONGDON, of Cattaraugus; A. X. PARKER, of St. Lawrence; A. B. HEPBURN, of the same county; MOOERS, of Clinton, and KERN, of Madison. All these may well be proud of their public records. They have each enjoyed with me innocent sport in the balmy air of the River of Rivers.

A prominent figure on the river for many years was THEODORE S. FAXTON. I first knew him in my boyhood-days, as one of that coterie of brainy men — PARKER, BUTTERFIELD, CHILDS and FAXTON — controlling in the office or from the driver's box those wonderful lines of post-coaches which radiated from Utica, reaching East, West, North and South, the uttermost parts of our noble State, just then emerging from a state of nature into an active, thriving, energetic Commonwealth of civilization and progress. THEODORE S. FAXTON was a prominent factor in this march of progress, keeping pace with the onward step; from the position of an humble stage-driver, he reached the higher rounds of life's ladder, dying universally honored and deeply mourned.

In marked contrast, there was another well-known Utican, a frequent and ever-welcome visitor; few in the State are ignorant of the name and fame of AMMI D. BARBOUR. For many years, as soon as the halls of legislation were opened to the annual inrush of the people's servants, BARBOUR, seeking no certificate from an avowed constituency, followed in their wake and quietly, from choice, took his stand "outside but close up to the bulwarks" — a cool, level-headed mind-reader, with a persuasively eloquent tongue and a well-lined pocket, he forced upon the ignorant or lucre-loving representative the course which, not perhaps leading to glory, would certainly be to the "material" profit of the legislator; active and efficient in the ranks, he was early made chief of staff by General Tweed, and finally became the undisputed King of the Lobby. Apart from his discreditable calling, BARBOUR was a man entertaining and interesting; he was the best posted of all others on the political history of parties as well as the inner character of politicians, and he had the rare faculty of an easy and pleasant recital. Above all else, in private life he was respected and esteemed by his neighbors as upright, honest and correct in his family and social relations and business dealings. He was an enthusiastic angler, but never wooed the finny people except his worthy wife and favorite grandson enhanced his enjoyment by their presence and participation.

I have met, with great pleasure and intellectual profit, Judges of every grade, who, hailing their vacation with the hilarity and abandon of the school boy, have hastened to doff the ermine, and donning the well-worn habiliments of secular days, concealing the dignified brow beneath the broad-brimmed palm-leaf, have sought the balmy air and cool waters of the Great River to recuperate their jaded minds and weary bodies. First, in strict compliance with legal rule, and in due order of judicial precedents, we welcome, marching forward, hand clasped in hand, those two inseparable disciples of Walton, Chief Judges ANDREWS and RUGER, whose names are written on a more enduring scroll than this fleeting note. I refrain from marring, by any attempt of mine, to laud their fame. We have met the pleasant countenances of CALVIN E. PRATT and his able and eccentric namesake, DANIEL. They each worthily represent the honor, dignity and learning of the Supreme Court, but they are boys again as they dart in and out, around and about, the rock-bound and grass-covered islands of the Great River.

I must not forget that there resides in the Summer days, in his tasteful cottage erected on consecrated ground — he would select no other — my fellow townsman and friend, GEORGE N. KENNEDY. He needs no eulogy at my hands, for he is proving for himself, by his untiring industry and acknowledged preeminence at the bar, the folly of that legislative dictum, "that a man's ability and power for intellectual work and honorable toil ceases at the age of seventy years."

I recall two other gentlemen of this grade of judges — one still in harness — both in deserved public esteem, whose pleasant smile and friendly grip have been seen and felt on the waters of the St. Lawrence, CHARLES MASON and PARDON C. WILLIAMS. It was here that PETER B. McLENNAN acquired that calm mind and sound judgment marking his course on the bench to-day.

As County Judge and a colleague in the Constitutional Convention of '67-8, Member of Congress, Secretary of State and State Senator, the mere recital of his official honors stamp HOMER A. NELSON, of Dutchess, as an able and trusted public man, and I can testify that he was a keen and successful angler, and, by natural sequence, a polished gentleman. JEROME FULLER, of Monroe, was another fellow member in the Convention of '67-8, and the recital of his official positions, all filled ably and well, are sufficient testimony of his acknowledged worth and character. He has filled the additional positions of County Judge of Monroe, Territorial Judge of Minnesota, Member of Assembly and State Senator, as well as that of successful angler on the bonny St. Lawrence. The legal learning, sound judgment and righteous administration of justice which marked the judicial lives of Judges VAN VORST, of New York, and SMITH, of Cortland, were never lessened by their keen appreciation and enjoyment of the unequaled attraction of our summer paradise.

Last, but not least, comes the beaming face of that true hearted and broad minded son of Madison, once its honored Judge, CHAS. L. KENNEDY.

I had firmly resolved early in my life on the river that whenever the opportunity offered to suit my taste and not wholly empty my pocket, I would

"Be monarch of all I surveyed,
With none my right to dispute ;
From the center all around to the sea,
The lord of the fowl and the brute "—

in the shape of an island in the St. Lawrence. My eye always rested lovingly and hopefully on an island in the broad channel immediately opposite to and about one-half mile distant from the docks of Clayton. In the "native directory" it had been christened "Shot Bag" to keep company with a near-by island and islet called respectively "Powder Horn" and "Cap Box," each so designated from its fancied resemblance to one of these necessary appendages to the shot gun. I early became acquainted with the owner, a gentleman by the name of LAWRENCE, a successful hat, cap and fur dealer in the city of New York. By the way, it might as well be noted right here, that he was an accomplished fly-caster, his daily catch of beauties being seldom second in number in the friendly struggle of the jovial anglers for preëminence. A pleasant, genial companion, he is gone never to return, but he is not forgotten. To return to my island. For a number of years I was advised that it was not for sale, and other spots were urged upon my attention, but I still hoped for my first choice, and finally declining health induced my friend to make me a proposition to part with it at the price of $400. At length, confirmed in his own belief by the judgment of others whom he considered experts, that the island would measure at least four acres, he closed the deal with myself and son-in-law, JAMES A. CHENEY, at $100 per acre; and when the survey demonstrated that $170 paid for 1 70-100 of an acre (the area of the island), with great disappointment, somewhat forcibly expressed, but with unhesitating adherence to his pledged word, the owner executed the deed of transfer. In family convention — from which I was carefully excluded — the name of "Shot Bag" was dropped, and the newly-acquired summer home was rechristened "Governor's Island." It was never under any "government," but the denizens, adults and children alike, took in health, happiness and all edibles within reach. There the cannon roared, the flags waved, the beacons shone, not with hostile intent, but as a cordial welcome to the coming, and a kindly farewell to the departing friend. These pleasant days covered seventeen joyous summers. That island is one of the brightest gems that adorn the water-encircled diadem of the Great River. It has now fallen under the dominion of one who, with rare taste and skill combined with a judicious expenditure of wealth, is constantly adding new attractions to the wonderful beauties of America's peerless summer resort. A hearty welcome to CHARLES G. EMERY. Others have met him on the Great River, and we all trust that many happy summers still await him on its restful bosom.

We have not deserted the river of our love and our pride; but, a little nearer its source, on a projecting point on old Grindstone — its primary rocks still showing the deep scars of the Glacial Period —" Lindenwold" displays its unmatched beauties, and the old starry flag of "Governor's Island," undimmed, waves over it, and the doors of the same modest but roomy cottage, stand wide open to all friends.

Excuse this apparently wide departure from the original text. It was partly necessitated as a means by which to bring into deserved notice my friends LAWRENCE and EMERY, and partly to authorize the use of my well-filled cottage registry, containing the names of "men I had met upon the Great River," thus rejuvenating a failing memory and rescuing from oblivion the river history of many who should not be forgotten.

The REV. DR. REESE, of Albany, was first met on the river, on the inside of St. John's Island, fighting manfully for and rejoicing over the capture of his first muskalonge, a beauty of over thirty pounds in weight; the occasion made us fellows, and began (for me) a pleasant acquaintance, renewed almost yearly for many summers past. This eloquent divine is ever welcome to Clayton, for he never fails to interest crowded audiences from the local pulpit on the appointed rest-days from secular labor. The Doctor is, like all good anglers, wholesouled, genial and an exceedingly interesting raconteur.

The REV. DR. CALTHROP, hailing from the Central City, fulfilling strictly and conscientiously his clerical duties, figures also as astronomer, expert, and peerless billiardist and chess-player, and excels in each. While at home he (rather too often) reads from the Sun, dire storm, destructive blizzard, drenching rain or parching drouth, his presence in the valley of the St. Lawrence always insures us beautiful sun-shine, placid waters, and abounding game for the angler.

Once upon a time there came into the legislative halls from the home of Conkling, a worthy, honest man, who answered equally and readily to either of the familiar names of "UNCLE DAVID" or "APPLE BARREL" GRAY. His heart was set upon the passage of his only bill; it was a bill "To regulate the size of Apple Barrels." Passing through the ordeal of the appropriate committee, it came before the full body of the Assembly for discussion and amendment. The naughty boys of that body offered and adopted so many incomprehensible and inconsistent amendments, that soon the honest old man did not know "where he was at." He appealed to me — to whom he had somehow been attracted — to solve the difficulty; I undertook the task, and soon the chairman announced, that "what was left of the bill was ordered to be engrossed for a third and final reading;" with bulging eyes and bated breath, Uncle DAVID asked "what was left?" He was blindly informed, that the title was intact, but that the staves, hoops and heads of the barrel were missing. He was at first somewhat inclined to blame me for the catastrophy, but he was persuaded to visit me in my summer home, where the Lethean effect of the "pellucid" waters, and the electric shock transmitted to his body by the strike of the bass through the line attached to his submerged hook, cured him of all suspicion, and he became, and still is, one of my warmest friends; but I have occasionally heard him, when overcome with sleep, after a heavy lunch on a grass-covered island, mutter "My next Apple Barrel Bill shall have the hoops nailed on, and the heads nailed in, *and I will attend to it myself.*"

On the river for many years the most marked man to be met was a Mr. SELLECK, from Newbargh. He was evidently a well educated person, and as a conversationalist, entertaining and instructive. Though totally blind he went everywhere without a guide, with a firm and assured step. He would walk from the hotel to the landing, and enter his boat without aid, and he seldom returned at nightfall with a smaller catch of the finny tribe than a full average of the return captures of the day. Report said that in his business as designer and manufacturer of artistic and decorated furniture, he had but few equals and no superiors.

I must not omit the military arm of the Nation. My register records their presence singly and in squads, veteran corps, and regiments, Kentucky colonels and "high privates," with waving banners and martial music. They were peacefully inclined, however; the bivouac and battle-field were memories. They march erect and step proudly to the beat of the drum, save when tempting forage was uncovered; then "double quick" and rapid rush broke down all lines, and discipline was ignored. From the many (few can be named "Facile Princeps"), stands forth the gallant SLOCUM. Not on the battle field, but when white-robed peace smiled on the beloved country he fought to save, he laid him down to die. History will keep ever green the sacred memory of this patriot soldier.

Make way for the heroic SNIPER, leading to the peaceful banks and enticing islands of the Great River the few remaining veterans of that noble regiment, which — when three of its gallant number had fallen with the flag they died to save, raising that starry emblem from the dying hands of its last defender, bearing it proudly forward — he rallied to victory; the sods of the valley now press upon his breathless form, but in the memory of the multitude who but knew him to love him, the patriotic deeds of General GUSTAVUS SNIPER will endure forever.

The name of General DAVIES stands high on the roll of fame among the noted cavalry leaders in the late Civil War, his clarion voice and flashing sabre gave victory to his gallant troopers in many a well fought fray; he is the same general on the waters of the Great river; cool, determined, untiring, he strikes for the royal muskalonge, and the trophies that adorn his wigwam are large in size and great in number.

The erect and noble form of the "Hero of

YACHTING ON THE ST. LAWRENCE.

Fort Fisher" looms above the waves of his native river; General in war, he is now guardian in peaceful days, of that ark of safety, the Constitution of our fathers, he so bravely helped to rescue from destruction, and stands as St. Lawrence's sentinel on the ramparts of the Nation's capitol. Though an eye was cheerfully lost amid the scenes of battle, he still, with one, single to his duty, fights bravely to protect and perpetuate for his country the rights so nobly defended on many a bloody field. All honor and praise to General NEWTON MARTIN CURTIS.

There is a "WYLIE" man, whose countenance is a familiar one on the long reaches and deep bays. Do not be deceived by surmising that the "D. D." which the name carries with it stands for "Doctor of Divinity." He is too wily and a little too wicked for that; but he was a good soldier and loyal man when the nation needed good soldiers and loyal men to compel and perpetuate an unbroken Union, and he is well entitled to be called "General." The only bad mark on his character ever discovered was his attempt to carry off, on a wager, a basket of champagne, as the reward of the superiority of his catch (with his own unaided rod and reel), in the number of lawfully sized bass by one day's fishing, over that of an antagonist (bound by the same requirements). He apparently won the match by a very narrow margin, and announced the victory to his shouting comrades with wilder shouts than theirs. But a few hours of sober reflection brought swift repentance, and on bended knee he humbly confessed that a brother conspirator from one boat and a venal guide from another, with no regard for lawful weight, had tumbled into his craft the larger number of his reputed victims, and he tearfully, but manfully, rolled into the cottage-door of his competitor, the coveted prize. He has been forgiven, and hopes are strong that by continued repentance of past deeds of wickedness and firm resolve of an honest future he may yet be allowed to write "D. D." as well in rear as in front of his patronymic, and thus wipe out forever any sinister meaning to the honored name of "Wylie."

Seventeen years have passed away since WILLIAM H. VANDERBILT and the lamented WEBSTER WAGNER came here to spy out the land. Both have passed to the "beyond," but their keen business eyes — we have reason to know — took in all the beauties and possibilities of the grand panorama spread before their vision, and the fruits of that visit are clearly noticeable in the increased comfort and ease of access hither from all parts of the Union, and under the wise and able management of their successors this will not be abated, but improved and amplified.

Not clothed in trappings of war but in the habiliments of peace, we look on the face and admire the soldierly bearing of one of the elite of that crack regiment, New York's only 7th, CHRIS WOLF, an island-dweller and ever a welcome comrade. The quiet, unobtrusive HICKS, with pleasant wife and daughter, not only guards, but makes, with cow and chicken, homelike and enviable, the upper gate of our archipelago.

Scarcely fifty years ago 1,500 of the Thousand Islands of this great river lay upon its glassy waters in the garb of Nature's clothing, save where, on the larger ones, blackened stumps marked the incipient effort of the husbandman or the ruthless swath of the wood-devouring steamer, then first invading the peaceful waters. To-day, in quiet bower and shady nook, on bold promontory or wide-spread lawn, in single sites and in varying groups, from lower Grenadier to upper Wolf, reaching as an outlying sentinel beyond the line where lake and river join, tiny cottage and palatial mansion mark an almost continuous city of grandeur and beauty — the imposing Crossmon at one extremity, and the towering Frontenac midway to the deep Ontario, inclose many other gorgeous resting places as homes for the flitting sojourner. As the swift-darting inhabitants below the water's surface, so on its bosom in almost equal numbers shoot hither and thither the ever-restless steamers — many at stated intervals on regular duty bound, many with banners flying and gladsome music, laden with the people from deserted town and village breathing the balmy air and drinking in the gorgeous beauties of the Great River, as with twinkling feet and glad shout they greet its glories. The trim-built, lavishly-furnished, flag-enveloped, swift-running yachts, alive with their crews of summer residents, add to the wild carnival of pleasure and happiness, and human shout, shrill whistle, sharp-clanging bell and barbaric music drive the rightful owners of the waters, frightened and alarmed, to the lowest depths and darkest caves of their watery kingdom.

Now many of these many men (and lovely women, too, God bless them!) "I have met upon the Great River." Time and space alike forbid a mere recital of their names; I must, therefore, be content with a brief notice of a few others who have been foremost, and who have not yet ceased their loving labors in adding to Nature's wonderful work on this unequaled river.

The widely-known and sincerely lamented scholar and scribe, the late Dr. HOLLAND, is with us no longer; but his warm love for his "Bonny Castle" has descended to his surviving family, who still enjoy, and each returning season make more beautiful, the delightful spot he loved so well.

The HAYDENS, PULLMAN, the large-hearted BROWNING, the coal king of the Lehigh valley, the denizens of Westminster Park, and many others, still intent upon gilding the refined gold of their incomparable Bay, all bear faces I have met upon the beautiful River. I have met many of the men who summer in assured safety and peaceful comfort under the Christian banner of the itinerant Methodists; among them my home neighbors, none of whom need go from their Central City to find witnesses to their worthy and Christian character. (Judge KENNEDY I have already named) WEEKS, HOLDEN, PENN, LEE, SPRAGUE, and scores of others, are men I am proud to say "I have met upon the Great River."

I even own up that I knew SAM GRINNELL, when he pastured his cow on his island, now studded with many beautiful cottages, and joyously welcomed the thirsty dwellers on Prohibition-1,000-Island-Park to his choice dispensary of contraband whisky.

Round Island is peopled with many worthy of notable mention. Across its head, facing the on-coming waters, stand four dwellings: First, the modest villa of DR. WHEDEN, the pioneer of the island-dwellers, followed by Messrs. HAYES, VAN WAGONEN, and JAMES J. BELDEN, ex-mayor and congressman, who, applying well-earned wealth with sound judgment and artistic taste to their work of pleasure, have erected houses of comfort and delight, the very embodiment of the poet and the painter's dream of loveliness. Another chief of the Central City, WM. B. KIRK, has applied a portion of his wealth to the adornment of this beautiful island, and these have found willing comrades to aid in making this cosy hamlet a beauty spot on the Great River.

As I pen these lines so many faces crowd upon my reviving memory, that my task must be abruptly closed or it will become endless. A few more of the multitude of those who deserve recognition and I have done.

No one who frequents the river can fail to know that always hilarious crowd, hailing from Albany, headed by JIM STORY, JOHN H. QUINBY, and CHARLIE GAY. At home, staid, steady, model business men. On the river—never offensive—but full to the brim, of fun and frolic, good anglers and genial companions.

There comes periodically to the river a quiet, unobtrusive but worthy and interesting gentleman. It is said that "Good wine needs no Bush," but a troll on the water and a lunch on the shore are made more enjoyable and satisfying whenever MR. "BUSH," of Buffalo counts as one of the party.

We entreat LUCIUS MOSES to bring back to the river himself with his delightful family; we yearn to hear once more the swish of his wonderful cast, as the fly tempts the bass to strike "twenty yards away."

In writing the name of Mr. BROWNING, of New York, there came back to me the remembrance of his brother-in-law, MR. SCOTT, who is an annual visitor, seldom failing a yearly return. Although a city man, he is old fashioned in dress and manners, though never other than a gentleman. Though easily approachable, he is naturally taciturn; an untiring angler, wind and wave never staying him. One day near the head of Hemlock, he was at anchor still-fishing for bass; a good sized perch was hooked, and he rapidly drew him up, and was rendered almost helpless by the onrush of a thirty-pound muskalonge, striking for his dangling perch. The big fellow landed with the perch, in the boat, and with the aid of the guide was killed. After a few moments delay, S., recovered sufficiently to ejaculate "GREAT SCOTT," the only words (the guide avers) that he uttered until he reached the dock at Clayton, three miles away.

Clustered on and around the hoary head of old Grindstone, the MORGANS and the LOV-ELLS, of New York, have brought refinement and artistic skill to adorn their summer homes, and in themselves have added acknowledged worth to the goodly society of our Summer City.

It would be very wrong and unjust if the men and women who dwell in inclement winter as well as in gentle summer on the banks of this world-famed stream were not recorded among the throng of those " I have met upon the Great River." In all ranks and conditions among them, they are the hosts and helpers of their welcome summer visitors; kind, considerate, helpful, never exacting or mercenary, they are always ready and obliging. Their character and conduct are in marked contrast with the reported greed, venality and robbery at other noted places of summer resort. I am glad to proclaim that I have met and have learned to respect and honor these constant dwellers in the valley of the Great River.

If life and health are spared, I trust to meet many old and to greet many new faces in the coming years, enjoying renovated health and needed relaxation from the ills and cares of busy life amid the scenes of grandeur and beauty nowhere so sure to be found as " Upon the Great River."

THOMAS G. ALVORD.

SYRACUSE, March, 1895.

We think no man or woman can rise up after reading Governor ALVORD's unique and entirely unapproachable remarks upon the people he has met, without a better feeling towards all mankind, and a most grateful sense of appreciation of this honored man, whose green old age has met with no blight, and whose frosted head bears no possible indication of any frost of heart. With thousands who love him and revere his matchless ability, we reëcho his own wish that he may yet be spared for many years to visit the Great River.

A BONAPARTE IN NORTHERN NEW YORK.

[The following excellent article is from the pen of Major J. H. Durham, of Cape Vincent, N. Y. Its insertion in this volume is considered proper and instructive because most of the people named were long ago residents of Cape Vincent, a town of many memories, which stands at the very head of those islands we are attempting to describe and to give their histories, as well as to make brief mention of those superior men who first settled on and near them, and were certainly the first to sound their praise and introduce them to the attention and knowledge of the American people.]

THE advent of Joseph Bonaparte, or Count de Survilliers (as he desired to be known), into Northern New York and upon the St. Lawrence, is scarcely explainable without some reference by way of introduction to Count James Donatien Le Ray de Chaumont, who was the son of Count Donatien Le Ray, the intimate friend of Franklin and Adams, and Morris, and a devoted adherent to the fortunes of the United States, who in a time of the utmost need imperiled his great fortune by coming to our assistance. He it was who sent a ship-load of powder to Boston; who furnished clothing for La Fayette's army, and fitted out three vessels of war to join the fleet under Commodore Jean Paul Jones.

Previous to the elevation of Joseph Bonaparte to the thrones, first of Naples and then of Spain, he and young Le Ray were students at the celebrated school of Juilly, near Paris; here their acquaintance ripened into an intimacy which, although interrupted by succeeding events, did not wholly cease, and so we find it renewed at a time when the friendship of a Le Ray was not to be despised, even by a Bonaparte, though twice a king. The young Le Ray, intimate at his father's house with such men as Franklin, Adams and Morris, had early learned lessons of Republican wisdom, and understood how to sympathize with the infant States in their struggle for freedom. His intercourse with these gifted statesmen did much to perfect a character naturally superior, and of which an intimate acquaintance wrote in after years as follows: "He had a strong mind, great penetration, sound judgment, a warm and affectionate heart, and a noble soul. He was guided through life by a high and chivalrous integrity." It was related that on one occasion a difference arose between the elder Le Ray and Robert Morris, then at the court of France. An umpire was to be chosen, and Robert Morris at once selected Mr. Le Ray's own son; the case was stated, and a decision in favor of Mr. Morris was the result. The citizens of Jefferson and Lewis counties, N. Y., owe much of their prosperity to his enlightened and liberal management; and by the citizens of Jefferson county especially he is affectionately remembered for his public-spirited improvements, his dignified and courteous demeanor, and the sympathy he never failed to express, not only in words, but practically, for whatever concerned the public welfare. He fully sympathized with all that his father did to aid the colonies in their struggle with Great Britain, and upon him it finally devolved to effect a settlement with them. It was a task of great difficulty. The depreciation of paper money, and the differing currencies of the States, were obstacles almost insurmountable. Tearing himself from the seductions of the most elegant court in Europe, and from the near prospect

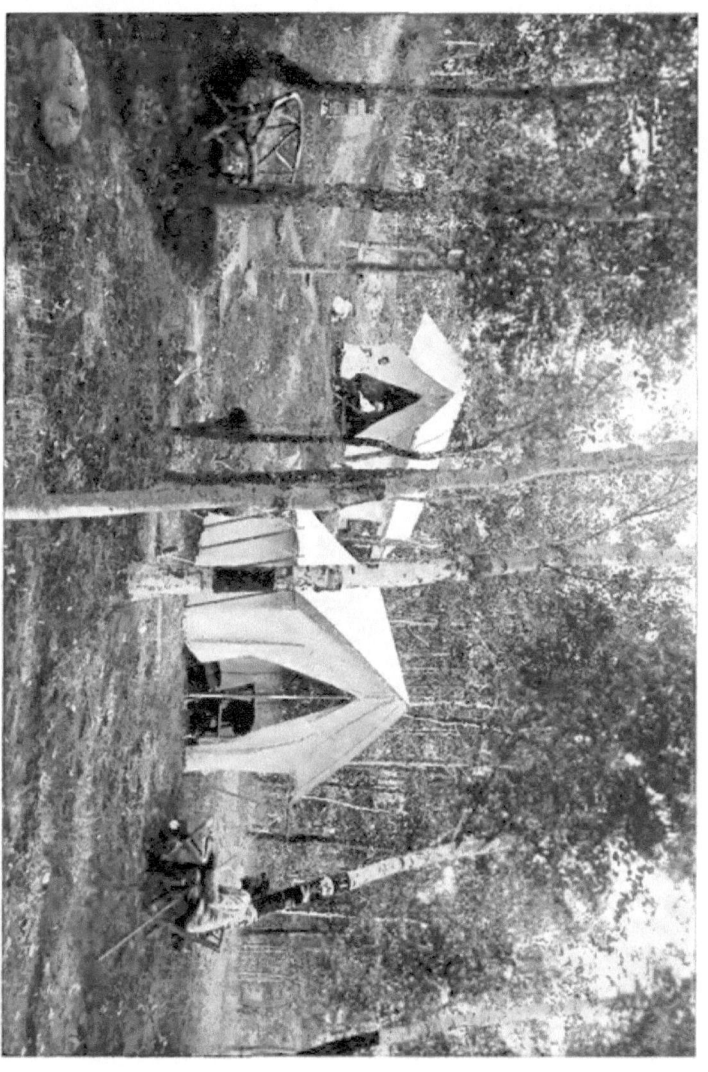

A SUMMER CAMP AT HAYNELL POINT.

of a brilliant marriage, he sailed for the United States, to distinguished citizens of which Franklin had given him letters; and yet, notwithstanding his talents and energy, strengthened by all the influence of Franklin, and Morris, and Adams, it was not until 1780 that a settlement was effected; just in time to save his father from a humiliating bankruptcy.

While in the United States he became acquainted with two men who largely influenced his subsequent career,—Gouverneur Morris and Count de La Foret, Consul-General of France,—who induced him to make heavy purchases of land In company with the latter, he purchased a large tract in Otsego county, and established as his agent there Judge Cooper, father of the great novelist. With the former he made extensive purchases in Northern New York, and by reason of these purchases it was that Joseph Bonaparte came upon the scene. In 1790, young Le Ray became a naturalized citizen of the United States, and married the daughter of Charles Coxe, Esq., of New Jersey, returning to France the same year. Between that and 1810, he had several times visited the United States; returning to France in that year, he settled upon his estates in Touraine, and busied himself in settling his affairs in Northern New York. The last meeting for more than a decade between young Le Ray and Joseph Bonaparte, was on the occasion of the signing of the treaty between France and the United States at Morte Fontaine, September 30, 1800, at which time they dined together. Fifteen years later came the downfall of Napoleon, and with him that of his family. Hearing that Joseph was at Blois, M' Le Ray hastened to offer his friendship. He was warmly welcomed, and the intimacy of former years was renewed.

One day while at dinner, a train of wagons passed the window near which they were sitting. Joseph, turning to M' Le Ray, said: "Mon ami, I remember that you have spoken to me of your large possessions in the United States. Do you still hold them? If so, I should like to exchange for a part of them some of the silver that I have in those wagons, which may be pillaged at any moment. Take four or five hundred thousand francs, and give me the equivalent in land." This M' Le Ray declined, saying: "It is impossible to make a bargain where I alone know the facts. "Oh," said Joseph, "I know you well, and I rely more upon your word than upon my own judgment."

A bargain was soon entered into, the terms of which were, that for 200,000 francs the elder Le Ray would give Joseph Bonaparte a letter to his son Vincent, then in the United States, instructing him to show to the ex-king a certain tract; when, if approved of by him after seeing it, the sale would be confirmed. If not approved, the money was to be returned. The bargain was consummated with a slight change in the terms of payment.

Some writers have asserted that Joseph Bonaparte's farewell to France was an escapade; but whether true or not, he reached the United States in 1815, and Northern New York in 1818. Of his career in New Jersey and elsewhere, this account has nothing to do, as it proposes to deal with his affairs in Northern New York and not elsewhere, unless it may be incidentally. On arriving in the United States he assumed the title of Count de Survilliers, by which name and title only he desired to be known. His purchase included the greater part of the town of Diana, in Lewis county, together with portions of several towns in Jefferson county, lying principally in the valley of the Black River and on the shores of Lake Ontario and the St. Lawrence river; the whole amounting to 150,000 acres, which was paid for in diamonds and silver. Subsequently, owing to the fact that diamonds had fallen to half their former value in market, other arrangements were entered into, and in 1820 the count accepted a tract of 26,840 acres, for which he paid $40,260.

He now memorialized the Legislature of New York to grant him the privilege of holding titles in his own name. In his memorial, he says: "Not being of the number of those who would wish to abandon this land of hospitality, where the best rights of man prevail, I am nevertheless bound to my own country by ties which misfortunes render sacred." The privilege solicited was granted by a special act, bearing date March 31, 1825. Having acquired his titles, the ex-king began to explore his possessions; and it is told of him that whenever it was possible, he traveled in great state. Under any circumstances, his private secretary, M. Carot, his cook, butler, valet and page constituted his suite; these, with the servants of his guests, of whom he usually entertained several, made up a train, which, in the eyes of the simple backwoodsmen of those days, formed a pageant long to be remembered. Those were the times when the old country tavern was in the ascendant; and how to dispose of such a retinue, became at times a problem too intricate for the rural host to solve.

On one occasion, when on his way to spend the winter in New York and Philadelphia, his train was unusually large, having for his guests, Count Pierre François Real, who was Chef de Police under the Emperor, and who then lived at Cape Vincent, Jefferson county; Emmanuel Count de Grouchy and General Desfurneaux, who, with their attendants, were also going to the metropolis, together with several distinguished gentlemen from Albany, who had been guests of Count Survilliers at Bonaparte lake. They halted in the evening at a well-known hostelry in the Mohawk valley, kept by a sturdy old Dutchman. As was by no means uncommon among those who were in company with Count Survilliers, a night of revelry followed; a kingly revel, where the guests were served on silver by Parisian waiters. The choicest vintages were served in Venetian-cut glass, and the costliest teas and coffees in Sevres china. First, drinking to the idol of their hearts, him who was even then breaking his heart against the bars of St. Helena, and whom they seldom for a moment forgot, they gave way to amusement and hilarity. Song and story followed in rapid succession, witticisms sparkled like the bead upon their champagne, while the worthy host, called here and there, often two ways at the same moment, was half crazed, and wholly bewildered. In the morning M. Carot, the Count's private secretary, called upon the landlord to present his bill. This was a poser; never before in that house, had a bill of items been asked for, but the crisis had come, and it must be met; and so the worthy Boniface, groaning over the unwonted mental exertion required, set slowly about his task. Aided by the "good frouw," whose qualifications as an accountant, were, if possible, fewer than his own, he finally, with much mental travail, produced a bill which seemed to meet the requirements; and with some trepidation in his manner, he presented it to M. Carot. It was a bill for $200. The astute secretary detected the exorbitant charges at a glance, and looked with dismay upon the final footing, the manifest result of an attempt to divide a large sum total among a few items only; the house as a matter of fact, having contributed but very little toward the entertainment.

Noticing the look upon his secretary's face, Count Survilliers demanded to see the bill. It was handed to him, and thence ran the gauntlet of the merry company, who, shouting with laughter at Mynheer's unique specimen of bookkeeping, nevertheless protested against his outrageous charges; which, allowing him the highest possible prices for labor and supplies, would scarcely amount to $50. The bill was returned to the landlord, and the exorbitant charges pointed out; in process of time an amended bill was brought in, which contained a very fairly itemized account amounting to $50, after which followed the crowning entry: "To making in mine house one d——d fuss, $150,"—thus triumphantly sustaining the original grand total. Saying "cheap enough, too," the ex-king ordered M. Carot, to settle the bill. For many years thereafter that same bill was in the possession of one of Albany's most distinguished citizens, who frequently exhibited it to his friends as a "model Mohawk-valley tavern bill."

Count Survilliers made a number of improvements in various parts of his domain, and expended money with a princely liberality, thereby benefiting many a poor man, who in those days would otherwise have handled money but rarely. At Natural Bridge, he erected a large framed house, with all the convenient accessories of a gentleman's summer residence and furnished it elegantly at a great expense. Here, for several seasons, the ex-king kept open house, and was visited at times by some of those whom, in his days of regal pomp and power, he had entertained at court in Naples and in Madrid. Among the more constant of his guests, however, were Count Real; the Peugnet brothers, Louis, Hyacinthe and Theophilus; Louis, having been a captain in the Emperor's body guard, an officer of the corps d'elite; still wore the cross of the Legion d'Honneur, placed upon his breast by the Emperor's own hand; General Rolland, Count Real's son-in-law Col. Jermoux, Camille Armand, and others, all living at Cape Vincent, where M. Le Ray had founded a prosperous village and erected a stately mansion, now the property of Mrs. Beaufort, and her sister, Miss Emeline Peugnet, daughters of Captain Louis Peugnet; estimable, refined ladies are they, well known far beyond the bounds of their village-home.

There are many circumstances which render it probable that these re-unions, in which M' Le Ray was by no means the least honored guest, and which he often reciprocated by gathering the entire company under his own roof, either in his stately chateau at Le Raysville, or in his house at Cape Vincent, were for the purpose of discussing matters of much greater importance than disquisitions on matters piscatorial, or the art of venery; although hunting and fishing was the ostensible object. The woods abounded in game, and the streams and the lakes with fish. A beautiful lake of some 1200 acres area, abounding in the choicest varieties of fish, and forming a part of the Count's domain, was but a few miles from his mansion, at Natural Bridge, N. Y. It is a beautiful sheet of water, with bold and rocky shores, its surface sprinkled with island gems, — an archipelago in miniature. On an eminence overlooking its shores the Count erected a commodious hunting lodge, and opened a road from the old State Turnpike to the lake, on which boats were launched and every possible convenience provided for both hunting and fishing, of which sports the Count was extremely fond; and yet, to use the phraseology of a man who worked on the building mentioned, and who is yet living at Natural Bridge: "They didn't seem to hunt and fish much a'ter all." This charming lake (Bonaparte, now named) is now the property of Hon. Joseph Pahud, a superior and most interesting gentleman, and he has erected a neat hotel there, a very paradise for anyone desiring rest, combined with fish and game.

That a scheme was formed to rescue the Emperor from the custody of Sir Hudson Lowe, and spirit him away to the United States, there can now be no doubt. The French residents of Cape Vincent, after the news of Napoleon's death was received, did not hesitate to avow that such had been their purpose. A well-known American naval commander, whose reputation for courage, skill and daring, even to recklessness at times, could not be questioned, was to have aided the scheme; and with his help, they hoped to succeed. It is also highly probable that, in some way, the exiles on St. Helena were made aware of the efforts on foot to secure their liberation. A letter written by Count Bertrand to Joseph Bonaparte on the death of the Emperor, after announcing the sad event, says of him: "The hope of leaving this dreadful country often presented itself to his imagination. Some newspaper articles added to, and excited our expectations. We sometimes fancied that we were on the eve of starting for America; we read travels; we made plans; we arrived at your house; we wandered over that great country, where alone we might hope to enjoy liberty. Vain hopes! Vain projects! which only made us doubly feel our misfortunes."

That Count Real erected a house at Cape Vincent for the reception of his adored Chief, is so well known in that locality that it "goes without saying;" and also that during its erection, Count Survilliers was oftener a visitor at Cape Vincent than at any other time. Then, too, his constant communication with this band of enthusiastic imperialists, and especially with Professor Pigeon, who was Private Secretary to Count Real, and who, no doubt, wrote every letter and every communication of whatever nature relating to their secret plans.

It was Prof. Pigeon who took a vow never to cover his head while Napoleon was a prisoner; and notwithstanding the severity of the winters in Northern New York, he steadfastly adhered to his resolution until the death of the Emperor released him from his vow.

During Joseph Bonaparte's last visit to Bonaparte Lake, a tragedy occurred that, for some time, threw a gloom over his daily life, which seemed impossible for him to shake off. Not far from Bonaparte Lake is Green Lake, a body of water not half the size of Bonaparte Lake, and as dismal, gloomy and repulsive as the other is delightful. Its shores are bold and rocky; and owing to a mass of fallen timber, which forms an almost impenetrable cheveaux de frieze around it, it is very difficult of access. Not far from the water's edge, at a point where the rocky wall almost reaches it, is a cave so dark and dismal that it became known as the "Cave of the Sepulchre," a name which a subsequent occurrence served to establish more completely, if possible, than it was before.

Among the attendants of the count, was a young Frenchman named Jean Vallois, who paid marked attention to the daughter of a French settler living in the vicinity. She was a beautiful girl, and it was not long before they were almost inseparable. It was especially their delight to take a boat and row away together among the islands, or climb the rocks to find some new view on which to feast their eyes. Count Survilliers was himself too fond of the fair sex to put any restraint on the loves of his followers, and so the liaison went on uninterrupted until it became apparent to all that a climax was not far distant. One day the young people announced their intention to visit Green Lake, which was but a short distance away. They were never seen again. Days lengthened into weeks, and weeks into months, and yet no trace of them was found. The woods were scoured far and wide in every direction, and the waters of Green Lake dragged in vain. Years sped on, and finally the old Frenchman and his wife died, and gradually the occurrence faded from recollection. In 1850 a party of hunters conceived the idea of exploring the Cave of the Sepulcher. Providing themselves with an abundance of material for lights and whatever else they deemed necessary, the exploration was made. Among the rubbish in the bottom of the cave some bones were found, which were thought to be those of an animal. One of the party, however, in looking closer, discovered a human skull, and further search revealed another; then some little trinkets were found; and finally a Spanish gold coin, on one side of which was stamped the head of Joseph Bonaparte. When these facts became known, it was remembered that Count Survilliers had often presented similar pieces to members of his suite, and to particular friends as souvenirs of some special occasion. This fact coupled with the medical testimony, that one of the skulls found belonged to a male and the other to a female, made the conclusion almost irresistible that these were none other than the remains of Jean Vallois and the French maiden so soon to become a mother. Whether it was deliberate suicide on the part of both, or whether they fell victims to a beast of prey, will never be known so far as human knowledge is concerned.

It would seem that a fondness for the fair sex was the dominant weakness of Count Survilliers. The story of his marriage to the little Quakeress of Bordentown, N. J., Annette Savage, has been told so often and in so many ways that it is now difficult to get at the real facts. It has been asserted that he contracted another marriage du covenance, in Philadelphia; but it is now known that the reputed Philadelphia wife was no other than the Bordentown lady; no longer Countess Survilliers, but Madame Delafolie. The result of that marriage was a beautiful daughter, who was named Caroline Delafolie, and who afterward married Col. Z. Howard Benton, by whom she had two children, Josephine and Joseph Bonaparte Benton. It was the ruling desire of Mrs. Caroline Benton's life to be acknowledged by the Bonaparte family; and when Louis Napoleon ascended the throne she journeyed to Paris, hoping to accomplish her purpose, and she is said to have succeeded. In Haddock's History of Jefferson county, p. 440, this subject is fairly handled. Through the kindness of Minister Washburn she was admitted to an audience with the Emperor, who received her favorably. On their return to the United States they gave glowing accounts of their reception at court, and of the appointment of their daughter Josephine to the position of maid of honor to the Empress Eugenie. The disastrous termination of the Franco-Prussian war forever ended any hopes that centered on Louis Napoleon, however willing he might have been to aid his kinsfolk.

There is a house yet standing in Evans' Mills which Count Survilliers erected for Madame Delafolie, and his summer residence at Natural Bridge is shown upon another page. He also built a stone house on the shore of Perch Lake, in the town of Pamelia, N. Y. This was also richly furnished throughout; the fireplaces were fitted with marble mantels, and the whole house was finished to correspond. This was intended for a winter residence, being within easy reach of his friends at Cape Vincent, and of the chateau of M. de Le Ray, at Le Raysville. This part of his domain was afterward sold to John La Farge, another French émigré, but now scarcely one stone stands upon another to mark what was once the dwelling of royalty. A nephew of Count Survilliers, Joachim Murat, was a frequent guest of his uncle, who presented him with a tract of land lying between the present villages of Antwerp and Theresa. Here the young man began business on a large scale. He caused a canal to be dug, a dam was built on Indian river, and a mill erected, a storehouse and dwellings put up, a town laid out on a grand scale, and every preparation made for a city in the wilderness, but it failed to materialize. While the young Murat possessed all the natural proclivities which constitute the modern "boomer," he was half a century in advance of the times; settlers failed to come, the development of the country was slow, the locality was off the natural lines of communication, so that after the expenditure of a fortune, he was forced to abandon the enterprise, and now but little remains to indicate the spot where he fondly hoped to rear the flourishing city of "Joachim."

In 1833, or it may be in the spring of 1834, Joseph Bonaparte returned to France, and Northern New York knew him no more. In 1835 his agent, Judge Joseph Boyer, sold all his remaining lands in Jefferson and Lewis counties to John La Farge. At this time, political events in France apparently favored a reinstatement of the Bonaparte family, and Count Survilliers, hopeful that the next turn of the political wheel would bring the Bonapartes to the surface, was anxious to be where his greatest interests lay, and where his personal efforts might be of some avail. With the sale of his landed estates, his interests in a country where, to use his own expression, "The best rights of man prevail," entirely ceased. Some three or four old men are yet alive,[*] who, in the capacity of guides or laborers for the ex-king, can relate some anecdote of him; but of his real life while in Northern New York, scarce anything is publicly known beyond what is embodied in this brief sketch. Of one who was king of Naples, who sat on the throne of Spain, whose brother was an emperor, and wore the diadem of the Cæsars, and whose acts have filled more pages of history than did those of Alexander the Great, it seems trifling indeed.

---

[*] In Haddock's History of Jefferson county, cited above, he mentions Hon. L. INGALLS, the veteran editor, of Watertown, N. Y., and Mr. BLANCHARD, of Natural Bridge, as well remembering Joseph Bonaparte. Mr. INGALLS was then a boy, and recollects the ex-king as a fat, full-chested, pleasant old man, delighting to sit in his doorway of a summer evening and throw pennies by handsful among the boys, to see them scramble and fight for them. Mr. BLANCHARD is past ninety, but is a remarkably bright old gentleman. He worked for the ex king upon the Natural Bridge dwelling, and tells how Joseph would don the dress of a workman, when the fit took him, and work in lathing the house, preparatory to plastering. He asserts that the ex king was companionable and agreeable, and readily approachable, always charitable and considerate.

THE MYSTERY OF MAPLE ISLAND.

BY MAJOR J. H. DURHAM.

Oh, that I were a painter! who could a picture make,
A fitting guide to be, into this Island mystery.

MAPLE ISLAND, on which the tragedy which I am about to relate took place, lies a little beyond the main steamboat channel on the American side, almost in front of, and in plain view from the balconies of the "Frontenac" on Round Island. It has an area of about six acres, and a high ridge extends across it from east to west, or nearly so, which is inclined to be precipitous on the north and north-west. For the most part, the island is covered by a thick undergrowth with here and there a few larger trees, excepting on the south side of the dividing ridge, where the timber has been cut away, leaving a triangular shaped clearing with its apex at the top of the ridge. There is nothing about it to attract especial attention.

Some time since, while glancing through the columns of Clayton's newsy weekly, On the St. Lawrence, I lighted upon a brief article which at once engrossed my attention. At this date I cannot give more than the substance of the sketch, having mislaid the clipping made at the time; but if my memory serves me it was headed: "The Tragedy of Maple Island;" at all events, if not this in exact terms, it conveyed the idea so forcibly that I read and re-read the article, vainly trying to recall something that I had read before, which in a vague, shadowy way seemed connected with it. The substance of the article in question is as follows:

In the summer of 1865, in the early part of June, a stranger made his appearance at the hotel in the little hamlet of Fisher's Landing, on the east bank of the St. Lawrence river, below Round Island, and opposite Thousand Island Park, which at that time had no existence. It was a singular fact that although he gave a name, which is not now remembered, he never signed the hotel register.

He was a broad-shouldered, dark-haired man, moustache and goatee, genteelly dressed, evidently not more than twenty-five years of age, probably less; of very agreeable manners, but very reticent, and with the characteristics of a Southerner. He spent his time chiefly in looking about the country, visiting, at times, the little village of Omar, and rowing in a skiff among the adjoining islands. He finally announced his intention of erecting a cabin on one of the islands, the better to enjoy his favorite pastime of fishing. He selected Maple Island as his place of residence, and at Clayton he purchased lumber and all the necessary materials for the structure, hired them transported to the island, engaged workmen to build it, bought a skiff with its outfit, and the furniture necessary for housekeeping, and in a short time occupied his island domicile. His food supplies — bread, butter, eggs, milk and vegetables — were obtained from farmers on Grindstone Island, and his groceries from Clayton. He made no intimate acquaintances, though, if a chance caller visited him, which was but seldom, he was treated courteously, but never invited to repeat the call. He was known to have quite a store of

books, and to amuse himself by playing upon the violin, as the strains of one were often heard proceeding from his cabin, which stood in a dense thicket against a wall of rock, and so hidden that it could not be seen from a passing skiff. The summer months sped away, and so quiet and undemonstrative was the stranger that he would have been almost entirely forgotten but for his semi-occasional visits to Clayton for supplies.

Very early in the autumn, and it may have been during the last days of August, several strangers made their appearance on the river, stopping for a time at Alexandria Bay, at Fisher's Landing, and at Clayton. As it was nothing unusual to see strangers at these places, no especial notice was taken of them further than that they all seemed to be Southerners. But for subsequent events, this would not have been remarked, as it was by no means an unusual thing for Southerners to visit the Thousand Islands, prominent even then as a resort for those who affected the rod and gun.

But an event took place which arrested the attention and aroused the sympathy of the people; a bloody mystery, which to-day is almost as great a mystery as ever, and one which will, in all probability, never be fully solved, until the day when all mysteries shall be made clear.

It was in September; the loveliest month on the St. Lawrence. As the poet Reade, sings:—

"The season where the light of dreams
Around the year in golden glory lies;—
The heavens are full of floating mysteries,
And down the lake the veiled splendor beams!
Like hidden poets lie the hazy streams,
Mantled with mysteries of their own romance,
While scarce a breath disturbs their drowsy trance."

It was on such an evening that a bright light was seen by residents of Clayton, on Maple Island. It was conjectured at once that the Hermit's cabin had caught fire, but as it was impossible to reach him in time to be of any assistance, and apprehending no personal danger to him, but little thought was given to the occurrence; further than that he was expected to come ashore for lodgings at a hotel; but as he did not come within a reasonable time, it was thought that he had rowed over to Grindstone Island, or down to Grenell's tavern, which stood where the Pullman Hotel now stands, and so nothing more was thought of the matter that night.

The next morning, some fishermen went ashore on Maple Island, and visited the spot where the cabin stood. They saw at once that something unusual had occurred. The ground was tramped as with many feet. Evidences of a desperate struggle were on every hand. Traces of blood were found on the bushes, and then robbery and murder was suspected. A careful search was instituted, and finally the body of the unfortunate occupant was found near the water's edge, on the lower end of the island. His throat was cut from ear to ear, and a knife thrust had nearly severed the heart. There was no clothing on the body except a pair of drawers, and across the breast three crosses were cut in a triangle, one cross forming its apex, and two its base. To the discoverers of the body, these had no especial significance. They saw nothing beyond plain murder and robbery. It might have been stated before, that the deceased was known to have plenty of money. He had always been a prompt and liberal paymaster, and whenever it had been necessary, owing to a lack of American money, he had offered English gold in payment for his purchases; and so, that he was murdered solely for his money, was the prevailing idea, and no significance attached to the crosses; and yet, these and these alone, furnished the clew which has nearly succeeded in tracing out the mystery.

The coroner was summoned, and after a patient examination, the principal facts as above stated were brought out, and a verdict rendered accordingly. The body was decently buried, the occurrence created a "nine day's wonder," and then passed out of mind; and but for the meager statement in the newspaper referred to, it would have never been revived, as there is to-day but one or two persons living who had an actual knowledge of the facts above stated. It must not be supposed that the newspaper article contained a tenth part of what is already related. It was by close and persistent search and careful inquiry, that these additional facts were gleaned, and they are presented here as a reason for, and an introduction to, what follows:

It was the month of April, 1865. The nation was jubilant. The long and bloody conflict had closed, and joy reigned triumphant everywhere. The country was ablaze with bonfires, and grand illuminations turned night into day. The evening splendors of the National Capital were unsurpassed, and the grand illuminations were made still more gorgeous by the display of fireworks. Bands of music serenaded the President, whose congratulatory speeches it seemed to many were tinged with a shade of melancholy. But a day was at hand; a day of gloom, and of darkness, and of woe, unparalleled in the history of the world. Were it not necessary, by reason of their being an important factor in this narrative, the sad events which plunged a nation into mourning and lamentation would not be here rehearsed. The inexpressible sadness which pervaded every countenance at the news of the assassination of Abraham Lincoln, was an index to the heartfelt pain within; and even now, though thirty years have rolled into the dim and misty past, I am unable to recall the terrible event, much less to transcribe, however briefly, its salient features, without experiencing again that fearful shock, which, like an electric current laden with woe and draped with disaster, ran from man to man and from camp to camp throughout our lines at Raleigh, where the corps to which the writer belonged was stationed. It was the same everywhere. All nature seemed clad in the habiliments of woe.

On the evening of the 14th day of April, 1865, the play "Our American Cousin" was in progress at Ford's Theater, on Tenth street, just above E street, Washington, D. C.; a large, plain brick edifice, now converted into a museum of war relics. In honor of the occasion and of the day's rejoicing, because the folds of the Nation's Flag had that day been once again flung to the breeze above the shattered ramparts of Fort Sumter, President Lincoln was to occupy the "Presidential box," which consisted of the two upper boxes on the left of the stage thrown into one. The box on that memorable evening was occupied by the President and Mrs. Lincoln, Major R. H. Rathbone and Miss Clara H. Harris. The house, holding nearly three thousand people, was filled with the wealth and fashion of the city.

At about 10 o'clock, when the second scene of the third act was on, a stranger worked his way into the proscenium box occupied by the Presidential party, and leveling a pistol close to the head of Mr. Lincoln, he fired; then drawing a knife he inflicted a severe wound upon Major Rathbone, who had seized him, and breaking away he sprang down upon the stage, flourished his knife and shouted: "Sic Semper Tyrannis!" and before the real position of affairs could be comprehended, he dashed across the stage, mounted a fleet horse, which was in waiting in the alley in the rear of the theater, and escaped.

That man was John Wilkes Booth, notoriously a rebel, an actor of some merit, but now an escaping murderer.

As soon as the audience realized the fact that the President was shot, the wildest excitement prevailed, and shouts of Hang him! Hang him! resounded from every part of the house. The dying President was borne to a private house — Mr. Peterson's, across the street — and prominent physicians and surgeons were summoned at once. It was soon discovered that there was no hope. Members of the cabinet assembled, together with other distinguished men, and stood mournfully grouped about the couch of the unconscious chief magistrate. An eye witness wrote thus: "The scene was one of extraordinary solemnity. The history of the world furnishes no parallel. Breathing his life serenely away, sensible to no pain and unconscious of all around, the Great Man of the nineteenth century lay, passing away to that immortality accorded by Providence to few of earth."

All the long, weary night the watchers stood around the couch. Day came at length, and at twenty-two minutes past seven o'clock on Saturday morning, April 15th, 1865, the spirit of Abraham Lincoln, freed from its earthly tenement, went to God who gave it, and the nation went into mourning.

It had been remarked that Secretary Seward was not among the members of the Cabinet who rallied around the bedside of their dying Chief; but when Surgeon-General Barnes reached the house, the reason was made clear. In substance, this is what happened to Surgeon-General Barnes: He was met in front of Willard's Hotel by an officer, on the night of the assassination, who informed him that the President was shot. Supposing that the deed had been done at the presidential mansion, he hurried to the surgeon-general's office to give orders for assistance, and there he found a summons to the bedside of Secretary Seward, who had also been attacked by an assassin. Believing that this occurrence was what gave rise to the story that the President was shot, he immediately hurried to the chamber of Mr. Seward. He found him lying upon the bed with one cheek cut open, and the flesh lying over on the pillow. The room presented a horrible appearance. Blood bespattered everything. The attendants were huddled into corners, frightened and helpless. No one seemed capable of giving a single detail of the terrible occurrence. Dr. Barnes immediately gave his attention to Mr. Seward, but shortly Dr. Norris came, and turning Mr. Seward over to his care, the surgeon-general proceeded to look after the assistant secretary, Mr. Frederick Seward, who was lying wounded and insensible in an adjoining room. Soon after, other surgeons came in, and from them he learned the distressing facts regarding the assassination of the President, and went at once to his bedside.

However strange it may seem to us of to-day, as we read the various and voluminous accounts of those occurrences, yet it is a fact, that not for several days afterward, did any one seem to grasp the idea that it was a preconcerted scheme of assassination — a concerted plot to take not only the life of the President, but of other prominent men also.

The one great overshadowing crime seemed to literally draw all attention to itself. Other transactions were dwarfed by it. Even the history of nations could produce no equal. True, Brutus slew Cæsar in the Roman Senate chamber, and Charlotte Corday murdered Murat in his bath; but neither instance paralleled this unheard of atrocity.

Gradually, however, as events began to unfold themselves, and the horizon of disturbance to clear, it was seen that the assassination was a part of a well-devised scheme, the only part, which, owing to some cause or causes unknown, had been carried into full effect. It soon became known also that the Metropolitan police had long been aware that a society called the Knights of the "Blue Gauntlet," the same in all essentials as that of the "Knights of the Golden Circle," existed in Washington; and they not only knew its place of meeting, but the names of many of the members. Not deeming it at all dangerous, but little attention had been paid to it, because the secrets of the "Knights of the Golden Circle," or rather the "Sons of Liberty," that being the real name of the organization, had become known, through the address of Timothy Webster, one of the most daring and skillful members of the secret service ever in the employ of the United States government; and who was captured in Richmond, tried, convicted and hanged as a spy by the orders of Gen. Winder, April 29, 1862.

A brief account of Webster's initiation into the secret society of the "Sons of Liberty" in the city of Baltimore, in 1861, may be given here as an illustration of the general character of the secret societies of that time, whose object was to aid the cause of the South, no matter under what name they masqueraded. Webster, it should be understood, had so ingratiated himself into the good graces of leading secessionists in Baltimore, that there was not the slightest suspicion afloat regarding him. On the contrary, he was so implicitly trusted that he visited unquestioned all parts of the South, making long visits to Richmond, where he was "Hail fellow, well met!" with prominent rebels, and their trusted agent in Washington, where they frequently sent him with important dispatches, the answers to which were to be delivered to the authorities in Richmond; but which, it is needless to say, reached other hands than those of Judah P. Benjamin, the rebel Secretary of War, for whom many of them were intended. Among other prominent rebels in Baltimore was one Sloan, a noted rebel, with whom Webster was on the most intimate terms. During Webster's absence on one of his southern trips, certain secessionists of Baltimore organized a secret society of which they were very desirous that he should become a member, and to Sloan, because he was an intimate friend, was delegated the duty of soliciting him to join. Seizing a favorable opportunity on Webster's return to the city, Sloan guardedly broached the subject.

"The fact is," said Sloan, "after you went away we formed a secret society."

"A secret society?"

"Yes; and we have held several meetings."

"Is it a success?"

"A perfect success. Some of the best in the town are among our members. We may be forced to keep silent, but they can't compel us to remain idle. We are well organized, and we mean undying opposition to a tyrannical government. I tell you, Webster, we will not down!"

"Never!" responded Webster, imitating the boastful tone and bearing of his friend Sloan. "It does not lie in the power of those white-livered Yankees to make slaves of Southern men! I should like to become a member of your society, Sloan."

"They all want you," said Sloan, eagerly. "We passed a resolution to that effect at our last meeting. We want the benefit of your counsel and influence."

"What is the name of your society?"

"The Sons of Liberty."

"When will your next meeting be held?"

"To-night."

"So soon?"

"Yes; and you are expected to attend. Have you any objections?"

"None whatever. But how will I get there?"

"I am delegated to be your escort."

"What is your hour of meeting?"

"Twelve o'clock."

"Ah! A midnight affair. All right, Sloan, you will find me waiting at the hotel."

Promptly at eleven o'clock Sloan appeared at the hotel, whence he and Webster proceeded toward the place of meeting. It was a dark and stormy night, and, as Webster thought, just the right sort of a night for concocting hellish plots and the performance of evil deeds. As Robert Burns says:

"That night, a chiel might understand,
The Deil had business on his hand."

Sloan led the way to a remote quarter of the city, and into a street which bore a particularly bad reputation. Stopping, he said:

"I must blindfold you, Webster, before proceeding any further. This is a rule of the order, which, under any circumstance, cannot be departed from."

Webster quietly submitted, and a thick bandage was placed over his eyes and securely fastened. Then Sloan took him by the arm and led him forward. Blindfolded as he was, Webster knew that they turned suddenly into an alley and passed through a gate which Sloan shut behind them. He also knew that they were in a paved court, probably in the rear of some building. Just then Sloan whispered:

"Come this way and make no noise."

The next moment he knocked in a peculiar manner against a door, and Webster knew it to be a signal. Immediately a guarded voice asked:

"Are you white?"

Sloan responded: "Down with the blacks."

A chain clanked inside, a bolt was withdrawn, the door creaked slightly on its rusty hinges, and they entered; immediately they began to climb a thickly carpeted stair, at the head of which they were challenged:

"Halt! Who comes there?"

"Long live Jeff Davis," answered Sloan.

Passing through another door, they entered an apartment in which there seemed to be several persons. A voice, meant to be impressive, demanded:

"Whom have we here?"

"A friend, Most Noble Chief, who wishes to become a member of this worthy league."

"His name?"

"Timothy Webster."

"Have the objects of this league been fully explained to him?"

"Most Noble Chief, they have."

"Mr. Webster, is it your desire to become a member of this knightly band?"

"It is."

Then came the ring of swords leaping from scabbards, and their clank as they met in an arch of steel above his head; and then the Noble Chief continued:

"You will now kneel upon your right knee, place your right hand upon your heart, and repeat after me the obligation of our brotherhood."

"I, Timothy Webster, a citizen of Baltimore, having been fully informed of the objects of this Association, and being in full sympathy and accord with the cause it seeks to advance, do solemnly declare and affirm, upon my sacred honor, that I will keep forever secret all that I may see or hear, in consequence of being a member of this league; that I will implicitly obey all orders, and faithfully discharge all duties assigned to me, no matter of what nature or character they may be; and that life or death will be held subordinate to the success and advancement of the cause of the Confederacy, and of the defeat of the bloody tyrants who are striving to rule by oppression and terrorism. Should I fail in the proper performance of any task imposed upon me, or should I prove unfaithful to the obligations I now assume, may I suffer the severest penalty awarded for treason and cowardice, and the odium belonging thereto, as well as the scorn and contempt of all true brother knights."

Again the swords clanked as they were returned to their scabbards, and the newly obligated member was commanded to arise. He obeyed, and the bandage was removed. At first he was blinded by the sudden light, but as his eyes became accustomed to it, he found himself surrounded by several stalwart men, all of whom wore dark cloaks and black masks.

"Mr. Webster," said the Chief, "I now pronounce you a Son of Liberty."

The masks were now removed, and to his relief, Webster discovered that the faces were all familiar. A cordial grasp of the hand was given by each in turn, and then they entered the principal council chamber, and Webster was escorted to a seat. In a few minutes the clock struck twelve, when every door was locked, and the real work of the order begun. There were some forty men present, and Webster noticed that they were from among the best citizens of Baltimore, the rowdy element not being represented. He was now instructed in the passes, signs and grips of the order, and especially in the rallying sign, which was three crosses, disposed in a triangle.

It is not necessary to say more under this head, our only design being to give the reader a brief sketch of the so often denied secret society of the South, which in time, by the aid of Clement L. Vallandingham, of Ohio, permeated the entire North, and which, but for a fortunate circumstance that took place in the city of Indianapolis in 1863, would have resulted in fire and bloodshed throughout several of the Northern States, and which years later found an individual culmination in a bloody tragedy on an obscure island in the Great River St. Lawrence.

Suffice it to say that in this case Webster listened to the schemes which were in preparation to destroy our National Capital, learned the names of the plotters and sympathizers in Washington, and in process of time so managed matters that this particular camp of the Sons of Liberty found itself immured behind the bars of the Old Capitol Prison.

As a further instance, it may be interesting to know that a shrewd detective, who is yet living, and whose name it is unnecessary to mention here, was sent from Cincinnati to Louisville, Kentucky, by order of Gen. George B. McClellan, for the purpose of uniting with the Brotherhood, in order that he might learn its secrets, methods of work, designs and plans, which he fully accomplished, being initiated, as a comparison of dates shows, at Louisville, only two nights later than was Webster at Baltimore. The initiatory ceremonies, grips, signs, passes and signals were found to be identical.

The Knights of the "Blue Gauntlet" had no names. The individual members were known only by numbers; and any order or direction from the Chief was always sent to a number and not to a name. With this, and a few other minor differences, the Sons of Liberty and the Knights of the Blue Gauntlet were the same. All this was known to the police, but never for a moment was there the slightest danger apprehended, so powerless for any real harm did the organization appear. That it was not more closely investigated, and entirely broken up, was a fatal mistake; realized when too late to be remedied. In fact, it had been but little more than a year since these secret meetings had been revived, and then more as a political factor than any thing else. To prevent the nomination and re-election of Abraham Lincoln was a consummation ardently desired by the friends of the Confederacy. With him no longer at the head of the government, a compromise would be effected, the war ended, and virtually victory would perch upon the flag of the South.

But from this semi-passive political position to one more pronounced was easy. All that was wanted was a leader. A man who, within himself, combined all the elements,— a strong will, unlimited zeal, unbounded enthusiasm, a strong personal magnetism, and a blind, unreasoning devotion to a cause whether right or wrong, coupled with an overwhelming desire for notoriety. Such a leader they found in John Wilkes Booth. As affording a slight insight into his character, an extract of a letter to the Washington Chronicle, written after the assassination, by A. D. Doty, of Albany, a soldier then in Carver hospital, Washington, is here given. He says: "At the commencement of the war, J. Wilkes Booth was playing an engagement at the Gayety Theater in Albany, N. Y., which city attested in action more eloquent than words its love for the old flag by displaying it from every roof and window, when the news came of the unholy attack on Fort Sumter. Booth, at that time, openly and boldly avowed his admiration for the rebels and their deeds, which he characterized as the most heroic of modern times; and he boasted loudly that the Southern leaders knew how to defend their rights, and that they would never submit to oppression. So vehement and incautious was he in his expressions, that the people became incensed and threatened him with personal violence, and he was compelled to make a hasty departure from the city. Before leaving, he attempted the life of an actress of whom he had become jealous. Finding his way to her room at midnight, he assaulted her with a dagger, fortunately inflicting but a slight wound. With the fury of a tigress she sprang upon him, and wrenching the weapon from his hand, in turn wounded him."

These episodes show that he was not only a virulent rebel, but was at heart an assassin. Not only was Booth a murderer, but he was a mercenary one. While he was willing to assassinate the President, he wanted pay for doing it. Notoriety it would bring, but with it he wanted gold.

All along during the war, and especially in the years 1863 and 1864, Canada's principal cities swarmed with Southerners. St. Catharines, Toronto, Kingston, Ottawa and Montreal, were especially favored by these gentlemen; some of whom were accredited agents of the Confederacy, while they were all engaged in plotting against the North, and setting schemes on foot worthy the palmiest days of Diabolus, for the destruction of our lake cities in the absence of their defenders who were fighting against treason and rebellion on Southern soil.

It has been already hinted that the secret order of the Knights of the Golden Circle had found a lodgement in some of the Northern States, especially in the States of New York, Indiana and Illinois; though Pennsylvania and Ohio were largely represented in their councils. In Michigan, Wisconsin and Iowa,

ENTRANCE TO LAKE OF THE ISLES.

the lodges were but few and far between. It was in Indiana and Illinois, that their great strength lay. In the former State there were 100,000 armed and organized knights, ready to do the bidding of their chiefs. These were in constant communication with the Southern emissaries who, under the protection of Canada, plotted treason, laid plans to capture steamers on the lakes and on the St. Lawrence river, fill them with armed men, and simultaneously descend upon Rochester, Buffalo, Detroit, Cleveland and Chicago, and firing them, rob, pillage, and murder, escaping to Canada as a place of safety. It was among the Confederate residents of Canada that the diabolical scheme was set on foot to scatter small pox throughout the cities of the North by means of infected rags.

While Indiana, under the magnetic inspiration of that greatest among the great war Governors, Oliver P. Morton, responded with alacrity to every demand upon her for troops, to an extent far beyond her quotas, sending to the front, as a matter of fact, more men in proportion to her population than any other State in the Union, she was also cursed to a much greater extent with that abhorred product of the rebellion, the "Copperhead;" who was also, whenever the opportunity offered, a Knight of the Golden Circle. It has been already stated that they numbered a hundred thousand. It is no idle statement. It can be verified by the muster rolls of the order, captured in Indianapolis, and now preserved in the archives of the State. A brief allusion to the facts, will refresh the memory of many of our readers, while the incident may be of some interest.

In 1863-4, Indianapolis was a great military camp. Sentries were stationed everywhere. The air was rife with rumors of an uprising in various portions of the State. The camps around the city were more closely guarded than ever. Emissaries of those inimical to the government had secretly poisoned the minds of many of the soldiers, and desertions were frequent. These were concealed in almost inaccessible places and carefully guarded against recapture. Bands of Southern sympathizers drilled openly in the fields. United States marshals were set upon by infuriated mobs, maltreated and murdered. Every citizen went armed. Fearful rumors of an impending outbreak permeated the community, but when, or how, or from what source the blow was to come, none could tell. Surmise was the only certainty. A sentry on duty at the Union depot was watching the unloading from a car a mass of boxes. They were consigned to Dodd & Co., merchants, at whose store was the "Repository of the American Bible Society," and these boxes were supposed to contain Bibles for distribution among the soldiers. One of the boxes was slightly shattered by the rough handling it received at the hands of those who were unloading the freight. A bit of metal gleaming through a crevice in the broken box attracted the soldier's attention.

"Nice lot of books them," he said to himself. "Silver plated Bibles, I reckon. Pretty durn tony them tract peddlers is gittin. Guess I'll have a look at one of 'em, anyhow."

A brief investigation revealed to the soldier the startling fact that the box contained revolvers. It suddenly occurred to him that he had heard that the firm of Dodd & Co. were suspected of being rebel sympathizers, though by no means outspoken. Unlearned, but with a shrewdness worth more in a case like this than all the diplomas ever issued from college halls, he at once decided how to act. Not a word did he breathe to his sergeant, nor to the officer of the guard. He saw clearly that it was a case requiring judgment, and yet promptness. Calling a comrade, he was about to send him to the General's headquarters with a note, when fortunately the General and two or three members of his staff came riding down Illinois avenue. As they neared his post, he saluted and then called to the General. In a few words he made known his discovery. The General dismounted and made a personal examination, satisfying himself that the statement was true. Sending for the officer of the guard, he ordered him to count the boxes and affix a private mark to each one, and then note carefully who came for them. Mounting his horse, he returned to headquarters.

By and by draymen came for the boxes, and, strangely enough, with every dray load that moved away, there loitered along on the opposite side of the street a lazy unconcerned looking citizen who always had business in the same direction the dray was going. The goods were unloaded in the rear of Dodd & Co.'s store, transferred to an elevator and sent above. Over this store, and three stores adjoining, in the third story, was an immense empty chamber which had never been utilized. It was one vast unfinished garret, as every one supposed.

There were times when early in the morning bits of paper, on which three crosses in a triangular form had been printed, were found pasted to fences, trees and tree boxes, or scattered loosely about; and so often did this occur that it was accepted as a sign — but a sign of what?

The next morning after the boxes were hoisted to the upper story of Dodd & Co.'s store, those triangular emblems were more numerous than ever before. So were the lazy men in citizen's clothes. They were disreputable men, too, because they were frequently seen to gather, two or three at a time, in the alley in the rear of the store, and drink from a bottle and then disappear. That night was a great business night for Dodd & Co. The store was thronged and never before were clerks so busy. Even the lazy citizen was there, having overcome his indolence so far as to make some slight purchases. Not having anything himself to do, he noticed what others were doing; and, among other things, he noticed that instead of going out the way they came in, that is to say, by the front door, they went out at the back door; slipped out, so to speak, singly; and, it seemed to him, as if desirous of not being observed. It also seemed to him that he could hear the noise of the elevator at work. A careful investigation showed that it was at work, and that the customers were going into the story above, probably to complete their purchases!

Be that as it may, a couple of hours later, all the lower part of the store was filled with soldiers, both front and rear, and squad after squad went up in the elevator, and then came the grand climax. The boxes of Bibles consigned to Dodd & Co. were found as marked and numbered. They were packed with navy revolvers and ammunition. But this was the least important of the capture. This turned out to be the general headquarters of the order for the State. In this room the Adjutant-General had his office. The rolls and reports of the order were found. The names of the members of every camp of the Knights of the Golden Circle in the State were there. It was a revelation. Men against whom not a breath of suspicion had ever found utterance, here stood revealed as officials high in the secret councils of treason. Correspondence with Jacob Thompson, Clement C. Clay and Larry McDonald, then in Canada as accredited agents of the Confederacy, was discovered; but over and above everything else, a plot to burn the cities already mentioned, and the time when a general rising was to take place, all was revealed. The conspirators stood aghast, with no word of excuse to offer. Under a strong guard they were marched away to the jail and to the military prison, and by early morning two Major-Generals of the order, one in La Fayette, and another in Evansville, together with several Brigadiers and Colonels, a score or more, were under arrest, and on their way by the first trains to the Capital City. Dodd, Horsey and Mulligan, the Bible operators, were tried among the rest, and in a few weeks there were no spare casemates in Fort La Fayette, and the Dry Tortugas was crowded. From that time a great fear fell upon the Knights of the Golden Circle in Indiana. Their collapse was as complete as it was sudden. Here and there in the strongest copperhead localities, an attempt was made to revive the order under new names, but it was a signal failure. It is a pleasure to be able to record the fact that the soldier who first discovered the "silver plated Bibles" was promptly promoted. His coolness and self-command at the time of the discovery made the detection of the conspirators certain. Had he been less shrewd, and informed his sergeant or lieutenant, the chances are that the find would have been known throughout the city in an hour; the evening paper would have displayed glaring headlines, and the chance to entrap the Knights of the Golden Circle would have been lost.

In the meantime, Chicago, Cleveland, Buffalo and other lake and river cities were warned, and had taken measures for their own safety. The Confederate plotters in Canada saw at a glance that the game was up. The chances of capturing steamers on the lakes, and transforming them into quasi vessels of war, were utterly destroyed; and so they turned themselves to the consideration of new schemes. They began to despair of conquering the North, and as a recompense for defeat they nourished revenge. Gradually this desire grew into a discussion as to ways and means, and finally led to the consideration of a method of relief for the South, which, could it be carried into effect, would be the crowning scheme of all. This was the assassination of Lincoln, Johnson, Seward, Grant, Sherman and Sheridan, and as many other prominent officers and men of affairs as could be reached and struck down at the same hour, through concerted action. This done, the South must be victorious. Visions of place and power in the future to those who could conceive and execute this daring scheme fired their ambition, and personal aggrandizement, more than pro patria, urged them on. But a tool must be found, and they had not far to look.

John Wilkes Booth was starring in Canada, and to him they instinctively turned. During his engagement in Toronto, a meeting took place at the Queen's Hotel. Booth knew enough about these men and some others then in Canada, not to be surprised at any scheme they might propose. Already they had perpetrated acts of villainy that if even half punished, would expatriate them for life. On the other hand they knew the man before them. They had fathomed his inordinate vanity, and well knew his sordid ambition. They ministered to the one, and made promises which, if fulfilled, would abundantly gratify the other. They assured him that the success of the scheme depended upon himself alone. That, if successful, unbounded wealth and fame to gratify the most ambitious would be his.

At first, Booth hesitated at the idea of wholesale murder. Another scheme had entered his fertile brain, and until that failed, there should be no murder; but if it failed, then— The plan was to kidnap the President and as many others as could be taken, gag them, convey them to a safe retreat, and when an opportunity offered, transfer them to the rebel capital. All these facts are substantiated by evidence on file in the government archives at Washington, among which is a letter written by Booth which reveals the entire scheme. The discovery of a house on —— street in Washington, with furnished underground apartments provided with manacles, and all the accessories of solitary confinement, is evidence indisputable. In an upper room of the same building the Knights of the Blue Gauntlet held their secret meetings, and finally plotted murder.

Throughout all his base designs the dramatic element in Booth was always uppermost. He planned a triumphal starring trip throughout the South. Full of this idea, he shipped his theatrical wardrobe from Canada, and when his plans had been successfully carried out, he would don the buskin once more, and become a theatrical star of the first magnitude, though his crime rather than his ability as an actor, should prove the drawing card. If assassination, which he now began to seriously contemplate, should be the final outcome of all this damnable plotting, what a Brutus he would become. That immortal creation of Shakspeare, Julius Cæsar, should be so modified, that Washington would become Rome, and Abraham Lincoln, Cæsar. Payne, and Atzeroth, and Surratt, and Harold, and half a score of others of a like character should be the grand conspirators, while he, the chief conspirator of all, the head, the director, the murderer par excellence, would be the Brutus. How realistic it would all be. A great Shaksperean tragedy, only modified in some particulars to adapt it to time and circumstance, played by a troupe whose leading characters were real assassins! What a triumph of the Thespian art! What a modern histrionic success! One thing only was lacking. Were it but possible to assassinate a veritable Lincoln at every presentation of the play, nothing more could be desired.

Booth soon discovered that his scheme of kidnapping could not be carried out. It was deemed too rash. He could find no one who would engage in the hazardous undertaking. Something must be done to satisfy, first, his own egotistic ambition, and, second, to earn the guerdon of blood, an earnest of which, in English gold, he had already received at the hands of his employers, the Confederate agents of the South.

Now he began to plan in earnest the villainous scheme of assassination. Furnished with abundant funds, he dropped an anchor to windward by depositing four hundred and fifty-five dollars, his own money, in the Bank of Ontario, at Montreal. This, with date of entry, was shown by his bank book, which was captured with Atzeroth.

Then came a search for the proper tools. Along the eastern boundary of Kentucky, bordering on Virginia, in a region of hills and mountains almost inaccessible, is a section of country which, for years, has been the home of family feuds, which have resulted in numerous murders, and, consequently in the growth of a class of men who held life very cheap, and to whom a bloody vendetta was but a recreation. In the midst of such associations, seven brothers, named Payne, had grown up. They were outlaws born, robbers by profession, and murderers from choice, though the sons of a Christian minister. So bold had they become, and so bloody their raids, especially on the homes of those mountaineers suspected of favoring the Union, that at length troops were sent into their neighborhood with instructions to kill or capture them. It was a cavalry force under the lead of an officer only too well disposed to carry out his instructions. The father was captured and imprisoned, and the sons made their escape. Three of them went to South America, and four of them to Florida, and thence to Canada. Two of them were engaged in the St. Albans raid, one escaped, and the other, Lewis Payne, under the assumed name of Wood, and by the direction of the Confederate agents in Canada, reported to Booth in Washington, where, later on, he was joined by John A. Payne, one of his brothers, whom he had left in Canada. Here, then, is a list of conspirators, all of whom have joined the Knights of the Blue Gauntlet— Booth, the two Paynes, one of whom was known as Wood, John H. Surratt, Sam Arnold, McLaughlin, Harold, John Lloyd, and several others, who took the alarm and escaped in time to avoid arrest.

The assassination of Murat by Charlotte Corday, of Normandy, is one of the conspicuous instances on record, that a woman may become an assassin; and even though we may applaud and justify her act, yet it was assassination; and because it was at the hands of a woman, its dramatic effect was increased tenfold. Keeping the dramatic effect in view, Booth determined to have a woman in this case, and it was not long before he became acquainted with the very person he needed.

Ten miles from Washington, in Prince George's county, Maryland, was a little crossroads hamlet called Surrattsville. The principal property there was a hotel; one of those fine old Southern hostelries which, when in the right hands, was as complete a home as a temporary stopping place can be made to be. The owner gave his name to the village and his property to his wife, and died peaceably, as a good landlord should. The wife carried on the hotel business for a while and then rented the property to one John Lloyd, removing with her son and several daughters to Washington. Early in the conflict, Surrattsville became a rebel post-office, and Mrs. Surratt a post-mistress. When she removed to Washington, John Lloyd looked after the mails. In renting her hotel, Mrs. Surratt reserved apartments for her own use whenever she chose to visit Surrattsville. Mrs. Surratt was a large, masculine woman, always self-possessed, and in her way, as dangerous a rebel as was ever Belle Boyd or Rose Greenhow. John Wilkes Booth could not have found a fitter agent in all Washington, and at her house in the city and her rooms in the country tavern Booth was ever welcome, and there treason took definite shape.

After the preliminaries had all been settled, a plan of escape was to be devised. To this end, Booth took a trip on horseback through lower Maryland as far as Leonardstown, professing to purchase land, but in reality to mark on his map every spot and place, and every road and crossing which might in the near future become useful. He had provided himself with one of the maps which was published for the rebel government by a copperhead firm in Buffalo, N. Y., but which was not full enough for his purposes, and so he made the needed corrections after personal examination.

The conspiracy made no undue haste. All the influence thereto was absorbed by Booth and Mrs. Surratt. He was the chief plotter and she his main stay. Even among the principals, assassination, though agreed upon, was never referred to except by implication. To have openly spoken of murder among themselves and in their most secret consultations, would not have been tolerated for a moment. It was against the canons of polite society. In this society Booth was at home; he was supreme; cool, vigilant and plausible; the chief command was easily accorded him, and he felt himself great in intellectual stature. Mrs. Surratt was too shrewd to embroil any member of her family in the conspiracy; and so it happened that young Surratt, though fully cognizant of everything, was sent north by his mother a day before the assassination. For a year or more he had been employed as a clerk in the office of the Commissary-General of Prisoners. He was a prominent member of the Knights of the Blue Gauntlet, and treasurer of the camp.

An extract or two from a letter of his to a cousin residing in New York, may be of interest:

"OFFICE OF THE COMMISSARY-GENERAL
OF PRISONERS,
WASHINGTON, D. C., Feb. 6, 1865.

'MISS BELLE SEAMAN:

"DEAR COUSIN, — I received your letter, and not being quite so selfish as you are, I will answer it in what I call a reasonable time. I am happy to say that we are all well and in fine spirits. We have been looking for you to come on, with a great deal of impatience. Do come, won't you? Just to think, I have never yet seen one of my cousins. But never fear, I will probably see you all sooner than you expect. Next week I leave for Europe, and may give you a call, as I go to New York. * * * I have just taken a peep in the parlor. Would you like to know what I saw there? Well, Ma was sitting on the sofa, nodding first to one chair, then another, and then the piano. Anna is sitting in a corner, dreaming, I expect, of J. W. Booth. Who is J. W. Booth? Well, she can answer that question. * * * But hark, the door-bell rings, and Mr. J. W. Booth, is announced. Just listen to the scampering. Such brushing and fixing. We all send love to you and family.

"Your Cousin,
"J. HARRISON SURRATT,
"541 H Street, between 6th and 7th streets."

Matters were now approaching a crisis. It was at first intended that the assassination should take place during the inauguration ceremonies, but it was finally decided to be too risky. When it became known that the President would appear in public at Ford's Theatre, the time for definite action was plain.

Booth's principal actors were now assigned their parts. John Harrison Surratt was to go north into Canada, and on hearing of the result, if all was right, he was to repair at once to Toronto and there claim the promised gold and make his way to Richmond. Atzeroth was to murder the Vice-president, Andrew Jackson; Lewis Payne, or Wood as he called himself, was to look after Seward; Sam Arnold and McLaughlin, were each to kill a cabinet officer, and John Lloyd, a general. John A. Payne, with two confederates, had gone to North Carolina to look after Sherman. Harold was the stage manager, and looked after the properties. Horses and arms were provided, and every possible avenue of escape cleared, even to cutting the telegraph wires around the city. On the very afternoon of the murder Mrs. Surratt visited Surrattsville and told John Lloyd to have the carbines which young Surratt had placed in his care, ready for immediate use, as they would be needed that night. Lloyd had sent his wife away on a visit. Three weeks before the murder, Harold told some friends that the next time they heard of him he would be in Spain; adding that there was "no extradition treaty with that country." John Lloyd told friends at Surrattsville that he would "make a barrel of money or that his neck would stretch." Atzeroth said in Port Tobacco that if he "ever visited that place again he would be rich enough to buy it."

On that fateful Friday night Ford's Theater was crowded. Long before the curtain rose, the "Standing room only" card was displayed at the ticket office window. Near the door, the lobby was crowded. Booth went on the stage, and from behind the scenes looked searchingly over the audience. Suddenly near the door, a voice was heard. It said:

"Nine o'clock and forty-five minutes!"

The words were repeated by other voices until they reached the sidewalk. While people wondered, the voice said again:

"Nine o'clock and fifty minutes!"

This also passed on as before, and then — after an interval —

"Nine o'clock and fifty-five minutes!"

The life of the President was growing shorter by intervals of five minutes each. The bells in the clock towers tolled out ten o'clock. Why, they knew not, but a shudder crept through the audience.

"Ten o'clock and five minutes!"

Another interval. Then:

"Ten o'clock and ten minutes!"

At this instant Booth entered the door of the theater, and the men who had so faithfully repeated the murder-laden minutes scattered as though a messenger of Death had approached. Five minutes more and the deed was done.

At the same moment Payne was scattering blood from room to room in Secretary Seward's home. Having murdered Mr. Seward, as he thought, and but for Robinson, the nurse, it would have been an accomplished fact, he mounted his horse and attempted to find Booth and Harold, but the selfishness of crime was uppermost, and they had gone and left him to his fate. The city was alarmed, and he fled to the open country; when near Port Lincoln, on the Baltimore pike, his horse stumbled and threw him headlong. Half stunned and bewildered, he arose and resolving to return to the city, attempted to disguise himself.

He threw away his bloody coat, which was afterward found, and from a sleeve of his woolen undershirt he fashioned a rude cap, and then, plentifully daubing himself with mud and clay, and shouldering a pick which he found in the intrenchments near by, he started for Washington.

He reached Mrs. Surratt's door just as the officers were arresting her. He was taken into custody. He had come, he said, to dig a ditch for Mrs. Surratt, who had hired him. With all the effrontery of crime, Mrs. Surratt protested that she had never before seen the man, and that she had no ditch to dig. The officers washed Payne's hands and found them to be soft and tender as a woman's. In his pockets they found tooth and nail brushes, and a delicate pocket knife. Unusual toilet implements to be found on the person of a digger of ditches.

Atzeroth's room at the Kirkwood was directly over that of Vice-President Johnson. He was there to do murder, but the opportunity failed, and his courage also. He fled in such haste that he left his weapons, a bowie knife and revolver, between the mattresses of his bed. Booth's coat was found in his room, and in the pockets were riding gauntlets, boxes of cartridges, a map of Maryland, published in Buffalo, and corrected by his own hand, a spur, and a handkerchief marked with his mother's name. Atzeroth fled alone, and when captured was at the house of his uncle in Montgomery county, Maryland. Sam Arnold and McLaughlin grew faint hearted and ran away, without making the slightest attempt to carry out their part of the programme.

It was not until Thursday night that the real intentions of Booth became fully known to the Knights of the Blue Gauntlet. John H. Surratt, before leaving the city on Thursday morning, confided the facts to a brother Knight. Confusion and terror ensued, and many of the band hurriedly fled from the city, and those who remained kept themselves in seclusion. Booth, with his accustomed duplicity, had kept them in ignorance, leading them to believe that the plan of abduction was the one to be pursued. So frightened were they that the lodge room, with its paraphernalia, was left undisturbed, and with it the cells in the basement still furnished, in which condition they were found by officers later on. Canada was a refuge for Southern rebeldom, and thither they fled.

Booth and Harold met immediately after the murder, and sped away at a gallop past the Patent Office, up and over Capitol hill, and away to the bridge which crossed the Eastern branch at Uniontown, and at midnight they drew rein at Surrattsville. Harold dismounted, and entering the bar procured a bottle of whisky which he handed to Booth, and then rushing up stairs he brought down one of the carbines which had been left there by John H. Surratt. One only was taken. The other, left in the hall, was found by the officers. As they started off, Booth said to Lloyd: "We have murdered the President of the United States and the Secretary of State." Before sunrise on Saturday morning they reached the house of Dr. Mudd. Here Booth's injured leg, one of the bones of which was broken when he jumped down upon the stage at the theatre, was set. A link in the chain of evidence was left here; Booth's riding boot had to be cut to get it from his foot, and his name was written in the inside of the leg on the lining. It was not noticed, and so it remained there until found by the officers in pursuit; one of the clews which revealed the route of the fugitives. They were concealed at Dr. Mudd's during the day, but at night, mounting their horses, they rode away in the direction of Allen's Fresh. It was to Allen's Fresh that Lloyd had sent his wife on a visit to get her out of the way. By the aid of a negro, to whom they gave five dollars, they reached the house of one Sam Coxe, at midnight. Coxe was a notorious rebel, and though the fact could not be fully established, enough was learned to convince all who heard his examination that he was well aware of the conspiracy.

The negro, whose name was Swan, remained at Coxe's until they were ready to go, when he was to pilot them further on their road. Notwithstanding the fact that Swan had seen them eating and drinking, the refugees when they left the house swore bitterly at Coxe for his lack of hospitality. This was to blind the negro; for after they had ridden about five miles, they told him that they now knew the road, and would no longer have need of his services; and giving him five dollars more they rode on. But Swan was a shrewd negro, and so he watched them until he saw them turn back to Coxe's again, where they were harbored from Sunday until the next Thursday.

The next move of the fugitives was to cross the Potomac. This was a move of some danger. Friday evening a white man was seen to bring a canoe to the shore and anchor it with a stone. Between seven and eight o'clock the next morning it disappeared, and in the afternoon some workmen saw two men land in a canoe on the south side of the Potomac, and strike across a ploughed field toward King George Court House. One of the men walked with a crutch. Booth was provided with a crutch at the house of Dr. Mudd. They were next heard of at the Port Royal Ferry, and then at Garrett's house. Now, the long-persecuted Unionists of Lower Maryland began to come forward and give important testimony, which under threats and intimidation they never before dared to whisper. They told of the meetings of the conspirators at Lloyd's Hotel in Surrattsville, and then Lloyd was arrested, Booth's carbine found, and three days later Lloyd confessed. A little party of detectives under the untiring Lovett overhauled the residence of Dr. Mudd, where they found Booth's boots. This was before Lloyd confessed, and was the first positive evidence the officers had that they were upon the trail of the murderers. Much of the after success of the pursuit was due to the careful work done by this little squad of detectives.

A second party, under the charge of Major O'Beirne, now took the field. Through these the hiding place of Atzeroth was discovered, and he was arrested. With this party was Captain Beckwith, Gen. Grant's chief cipher operator, who tapped the wire at Point Lookout, and thus put the War Department in momentary communication with the theater of events. By this time the troops were assembling in various parts of the country in considerable numbers. Seven hundred men of the Eighth Illinois Cavalry, six hundred men of the Twenty-second Colored Volunteers and one hundred of the Sixteenth New York were patrolling the country by detachments, while Major O'Beirne and Col. Wells, with a force of cavalry and infantry, swept the entire peninsula with a line of skirmishers deployed in close intervals. Major O'Beirne, with his detectives, then crossed the Potomac and found where the fugitives had landed from the canoe on Boone's farm. This was another link in the chain which gave a clew to their route.

Now comes the chief of the secret service, Col. Lafayette Baker, on the scene. Absent from Washington at the time of the murder, he returned three days after, by order of Secretary Stanton, and engaged at once in the search for Booth. He possessed himself of all the War Department knew regarding the matter, and then acted. His first find was a negro who saw Booth and Harold when they crossed the Potomac.

Sending to General Hancock for twenty-five cavalrymen and an officer, Lieutenant Edward P. Doherty, he sat down to his maps to decide upon the probable route of the fugitives. He knew that they would not keep close to the coast owing to the difficulty in crossing swamps and rivers, nor would they take any direction leading east of Richmond, where they were likely at any time to strike our lines. He soon decided that they would be most likely to pass through Port Royal,

and there he hoped to intercept them. The little force of cavalry detailed from Company G, 16th N. Y., under the command of Lieutenant Doherty, having reported, he placed them under the command of Lieutenant-Colonel Conger, of Ohio, and Lieutenant L. B. Baker, of New York, and sent them direct to Belle Plain, on the lower Potomac, from thence to scour the whole country north of Port Royal. Here they found a negro who had driven two men, in his wagon, a short distance toward Bowling Green. These men answered the description of the fugitives. The ferryman who took the party across the Rappahannock gave them information of the utmost importance, though wrung from him by threats. They learned that the two men were at that moment lying at the house of one Garrett, which they had passed some time before. Retracing their steps, the nearly exhausted cavalrymen reached Garrett's at two o'clock in the morning. It was a pale moonlight night. The plain old farmhouse was dimly seen through a locust grove. It stood about three hundred yards from the road, and behind it an old weather-beaten barn, some long corn cribs, and a cattle shed.

Entering the roadside gate, the troops rode up to the house. Lieutenant Doherty picketed the premises, and then rode up to a side entrance and rapped. An old man in his night clothes, with a candle in his hand, made his appearance. It was Garret.

"Where are the men who are staying with you?" asked Doherty.

"They are gone," he said. "They went to the woods this afternoon."

In the meantime a lad, John M. Garrett, had been found by one of Doherty's men in a corncrib. Questioned in earnest, he saw that evasion would not do, and at once revealed the fact that Booth and Harrold were asleep in the barn. Doherty had already threatened to search the house, and the women were up and dressed, but this news changed the programme.

The troops were dismounted and the barn surrounded. Baker hailed the persons inside, who could now be heard stirring.

Lieut. Baker called to them: "We are about to send in the son of the man in whose custody you are found. Surrender your arms to him, and give yourselves up or we will fire the place."

There was no answer. The door was opened and young Garret pushed inside, appealed to them to surrender. With an oath Booth said: "Get out of here. You have betrayed us." The boy slipped out again as the door was slightly opened, and reported that his errand had failed.

The summons was repeated by Baker. "You must surrender! Give up your arms and come out! There is no chance for escape. We give you ten minutes to make up your minds."

Then came the demand: "Who are you, and what do you want with us?"

Baker again said: "We want you to deliver up your arms and become our prisoners."

After a lapse of some minutes, Baker hailed again: "Well, we have waited long enough; come out and surrender, or we'll fire the barn."

Booth answered: "I am a cripple, a one-legged man. Withdraw your forces twenty-five paces from the door, and I will come. Give me a chance for my life. I will never be taken alive."

"We did not come here to fight, but to capture you. Surrender, or the barn will be fired," said Doherty.

"Well, then, my brave boys, prepare a stretcher for me," cried Booth.

Then there was a pause, during which a discussion between Booth and his companion was heard. Booth said, "Get away from me. You're a —— coward, and want to leave me in my distress; but go — go! I don't want you to stay — I won't have you stay!" Then he shouted: "There's a man inside here who wants to surrender."

Then Harold rattled at the door, and begged to be let out, saying, "I want to surrender."

"Hand out your arms, then," said Doherty.

"I have none."

"You are the man who carried the carbine yesterday; bring it out."

"I haven't got any." In a whining tone.

Booth then said: "On the word and honor of a man and a gentleman, he has no arms with him. They are mine, and I have them."

Harold came to the door, was seized and pulled out by Doherty, handcuffed and turned over to Corporal Newgarten.

Booth then made his last appeal. "Captain, give me a chance. Draw off your men and I will fight them singly. I could have killed you six times to-night, but I believe you to be a brave man, and would not murder you. Give a lame man a show."

It was too late for further parley. Before he had ceased to speak Colonel Conger slipped around to the rear of the barn, and drawing some loose straws through a crack set them on fire. They were dry and soon in a blaze lighting up every part of the great barn. At sight of the fire Booth dropped his crutch and carbine and crept on his hands and knees to the spot hoping to see the incendiary and shoot him down. Then he turned upon the fire as if to leap upon and extinguish it; but it had gained too much headway. Turning, he made for the door, resolved not to die alone, when Sergeant Boston Corbett, thinking that he was about to shoot Lieutenant Doherty, fired with the intention of hitting him in the arm, but instead of the arm the bullet struck him in the head, barely an inch from the spot where the assassin's bullet struck the murdered President.

It was first thought that he had shot himself. He fell into the arms of Lieutenant Doherty, who brought him out of the burning barn and laid him upon the grass. Water was brought and dashed upon his face, and he revived. He was then carried to the porch of the house and laid upon a mattress. Brandy and water was given him, and when able to speak he said: "Useless, useless." The soldiers extinguished the fire. Booth muttered "Kill me! Kill me!" Brandy was given him every minute, and the doctor who lived six miles away, arrived but could do nothing. Booth asked to have his hands raised so that he could see them; his arms were paralyzed, so that he knew not where they were. When they were shown him, he muttered: "Useless, useless!" They were his last words; applicable not only to his hands, but to his whole life. "Useless." And so he died. His remains were sewed up in a saddle blanket, placed in a rickety old wagon drawn by an ancient relic of a horse, and the march to Washington was begun. The arms found with him were a knife, a repeating carbine and a pair of revolvers. A diary, bills of exchange and Canada money were found on his person. Harold was mounted on a horse, his legs tied to the stirrups, and placed in charge of four men, and the cortege of retributive justice moved on.

"Though the mills of God grind slowly,
Yet they grind exceeding small;
Though with patience He stands waiting,
With exactness grinds He all."

Ferrying once more at Port Royal they pushed on for Belle Plain, reaching there about three o'clock in the afternoon, when they embarked for Washington, where a few only were permitted to see the corpse for the purpose of identification. That this should be complete, the Secretary of War directed Col. Baker to summon a number of witnesses residing in Washington who had previously known Booth. Six witnesses, who had for years known him intimately, were examined, and identified the remains. Surgeon-General Barnes cut from the neck about two inches of the spinal column through which the bullet had passed. This is in the Government Medical Museum in Washington, and is the only relic of the assassin's body in existence. No further mutilation of the remains took place in the slightest degree. Following the further instructions of the Secretary of War as to the disposition of the body, it was taken directly from the gunboat to the old penitentiary building adjoining the arsenal grounds, and there in a cell a large flat stone was raised from the floor, a rude grave dug, the body dropped in, and so ended the funeral obsequies of John Wilkes Booth, the assassin.

Atzeroth, Payne, Harold and Mrs. Surratt were tried, convicted and hanged. The execution took place on the 9th of July, 1865.

Others, no doubt equally guilty in intent, escaped; and the movements of some of these will be set forth in this narrative. Into the details of the trial and execution, I need not enter. Complete accounts may be had from other sources, no doubt well known to the reader. From this point the narrative will press steadily on toward the "Mystery of Maple Island."

Much of what is yet to be said is but a compilation of existing records, published and unpublished, some of which have been kindly loaned to the author of this chapter. The reader will remember that John A. Payne was sent to North Carolina to look after General Sherman, and the first clue to his whereabouts at the time of the assassination, is found in the following correspondence, which we give early.

"MOOREHEAD CITY, NORTH CAROLINA,
May 5, 1865.

"Hon. WILLIAM H. SEWARD, Secretary of State:

SIR:—Enclosed you will find a letter which I found floating in the river by the new Government wharf, at this place, on the evening of the 2d inst. It was not until late last night that I succeeded in learning its purport, it being in cipher. Having learned its nature, I lose no time in transmitting it to you. I also send a copy of the letter as translated. The letter evidently had not been opened when thrown in the river. I think the fiend was here awaiting the arrival of General Sherman, but learning that he had gone by way of Wilmington, and being pressed by detectives, threw it overboard.

CHAS. DENET.

"P. S.—If the letter should lead to anything of importance, so that it would be necessary that I should be seen, I can be found at 126 South H st., between 6th and 4½ sts. I am at present engaged in the Construction Corps, Railroad Department, at this place. Will be in Washington in a few days."

The following is a translation of the cipher letter. It was one of those ciphers which are readily translatable when the key is known, and even that is not so very difficult to discover. The government experts were familiar with it, having often seen the same cipher in captured rebel correspondence. Hence it was easy to see that Mr. Denet's ingenuity had given him the key to the true meaning of the epistle.

[Translation.]

"WASHINGTON, April 15, 1865.

"DEAR JOHN—I am happy to inform you that Pet. has done his work well. He is safe and old Abe is in hell. Now, sir, all eyes are on you—you must bring Sherman. Grant is in the hands of Old Gray ere this. Red Shoes showed lack of nerve in Seward's case, but fell back in good order. Johnson must come. Old Crook has him in charge. Mind well the Brother's Oath, and you will have no difficulty. All will be safe, and we will enjoy the fruit of our labors. We had a large meeting last night—all were bent on carrying out the programme to the letter. The rails are laid for safe exit. Old—always behind—lost the pass at City Point. Now, I say again:—The lives of our brave officers and the life of the South depends upon the carrying this programme into effect. No. 2 will give you this. It is ordered that no more letters be sent by mail. When you write again, sign no real name, and send by some of our friends who are coming home. We want you to write us how the news was received there. We receive great encouragement from all quarters. I hope there will be no getting weak in the knees. I was in Baltimore yesterday. Pet. has not got there yet. Don't lose your nerve.

"No. FIVE."

O. B.

That this delicious bit of treasonable correspondence was sent to John A. Payne there is little or no doubt. From it we also learn that "Pet." was John Wilkes Booth; "Red Shoes," Wood, alias Lewis Payne, and "Old Crook," Atzeroth. The letter was evidently written early on the morning after the assassination, and placed in the hands of No. 2, to convey to Payne. It further shows that there was a meeting of the Brotherhood of the Blue Gauntlet on the very night of the assassination; or, if not of them as a camp, of some of them as a band of conspirators.

General Sherman's change of route threw Payne out in his calculations. The ordinary route from Raleigh, where Gen. Sherman's headquarters were at the time, to Washington, was by rail via Goldsborough and New Bern to Moorhead City, thence by steamer to Washington. There is no doubt, as Mr. Denct suggests, that Payne was on the watch at Moorhead City, but learning that Sherman had gone to Washington via Wilmington, and hearing, as he could not fail to hear, the result of the assassination, he lost heart, rid himself of every thing of a suspicious nature, and fled.

We will probably strike his trail again before our narrative closes. The following letter, dated at Buffalo, N. Y., is of no little interest, because it verifies in a degree what has already been stated.

"BUFFALO, N. Y., April 18, 1865.

"Hon. E. M. STANTON, Secretary of War, Washington, D. C.:—My Dear Sir:—Business has called me to Toronto, C. W., several times within the past two months; and while there, I have seen and heard some things which may be of service to the government.

"About five weeks ago, I saw at the Queen's Hotel, Toronto, a letter written by the late John Y. Beale, just previous to his execution, which, after speaking of his mock trial, unjust sentence, the judicial murder that was to be perpetrated by his execution, etc., called upon Jacob Thompson to vindicate his character before his countrymen of the South, and expressed his belief that his death would be speedily and terribly avenged. The letter itself was addressed to Colonel J. Thompson, Confederate Commissioner at Toronto, but the superscription on the envelope, which was in a different handwriting read simply, J. Thompson, Toronto, Canada. This circumstance caused it to be delivered to a Mr. Thompson for whom it was not intended. I was permitted to peruse, but not to copy, the letter. I was informed, at that time, that the friends of Beale were banded together for the double purpose of avenging his death, and aiding the rebel government. I have heard the same statement repeated many times since, and have been frequently told by citizens of Toronto that some great mischief was being plotted by refugees in Canada. For more than a month General Dix's name was mentioned in my hearing in connection with the threatened vengeance. Regarding all such stories as idle tales, I never repeated them. Last Friday evening, while sitting in the office of the Queen's Hotel, I overheard a conversation between some persons sitting near me, which convinced me that the plot to murder the President was known to them. The party was mourning over the late rebel reverses, commenting upon the execution of Beale, the extradition of Bueley, etc., and then they cheered themselves after this fashion : "We'll make the damned Yankees howl yet." "Boys, I'll bet that we'll get better news in fortyeight hours." "We'll have something from Washington that will make people stare." Their words at the time seemed to me to be simply vulgar and profane, and implying idle threats which could never be executed. The next morning (Saturday, April 15), when I heard of the assassination, I could not help feeling that the party were implicated in the act. On Saturday, I met two of them in company with Ben Young, and one or two others of the St. Albans raiders, in the bar-room at the Queen's. One said, "Good news for us this morning," and another, "Damn well done, but not enough of it." Raising their glasses, one said, "Here's to Andy Johnson's turn next, to which another responded, "Yes, damn his soul." On relating this circumstance to Hon. E. G. Spaulding and others, they were of the opinion that I should communicate them to your Department. For my own part, I beg to refer to Hon. Ira Harris, of the Senate, and Hon. John A. Griswold, of the House."

"I am, my dear sir, very truly yours,

G. C."

Mr. C. is a respectable lawyer in this city, and his statements are entitled to credit.

E. G. S.

BUFFALO, N. Y.

The letter speaks for itself, and needs no comment. The only criticism to offer is not upon the letter, but upon the writer. Had he been possessed of the shrewdness which the average lawyer ought to possess, he would have written to the War Department long before. Written at the time it was, it only showed how great was the lack of detective ability which every great lawyer possesses in some degree. In the writer, it only verified the old adage about "locking the stable after the horse is stolen."

The next letter in evidence throws a ray of light on the trail of John Harrison Surratt, and also, from the description, of John A. Payne. It is from one of the many detectives which were sent into Canada on a hunt for the escaped conspirators. It is dated at Montreal on the 27th of April. Its great length precludes its insertion in full, but we give the salient portions; those relating directly to the subject in hand. Just here, it may be well to note that a prominent Englishman in Montreal, who, previous to the assassination of the President, was a strong sympathizer with the South, and was well acquainted with the Confederate agents in Canada, and fully informed of their plans and movements, said that the murder of the President was too much for him; and he told Alderman Lyman, of that city, that the Southern agents had heard from the party who murdered the President, and that they expected him in Montreal within forty-eight hours; and if not the principal, one closely connected with the assassination. This information the agents received on the 20th of April. The reader will bear the date in mind, as he reads the extracts from the detective's letter:

"MONTREAL, April 27, 1865.

"COLONEL L. C. BAKER:

"Dear Sir — While in Burlington (Vt.), I obtained a white linen handkerchief, which was dropped in the Vermont Central Depot, on Thursday evening April 20, by one of three strange men who slept in the depot all Thursday night. These men came from the steamer Canada, Capt. Flagg. She was very late that evening, and did not connect with the train north, to Montreal, which leaves at 7 o'clock, P. M. They came into the depot between seven and a half and eight o'clock, after the night watchman went on duty. They had no baggage. They were all rather poorly dressed, and looked hard, worn out, and tired. The watchman asked them which way they were going; they said "to Montreal." When told that they could not go that night, they said that they knew it. He asked them if they wanted a hotel; they said no, that they were going to stay in the depot. They did not seem to have much to say or do with each other. They curled up on seats in different parts of the room, and went to sleep, and remained quiet all night. The watchman awakened them about 4 o'clock in the morning to take the train, which they did. After they left he picked up two dirty pocket handkerchiefs where they had slept. While looking them over, he found the name of J. H. Surratt No. 2, on one of them. B., the watchman, got his mother to wash the handkerchiefs, and on Saturday he went to the city, and told the circumstance of finding them. Detective G. C. got the handkerchief from B, and I got it from him. Enclosed you will find it. B. said that one of the men was tall and the others short. He identifies the likeness of Surratt, as being one of the men. I then found the conductor who ran the train to Essex Junction that morning, and he too, fully identified Surratt's likeness as being one of the men. I next found C. T. Hobart, who runs the through train to St. Albans, Vermont. He gave a description of two men only who boarded his train at Essex Junction on Friday morning, April 21, at 5.05 o'clock. One was a tall man, broad shoulders, otherwise slim, straight as an arrow, did not look like a laborer, though dressed rather poor; had on a loose sack coat, cassimere shirt, light colored pants, and a tight fitting skull cap. His hair was black as jet and straight; no beard; was young, not more than twenty-one or twenty-two. The other man was not much over five feet, thick set, short neck, full face,

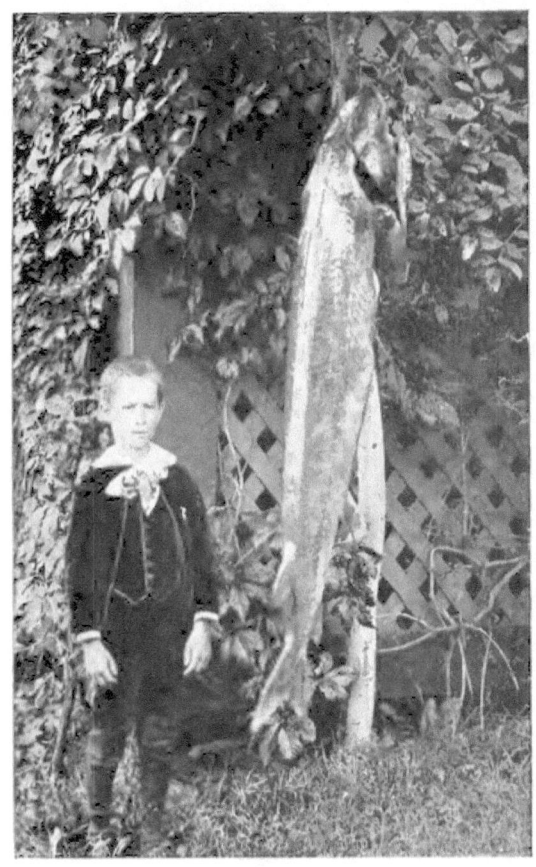

A STURGEON CAUGHT IN THE ST. LAWRENCE.

sandy complexion, sandy chin whiskers and no other beard. He wore a soft black-felt hat, dark-colored sack coat, light-colored pants, and a reddish-colored flannel shirt. He had but little to say; let the tall man do the talking. They both got off the train at St. Albans. He felt as if they were a pair of assassins, and in speaking to a friend about the matter, he gave vent to his suspicions. He fully identified Surratt's picture as that of the tall one, and said that he would know him anywhere. * * * There is no doubt that Surratt is in this province, together with some others, but whom I cannot tell. Enclosed I send you a likeness of one of the Paynes, of whom there are seven brothers, all Kentuckians. Three of them are said to be in South America, one is in jail at St. Albans, and the others are here unless you have them with you. The picture is marked on the back. If of no use, please send it back to the owner. I am going out along that portion of Canada bordering on Maine, Vermont and New York. Many rebels are in there. Young Saunders and others are there now. Porterfield, a dangerous rebel, is making preparations to go to Nashville; ought not to be allowed. Trowbridge, another, has gone to Detroit. Respectfully, etc.,
————.

It was that very picture of "one of the Paynes," which fully revealed the identity of the man Wood, who attempted the assassination of Secretary Seward. It was, in fact, his own portrait taken in Montreal, some time previous to starting for Washington to report to John Wilkes Booth. The next communication is addressed to Secretary Stanton. It was dated at Montreal on the 29th of April, 1865. We append an extract or two:

"HON. E. M. STANTON, Secretary of War:

"Dear Sir,—There is no doubt that J. H. Surratt and John A. Payne were in the city yesterday, and that they left last night in company with Clement C. Clay and others probably for Toronto. I am a private detective here, without authority to act for your government. I looked the city over for G., one of Baker's men, but found that he left for the border townships yesterday morning, so I failed to see him. * * * I am not at all certain that they went to Toronto; it is only my opinion. They may have gone to Three Rivers, as there are a great many Southern refugees there, or to Tanner, where it is said that John A. Payne has heretofore spent a great deal of his time, together with three of his brothers. Respectfully, etc.,
————.

About this time a letter was received at Washington, post-marked Detroit, but written at Tanner, Canada, by one John P. H. Hall, of that place, and directed: "To Andrew Johnson, President of the United States, or other authority." Its contents are as follows:

"With certainty I state to you that John A. Payne, and thirteen others, are sworn to murder Andrew Johnson, E. M. Stanton, L. S. Fisher, and others, within thirty days from April 23d, 1865. The arrangements are all made and in progress toward execution. I do not know where John A. Payne is now. He was at Montreal when this plot was projected. His brother (whose name I do not recollect) is implicated. Seven of the plotters are at Washington, four at Bedford, Pennsylvania, and the thirteenth is with Payne. These are plain facts. Do not reveal this, but arrest John A. Payne and his brother. I send this to Detroit to avoid suspicion.

Yours, etc.,
" ———— ————."

The Montreal private detective was right in his opinion, at least so far as Clement C. Clay was concerned; because, among many other names registered at the Queen's Hotel, Toronto, on the evening of April 29, 1865, was that of C. C. Clay. Whether Surratt and Payne were in his company remains to be seen. Jacob Thompson and Larry McDonald were already there.

So far, the testimony as to the whereabouts of John H. Surratt is fairly complete. In the absence of direct and absolute proof, it may, at all events, be accepted as strong circumstantial evidence. We now present yet another letter, written by a colored man, which, though anonymous, and as such not entitled to take rank as evidence, yet it harmonizes so well with what has been already learned that it seems worthy of some credence. At all events, it is here given place, and left to the judgment of the reader.

The letter is postmarked "Niagara Falls," and is dated "Monday, May 2nd, 1865," and directed "To the Secretary of War, Washington, D. C." The writer says:

"I beg of you not to let any one see this letter. I dare not sign it for fear that my name may somehow come out. I send you my name and business on a separate paper so that you may judge whether I have an opportunity to learn what I tell you. Be sure to destroy it. I send this to be mailed at Niagara Falls, because a letter directed to you and

dropped into this post-office, would be read by Jake Thompson before it was sent out, if it was ever sent at all. What I want you to know is that there is an awful nest of rebels here at this time. Clay, Surratt and John A. Payne are here. They came Saturday with a lot of others. Surratt and Payne skipped out last night and now there is the very devil to pay. It seems that Surratt was the treasurer of some society that was hired to murder President Lincoln and a lot of others, and that Jake Thompson took the gold out of the bank here and paid it over to him and Payne, and that they were to divide it among the others; but they skipped out and now they can't find hide nor hair of them. I wouldn't like to be in their shoes if the gang gets them, and they are going in pursuit. They are plotting now to murder a lot more in revenge for the killing of Booth, and if Payne and the rest are hung they say that they will burn Washington. You can't tell how much I hear, and of course I don't hear it all, as I am only in the room when I take liquor to them, which is pretty often though, but one of the girls hears heaps and tells me all about it. Anyway, you folks in Washington ought to look out. I hope you will catch and hang every one of them, especially Jake Thompson. I hate him. That is all I can write now.
" ———— ————."

But little more remains to be said, and that is scarcely more than conjecture. This much is positively known. A sharp lookout for J. H. Surratt and John A. Payne, was kept at St. Catharines, Canada, for some time. That city was a great place of resort for Southern rebels, among whose citizens they found a welcome, especially among a certain class. Then, too, Col. Beverly Robinson, of Virginia, was the proprietor of a fashionable hotel there, which became a noted resort for Southerners and Southern sympathizers, and where rebellion against the Government of the United States was as openly discussed as it ever was in Charleston, South Carolina, where it originated. But the rebellion went down with a crash and so did Beverly Robinson's hotel business, to the sorrow of several capitalists of St. Catharines, whose only security for heavy loans was a life insurance policy, and the "honah, sah," of Col. Beverly Robinson, one of Virginia's F. F. V.'s, on neither of which as late as 1881, had they ever realized a cent. Whether the indebtedness has since been canceled, this deponent saith not.

But John H. Surratt and John A. Payne were too shrewd to visit St. Catharines. The former made his way to Three Rivers, Quebec, where he was protected for a time by Father Boucher, a Catholic priest. He went thence to Italy, enlisted in the Papal Zouaves, was exposed by another Papal soldier by the name of Massie, extradited, tried and acquitted in Washington in 1868, and now lives in Baltimore. A man bearing the description of John A. Payne, was seen in the vicinity of Sharbot and Rideau lakes, Ont., and at Smith's Falls during the latter part of May, 1865, and shortly afterward at Gananoque, where he stayed for a day or two, and then settling his hotel bill, in payment of which he offered a gold piece of English coinage, he left, no one knew whither. Was it John A. Payne who made his appearance at Fisher's Landing? The description and the time tally well. It may with some show of reason be asked: If he wanted to hide himself effectually among the islands, why did he not choose some spot among the myriad islands of the Admiralty group near Gananoque, or in the Navy group below? Evidently he was a shrewd observer. He well knew that the defrauded Brotherhood would hunt him to the death, but he also knew that they would be unlikely to venture to the American side of the St. Lawrence; while they would search every island in the Canadian Channel. He knew, too, that Baker's government detectives, would never think of looking for him on the United States side of the line. Besides, had he located in either of the island groups mentioned, the Admiralty, for instance, his supplies would necessarily be drawn from Gananoque, a dangerous point for him to visit. If in the Navy group, it was not easy to procure needed supplies, without travelling some distance. Then, too, the main channels of steamboat travel at that time, especially for the Canadian steamers, passed through those groups.

Locating where he did — if indeed it was him, showed great shrewdness. Maple Island is at some distance from any of the regular lines of steamboat travel, and from any of the channels taken by excursion steamers, which, at that time, were few and far between; and while the island is by no means hidden, that fact of itself was an element of safety; because no one would think of searching an island so open to the view of every one. That a party of five or six men made their appearance in Gananoque in the month of August, 1865, making inquiries about a man who answered the description of John A. Payne, already given, is a fact that may be easily substantiated. They affirmed that they all belonged to a party of workmen who had been employed near Montreal, and that the man for whom they were looking drew the pay for them, and then ran away. They had followed him to Smith's Falls, and from there could get no further trace of him.

There is some significance, too, in the fact that after the burning of the cabin on Maple Island, nothing more was seen of the party of supposed Southerners, who had for some days previous sojourned at the Hubbard and Walton Houses in Clayton.

But of yet greater significance is the fact that the fateful sign of the three crosses was cut upon the breast of the murdered hermit. That of itself is almost positive evidence that he met his doom at the hands of the Brotherhood, and that not robbery only, but revenge, was a prime factor in the assassination.

Scores of instances can be produced where the bodies of those who fell victims to the relentless oaths of the secret Brotherhoods of the South during the rebellion were marked in like manner. Even the " Ku Klux Klans " of 1866, '67 and '68, during the reconstruction

"LITTLE FRAUD," BELOW FAIRY LAND.

period, left in many instances the same bloody sign upon the breasts of their murdered victims.

Reader, the testimony is all in ; whatever may be its value as evidence, it is wholly a matter of record, accessible to those who care to investigate. The writer has sought far and wide for additional proofs, but they could not be found by him ; and now the judgment remains with you ; for with this paragraph, he submits for your decision THE MYSTERY OF MAPLE ISLAND.

OLD FORT FRONTENAC AND MODERN KINGSTON.

MORE than two centuries ago, the aboriginal dwellers along the River St. Lawrence, and on the islands which form its wondrous archipelagoes, witnessed a display never before seen on the inland waters of the great western continent. First came an advanced guard of canoes, disposed in four lines, followed by two large bateaux, gay with flags and banners; then other lines of canoes bringing up the rear — the whole constituting a flotilla of 120 boats, conveying a force of French troops, 400 or more, under the command of Louis de Buade, Count de Frontenac, whose mission was to establish the first military post of any note above Montreal at the place called by the Iroquois "Kataroquoi," which, interpreted, means: "A land of many lakes;" — the Kingston of to-day.

The flotilla was met by a deputation of the oldest and most influential chiefs of the great confederation of the Five Nations, who saluted the Admiral, according to the journal of Count de Frontenac, "with evidence of much joy and confidence;" and was by them guided into "one of the most beautiful and agreeable harbors in the world, capable of holding 100 of the largest ships," into which from the north flows the waters of the Cataraqui, from the west and southwest those of that most beautiful of bays the Bay of Quinte, and rounding in from the south the waters of Lake Ontario.

With bugle-call and beat of drum, and with salvos of artillery, banners waving, and all the "pomp and circumstance" of military display, the flotilla landed on the point now occupied by the Tete du Pont Barracks. Two years previous, M. de Courcelles had selected this spot as a suitable site for a fort, the lines for which, under his direction, were marked out by M. de Talon. On July 13, 1673, a grand council, consisting of the Iroquois deputation on one side and Count Frontenac and the French officers on the other, assembled at the tent of the Admiral. The pipe of peace was smoked, and Garakontie, a distinguished chief, opened the council with a speech in which he expressed the utmost respect for the Great Father Onnontio. Count Frontenac answered in a speech expressing great pleasure at meeting his Indian children, and after a distribution of presents to all, men, women and children, the council was broken up, only to be repeated a few days later with another still more formal and elaborate.

While the Count was amusing his aboriginal friends, work on the fort was pushed with the greatest vigor. The ground was cleared, trenches dug, palisades set, and the keel of a vessel laid, which, when completed, would give him the command of Lake Ontario. The command of the fort was given to M. de la Salle, to whose comprehensive schemes it owed its existence. Charlevoix explains the object of its erection. He says: "There was formerly a great trade here, especially with the Iroquois, and it was to entice them to us, as well as to hinder their carrying their skins to the English and to keep these savages in awe, that the fort was built." But not even Charlevoix had comprehended the wider plans of La Salle. Born of a wealthy burgher of Rouen, La Salle came to Canada when twenty-two years of age, filled with the dream of reaching China by way of the Ottawa river. He was endowed with great firmness and perseverance, and was eager to distinguish himself in the ranks of the great discoverers. Having read Joliet's report of the great river, the

Mississippi, to take possession of the vast region south of the great lakes, which is watered by its confluents, became the dream of his life and the summit of his ambition. To this end, Fort Frontenac was the first step, the next was Niagara. But Fort Frontenac must first be completed. In 1674, he secured a grant of the fort, a large tract of the surrounding country and the adjacent islands. The original fort was enlarged and enclosed with ramparts and bastions of stone, and contained, in addition to a range of barracks and officers' quarters, a well, a mill, a bakery and a forge. Where now stands the oldest portion of Kingston, a village of French colonists grew up. A village of Iroquois, and the chapel and Presbytery of the Recollet Friars were near by. Here was a little Kingdom over which La Salle reigned supreme; and had not

"His vaulting ambition o'er leaped itself."

he might have made of Kingston a place of great importance, scarcely second to Montreal. But to the west and south, against the stubborn resistance of both Jesuit Fathers and Canadian traders, he was determined to push his way. Building a vessel at Frontenac, he sailed to Niagara, and there established a "palisadoed fort," built and launched a vessel on Lake Erie, which was lost with her first cargo of furs, and finally after encountering and overcoming obstacles that would have deterred a less determined man, he sailed down the Father of waters to the Gulf of Mexico, and finally perished through the treachery of a follower. All this is but a part of the history of the New France.

The infamous Denonville, who succeeded La Salle in command of Fort Frontenac, by his imprisonment and transportation to France of several Iroquois chiefs, where they died in confinement condemned to the galleys, brought about a terrible retribution, which culminated in the massacre of the innocent inhabitants of Lachine, the desolation of the country around Cataraqui, and the destruction of the fort, which was demolished by the Indians. On his recall to the place, Count de Frontenac found the country devastated, and smoking ruins in the place of prosperous villages; and, what was more portentous, a dim war-cloud was rising upon the horizon line between the New France and the New England, which boded evil days in the near future. This spurred him on to rebuild the fort, which he did at once.

But despite his forebodings, a half century of tranquility followed, and so little did the country progress, that after Count Frontenac's death in 1698, the fort and settlement at Cataraqui were almost completely lost sight of, and yet his fears were prophetic; for France was soon to lose her possessions in the New World, and after Quebec, Fort Frontenac was to feel the force of the blow, directed by Gen. James Abercrombie, and delivered by Col. John Bradstreet on August 25, 1758.

The garrison of the fort had been withdrawn to protect another point, leaving only seventy men under the command of a gallant officer, M. de Noyan. Bradstreet erected a battery where the market-place now is, and soon compelled the garrison to capitulate, but on such terms as brave men are entitled to. What was of yet greater importance to the English, the surrender of the fort included the French navy on Lake Ontario, consisting of twenty-two vessels, eighty pieces of artillery, and a large quantity of small arms and ammunition.

In the beginning of the Kingston of to-day, traces of the old fort and of the breast-works erected by Col. Bradstreet were visible for many years. In fact a bastion of the old fort is yet traceable on the parade of the Tete du Pont Barracks. For many years a few French and Indian families loitered in the vicinity, but it was not until the coming of the U. E. Loyalists at the close of the War of the Revolution, that the place sprang into notice. During that war, all the military and naval operations were transferred to Carlton Island, in the south channel of the St. Lawrence river, where, in 1778, a strong fort was erected by order of Gen. Sir Frederick Haldimand, after whom it was named.

The first little band of loyalist refugees were guided to this point by Captain Grass, who had once been a prisoner in Fort Frontenac.

Coming from New York by way of the St. Lawrence, they left their families at Sorel, returning there to winter, and in the spring took up their grants at Cataraqui, came up the river with their families in bateaux, and taking possession, a second band of "Pilgrim Fathers," seeking a sanctuary because of persecution, and founding at once a nation and a party.

As in all new settlements, for many years life was exceedingly primitive; a mortar and pestle was their mill, and not unfrequently was a farm sacrificed in order to live. So great became the needs of the infant settlement that 1788 was long remembered as the "famine year," because of the terrible drouth, which almost entirely destroyed the crops, and reduced the people to the verge of starvation.

With all its drawbacks, Kingston became a place of consequence; trade increased, the building of a grist-mill on the Cataraqui river was a material help, exports of home-raised products increased, the settlers began to replace their home-made fabrics with clothes of foreign manufacture, shops increased, so that what is now known as Princess street, the principal street of the city, was then called "Store street."

It was not until 1812, however, that Kingston came prominently into notice; but as the principal Canadian port on Lake Ontario and at the head of the St. Lawrence river, with a magnificent harbor, and so situated that it became an easy post of observation on Sackets Harbor, an important post of the United States, it could not be neglected; but on the contrary it sprang into importance at a bound. A government dock yard occupied the grounds where the Royal Military College buildings stand, while the bay between that and the slope of the present Fort Henry, was the mooring ground for vessels of war. During this war, the original Fort Henry was begun, a series of block houses were erected, which, connected by long stockades, were deemed sufficient for the defense of the city. Later a chain of massive Martello towers and stone walls took the place of the log block houses and stockades. The tall towers, with their conical red caps, look well as we approach Kingston by steamer, while the modern Fort Henry, which was not erected until more than twenty years after the war of 1812-15, looks down upon us from the summit of the hill with a sort of grim defiance, more the result of decay than of strength. Fort Frederick, an earth work in front of the Military College, is really a strong point in the defenses of Kingston. As for the rest, they can scarcely be excelled as a ——— show; in which their greatest rival on this continent is the system of fortifications which defend the entrance to the Bay of San Francisco.

For many years Kingston has been especially eminent as an educational point. In 1786, Dr. Stuart, the first clergyman and the first teacher in Upper Canada established a "Grammar School," and in 1805 the schools of Kingston had attained such prominence that Rochefoucauld deemed them worthy of a somewhat extended notice in his memoirs. In 1840 the University of Queen's College was founded, and its growth has been that of Canada, and its record of work done, a noble one. Its hopes for the future are bright.

The Royal Military College, the "West Point of Canada," is treated at length in another chapter; but, in addition to Queen's University, with its Departments of Arts, Science, Law and Divinity, there are the Women's Medical College, and the Royal College of Physicians and Surgeons, both of which are affiliated to the Queen's University. The Collegiate Institute consists of the two older High Schools, among whose graduates have been Premiers of the Province and of the Dominion.

Kingston at one time narrowly escaped being the capital of Upper Canada. In fact it was here that Lieut.-Governor Simcoe was sworn into office, in an old wooden church which fronted the market place,—his first Cabinet chosen and writs issued to convene the Legislature. The new Legislature met once at Niagara, and then adjourned to York, now Toronto, which place, as a matter of fact, had been already decided upon as the future capital of the Upper Province. The "Old Borough" of Niagara has always been

ONE OF THE MARTELLO TOWERS, KINGSTON, ONT.

excessively proud of the fact that it was for a time the capital of Upper Canada; but as between it and Kingston, honors are fairly easy. In 1840-44, however, Kingston became the seat of government of the United Provinces, until its removal to Ottawa.

Back of Kingston is a most unpromising region of country so far as looks is concerned, though rich in minerals, chiefly iron, lead and phosphates, which the Kingston and Pembroke Railway has opened up and made tributary to Kingston, thereby increasing the prosperity of the place more than any other road has done; and whenever all this rich mineral country is fully developed, Kingston will become a city of far greater importance than the most sanguine of her citizens have yet dreamed of.

Among the latest improvements in Kingston, is the Electric Street Railway, than which no other city can boast a better. Compact and complete, with a service in every way satisfactory, with elegantly equipped cars supplied with the very latest electrical appliances, finely furnished, heated and lighted by electricity in the winter and furnished with elegant observation cars in summer, it is one of Kingston's most enjoyable attractions.

Forming a belt line, which completely encircles the city, it branches out to the outlying town of Portsmouth, to the Kingston Penitentiary, to Rockwood Insane Asylum, and to the beautiful and popular grounds of Lake Ontario Park, whose shaded shores sloping away to the lake, afford an enchanting view of Old Ontario and the river St. Lawrence, interspersed with island gems, a scene of surpassing loveliness. A separate branch of the road runs to the historic Cataraqui Cemetery, the chosen resting place of many of Canada's cherished dead; men prominent in her affairs, who made her history glorious, whose memories will ever remain green in the hearts and homes of her people, and to whose tombs a visit is but a brief pilgrimage,— of patriotism to the citizen, of admiration and respect, to the visitor; because true greatness and worth have no nationality.

Starting at the foot of Brock street, near the landing of the steamers of the Thousand Island and St. Lawrence River Steamboat Companies, the Electric Belt Line runs along Ontario street, past the Town Hall and City Buildings, the Kingston and Pembroke Railway Station, the Hotel Frontenac and the station of the Grand Trunk Railway, up William street to King, and thence along King, the street of residences, past many of the finest homes of Kingston's citizens, past the great buildings of the Merchant's Bank, and of the Bank of Montreal, along the southern edge of the City Park to McDonald Park with its formidable guns and Murney Tower Fort.

Here the line turns to the right on Barrie street and runs along the west side of the City Park, beneath a magnificent arch of grand old elms, a beautiful avenue graced with many elegant homes. Turning on Union street comes the Cricket Field, the sporting grounds of Kingston's athletes; and next the Court House and County Prison, both large and imposing structures. Next we have views of the Government Drill Shed, the Skating and Curling Rinks, the Queen's College, the Infant's Home, the Kingston City Hospital, and several beautiful country residences belonging to English families, surrounded by elegant grounds and extensive lawns, and then we arrive at the junction at the corner of Alfred and Union streets. From this point we may continue out Union street, visiting the Penitentiary, Portsmouth, the Insane Asylum, or Lake Ontario Park, above referred to. To inspect the Penitentiary or Rockwood Asylum, permission may be obtained on application to the warden, and visitors will find both very interesting.

To make this side trip, we change cars at Alfred street. Returning to that point, we again change to the Belt Line, and proceed to swing around the grand circle. First come the buildings and grounds of Victoria School and the Collegiate Institute, and also Victoria Park, and the next turn brings us to the junction on Princess street, the business and commercial street of the city, gorgeous in display and a veritable hive of trade and traffic. At the junction on Princess street, we may change cars for Cataraqui Cemetery, and in a few minutes exchange the busy hum of the city for a scene of rural quiet. Continuing down Princess street, however, in addition to the great mercantile houses of the city, we see the imposing buildings of the Young Men's Christian Association, St. Andrew's Church, Kingston Business College, the Opera House, and pass within a block of the great Catholic Cathedral. Turning again from Princess to King, and from King to Brock, we pass down Brock, past the Market Square, having swung around the entire circle in forty minutes — that is to say, the Belt Line proper, leaving the branch excursions out of the question. In that time we have seen the largest part and the most interesting objects of interest in this old historic city, excepting, of course, the trips to Portsmouth, the Penitentiary, the Asylum and Ontario Park, and to Cataraqui Cemetery. These taken, will add to the time, but are well worth the expenditure of both time and money. During the summer months, the Belt-Line cars run every five minutes, reducing the time of waiting to a minimum. Passengers may, if they choose, reverse the order of the trip, and swing around the circle in the opposite direction. Should such be the case, then must our brief description also be read in reverse order. In any case, we have arrived at our starting point, near the steamer landing, and if an excursionist, we may go on board at our leisure.

There are few finer views to be had than from the deck of the Empire State, as she swings away from her wharf on a pleasant morning for a run down among the Thousand Islands. The sun, rising in all its splendor, gilds the highlands of Wolfe Island, and lights up the broad expanse of Lake Ontario, that stretches away to the western horizon, which stoops to bathe itself in its limpid waters. Simcoe and Garden Islands are sharply defined, Batteau Channel looks like a wide canal cut through solid limestone; away beyond the long bridge is the winding Cataraqui, and then the eye catches the tower of Barriefield Church, and sweeps along the ridge until it rests on Fort Henry, with the Military College and Fort Frederick at its base. On the other hand the eye catches the city buildings in the foreground, and then spire and dome and tower follow in succession, until the buildings of Rockwood Asylum appear in the distance, and the beautiful Bay Quinte coyly permits a charm to be seen, and as quickly hides it from view. Swinging past Cedar Island with its picturesque Martello tower, we enter the broad channel and speed away down the river, leaving behind us a scene long to be remembered — and one of the most ancient, honorable and historic of all the cities of Canada — a grand country, larger in area than the whole United States.

H. WALTER WEBB.

SOME writer for a New York newspaper, under date of August 18, 1894, lets himself loose in the following style:

"While Dr. Chauncey M. Depew is dividing his time in Europe between talking horse and diplomacy with Lord Roseberry, Rhine wine and yachts with the German Kaiser and anarchy and politics with President Casimir-Perier, of France, his job, as the president of the New York Central Railroad and authority on almost everything pertaining to railroads, is being held down by a young man who is not so well known as he, but who is thought by men who know, to be an altogether better president of railroads than the talented Dr. Depew. Dr. Depew's 'sub' is about twenty-five years younger than himself, and he can probably outrun and outbox his superior and do a lot of things that the doctor's stiffened joints would not possibly permit him to undertake. He is very much quieter than the doctor, and while he may not have as many

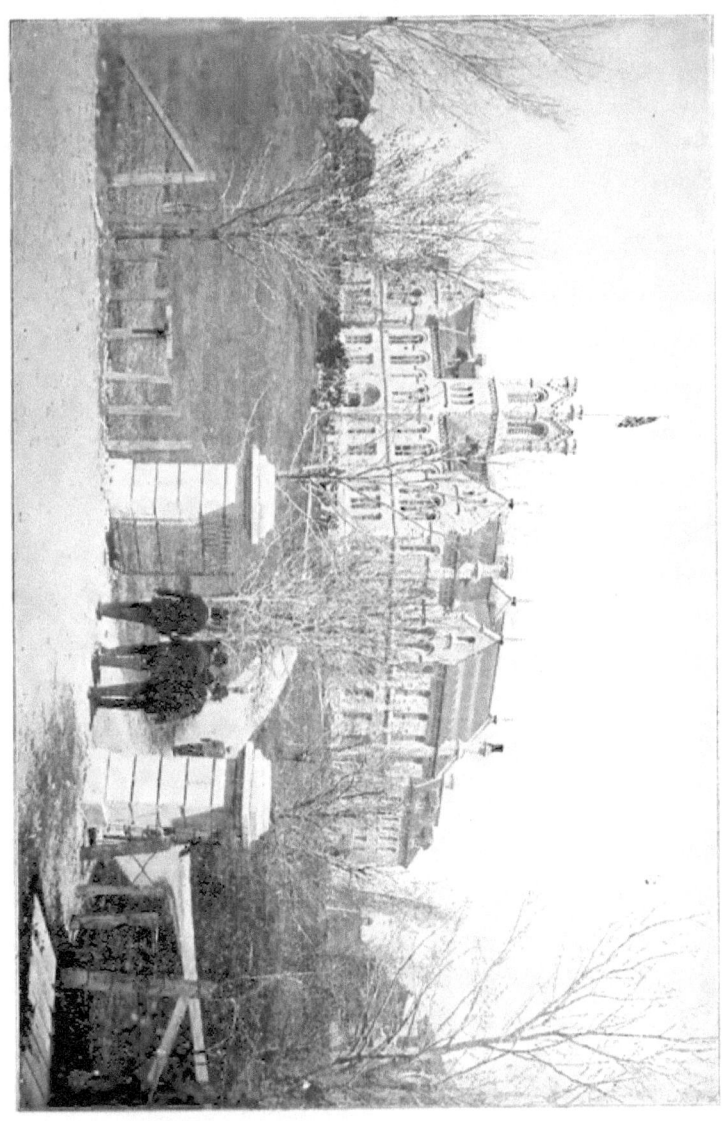

QUEEN'S UNIVERSITY, KINGSTON, ONT.

friends, those who talk with him every day say that he can give his chief points in the line of 'hustling.' Although he was not altogether unknown four years ago, it was not until then that his genius as a railroad manager brought him prominently before the public. Mr. Depew was then, as now, in Europe hobnobbing with the big guns over there, while Cornelius Vanderbilt, who owns most of the New York Central Road and who hires Mr. Depew at a fancy salary, was somewhere in Africa."

This screed reads well, and desiring to know more of this man who has proven himself able to "hold down" the great Chauncey's seat, we have taken some pains to make inquiries about him. We are told that in the spring of 1890 the directors of the New York Central Railroad determined to make some changes in the organization—changes which involved promotion of some of the abler officers of the road. Among other things which they voted to do was the creation of a new department, the head of which was to be elected third vice-president of the system, and to have supreme direction of the traffic of the road, both passenger and freight. He was to be held, in short, responsible for the management of such business as was offered to the company. The choice for this responsible office fell upon H. Walter Webb, and only a few weeks later this young man found himself face to face with a strike which was more threatening than any that had occurred upon the road, perhaps in its existence, certainly since the great strike year of 1877.

Two years later Vice-President Webb was called to face another emergency of the same sort, and these two experiences fixed attention upon him as one of the great railway managers of the United States. Men who do not know Major Webb are asking one another something about his personality and his intellectual qualities, as the generalship he displays not only in strike crises, but in those more silent but in some respects equally desperate battles which railroad companies as competitors of other railroad companies are constantly fighting.

In New York Major Webb is well known, but elsewhere, although he has gained wide repute, there is little knowledge of the manner of man he is. The story of his career contains much that is instructive and interesting.

Major Webb is one of the sons of that distinguished politician and editor of the time when the Whig party was fighting its battles, Gen. James Watson Webb. Great as were Gen. Webb's achievements in the political world, when he came to old age he took greater pride in the promise which was already beginning to be fulfilled, of raising a family of boys who would gain distinction, perhaps, equal to that which was gained by the famous Field, or Washburn, or Wolcott families.

Walter Webb, in his youth, showed some taste for engineering, and he was placed in the Columbia College School of Mines, which is the scientific department of that institution, and was at the head of his class some twenty years ago. After graduation, however, young Webb felt some inclination toward a career at the bar. He gratified it to the extent of studying, being admitted, and hanging out his shingle for a brief time. His legal education was of value to him, though only in other achievements toward which he began to drift soon after he opened his office. An opportunity was presented for him to go into the banking and brokerage business, and for some years he was busy in studying the mysteries of Wall street, and in learning the market value of the securities there dealt in.

Almost incidentally he drifted into the railway business. His brother, Dr. Seward Webb, who married one of the daughters of William H. Vanderbilt, became interested in the Palace Car Company which the Vanderbilts controlled, and when Webster Wagner, the president of that company, met his sudden death, having been crushed between two of his own cars in a railway collision, Dr. Webb became president of the company, and invited his brother to accept an official post in connection with it. Walter Webb had not been in the railway business a month before both he and his employers discovered that he had peculiar qualifications for this business. It seemed to fascinate him. He was no pompous official, fond of sitting in richly carpeted rooms and issuing orders with heavy dignity. He was everywhere. He studied the science of railway car building; he skirmished around among the shops; he was not afraid of dirt, nor of putting on a jumper and a pair of overalls, if necessary, and as a consequence he soon had not only mastered those duties he was employed to perform, but being full of suggestions and devoted to his avocation, he was rapidly promoted. He served, while an officer, really an apprenticeship, working harder than any other employé, never thinking about hours or salary, but only bent on learning the business.

In the railway business such a person moves rapidly toward the top. The history of railway corporations in the United States furnishes many such instances. Social influence, political pulls, as they are called, family prestige, count for nothing in the development of railway men. Nothing but fidelity and capacity have any influence with directors in the selection of executive officers. Any other course would be perilous.

Therefore, when the time came for this corporation, one of the greatest in the world in railway management, to place a competent man at the head of its traffic business, Major Webb was selected, and so thoroughly has he justified that choice that at the time when President Chauncey M. Depew was considering the invitation of President Harrison to become the successor of Mr. Blaine, as Secretary of State, it was understood in railway circles that Major Webb would be chosen president of the New York Central, in case Depew resigned that office.

Chief among Major Webb's qualifications for this work is his devotion to business. His college training as an engineer has served him well, and his legal knowledge has been of great value to him in the two great emergencies which he was called of a sudden to face, when many of the employés of the road went out on strike. He lives not five minutes' walk from his office, and he is frequently there as early as 7 o'clock in the morning. In the summer, when he is at his country place, he takes the first train into the city, while the bankers and brokers and professional men who live near him, do not follow until two or three hours later. He rarely leaves his office before 6 o'clock, and sometimes is there until late at night. His office is a place of comfort, but not of luxury. Major Webb is democratic in his relations with men, and none of the red tape which prevails in some of the great corporation offices annoys visitors who desire to see him. If a delegation from the engineers or switchmen, or from any of the other employés call, Major Webb receives them in a manner which does not lower their self-respect. There is neither condescension nor haughtiness in his relations with them. Major Webb will receive hard-handed employés, and within an hour be in association with a group of millionaires, fellow-directors of his in the great bank which is located near his office, and his manner is the same in each case. He treats everybody in a business-like way. He is quick-spoken, prompt, decisive, without being curt or brusque.

As a railroad man, he is what is called a flyer. Like William H. Vanderbilt, he is fond of going fast, and when business calls him to a remote point, he will order a locomotive attached to his special car, and within half an hour after the decision is taken, will be flying over the rails at the rate of a mile a minute. He is absolutely fearless in his travels, as William H. Vanderbilt was. Business men may see him in the afternoon of one day, and hear of him the next morning at Buffalo, 450 miles away. This does not indicate restlessness, but energy. Major Webb is one of the most quiet, self-contained and serene-mannered of all our railway managers.

When, just after he became vice-president, he was called upon to face a most dangerous strike, railway men said that he had been put to the test too early, and some of them feared that he would not be equal to the responsibility. Depew was in Europe. Cornelius Vanderbilt in Newport, and members of the executive board scattered here and

MR. H. WALTER WEBB,

3d Vice President N. Y. C. & H. R. R. R.

there. Major Webb immediately made of his office a campaign-place. He collected his staff about him. The strikers had control of the approaches to New York city, and traffic was paralyzed. He first took pains to discover how many of the men were out, and also to learn what their precise grievance was. If it was a question of time or wages or any other thing over which there had been misunderstanding or business disagreement, he believed that the trouble could be speedily settled. He found, instead, that it was a matter of discipline, that the men protested against certain rules which the subordinate officers had found necessary, as they believed, in order to maintain discipline. The strikers objected to the discharge of certain men who were reported disobedient or incompetent, and when Major Webb heard this, he said, in a quiet way, to his staff: "This is a point this company cannot yield. The stockholders must retain the right to manage, in their own way, this property."

Then he called upon his resources. He sent agents to procure men to take the places of the strikers. He called upon the police force of New York for protection, and got it. Night and day for seventy-two hours he left his office for only a few moments at a time. He caught catnaps, and two nights did not sleep a wink. And, when the railway men connected with other lines found out what he was doing, they said: "There is a young general in command at the Grand Central Station."

In his conferences with leaders of labor associations, Major Webb's legal knowledge was of great service to him, and Mr. Powderly himself, who met him in conference several times, was greatly impressed by his tact, coolness, good temper, and his firmness as well.

When Mr. Depew returned from Europe, not a sign of the strike appeared. Cornelius Vanderbilt, constantly informed over the wire at his Newport home of what was going on, deemed it unnecessary to come to the city.

At the first mutterings of the strike in Buffalo, information of which was sent to Major Webb by telegraph, he touched his electric bell, the messenger who answered received an order which was taken to the proper authority, and within half an hour Major Webb was aboard his private car, speeding over the tracks at the rate of fifty miles an hour; and before dawn next morning he was in Buffalo. His part in that convulsion is a matter of recent history, and unnecessary to describe here.

In physical appearance, as his photogravure picture shows, Major Webb does not at all suggest the typical railway manager. He is of slight figure, medium stature, erect in carriage. He cares nothing for social pleasures of the fashionable set. His home and his office are his life. He is not a club man. He takes no conspicuous part in politics, although he has strong political views; but it is safe to say that not a dozen men employed by his company know whether he is a Republican or a Democrat. He is a strong churchman, being a vestryman, and one of the most active members of one of the New York uptown Episcopal churches; and if the millionaires contributed sums proportionate to their wealth as great as those he gives for church work, his church would have an enormous income. Major Webb is a great believer in the future possibilities of fast railway travel. He has studied this development with great care, and with such results that he is now running daily the fastest railway train in the world, making nearly a mile a minute consecutively for 450 miles. His experiments have shown that the old idea that very fast traveling does not pay, is an error, but he says that in order to make it pay, the cars must be light but strong, the service sufficient but not luxurious, and the carrying capacity limited, so that an engine will not be compelled to draw too heavy a train.

Chauncey M. Depew has the reputation of being the most accessible to newspaper men of all the distinguished men in New York, yet he is not more so than Major Webb. Any respectable newspaper man is welcome to his office at all times, and he treats such callers as though they were men, and like one who respects their calling. The reporter has yet to be found who has got of Major Webb a suggestion that a puff or a bit of praise would be pleasing. He will not talk about himself, but will cheerfully give all the news which he has, provided it is consistent with the policy of the road to make publication of it. If it is not consistent, he says frankly: "That is something I cannot talk to you about just now. Perhaps I may be able to do so to-morrow."

Perhaps this disposition is partly due to his recollection of the fact that his father was a newspaper man who always treated the humblest of reporters with great respect. At the time Gen. Webb was approaching death, and the various newspapers of New York sent reporters to his home, so that immediate information of his death might be obtained. Gen. Webb used to say to his sons: "Are you taking good care of the newspaper men? If any of them have to wait long, show them some hospitality. Give them a glass of Madeira and a sandwich or biscuit, and do not forget that the newspaper reporters as a class are hard-working, fair-minded, intelligent men, who should be treated exactly as any other business man is, who comes to you on business matters." Whether this injunction accounts for the treatment the Major and his brothers give newspaper men or not, the fact remains that they all are thus minded when they receive representatives of the press.

The general impression in railway circles is, that when President Depew retires from official connection with the New York Central, Major Webb will be his successor.

HIS CONNECTION WITH THE ROADS OF NORTHERN NEW YORK.

What we have thus far said relates to Mr. Webb's connection with the main lines of the Central corporation, the extent of which all our readers understand, for that system is one of the largest in the world, and is managed with a degree of judgment and practical capacity that has elicited the wonder of travellers who are familiar with the great lines both in Europe and America. But it is in Major Webb's connection with our own northern line that he has been brought more directly into official relations with our own people. When the New York Central, on March 14, 1891, leased the lines of the R. W. & O. Road, Major Webb was placed in complete control of that entire system, and became the managing officer, the supreme executive head. Almost from the very week he assumed control, the beneficence of his management has made itself manifest. He began the great work of raising the newly-acquired property to the high standard of the trunk line. This necessitated new bridges, new rails, and the accomplishment of almost a process of new construction — entirely so in some localities. The outlay for these improvements has been enormous, reaching $2,000,000 of which $600,000 has been expended in the construction of new bridges, built of steel and iron. The bridges upon the whole line are now as good as any in the country.

The entire road-bed has been re-ballasted, and in most of it new ties have been placed, and the number of the same per mile has been increased. New steel rails have been laid, weighing 70 and 72 pounds to the lineal yard, and the equipment has been correspondingly improved by the addition of standard locomotives of the heaviest pattern, which could not be run over the old R. W. & O., but which now, under the new improvements — steel rails, perfect road-bed, and strong bridges — are allowed to run at high speed, and haul heavy trains. New passenger cars have been added; in fact, the road has been virtually re-constructed. Freight rates have been reduced, and the general conditions have been greatly improved. Among other things, several enterprises in Northern New York have been assisted; and all this has been done by hard work, and under the plans made and supervised by Mr. Webb.

For such labors, so well done, too much praise cannot be given this young man, who might have chosen ease, but prefers work. All that he touches he benefits. He has raised the old R., W. & O. R. R. system from a decaying condition, with worn material and weak bridges, to become a grand roadway in itself, the natural ally of the great trunk system with which it makes close connections, with vestibuled trains, and in summer with its steady-running "flyers" that cross the country at forty miles an hour in entire safety. The value of such a system, so connected, adds to the value of every acre of land in Northern New York, and is of interest to the poorest man as well as to the richest. The remarkable freedom from personal accidents to passengers during the year 1894 affords the best possible guaranty that the system is well and safely managed. Speed and comfort are two conditions demanded by modern travellers; but the perfect combination is a rare one. On most American railroads, high speed is only possible at the expense of danger and discomfort. To combine comfort and safety with the greatest speed, perfect equipment and absence of sharp curves are necessary. This is certainly the case with the R., W. & O. system. Its great eastern and western outlets, the New York Central and Hudson River Roads, hold the world's championship for long distance fast trains, won by recent improvements in equipment and locomotive-building, that fairly mark an epoch in railroading; and its hundred-ton engines, borne on massive rails weighing 120 pounds per yard, now skim with perfect safety around curves at the rate of fifty-five miles an hour. The solidest of road-beds is needed to withstand this marvelous speed, and to bear the enormous locomotives and trains; what it does with safety is impossible to other railroads of inferior equipment, or built with sharp curves. Excepting the Great Western of Canada, which has one air-line reach of 100 miles, the New York Central straight tracks exceed those of any other railroad in the world.

J. A. H.

THEODORE BUTTERFIELD.

MR. BUTTERFIELD comes into the transportation system of Northern New York by what may be called "natural inheritance." His grandfather, the Honorable John Butterfield, of Utica, was the originator of the American Express Company, which was started under the firm of Wells, Butterfield & Company. He also raised the money and built the first Western Union Telegraph Line, which was called the Morse Line Telegraph at that time, and was a director in the New York Central in its early stages, and one of the promoters and capitalists who built the Utica and Black River road, which started in opposition to the Rome and Watertown road, because they could not agree on a starting point, as the capitalists of Northern New York wanted to start from Herkimer; the Utica people would not hear to that, and were bound to start from Utica; so the other people started from Rome, and the Utica people, not to be outdone, started their road from Utica, which was built up to Boonville, and finally extended to Ogdensburgh, Clayton and Sackets Harbor. John Butterfield also started and owned the famous Pony Express or Overland Mail, which was the precursor of the Pacific railroads.

Theodore Butterfield's uncle, Major-General Daniel Butterfield, was the first general superintendent of the American Express Company, and also was chief of staff of the various commanders of the Army of the Potomac, and gave the celebrated order, by direction of General Meade, to the corps commanders to fight Lee at Gettysburg, the battle that nearly broke the back of the Confederacy.

Mr. Butterfield has been connected with the railroads of Northern New York for 20 years. He began as chief clerk in the accounting department of the old Utica & Black River railroad, at Utica, and was soon after made general ticket agent, and then general passenger agent of that road; and, as the road grew, he was made general freight and passenger agent. He remained in that position until the consolidation with the Rome, Watertown & Ogdensburg railroad, when he was appointed general passenger agent of the R., W. & O. R. R., and has held that position under the consolidation of that system with the New York Central & Hudson River R. R.'s. When first appointed he was the youngest general ticket agent in the United States. His experience as assistant to the general superintendent, and in the operating department of the Utica & Black River railroad, made him familiar with all departments of railroading, and that is the secret of his success in the passenger business, as he thoroughly understands the details in railroading, and has in addition rare executive ability. He is the originator of the long-distance excursions, such as the New York, Washington and Chicago excursions; and the idea of attaching sleeping-cars and drawing-room cars to excursion trains, now generally adopted, originated with him.

At the time of his appointment he was the youngest general passenger agent in the United States. He is beyond all doubt the most popular railroad man in Northern New York, the best known and most appreciated. With a clear head and ample knowledge of all railroad matters, his suggestions at the meetings of the passenger agents of the whole country are always listened to with the closest attention, and usually adopted.

THEODORE BUTTERFIELD.

COL. ZEBULON HOWELL BENTON.

COLONEL ZEBULON HOWELL BENTON.

(Copied from Wallace's Guide to the Adirondacks.)

THERE was probably no more romantic, picturesque or conspicuous figure connected with the chronicles of Lake Bonaparte than Colonel Zebulon H. Benton. The accompanying engraving faithfully represents his appearance in daily life. He invariably dressed with the nicest regard to minute particulars, in peaked felt hat, long black coat and ruffled shirt — every article faultlessly neat. With his fresh, ruddy complexion, clean-shaven face, rich growth of snow-white hair, graceful carriage, and form almost as lithe and perfect, at the ripe age of 82, as if in the flower of youth and strength, he seemed the embodiment of a gentleman of the old regime.

Colonel Benton was born in Apulia, N. Y., January 27, 1811, and the details of his checkered life would fill a book. We can only briefly allude to the following facts: He was a cousin of Thomas Hart Benton, the great Missouri statesman, and consequently a kinsman of his daughter, Jessie Benton Fremont, the noted wife of the famous "Pathfinder." In the war of the Rebellion he received an appointment on the staff of General Fremont, but before he could arrange to take the position the general was suspended. He was also a relative of the eminent novelist, James Fenimore Cooper. From his very boyhood he led an extremely active life, and before he was fairly out of his teens he was entrusted by his employers with commissions of the utmost importance, which he brought to successful consummation. He was engaged from time to time in great enterprises, especially those of land, mining and railroading. The capital invested in these sometimes exceeded a million dollars. His ventures, often gigantic, were not confined to Lewis and St. Lawrence counties, but extended into the Canadas, to the Gulf of Mexico, and even into South America. The mines at Rossie, Clifton, Jayville and Alpine are examples of these operations. We are convinced that the Carthage & Adirondack Railway owes its existence to Colonel Benton and to Hon. Joseph Pahud, of Harrisville, N. Y., as they were unceasing in their efforts to establish that line to the Jayville mines.

From the Carthage Republican, Philadelphia Press and other reliable sources, we glean the following interesting information: Soon after the arrival of Joseph Bonaparte in this country, he met and loved a beautiful Quakeress, by the name of Annette Savage, a member of a family of high respectability, residing in Philadelphia, descendants of the celebrated Indian princess, Pocahontas. They were subsequently married in private by a justice of the peace in that city. Two daughters were the fruit of this union, one of whom died in infancy. The other was christened Charlotte C. Soon after arriving at maturity, she became the wife of Colonel Benton. Their marriage resulted in seven children. The five surviving bear the appropriate names of Josephine Charlotte, Zenaide Bonaparte, Louis Joseph, Zebulon Napoleon and Thomas Hart.

Mrs. Benton, having obtained a letter of introduction from General Grant to Hon. Elihu B. Washburn, United States Minister to France, and one also from Dr. J. DeHaven White, the eminent Philadelphia dentist, to his former pupil, Dr. Evans, the dental surgeon of Louis Napoleon, repaired to Paris in 1869. She obtained audience with the Emperor, and received immediate recognition as the daughter of Joseph Bonaparte; and by his imperial will and the laws of France, the union of her parents was confirmed and her legitimacy established. Honored by an invitation to attend the French court, she and two of her children were there kindly and cordially entertained by the Emperor and Empress, who presented her with valuable souvenirs upon the occasion. Napoleon often expressed great regret that he did not know his cousin earlier, so that he might the sooner have bestowed upon her children the places to which, by birth, they were entitled. He presented her with her father's palace; but this was lost through the downfall of the empire and of that ill-fated royal family. Mrs. Benton attended Napoleon during his imprisonment in Germany, and a short time afterward (1871) returned to America. She was a woman of remarkable beauty and talent, and of most lovely characteristics. Her eyes were large, dark and lustrous, and, like the Colonel's, never dimmed by age. Receiving a fine education, in Europe and in this country, she early developed great versatility in writing. Many brilliant articles in various papers and magazines were the productions of her pen, and she was the author of a book of rare merit, entitled "France and her People." She died December 25, 1890, at Richfield Springs. Her husband, the subject of this sketch, died May 16, 1893, closing an unique, interesting and wonderfully romantic life.

MAJOR JAMES HERVEY DURHAM,

So well and favorably known among the Thousand Islands, is the youngest son of John Perrin Durham, who came from County Durham, in the north of England, with his father William Egbert Durham, just at the close of the Revo- P. became first an ensign in the Fraser Rifles, and finally a major in that noted regiment. James H. Durham, the subject of this sketch, was born in Syracuse, N. Y., December 17, 1821, and in 1831 went with his parents into the

MAJOR JAMES HERVEY DURHAM.

lution, at the age of two years. William E. was a major in the British army, but becoming disgusted with the license given to the Indians to murder and scalp their prisoners, he threw up his commission, returned to England, and finally emigrated to the United States. John wilds of Ohio, on a farm five miles from the nearest inhabitant. He attended the district schools for a time, then the seminary at Norwalk, O., Baldwin Institute, Berea, O., and Oberlin College. He entered the 2nd Dragoons, U. S. A., in 1849, serving up to th breaking out of the Rebellion. He was a member of B Co., Capt. Blake, 9th Indiana Vols., under Colonel, afterward Gen. Robert H. Milroy, in the first three months' campaign in West Virginia. He reported to Gen. George B. McClellan at Grafton, West Va., and was sent by him on important scouting service; was in the battles of Phillipi, at Laurel Hill, and Carrick's Ford. At the close of the three months' campaign, he was appointed by Gov. Oliver P. Morton to the command of a camp near Indianapolis, and finally went to the front as 1st Lieutenant and Adjutant of the 33rd Indiana Volunteers, Col. Coburn. Resigning from that command at the end of eighteen months' service, he became Major of cavalry, and later was connected with the artillery of the 23rd corps, under Gen. Schofield. He was once in Libby prison, and the Andersonville stockade fifteen days He participated in several of the hardest-fought battles of the war, and was several times wounded. He has an honorable discharge and is a pensioner. He is the author of our history of Cape Vincent but not of this sketch.

GENERAL WILLIAM H. ANGELL

WAS long prominently connected with the interests of the St. Lawrence, and legitimately belongs with those who are entitled to prominent remembrance in any history of the Upper St. Lawrence and of the Thousand Islands. He is remembered with pleasure by the older citizens of Clayton and of Jefferson county, for he was a man of great business capacity and force. Many buildings in Watertown bear silent witness of his manner of construction — notably the Taggart Bros'. mill at the lower falls, and the water-reservoir, now over forty years in use. He was born in Burlington, Otsego county, N. Y., in 1797, one of a family of ten children. When only ten years of age he left home, and thenceforward earned not only his own living, but helped to care for the less able members of the family. At fourteen he gave his father $200 for his "time"— that is, for the time he would be a minor, and his father would, therefore, be legally entitled to his earnings. The General came into Jefferson county about 1815. He first located at Smithville, where he went into business with old-time Jesse Smith. When less than twenty years of age he bought over $3,000 worth of goods, and from Smithville, went to Clayton. Several years later (about 1834) he was at Sackets Harbor. In 1824 he had married Miss Harriet Warner. Seven children were born to this union, four of whom are still living. While at Sackets Harbor the General became associated in the management of the Sackets Harbor Bank, which was later merged into the Bank of Watertown, of which, about 1842, General Angell became sole owner. In 1858 his beloved wife died — a lady well remembered in Watertown for her devotion to charity and Christian works. The deserving poor never had a better friend, for what she gave was given with a grace and gentleness that made the action doubly endearing.

In 1860, General Angell married Miss M. Louise Judson, cousin of the late Gen. R. W. Judson, of Ogdensburg. She was an accomplished lady, the pattern for a kind, dutiful wife. In 1861, at the beginning of the civil war, the General removed to New York, where he become interested in several city contracts, and in 1862 he removed his family to that city, which was thenceforth his home. By nature he was too active to relish a life of idleness, and he took up several means of acquiring wealth, among others extending the circulation of his bank from $29,000 to $80,000. He was also largely interested in the Continental Steel Works at Maspeth, Long Island. In 1863 the imposition of a tax of ten per cent upon the circulation of State Banks, drove them out of business. In 1871, General Angell had accumulated enough means to make home comfortable, and in that year he removed to Geneseo, expecting to spend there several years in the enjoyment of needed rest and a release from the cares of business. But his hopes were to be disappointed. On the 1st of July, 1872, he was his home early in life, instead of Watertown, he would have taken rank with George Law and the elder Vanderbilt, for he was their superior in shrewdness of management, in perspicuity, in ability to predict the rise or fall of cereals or articles of general consump-

GENERAL WILLIAM H. ANGELL.

taken ill, and after great suffering, died at Geneseo on November 26, 1872.

Viewed in the light of his varied and eventful career, General Angell was a character difficult to reproduce. He had a noble soul, which scorned little things. He was undoubtedly superior to the average able business men of his day—and had he made New York city tion. He was a firm friend, and he had many friends, for he was a friendly man, democratic in his ways, easily approached, never elated by success, nor intimidated by adversity. From 1820 to 1861, he was a conspicuous figure in Jefferson county, and his removal was a source of sincere regret.

J. A. H.

THE THOUSAND ISLANDS IN AUTUMN.

CONTRIBUTED BY MR. S. E. BRIDGMAN.

THE POT-HOLES.

ALL who have ever inhaled the breath of its forest trees, rambled over secluded fields or sailed into quiet and remote inlets, know the charm of these islands. But Nature is a coy maiden, and reserves her full glory for those who appreciate her worth and tarry till Autumn. Then she robes herself in scarlet; she clothes herself from day to day in garments of beauty, changing from grave to gay. Under a cloudy sky the gray and the brown are worn in harmony with the upper world. Then, when the autumn sun gladdens us by his beams, she twines into her robes the delicate coloring which art tries in vain to rival. The excursions in and around among the Islands reveal visions of exquisite beauty. The golden air, the quiet waters, the flaming sentinels which wave their crimson banners, from crag and peak, the bold precipitous rocks with their granite sides stand out in relief, and fascinate the traveller as he winds in and out among these wonderful channels.

We have rambled alone in wooded paths, out and away from the busy world outside, with only now and then a herd of cows for company. With crumpled horns and tinkling bell, their large eyes look lustrously upon us as if we were intruders. The crows sail over our heads and saucily call to us. The crane flutters up from the river side and flees away, his long, slender legs giving a most ridiculous appearance as he mounts the upper air. The little snake, with color rivaling that of the brilliant foliage, startles us as he crosses our path, but tarries not to make an acquaintance. The goldenrod bows in mock humility as we pass her by. We walk under sturdy oaks and graceful pines, each adorned in their own peculiar green. The trees of the summer cover us with their brown leaves and speak to us of their past beauty. Blackened stumps give a tinge of sadness to the landscape so fair and beautiful and tell of forest fires. We climb up and stand on rocky ledges and catch glimpses of islands, lakes, bays, river, which glimmer in the afternoon sun, and a pathway of rosy light lies between us and distant shores. We plunge into dark ravines and stand amid shattered remnants of titanic rocks, which tell of the storms of the elements before man was. We descend to the water's edge, and gather the pure white lily, blossoming under the massive masonry, which guards it from the wayfarer. We shout for joy as we ramble over this enchanted ground, and our voice is caught up and thrown back to us from the palisades above. Our call to the genii of the hills is answered, but only in mockery. So we ramble on, now carefully picking our way under boulders that have been tossed by giant arms from the heights above, and which if loosened as we pass would give us a burial and a monument, such as but few heroes have had. Suddenly, on a rocky promontory, away from hurrying footsteps, and far from ordinary rambles, we are startled by a vision of another world. We stand before no burning bush which blazes unconsumed, but we hear the

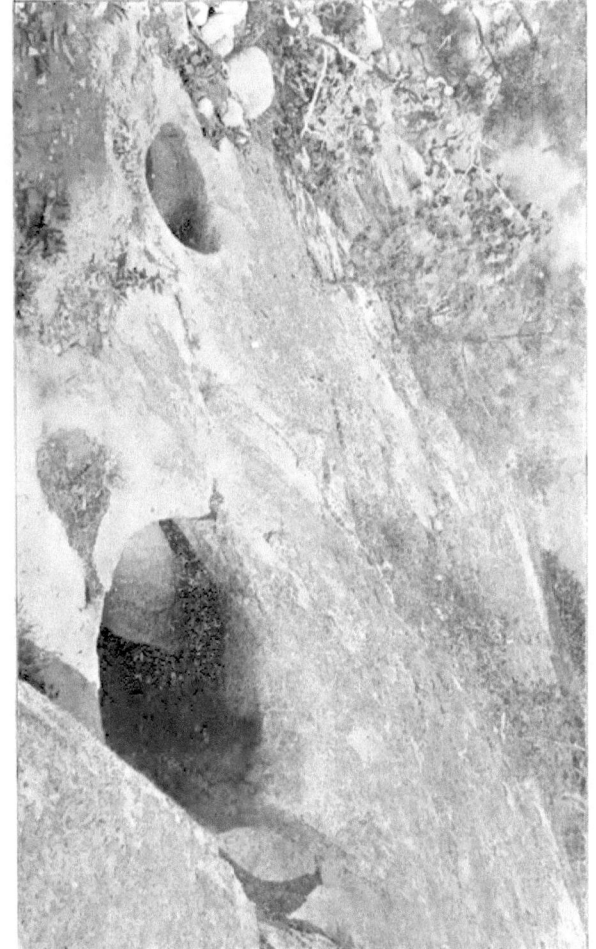

REMARKABLE POT HOLES NEAR THE PALISADES, IN EEL BAY.

voice from out the silence saying, "Take the shoes from off thy feet, for the place whereon thou standest is holy ground."

THE POT-HOLES

Before us is an inclined and solid rock stretching down to the watery edge, which instantly carries us back, beyond the "A. D.," beyond the "B. C.," beyond all human computation, back, back to the aeons of the past. In the center of this great rock is a well of water some ten to twelve feet deep, rising to within about five or six feet of the surface. No curb protects it. That would be mockery. It is well that we should not be reminded of man, when we stand by a well that was ages old when Jacob in Palestine immortalized his name by giving it to the one he dug for himself and cattle. We leaned over its side and looked down into its depths. Carved, planed, smoothed, with no mark or crevice down its granite sides, it has stood the vast centuries, telling of the "ice age" of glacial avalanche, but more clearly telling the story of a tireless workman patiently working along the ages. In the far away past a little depression had been made in the rock. A small boulder was placed loosely in the center. Then the storm of waters flowed over the old, old world. For a time it circled playfully around in its rocky bed and wore away the rock to make for it a smooth resting place. It never dreamed that it was making for itself a grave, that would, perhaps, be seen by mortal man who then had no existence. After age upon age had passed, it woke to find itself helpless to escape. Round and round in its agony it whirled in a circle, grinding and tearing its cage and ever sinking deeper and deeper into the abyss which it was making for itself. Is it a wonder that in the deep silence, the great bay before us, the forest behind, we stood in awe before this relic of the Eternal Fray? Just below it is a smaller well, it, too, telling the story of its grander neighbor and holding in its depths the instrument used for the work of alteration.

We are not geologists, and the professors may smile at a layman's philosophy, but one cannot be blamed for a little imagination when standing by such a well, in the calm and haze of a autumnal day, with nature singing the doxology about him.

We travel farther on; now in green pastures and by still waters, then over majestic walls of masonry which form fortresses and barriers that could stand the assault of a nation's batteries. At last we come out upon a plateau of rock, smooth and glossy almost as glass, it also having an unknown history. In its center is a massive granite boulder, a lonely giant stranded on the rock. Ask where it came from and only the echo answers "where?" Where in the world is there so enticing a place as "The Thousand Islands?"

THE WHITTLESEY AFFAIR.

IN giving an extended notice of this Whittlesey episode, we are perhaps open to the criticism of making a great deal out of a comparatively unimportant matter; but there is so much of tragedy in the story, and it affords so striking an illustration of the soul-destroying influence of a dishonest greed for money, that the tale rises above a mere relation, and becomes a great moral lesson. In that light we present it as a legitimate chapter of history.

Samuel Whittlesey, originally from Tolland, Ct., had removed, about 1808, to Watertown, and engaged in business as a lawyer. On the 12th of February, 1811, he received the appointment of district attorney for the territory comprised in Lewis, Jefferson and St. Lawrence counties, and on the 6th of February, 1813, he was superseded by the appointment of Amos Benedict, who had preceded him. Events connected with this, led to some sympathy for him, and the office of brigade paymaster, which had been tendered to Mr. Jason Fairbanks, was by him declined in favor of Whittlesey, and he, with Perley Keyes, became security for the honest discharge of the duties of the office. At the close of the war a large amount of money being due to the drafted militia, for services on the frontier, Whittlesey went to New York, accompanied by his wife, to obtain the money, and received at the Merchants' Bank in that city $30,000, in one, two, three, five and ten-dollar bills, with which he started to return. At Schenectady, as was afterwards learned, his wife reported themselves robbed of $8,700, an occurrence which greatly distressed and alarmed him, but she advised him not to make it public at that moment, as they might thereby better take steps that might lead to its recovery, and on the way home, she in an artful and gradual manner persuaded him that if they should report the robbery of a part of the money, no one would believe it, as a thief would take the whole, if any. In short (to use a homely proverb), she urged that they might as well "die for an old sheep as a lamb," and keep the rest, as they would inevitably be accused of taking a part. Her artifice, enforced by the necessities of the case, took effect, and he suffered himself to become the dupe of his wife, who was doubtless the chief contriver of the movements which followed. Accordingly, on his return, he gave out word that his money had been procured, and would be paid over as soon as the necessary papers and pay-roll could be prepared. In a few days, having settled his arrangements, he started for Trenton on horseback, with his portmanteau filled, stopping at various places on his way, to announce that on a given day he would return, to pay to those entitled, their dues, and in several instances evinced a carelessness about the custody of his baggage that excited remark from inn-keepers and others. On arriving at Billings' tavern at Trenton, he assembled several persons to whom money was due, and proceeded to pay them, but upon opening his portmanteau, he, to the dismay of himself and others, found that they had been ripped open, and that the money was gone! With a pitiable lamentation and well-affected sorrow, he bewailed the robbery, instantly despatched messengers in quest of the thief, offered $2,000 reward for his apprehension, and advertised in staring handbills throughout the country, in hopes of gaining some clew that would enable him to recover his treasure. In this anxiety he was joined by hundreds of others, who had been thus indefinitely delayed in the receipt of their needed and rightful dues, but although there was no lack of zeal in these efforts, yet nothing occurred upon which to settle suspicion, and with a heavy heart, and many a sigh and tear, he returned home, and related to his family and friends his ruin. As a natural consequence, the event became at once the absorbing theme of the country, for great numbers were affected in their pecuniary concerns by it, and none more than the two endorsers of the sureties of Whittlesey. These gentlemen, who were shrewd, practical and very observing men, immediately began to interrogate him, singly and alone, into the circumstance of the journey and the robbery, and Fairbanks in particular, whose trade as a saddler led him to be minutely observant of the qualities and appearances of leather, made a careful examination of the incisions in the portmonteau, of which there were two, tracing upon paper their exact size and shape, and upon close examination, noticed pin holes in the margin, as if they had been mended up. Upon comparing the accounts which each had separately obtained in a long and searching conversation, these men became convinced that the money had not been stolen in the manner alleged, but that it was still in the possession of Whittlesey and his wife. To get possession of this money was their next care, and, after long consultation, it was agreed that the only way to do this, was to gain the confidence of the family, and defend them manfully against the insinuations that came from all quarters that the money was still in town. In this they succeeded admirably, and from the declarations which they made in public and in private, which found their way directly back to the family, the latter were convinced that, although the whole world were against them in their misfortunes, yet they had the satisfaction to know that the two men who were the most interested were still by their side. To gain some fact that would lead to a knowledge of the place of deposit, Messrs. Fairbanks and Keyes agreed to listen at the window of the sleeping room of those suspected, which was in a chamber, and overlooked the roof of a piazza. Accordingly, after dark, one would call upon the family and detain them in conversation, while the other mounted a ladder and placed himself where he could overhear what was said within, and although they thus became convinced that the money was still in their possession, no opinion could be formed about the hiding place. Security upon their real estate was demanded, and readily given.

A son of the family held a commission in the navy, and was on the point of sailing for the Mediterranean, and it was suspected that the money might thus have been sent off, to ascertain which, Mr. Fairbanks, under pretext of taking a criminal to the State Prison, went to New York, made inquiries which satisfied him that the son was innocent of any knowledge of the affair, and ascertained at the bank the size of the packages taken. He had been told by Whittlesey that these had not been opened when stolen, and by making experiments with blocks of wood of the same dimensions, they readily ascertained that bundles of that size could not be got through an aperture of the size reported, and that instead of a seven it required an eighteen-inch slit in the leather to allow of their being extracted. Some facts were gleaned at Albany that shed further light, among which it was noticed that Mrs. Whittlesey at her late visit (although very pennrious in her trade) had been very profuse in her expenses. After a ten-days' absence Mr. Fairbanks returned; his partner having listened nights meanwhile, and the intelligence gained by eves-dropping, although it failed to disclose the locality of the lost money, confirmed their suspicions. As goods were being boxed up at Whittlesey's house at a late hour in the night, and the daughters had already been sent on to Sackets Harbor, it was feared that the family would soon leave; decisive measures were resolved upon to recover the money, the ingenuity and boldness of which evince the sagacity and energy of the parties. Some method to decoy Whittlesey from home, and frighten him by threats, mutilation or torture, into a confession, was discussed, but as the latter might cause an uncontrollable hemorrhage, it was resolved to try the effect of drowning. Some experiments were made on their own persons, of the effect of submersion of the head, and Dr. Sherwood, a physician of the village, was consulted on the time life would remain under water. Having agreed upon a plan, on the evening before its execution, they repaired to a lonely place about a mile south of the village, screened from the sight of houses by a gentle rise of ground, and where a spring issued from the bank and flowed off through a miry slough, in which, a little below, they built a dam of turf that formed a shallow pool. It was arranged that Mr. Fairbanks should call upon Whittlesey, to confer with him on some means of removing the suspicions which the public had settled upon him, by obtaining certificates of character from leading citizens and officers of the army; and that the two were to repair to Mr. Keyes's house, which was not far from the spring. Mr. Keyes was to be absent repairing his fence, and to leave word with his wife that if any one inquired for him, to send them into the field where he was at work. Neither had made confidants in their suspicions or their plans, except that Mr. Keyes thought it necessary to reveal them to his son, P. Gardner Keyes, then seventeen years of age, whose assistance he might need, in keeping up appearances, and in whose sagacity and fidelity in keeping a secret he could rely.

Accordingly, on the morning of July 17th (1815), Mr. Keyes, telling his wife that the cattle had broken into his grain, shouldered his axe and went to repair the fence which was thrown down, and Mr. Fairbanks called upon Whittlesey, engaged him in conversation, as usual, and without exciting the slightest suspicion, induced him to go up to see his partner, whom they found in a distant part of the field at work. Calling him to them, they repaired as if casually to the spring, where, after some trifling remark, they explicitly charged him with the robbery, gave their reasons for thinking so, and told him that if he did not instantly disclose the locality of the money, the pool before him should be his grave. This sudden and unexpected charge frightened their victim; but with a look of innocence he exclaimed, "I know nothing of the matter." This was no sooner said than he was rudely seized by Mr. Keyes and plunged headforemost into the pool, and after some seconds withdrawn. Being again interrogated, and assured that if the money were restored, no legal proceedings would be instituted, he again protested his innocence, and was a second time plunged in, held under several moments and again withdrawn, but this time insensible, and for one or two minutes it was doubtful whether their threats had not been executed; but he soon evinced signs of life, and so far recovered as to be able to sit up and speak. Perhaps nothing but the certain knowledge of his guilt, which they possessed, would have induced them to proceed further; but they were men of firmness, and resolved to exhaust their resource of expedients, rightly judging that a guilty conscience could not long hold out against the prospect of speedy death. He was accordingly addressed by Mr. Keyes in tones and emphasis of sober earnest, and exhorted for the last time to save himself from being hurried before the tribunal of Heaven, laden with guilt—to disclose at once. In feeble tones he re-asserted his innocence, and was again collared and plunged in, but this time his body only was immersed. It had been agreed in his hearing, that Fairbanks (being without a family) should remain to accomplish the work, by treading him into the bottom of the slough, while Keyes was to retire, so that neither could be a witness of murder if apprehended; and that on a given day they were to meet in Kingston. Keyes paid over about $90 to bear expenses of travel, and was about to leave, when the wretched man, seeing these serious arrangements, and at length believing them to be an awful reality, exclaimed, "I'll tell you all about it!" Upon this, he was withdrawn, and when a little recovered, he confessed, that all but about $9,000 (which he now, for the first time, stated to have been stolen at Schenectady), would be found either under a hearth at his house, or quilted into a pair of drawers in his wife's possession. Mr. Keyes, leaving his prisoner in charge of his associate, started for the house, and was seen by his wife, coming across the fields, covered with mud, and, to use the words of the latter, "looking like a murderer;" and although in feeble health, and scarcely able to walk, she met him at the door, and inquired with alarm, "What have you been doing?" He briefly replied, "We have had the old fellow under water, and made him own where the money is;" and hastily proceeding to the village, related in a few words to his friends, Dr. Paul Hutchinson and John M. Canfield, the facts, and with them repaired to the house of Whittlesey. Seeing them approach, Mrs. Whittlesey fled to her chamber, and on their knocking for admission, she replied that she was changing her dress, and would meet them shortly. As it was not the time or place for the observance of etiquette, Mr. Keyes rudely burst open the door, and entering, found her reclining on the bed. Disregarding her expostulations of impropriety, he rudely proceeded to search, and soon found between the straw and feather bed, upon which she lay, a quilted garment, when she exclaimed: "You've got it! My God, have I come to this?" The drawers bore the initials of Col. Tuttle, who had died in that house, under very suspicious circumstances; were fitted with two sets of

THE "BON VOYAGE" ENTERING ALEXANDRIA BAY.

buttons, for either the husband or wife to wear, and contained about thirty parcels of bills, labelled, "For my dear son C——, 250 of 5;" "For my dear daughter E——, 150 of 3," etc., amounting to $15,000 to her five children; the remainder being reserved for her own use. The garment also contained a most extraordinary document, which might be called Her Will, and about which she expressed the most urgent solicitude, imploring, "That you have children as well as me!" It was soon after published in the papers, and was as follows:

"It is my last and dying request, that my children shall have all the money that is contained in the papers which have their names on, which is $3,000 for each; and let there be pains and caution, and a great length of time taken to exchange it in. God and my own heart knows the misery I have suffered in consequence of it, and that it was much against my will that it should be done. I have put all that is in the same bank by it, that I had from prudence, and a great number of years been gathering up; and when I used to meet with a bill on that bank in your possession, or when I could, I used to exchange others for them, as I supposed it was the best, and would be the most permament bank. You know the reason of your taking this was, that we supposed that from the lock of the small trunk being broken, and the large one being all loose, and the nails out, that we were robbed on the road of $8,700. You know that I always told you, that I believed it was done in the yard, where you, as I told you then, put the wagon imprudently in Schenectady. Oh! how much misery am I born to see, through all your improper conduct, which I am forced to conceal from the view of the world, for the sake of my beloved off-springs' credit, and whereby I have got enemies undeservedly, while the public opinion was in your favor! But it fully evinces what false judgments the world makes. Oh! the God who tries the hearts, and searches the veins of the children of men, knows that the kind of misery which I have suffered, and which has riled and soured my temper, and has made me appear cross and morose to the public eye, has all proceeded from you, and fixed in my countenance the mark of an ill-natured disposition, which was naturally formed for loves, friendships, and other refined sensations. How have I falsified the truth, that you might appear to every advantage, at the risk and ill-opinion of the sensible world towards myself, when my conscience was telling me I was doing wrong; and which, with everything else that I have suffered since I have been a married woman, has worn me down and kept me out of health; and now, oh! now, this last act is bringing me to my grave fast. I consented because you had placed me in the situation you did. In the first place you were delinquent in the payment to the government of eighteen or nineteen hundred dollars. Then this almost $9,000 missing, I found when you came to settle, that you never could make it good without sacrificing me and my children, was the reason I consented to the proposal. I did you the justice to believe that the last sum had not been missing, that you would not have done as you did: but I am miserable! God grant that my dear children may never fall into the like error that their father has, and their poor unfortunate mother consented to! May the Almighty forgive us both, for I freely forgive you all you have made me suffer."

The money being counted, and to their surprise found to embrace a part of the sum supposed to be stolen, Mr. Keyes went back to release Whittlesey. The latter, meanwhile, had related the circumstances of the robbery, and anxiously inquired whether, if the whole was not found, they would still execute their purpose; to which Mr. Fairbanks replied in a manner truly characteristic, "that will depend on circumstances." No one was more surprised than Whittlesey himself, to learn that most of the money was found, and that he had been robbed at Schenectady by his own wife. He begged hard to be released on the spot, but it was feared he would commit suicide, and he was told that he must be delivered up to the public as sound as he was taken, and was led home. The fame of this discovery soon spread, and it was with difficulty the villagers were restrained from evincing their joy by the discharge of cannon. Mr. Whittlesey was led home and placed with a guard in the room with his wife, until further search; and here the most bitter criminations were exchanged, each charging the other with the crime, and the wife upbraiding the husband with cowardice for revealing the secret. The guard being withdrawn in the confusion that ensued, Mrs. Whittlesey passed from the house, and was seen by a person at a distance to cross the cemetery of Trinity church, where, on passing the grave of a son, she paused, faltered and fell back, overwhelmed with awful emotion; but a moment after, gathering new energy, she hastened on, rushed down the high bank near the ice-cave, and plunged into the river. Her body was found floating near the lower bridge, and efforts were made to recover life, but it was extinct.

The sympathies of the public were not withheld from the children of this family, who were thus cast penniless and disgraced upon the world. Many details connected with the affair we have not given; among which were several attempts to throw suspicion upon several parties by depositing money on their premises, writing anonymous letters, etc.; which served but to aggravate the crime by betraying the existence of a depravity on the part of the chief contriver in the scheme, which has seldom or never been equaled. The marked bills amounting to $400 had been dropped on the road to Sackets Harbor, and were found by Mr. Gale, who prudently carried them to a witness, counted and sealed them and after the disclosure brought them forward. Mr. Whittlesey stated that he expected some one would find and use the money, when he could swear to the marks, and implicate the finder. Mr. Gale, upon hearing this, was affected to tears, and exclaimed: "Mr. Whittlesey, is it possible you would have been so wicked as to have sworn me to State Prison for being honest!"

Mr. Whittlesey remained in Watertown nearly a year, and then moved to Indiana, where he afterwards became a justice of the peace and a county judge, and by an exemplary life won the respect of the community; and although the details of this affair followed him, yet the censure of opinion rested upon the wife.

Congress, on the 11th of January, 1821, passed an act directing the Secretary of the Treasury to cancel and surrender the bond given by Whittlesey and endorsed by Fairbanks and Keyes, on condition of the latter giving another, payable with interest in two years, for the balance remaining unaccounted for—thus virtually closing up a business arrangement which had been a continued occasion for anxiety and trouble to them through successive years.

In speaking of the Whittlesey matter, to the author of this History, Mr. Fairbanks said:

Before we executed our plan we had positive evidence of his knowledge of the transaction and of his guilt; and, on the strength of that, we did not expect to proceed to extremities further than to frighten him until he informed us where the money was secreted. But his stubbornness held out much longer than we supposed it would or could. When we put the evidence of his guilt before him in such a plain manner his looks were evidence of it. We informed him that there was no doubt about it, and I believe that there is not one case in a thousand where evidence was so palpable as in this case. But Lynch Law is a dangerous one, and I would not advise it. But with other guilty parties who have stolen from me and been detected, I believe I have used more mild and lenient measures. I have probably caught twenty persons pilfering from me, and I have always made them give me a confession in writing, and then promised them, that as they had relatives who would be disgraced by their conduct, I would keep it a profound secret until they committed the crime again, when I would prosecute them. I found this plan the surest method of reforming them.

THE "PATRIOT" WAR.

COPIED FROM HADDOCK'S HISTORY OF JEFFERSON COUNTY, N. Y.

DURING the fall of 1837 there occurred one of the most curious, and what would now be classed as inexcusable and insane, episodes that Jefferson county and the whole northern frontier had ever witnessed — nothing more nor less than a popular effort on the part of American citizens to overthrow the government of Canada by an unwarranted invasion of the frontier towns, expecting to arouse the people to immediate participation in the rebellious effort as soon as a stand should have been made. Ridiculous as this affair appears at this day, it was a popular and an enthusiastic effort at the time, drawing into its service many educated and apparently levelheaded men, and meeting with an amount of sympathy in Northern New York that was really astonishing.

There had been for some time considerable discontent in Canada, some claiming that they were virtually shut out from proper participation in the government, and their repeated efforts to obtain better legislation had been disregarded. This discontent was more pronounced in the Lower Province, where the French Canadians had great influence, and had never in their hearts yielded a loyal support to the English rule over a country which had once belonged to France. It was said at the time that the charges made by the Canadians against their rulers were greater than the causes that separated the American colonies from the English. The Reform party in Parliament of the Upper Province was led by William Lyon McKenzie, and Papeneau was the leader in the Lower Province. The Home Government sustained all the alleged oppressive acts of the local government. The Reform party refused to vote supplies for the support of the government, and the Parliaments were dissolved. The excitement had become great all through the provinces, extending to the frontiers on this side. The parliament buildings at Montreal were burned. The first collision between the Reform parties and the Tories, in the Upper Province, was on Yonge street, Toronto, where several were killed. The feeling now became very intense. The reform party contained many determined and resolute men, but they desired relief from British oppression through peaceful means. They had never contemplated a resort to arms, but the feeling in both provinces was aroused to such an extent that it could not be peaceably controlled. The feeling for the " relief " of Canada seemed to pervade all classes; secret societies were formed in the principal towns on this side as well as many on the Canadian side of the river. They were called Hunter's Lodges, and had signs and pass-words by which they could recognize each other.

In the summer of 1837, William Lyon McKenzie and Gen. Van Rensselaer, with 300 men, established themselves on Navy Island in Canadian waters, between Chippewa and Grand Island, in the Niagara river. Reinforcements came to Navy Island from the American side. The little steamer "Caroline" was chartered to carry passengers and freight to the island from Buffalo. On the night of November 29, 1837, while this steamer was moored at Schlosser's wharf, a captain in the English army with a company of British soldiers, boarded her and set her on fire, and cutting the boat loose, sent her adrift over Niagara Falls. One Captain Alexander McLeod, while on a debauch at Niagara, made his boast that he was one of the gang that burned the Caroline. He was arrested for the murder of Durfee. His trial was commenced at Canandaigua, but it was considered unsafe and he was removed to Utica. His defense was that he acted under the authority of the British government. He proved an alibi and was acquitted, being defended by able Canadian lawyers. The outrage was complained of by Governor Marcy to Martin Van Buren, then President of the United States, but no demand on the British government was ever made. The President issued a proclamation forbidding all persons from aiding or assisting, in any way, the rebellious acts of any people, or collection of people who interfered with the execution of the laws of a friendly nation, declaring all such persons outlaws and not entitled to the protection of the American government.

Great preparations were soon made for an attack upon Kingston, while the St. Lawrence was bridged with ice. On the night of February 19, 1838, the arsenal at Watertown, N. Y., was broken into and 400 stand of arms were taken. The arsenals at Batavia and Elizabethtown were also plundered. On the 20th of February patriots began to flock to French Creek in large numbers with a supply of arms and ammunition, consisting of 1,000 stand of arms, twenty barrels of cartridges and a large store of provisions. It was intensely cold, and the men suffered from exposure. General Rensselaer Van Rensselaer, a son of General Van Rensselaer, of the war of 1812, was to assume the command. Either through the cowardice of the officers or the men, no man saw Canadian soil, and after much talk of bravery the men dispersed to their homes. It was reported that Colonel Bonnycastle, at the head of 1,600 men, was coming from Kingston to make an attack upon the town, and through fear and of the loved ones at home, the patriots scattered without much ceremony, leaving all their arms and ammunition behind. This flight homeward was as ridiculous as their attempt was insane.

On the night of May 30, 1838, the Canadian steamer, Sir Robert Peel, which was commanded by John B. Armstrong, on her way from Brockville to Toronto, with nineteen passengers and about £20,000 in specie for paying off the troops in the Upper Province, was taking on wood at McDonnell's wharf, in the southern channel of the St. Lawrence, above Alexandria Bay, when a company of men, led by "Bill" Johnston, the alleged hero of the Thousand Islands, disguised and painted like savages, armed with muskets and bayonets, rushed on board, shouting, "Remember the Caroline." The night was dark and rainy. The passengers (who were asleep in the cabin) together with the crew were ordered on shore. The boat was then pushed out into the river and burned. The sunken hull can be seen there to this day. Heavy rewards were offered for the apprehension of the offenders by both governments. Twelve of the band were arrested and held in the Watertown jail for about six months. On the 2d of June, Anderson was indicted and held for arson in the first degree. He was tried before John P. Cushman, one of the circuit judges, and defended by Calvin McKnight, Benjamin Wright, John Clark and Bernard Bagley. After a deliberation of two hours the jury brought in a verdict of "not guilty." After a time the others were released on their own recognizance, and were never subjected to a trial.

William Johnston was born in Lower Canada and became a confidential friend of William Lyon McKenzie. He became a leader in the Reform party, and afterwards removed to French Creek. He was a man of great energy, and bore a fair reputation. Johnston was now considered the patriotic commander, and a band under his command fortified themselves on one of the islands within the Jefferson county line. His daughter, Kate Johnston, held communication with them and furnished them with provisions and supplies. It was at this time that Johnston published the following curious manifesto — which is, so far as the writer knows, the only instance in which an outlaw had the "cheek" to declare war from his place of hiding against a friendly nation:

"I, William Johnston, a natural born citizen of Upper Canada, do hereby declare that I hold a commission in the Patriot service as commander-in-chief of the naval forces and flotilla. I commanded the expedition that captured and destroyed the Sir Robert Peel. The men under my command in that expedition were nearly all natural born English subjects. The exceptions were volunteers. My headquarters are on an island in the St. Lawrence without the line of the jurisdiction of the United States, at a place named by me Fort Wallace. I am well acquainted with the boundary line and know which of the islands do, and which do not, belong to the United States. Before I located my headquarters I referred to the decisions of the commissioner made at Utica, under the sixth article of the treaty of Ghent. I know the number of the island and know that by the division of the commissions it is British territory. I yet hold possession of the station and act under orders. The object of my movement is the independence of the Canadas. I am not at war with the commerce or property of the United States.

"Signed this 10th day of June in the year of our Lord one thousand eight hundred and thirty-eight.
"WILLIAM JOHNSTON."

The effect of this manifesto was quite important, as it was distributed through all the provinces and in all parts of the frontier States. The excitement along the frontiers grew more intense. Sir Allan McNab, the governor-general, fearing for the safety of his life, had resigned, and in returning to England passed through Watertown disguised as a laborer. He was recognized by Jason Fairbanks while sitting on a wheelbarrow in front of Gibson's tavern, waiting for the stage for Utica. Being advised by some of the leading men that he need have no fear of danger while travelling through the States, he changed his disguise and assumed his former dignity. Lord Durham succeeded him as governor-general. The secret lodges were now making large additions to their membership. It had now become evident that a stand was to be made somewhere for the threatened invasion.

On the 10th of November, two schooners, the "Charlotte," of Oswego, and the "Isabelle," of Toronto, left Oswego with arms and ammunition and about 300 men for some Canadian point on the St. Lawrence. The steamer "United States" left Oswego on the following morning for the same destination, touching at Sackets Harbor and taking on board about 100 men, besides arms and ammunition. The schooners had proceeded as far as Millen's Bay, below Cape Vincent, and the steamer "United States" coming up took them in tow, one on each side. There were now about 500 men on board the boat, all young, destined for some point known to but very few, if any, except the officers. They were fully officered, Gen. J. Ward Birge holding the appointment of commander-in-chief. He was very sanguine, but his subsequent acts made him conspicuous as a coward. These vessels being well supplied with field pieces, small arms, ammunition and provisions, started on the morning of the 17th of November, down the river. When passing Alexandria Bay, Charles Crossmon, one of these "patriots," then a young man of twenty years, full of patriotic impulses, little thought that one day at this point a beautiful tourist home should bear his name.

The boats swept down the river until abreast of Prescott. At that point the schooners were detached, and dropped down to Windmill Point, about a mile below the city, where stood an abandoned windmill.

In trying to land, the schooners ran aground, one near the point and the other farther down the river. About 250 men landed from the schooners, and the greater part of the guns and ammunition, together with one twelve pounder and two brass seven pounders were brought down. They then took possession of the windmill, which they held with three other stone buildings. The schooners, after getting afloat with the balance of the men and ammunition, sailed for Ogdensburg. This looked rather discouraging to the men in the windmill, to see these schooners leave them with many of their men and nearly all of their provisions and ammunition. Colonel Worth and the United States Marshal, Garrow, afterwards seized the vessels and all of their cargoes. Prospects began to darken for the Patriots. They were deserted by nearly all of their officers. General Birge wilted at the first chance of facing British bullets. It happened that among the Patriot band was a Polish exile, Niles Sobeliteki Van Schoultz, who came from Salina. He was of noble birth, his father being an officer of high rank, and he himself had been an officer in the Polish service. He had been deluded into the project of freeing Canada from "tyranny and

river. They landed at Prescott. It was now evident that some fighting was to be done. Von Schoultz gave great encouragement to his men, advising them to brave the British bullets and stand by each other to the last man. They agreed to follow wherever he should lead.

The British steamers were now patroling the river, and occasionally firing shots at the wind-mill. One shot was fired at the steamer

BAT-WING SAIL.

oppression." In the emergency he was now placed in command. It had all along been understood that as soon as a stand was made by any Patriot force, the Canadians would flock to their standard. In this they now found themselves grossly deceived; not a single man came to their relief. They were looked upon as brigands and robbers. On the morning of the 18th, three Canadian steamboats, the "Coburg," the "Experiment" and the "Traveller," with about 400 regular troops from Kingston, were seen coming down the

"United States" while in American waters passing through her wheel house, killing the man at the wheel. The British troops, under Colonel Dundas, came marching from Prescott to annihilate the Patriots. Van Schoultz marched his men out of the building into the field. They formed in line behind a stone fence, which they used as a breast-work. The British commenced firing when about 150 yards away, and continued their firing as they advanced, without doing any injury. The "Patriots" held their fire until the enemy had advanced to within fifteen rods, and then they got the order to fire. This broad-side resulted in killing thirty-six British soldiers, and wounding many others. The British fell back, but the firing continued on both sides. This was followed by the withdrawal of the "Patriots"—some into the wind-mill, and others occupying the outhouses, but continuing their fire at long range. The cannon shots aimed at the mill glanced off and produced no effect upon the walls. The battle raged three hours and twenty minutes, during which time six of the Patriots had been killed, and twenty-one wounded. It was estimated that seventy-five of the British lay dead upon the field, and 150 were wounded. Colonel Dundas now sent a flag of truce, asking a cessation of hostilities for an hour, that he might remove his dead and wounded, which was cheerfully granted by Von Schoultz.

The strife was watched with intense interest by a large crowd of people at Ogdensburg, directly opposite. The river now being clear, Hon. Preston King, with a few volunteers, chartered the "Paul Pry" to go over and get the Patriots away from the wind-mill. This was done probably by consent of the British forces. The boat went over, but only a few of the men chose to leave. Jonah Woodruff, the artist, afterwards the sleeping-car inventor and proprietor, was one of those who came away on the "Paul Pry." As time was precious, the night dark and the limit of the truce uncertain, the men in the mill irresolute and under poor military subjection, Mr. King and his party were forced to leave with but few, when all could have been saved.

About 10 o'clock on the third day the British regulars, reinforced with about 1,000 militia, came bearing down upon this almost defenseless band in the old mill. They had but little ammunition left, but they resolved to sell their lives as dearly as possible. The troops continued firing their cannon and volleys of musket balls, however, without perilous effect. At length Von Schoultz ordered a cannon loaded with musket balls, spikes and pieces of iron placed in the door of the mill, and at an opportune moment it was discharged, killing twenty-five of the British and wounding as many more. This threw them into confusion, and they retreated.

At length Von Schoultz saw that his men could not stand another charge, and, with much reluctance, sent out a flag of truce, the bearers of which were immediately taken prisoners. They then displayed a white flag from the top of the mill, but no notice was taken of it. Towards night Colonel Dundas sent out a flag demanding a surrender of the men at his discretion. Von Schoultz offered to surrender as prisoners of war, but Colonel Dundas would grant no conditions. Finally the little band, finding opposition hopeless, gave themselves up without terms into the hands of the British commander.

Thus ended one of the most foolish and ill-conceived expeditions that was ever undertaken. Nineteen of the patriots were killed, thirty-five were wounded and about 190 were taken prisoners. The latter were placed on board the steamers and taken to Kingston, where they were confined in Fort Henry. It was estimated that about 125 of the British were killed and 200 wounded.

The prisoners were confined in squads of fifteen to twenty in small rooms in the fort, and placed under a strong guard. Sir George Arthur had decided that they were brigands and must be tried by a court martial, to be composed of seven field officers and seven captains of the line.

The serious condition of these prisoners excited the sympathy of the people of Jefferson county as well as of their friends, and meetings were held in all the towns under great excitement, petitions being circulated far and wide and extensively signed. These were presented to Sir George Arthur, the governor-general, asking clemency for these poor deluded victims. The best legal talent in the State volunteered their aid in defence of the prisoners, and in mitigation of their condition. William H. Seward, Philo Gridley, Hiram Denio, Joshua A. Spencer, Bernard Bagley and George C. Sherman, all united and used their best efforts in appealing to the governor-general for clemency.

The court convened on the 28th of November; Daniel George being the first prisoner to be tried, pleaded not guilty. When he was taken from the steamer, papers were found in his pockets commissioning him as paymaster of the eastern division of the Patriot army. Von Schoultz was then brought before the court for trial. He employed the barrister, Sir John McDonald, to aid him in his defense. He pleaded guilty. He sent a written appeal to the governor-general, in which he stated that he was deluded into joining in the invasion of Canada by the gross misrepresentations of such men as J. Ward Birge and William Lyon McKenzie, who claimed to know the sentiment and wishes of the people of Canada, and that they would be received with open arms. Also, that the militia, when called out, would flock to their standard. All of which proved to be a base delusion. He asked for mercy at his hands. Every means of influence which could be brought to bear upon the governor-general by such men as Judge Fine, Silas Wright and a host of others, could not change his determination of executing all the officers and leaders.

Dorephus Abbey, a former newspaper editor of Watertown, was the next to be tried. He was captured while carrying a flag of truce, and was next in rank to Von Schoultz. Next was Martin Woodruff. All of these, after trial, namely: Daniel George, Nicholas Von Schoultz, Dorephus Abbey and Martin Woodruff were sentenced by Sir George Arthur to be hanged, and this sentence was carried out December 8th. Von Schoultz made his will, giving, among his many bequests, $10,000 for the benefit of the families of the British soldiers who were killed at the battle of the Windmill. He also wrote the following pathetic and farewell letter to his friend, Warren Green, of Syracuse:

"DEAR FRIEND.—When you get this letter, I shall be no more. I have been informed that my execution will take place to-morrow. May God forgive them who brought me to this untimely death. Hard as my fate is, I have made up my mind to forgive them, and do. I have been promised a lawyer to write my will—intend to appoint you my executor. If the British government permits it, I wish my body delivered to you and buried on your farm. I have no time to write more because I have great need of communicating with my Creator to prepare myself for His presence. The time allowed me for this is short. My last wish to the Americans is, that they will not think of avenging my death. Let no further blood be shed. And believe me, from what I have seen, all the stories which were told of the sufferings of the Canadian people were untrue. Give my love to your sister, and tell her that I think of her as I do of my own mother. May God reward her for her kindness. I further beg of you to take care of W. J. so that he may find honorable bread. Farewell, my dear friends. May God bless you and protect you.
"*December* 18.
"N. VON SCHOULTZ."

Joel Peeler and Sylvanus Sweet were executed, January 11, 1839. Sylvester Lawton, Duncan Anderson, Christopher Buckley, Russell Phelps and Lyman H. Lewis were sent to the scaffold, February 11. They were followed by Martin Van Slyke, William O'Neal and James Cummings. The officers now having all been dealt with, they made quick work trying the men under them. The prisoners were brought into court in squads of from ten to fifteen, and asked a few questions, and were then returned to their quarters. They all expected that their doom was sealed, and were anxiously awaiting their death warrants. But a powerful influence was brought to bear upon Governor-General Arthur, and he finally decided that there would be no more executions, and went so far as to say that a number of them would be pardoned. The court had adjourned from January 4th to February 26th. The prisoners were allowed to receive visits from their friends, but under close guard. On the 5th of April the steamer "Commodore Barry" arrived at Sackets Harbor with twenty-two prisoners, pardoned by the governor-general. And on the 27th of April, thirty-seven more pardoned prisoners arrived at the same place. All released were under twenty-one years of age. The balance of the men remained in the fort all summer, uncertain as to their fate, whether they would be pardoned or banished. On the 17th of September, 1839, orders were given to prepare for departure, and ninety-five of them were heavily ironed, placed in canal barges and taken to Montreal, and there, with another lot of prisoners, making about 150 in all, were put on board the ship "Buffalo," bound for Van Dieman's Island.

February 13, 1840, after an uneventful voyage, they landed in the harbor of Hobart Town. After the inspector had taken a description of them, the governor, Sir John Franklin, who afterwards died during a voyage of exploration to the Arctic region, came to see them, and after looking them over, read their sentence, which was banishment for life. He was happy to learn of the captain of the "Buffalo" that they had behaved remarkably well during the voyage. He also informed them that they would be placed at hard labor on the public roads with other convicts, and that with good behavior, after three years, they would be granted tickets of leave, which would give them the liberty of the island.

After three years of this service, they were granted tickets of leave, but were confined within certain limits, and obliged to report at the station every Saturday night. If they so desired, they could be changed from one district to another. The deliverance from the heavy work they had hitherto endured was a blessing, and gave them new life. A reward of a pardon and free passage to America having been offered by the governor to any of the convicts who would capture some bushrangers who were infesting the island, W. Gates, Stephen Wright, Aaron Dresser and George Brown succeeded in discovering the hiding-place and capturing two of the rangers. They were pardoned, and, after a long voyage, returned to America, having served five years of a convict's life.

In September, 1845, the governor commenced to deal out pardons of ten and fifteen at a time. He thought it not quite safe to liberate too many at once. During the year 1846, all of the Canadian prisoners had received pardons excepting some few whose behavior did not entitle them to such a reward.

Thus ended the Patriot war. It was not without some beneficent results to the Canadas, for the home government granted them a new charter, by which the provinces were united into a dominion with a parliament. The Tories were defeated in the parliament, and the Reform party, after driving them from power, assumed control of the State. Even the outlaw, William Lyon McKenzie, was restored to citizenship, and was for many years a member of parliament, and the premier of the government. A curious phase of the Patriot troubles was the effect on the political heads of National and State governments. President Van Buren and Governor Marcy were both soundly denounced by many newspapers for performing their duty in enforcing the neutrality laws, and lost many votes in the frontier States. Marcy was succeeded by Seward, and on the day the election of Harrison was announced in Washington, the boys shouted about the White House the refrain: "Van! Van! is a used-up man." And even General Scott attributed his failure to receive the Whig nomination at the Harrisburg National Convention to the machinations of Col. Solomon Van Rensselaer, a delegate from New York, who held a spite against General Scott for having "squelched" his son, the general in command at Navy Island.   J. A. H.

During the "Patriot" war, Watertown and the adjoining towns were filled with expatriated "Patriots" who had fled from Canada to avoid arrest and imprisonment for alleged treason. Watertown being the headquarters of the Canadian leaders, William Lyon McKenzie, Van Rensselaer, and others, were located at the old stone Mansion House, kept by Luther Gilson, on the site of the present Iron block. The old hostelry was crowded with the patriots. During the early winter of 1838, the then governor-general of Upper Canada, who had been recalled from his position by the British government, was ordered to return. This notable official was Sir Francis Bond-Head, an ex-officer of the British army, and thoroughly despised in Canada. Wishing to reach New York to sail for England, he undertook to make the journey by stage to Utica via Watertown. Not desirous of meeting his expatriated subjects for fear of recognition and possible insult, he determined to pass through incognito. Leaving Kingston during the night, accompanied by a prominent citizen of that city, to whom he acted the part of valet (or gentleman's gentleman), he arrived safely next morning by wagon and driver, hired as an "extra." The driver, not being informed as to the quality or rank of his passengers, drove straight to the Mansion House, and landed his man at the headquarters of his enemies. It was just after the breakfast hour, and the lobby was filled with the Patriot community, who recognized the Kingston citizen and greeted him cordially, but did not recognize the valet, who discreetly kept in the back ground. Prominent among the Patriot leaders at the hotel was Hugh Scanlon, an Irish-Canadian, a bright and shrewd fellow. After a short time, Scanlon noticed that the valet was missing, and his suspicions were aroused, so he began to hunt him up. After looking high and low and all around the public square without finding him, he continued to search elsewhere, and at last found the lost valet cosily sitting on a wheelbarrow near the stables. Walking up to the late governor-general, he recognized him at once. Introducing himself, Scanlon invited him to breakfast and to meet his late subjects, assuring him that he would be welcome, and receive every courtesy due his rank. The governor accepted the invitation and came forward. He was met by all in a courteous and friendly way, and was assisted in his arrangements for departure. He left town in a coach and four, with cheers, and without a single uncomplimentary remark.

A. J. F.

SIGNALING THE "NORTH KING," OF THE CANADIAN LINE.

MR. JOHN A. HADDOCK'S

CELEBRATED BALLOON VOYAGE WITH PROFESSOR LA MOUNTAIN.

IT is now about thirty-five years since the undersigned made the memorable balloon voyage with Professor LaMountain — a voyage intended to be short and pleasant, but which resulted in a long and most disastrous one, entailing the loss of the valuable balloon, and seriously endangering the lives of the travellers. Since then, LaMountain, after serving through the great rebellion, has made his last "voyage," and has entered upon that existence where all the secrets of the skies are as well defined and understood as are the course of rivers here on the earth.

To fully understand my reasons for making the trip, some leading facts should be presented:

1. There had been, all through the year 1859, much excitement in the public mind upon the subject of ballooning. In August of that year, I returned from Labrador, and found that the balloon Atlantic, with Wise, Hyde, Gaeger and LaMountain, had been driven across a part of Lake Ontario, while on their great trip from St. Louis to New York city, and had landed and been wrecked in Jefferson county, N. Y., and the people of that whole section were consequently in a state of considerable excitement upon the subject of navigating the air.*

2. I had heard of other newspaper editors making trips in balloons, had read their glowing accounts, and it seemed to me like a very cunning thing. Desiring to enjoy "all that was a-going," I naturally wanted a balloon ride, too, and therefore concluded to go, expecting to be absent from home not more than ten or twelve hours at the longest, and to have a good time. Being a newspaper man, and always on the alert for news, I had also a natural desire to do all in my power to add to the local interest of my journal, and for that reason felt a willingness to go through with more fatigue and hazard than men are expected to endure in ordinary business pursuits.

3. I felt safe in going, as I knew that LaMountain was an intrepid and successful aeronaut, and I thought his judgment was to be depended upon. How he was misled as to distance, and how little he knew, or any man can know, of air navigation, the narrative will readily demonstrate.

---

* The Wise named above was the celebrated aeronaut, Professor John Wise, of Lancaster, Pa.; and I may here remark that the trip made by him and his associates is by far the longest on record. Leaving St. Louis at about 4 P. M., they passed the whole night in the air, were carried across the States of Illinois, Indiana, a portion of Ohio and Michigan, over the whole northwestern breadth of Pennsylvania and New York, and were at last wrecked in a huge tree-top near the shore of Lake Ontario, at about 3 P. M. the next day, escaping with severe bruises, but without broken bones, after a journey of eleven hundred miles. These adventurers did not travel as fast, nor encounter the perils that awaited us, but they made a longer voyage. It was with this same balloon Atlantic that LaMountain and myself made our trip; but it had been reduced one-third in size, and was as good as new. John Wise afterwards lost his life in a balloon, but just where he perished was never known. Gaeger was a manufacturer of crockery, and he died in Massachusetts. Hyde is publishing a newspaper in one of the western States. LaMountain died in his bed at Lansingburgh, N. Y., about 1884.

With these explanations, I will proceed with my original narrative, nearly as written out at the time.

Nearly every one in Watertown is aware that the second ascension of the balloon Atlantic was advertised for the 20th of September, 1859. The storm of that and the following day obliged the postponement of the ascension until the 22d. Every arrangement had been made for a successful inflation, and at 27 minutes before 6 P. M., the glad words "all aboard" were heard from LaMountain, and that distinguished aeronaut and myself stepped into the car. Many were the friendly hands we shook—many a fervent "God bless you," and "happy voyage," were uttered—and many handkerchiefs waved their mute adieus. "Let go all," and away we soared; in an instant all minor sounds of earth had ceased, and we were lifted into a silent sphere, whose shores were without an echo, their silence equaled only by that of the grave. No feeling of trepidation was experienced; an extraordinary elation took possession of us, and fear was as far removed as though we had been sitting in our own rooms at home.

Two or three things struck me as peculiar in looking down from an altitude of half a mile: the small appearance of our village from such a height and the beautiful mechanical look which the straight fences and oblong square fields of the farmers present. As we rose into the light, fleecy clouds, they looked between us and the earth like patches of snow we see lying upon the landscape in springtime; but when we rose a little higher the clouds completely shut out the earth, and the cold, white masses below us had precisely the same look that a mountainous snow-covered country does, as you look down upon it from a higher mountain. Those who have crossed the Alps—or have stood upon one of the lofty summits of the Sierra Nevada, and gazed down upon the eternal snows below and around them, will be able to catch the idea. In six minutes we were far above all the clouds, and the sun and we were face to face. We saw the time after that when his face would have been very welcome to us. In eight minutes after leaving the earth, the thermometer showed a fall of 24 degrees. It stood at 84 when we left. The balloon rotated a good deal, proving that we were ascending with great rapidity. At 5:48 the thermometer stood at 42, and falling very fast. At 5:50 we were at least two miles high — thermometer 34.

An unpleasant ringing sensation had now become painful, and I filled both ears with cotton. At 5:52 we put on our gloves and shawls — thermometer 32. The wet sandbags now became stiff with cold — they were frozen. Ascending very rapidly. At 5:54 thermometer 28, and falling. Here we caught our last sight of the earth by daylight. I recognized the St. Lawrence to the southwest of us, which showed we were drifting nearly north. At 6 o'clock we thought we were descending a little, and LaMountain directed me to throw out about 20 pounds of ballast. This shot us up again — thermometer 26, and falling very slowly. At 6:05 thermometer 22 — my feet were very cold. The Atlantic was now full, and presented a most splendid sight. The gas began to discharge itself at the mouth, and its abominable smell, as it came down upon us, made me sick. A moment's vomiting helped my case materially. LaMountain was suffering a good deal with cold. I passed my thick shawl around his shoulders, and put the blanket over our knees and feet. At 6:10 thermometer 18. We drifted along until the sun left us, and in a short time thereafter the balloon began to descend. We must have been, before we began to descend from this height, 3¼ miles high. At 6:32 thermometer 23; rising. We were now about stationary, and thought we were sailing north of east. We could, we thought, distinguish water below us, but were unable to recognize it. At 6:38 we threw over a bag of sand, making 80 pounds of ballast discharged, and leaving about 120 pounds on hand. We distinctly heard a dog bark. Thermometer 28 — and rising rapidly. At 6:45 the thermometer stood at 33.

At 6:50 it was dark, and I could make no

more memoranda. I put up my note book, pencil and watch, and settled down in the basket, feeling quite contented. From this point until next morning I give my experience from memory only. The figures given were made at the time indicated, and the thermometric variations can be depended on as quite accurate.

We heard, soon after that, a locomotive whistle, and occasionally could hear wagons rumbling over the ground or a bridge, while the farmers' dogs kept up a continual baying, as if conscious there was something unusual in the sky. We sailed along, contented and chatty, until about half-past eight o'clock, when we distinctly saw lights below us, and heard the roaring of a mighty water-fall. We descended into a valley near a very high mountain, but, as the place appeared rather forbidding, we concluded to go up again. Over with 30 pounds of ballast, and sky-ward we sailed. In about 20 minutes we again descended, but this time no friendly light greeted us. We seemed to be over a dense wilderness, and the balloon was settling down into a small lake. We had our life-preservers ready for use, but got up again by throwing out all our ballast, except perhaps 20 pounds. LaMountain now declared it was folly to stay up any longer, that we were over a great wilderness, and the sooner we descended the better. We concluded to settle down by the side of some tall tree, tie up, and wait until morning. In a moment we were near the earth, and as we gently descended I grasped the extreme top of a high spruce, which stopped the balloon's momentum, and we were soon lashed to the tree by our large drag-rope.

We rolled ourselves up in our blankets, patiently waiting for the morning. The cold rain spouted down upon us in rivulets from the great balloon that lazily rolled from side to side over our heads, and we were soon drenched and uncomfortable as men could be. After a night passed in great apprehension and unrest, we were right glad to see the first faint rays of coming light. Cold and rainy the morning at last broke, the typical precursor of other dismal mornings to be spent in that uninhabited wilderness. We waited until 6 o'clock in hopes the rain would cease, and that the rays of the sun, by warming and thereby expanding the gas in the balloon, would give us ascending power sufficient to get up again, for the purpose of obtaining a view of the country into which we had descended. The rain did not cease, and we concluded to throw over all we had in the balloon, except a coat for each, the life-preservers, the anchor and the compass. Overboard, then, they went — good shawls and blankets, bottles of ale and a flask of cordial, ropes and traps of all kinds. The Atlantic, relieved of this wet load, rose majestically with us, and we were able to behold the country below. It was an unbroken wilderness of lakes and spruce — and I began then to fully realize that we had, indeed, gone too far, through a miscalculation of the velocity of the balloon. As the current was still driving us towards the north, we dare not stay up, as we were drifting still farther and farther into trouble. LaMountain seized the valve-cord and discharged the gas, and we descended in safety to the solid earth. Making the Atlantic fast by her anchor, we considered what was to be done.

We had not a mouthful to eat, no protection at night from the wet ground, were distant we knew not how far from any habitation, were hungry to start with, had no possible expectation of making a fire, and no definite or satisfactory idea as to where we were. We had not even a respectable pocket knife, nor a pin to make a fish hook of — indeed, we were about as well equipped for forest life as were the babes in the woods.

After a protracted discussion, in which all our ingenuity was brought to bear upon the question of our whereabouts, we settled in our minds (mainly from the character of the timber around us), that we were either in John Brown's tract, or in that wilderness lying between Ottawa City and Prescott, Canada. If this were so, then we knew that a course south by east would take us out if we had strength enough to travel the distance.

TRAMPING IN THE WOODS.

Acting upon our conclusion, we started through the woods towards the south-east. After travelling about a mile we came to the bank of a small stream flowing from the west, and were agreeably surprised to find that some human being had been there before us, for we found the stumps of several small trees and the head of a half-barrel, which had contained pork. I eagerly examined the inspection-stamp; it read:

"MESS PORK."
"P. M."
"MONTREAL."

This settled the question that we were in Canada, as I very well knew that no Montreal inspection of pork ever found its way into the State of New York. Although the course we had adopted was to be a south-easterly one, we yet concluded to follow this creek to the westward, and all day Friday we travelled up its banks — crossing it about noon on a floating log, and striking on the southern shore, a "blazed" path, which led to a deserted lumber road, and it in turn bring us to a log shanty on the opposite bank. We had hoped this lumber road would lead us out into a clearing or a settlement, but a careful examination satisfied us that the road ended here, its objective point evidently being the shanty on the other bank. We concluded to cross the creek to the shanty, and stay there all night. Collecting some small timbers for a raft, LaMountain crossed over safely, shoving the raft back to me. But my weight was greater than my companion's, and the frail structure sank under me, precipitating me into the water. I went in all over, but swam out, though it took all my strength to do so. On reaching the bank I found myself so chilled as scarcely to be able to stand. I took off all my clothes and wrung them as dry as I could. We then proceeded to the shanty, where we found some refuse straw, but it was dry, and under a pile of it we crawled — pulling it over our heads and faces, in the hope that our breath might aid in warming our chilled bodies. I think the most revengeful, stony heart would have pitied our condition then. I will not attempt to describe our thoughts as we lay there; home, children, wife, parents, friends, with their sad and anxious faces, rose up reproachfully before us as we tried to sleep. But the weary hours of night at last wore away, and at daylight we held a new council. It was evident, we argued, that the creek we were upon was used by the lumbermen for "driving" their logs in the spring freshets. If, then, we followed it to its confluence with the Ottawa or some stream which emptied into the Ottawa, we would eventually get out the same way the timber went out. The roof of the shanty was covered with the halves of hollow logs, scooped out in a manner familiar to all woodsmen. These were dry and light, and would make us an excellent raft. Why not, then, take four of these, tie them to cross-pieces by wythes and such odd things as we could find around the shanty, and pole the craft down stream to that civilization which even a saw-log appeared able to reach. Such, then, was the plan adopted, although it involved the retracing of all the steps hitherto taken, and an apparent departure from the course we had concluded would lead us out.

Without delay, then, we dragged the hollow logs down to the creek, and LaMountain proceeded to tie them together, as he was more of a sailor than myself. We at last got under way, and, as we pushed off, a miserable crow set up a dismal cawing — an inauspicious sign. We poled down the stream about a mile, when we came abruptly upon a large pine tree which had fallen across the current, and completely blocking the passage of the raft. No other course was left us but to untie the raft, and push the pieces through under the log. This was at last accomplished, when we tied our craft together again, and poled down the stream. To-day each of us ate a raw frog (all we could find), and began to realize that we were hungry. Yet there was no complaining — our talk was of the hopeful future, and of the home and civilization we yet expected to reach. Down the creek we went, into a lake some four miles long, and into which we of course supposed the stream to pass, with its outlet at the lower end. We followed down the northern bank, keeping always near the shore and in shallow water, so that our poles could touch the bottom, until we reached the lower extremity of the lake, where we found no outlet, and so turned back upon the southern shore in quest of one. On reaching the head of the lake, and examining the stream attentively, we found that the current of the creek turned abruptly to the right, which was the reason of our losing it. We felt happy to have found our current again, and plied our poles like heroes. We passed, late in the afternoon, the spot where we had at first struck the creek, and where we stuck up some dead branches as a landmark which might aid us in case we should, at a future time, attempt to save the Atlantic.

When night came on we did not stop, but kept the raft going down through the shades of awful forests, whose solemn stillness seemed to hide from us the unrevealed mystery of our darkening future. During the morning the rain had ceased, but about 10 o'clock at night it commenced again. We stopped the "vessel" and crawled in under some "tag" alders on the bank, where our extreme weariness enabled us to get, perhaps, half an hour's sleep. Rising again (for it was easier to pole the raft at night in the rain down an unknown stream amidst the shadows of that awful forest than to lie on the ground and freeze), we pressed on until perhaps 3 in the morning, when pure exhaustion compelled us to stop again. This time we found a spot where the clayey bank lacked a little of coming down to the water. On the mud we threw our little bundle of straw, and sat down with our feet drawn up under us, so as to present as little surface to the rain as possible. But we could not stand such an uncomfortable position long, and as the daylight of the Sabbath broke upon us, we were poling down the stream in a drizzling rain. At 8 o'clock we reached a spot at which the stream narrowed, rushing over large boulders, and between rocky shores. This was trouble, indeed. To get our raft down this place, we regarded as well-nigh hopeless. We tied up and examined the shore. Here, again, we found unmistakable marks left by the lumbermen, they having evidently camped at this point, to be handy by in the labor of getting the timber over this bad spot in the stream. The rapids were about a third of a mile long, and very turbulent. After a protracted survey we descended the bank, and thought it best to abandon our raft, and try our luck on foot again. After travelling about a mile, we found the bank so tangled and rugged, and ourselves so much exhausted, that satisfactory progress was impossible. So we concluded to go back, and if we could get the raft down, even one piece at a time, we would go on with her — if not, we would build as good a place as possible to shield us from the cold and wet, and there await with fortitude that death from starvation which was beginning to be regarded as a probability. This was our third day of earnest labor and distressing fatigue, and in all that time we had not eaten an ounce of food, nor had dry clothing upon us.

Acting upon our resolution, we at once commenced to get the raft down the rapids, and I freely confess that this was the most trying and laborious work of a whole life of labor. The pieces would not float over a rod at a time, before they would stick on some stone which the low water left above the surface, and then you must pry the stick over in some way, and pass it along to the next obstruction. We were obliged to get into the stream, often up to the middle, with slippery boulders beneath our feet. Several times I fell headlong —completely using up our compass, which now frantically pointed in any direction its addled head took a fancy to. The water had unglued the case, and it was ruined. After long hours of such labor, we got the raft down, and LaMountain again tied it together. Passing on, in about an hour, we came to a large lake, about ten miles long by six broad. Around it we must of course pass, until we should find the desired outlet. So we turned up to the right, and pressed on with as much resolution as we could muster. To-day we found one clam, which I insisted LaMountain should eat, as he was much weaker than myself, and had eaten nothing on the day we went up.

Part of this day LaMountain slept upon the raft, and I was "boss and all hands." As the poor fellow lay there, completely used up, I saw that he could not be of much more assistance in getting out. Erysipelas, from which he had previously suffered, had attacked his right eye; his face was shriveled so that he looked like an old man, and his clothes were nearly torn from his body. A few tears could not be restrained, and my prayer was for speedy deliverance or speedy death. While my companion was asleep, and I busily poling the raft along, I was forced to the conclusion, after deliberately canvassing all the chances, that we were pretty sure to perish there miserably at last. But I could not cease my efforts while I had strength, and so around the lake we went, into all the indentations of the shore, keeping always in shallow water. The day at last wore away, and we stopped at night at a place we thought least exposed to the wind. We dragged the end of our raft out of the water, and laid down upon the cold ground. We were cold when we laid down, and both of us trembled by the hour, like men suffering from a severe attack of the ague. The wind had risen just at night, and the dismal surging of the waves upon the shore, formed, I thought, a fitting lullaby to our disturbed and dismal slumbers.

By this time our clothes were nearly torn off. My pantaloons were split up both legs, and the waistbands nearly gone. My boots were mere wrecks, and our mighty wrestlings in the rapids had torn the skin from ankles and hands. LaMountain's hat had disappeared; the first day out he had thrown away his woolen drawers and stockings, as they dragged him down by the weight of water they absorbed. And so we could sleep but little. It really seemed as though, during this night, we passed through the horrors of death. But at daylight we got up by degrees, first on one knee and then on the other, so stiff and weak that we could hardly stand. Again upon the silent, monotonous lake, we went—following around its shore for an outlet. About 10 o'clock we came to quite a broad northern stream, which we thought was the outlet we were seeking, and we entered it with joy, believing it would take us to our long sought Ottawa. Shortly after entering this

THE POP-CORN MAN, KNOWN AS OLD "JUST ABOUT."

stream it widened out, and began to appear like a mere lake. We poled up the westerly shore for about seven miles, but found ourselves again deceived as to the outlet — the water we were upon proving to be another lake or bayou. We had gone into this lake with the highest hopes, but when we found that all the weary miles of our morning travel had been in vain, and had to be retraced, my resolution certainly failed me for a moment. Yet we felt that our duty, as Christian men, was to press forward as long as we could stand, and leave the issue with a higher Power

It had now been four full days since we ate a meal. All we had eaten in the meantime was a frog apiece, four clams and a few wild berries, whose acid properties and bitter taste had probably done us more harm than good. Our strength was beginning to fail very fast, and our systems were evidently undergoing an extraordinary change. I did not permit myself to think of food — the thought of a well-filled table would have been too much. My mind continually dwelt upon poor Strain's sufferings on the Isthmus of Darien (then lately published in Harper's Magazine). He, too, was paddling a raft down an unknown stream, half starved, and filled with dreadful forebodings. But I did not believe we could hold out half as long as he had. Besides, he was lost in a tropical country, where all nature is kind to man: he had fire-arms and other weapons with which to kill game. We were in a cold, inhospitable land, without arms, and utterly unable to build a fire. Strain was upon a stream which he knew would eventually bear him to the sea and to safety; while we were upon waters whose flow we positively knew nothing about, and were as much lost as though in the mountains of the moon. Yet we could not give it up so, and tried to summon up fresh courage as troubles appeared to thicken around us. So we turned the raft around, and poled it in silence back towards the place where we had entered this last lake. We had gone about a mile when we heard the sound of a gun, quickly followed by a second report. No sound was ever so sweet as that. We hallooed as loud as we could, a good many times, but could get no response. We kept our poles going quite lively, and had gone about half a mile, when I called LaMountain's attention to what I thought was smoke curling up among the trees by the side of a hill. My own eyesight had begun to fail very much, and I felt afraid to trust my dull senses in a matter so vitally important. LaMountain scrutinized the shore very closely, and said he thought it was smoke, and that he believed there was also a birch canoe on the shore below. In a few moments the blue smoke rolled unmistakably above the tree tops, and we felt that

WE WERE SAVED!

Such a revulsion of feeling was almost too much. We could hardly credit our good fortune, for our many bitter disappointments had taught us not to be very sanguine. With the ends of our poles we paddled the raft across the arm of the lake, here, perhaps, three-quarters of a mile wide, steering for the canoe. It proved to be a large one, evidently an Indian's. Leaving LaMountain to guard and retain the canoe, in case the Indian proved timid and desired to escape from us, I pressed hurriedly up the bank, following the footprints I saw in the damp soil, and soon came upon the temporary shanty of a lumbering wood, from the rude chimney of which a broad volume of smoke was rising. I hallooed — a noise was heard inside, and a noble-looking Indian came to the door. I eagerly asked him if he could speak French, as I grasped his outstretched hand. "Yes," he replied, "and English, too!" He drew me into the cabin, and there I saw the leader of the party, a noble-hearted Scotchman named Angus Cameron. I immediately told my story; that we had come in there with a balloon, were lost, and had been over four days without food—eagerly demanding to know where we were. Imagine my surprise when he said we were ONE HUNDRED AND EIGHTY MILES DUE NORTH OF OTTAWA, near 300 miles from Watertown, to reach which would require more than 500 miles of travel, following the streams and roads. We were in a wilderness as large as three States like New York, extending from Lake Superior on the west, to the St. Lawrence on the east, and from Ottawa, on the south, to the Arctic circle.

The party consisted of four persons — Cameron and his assistant, and a half-breed Indian (LaMab McDougal) and his son. Their savory dinner was ready. I immediately dispatched the young Indian for La-

Mountain, who soon came in, the absolute picture of wretchedness. All that the cabin contained was freely offered us, and we BEGAN TO EAT. Language is inadequate to express our feelings. Within one little hour the clouds had lifted from our sombre future, and we felt ourselves to be men once more — no longer houseless wanderers amid primeval forests, driven by chance from side to side, but inspired by the near certainty of seeing home again and mingling with our fellows once more in the busy scenes of life.

We soon learned from Cameron that the stream we had traversed with our raft was called Filliman's creek — the large lake we were then near was called the Bos-ke-tong, and drains into the Bos-ke-tong river, which in turn drains into the Gatineau. The Gatineau joins the Ottawa opposite the city of that name, the seat of government of Canada. Cameron assured us that the Bos-ke-tong and Gatineau were so rapid and broken that no set of men could get a raft down, no matter how well they knew the country, nor how much provisions they might have. He regarded our deliverance as purely providential, and many times remarked that we would certainly have perished but for seeing the smoke from his fire. He was hunting timber for his employers, Gilmour & Co., of Ottawa, and was to start in two days down the Gatineau for his headquarters at Desert. If we would stay there until he started we were welcome, he said, to food and accommodations, and he would take us down to Desert in his canoe, and at that point we could get Indians to take us further on. He also said that he had intended to look for timber on Filliman's creek, near where the balloon would be found, as near as we could describe the locality to him, and would try to look it up and make the attempt to get it to Ottawa. This would be a long and tedious operation, as the portages are very numerous between the creek and Desert—something over 20—one of them three miles long. Over these portages, of course, the silk must be carried on the backs of Indians.

After eating all I dared to, and duly cautioning LaMountain not to hurt himself by over-indulgence, I laid down to sleep. Before doing so, I had one of the men remove my boots, and when they came off, nearly the whole outer skin peeled off with the stockings. My feet had become parboiled by the continual soakings of four days and nights, and it was fully three months before they were cured.

After finishing up his business in the vicinity where we found him, on Friday morning (our ninth day from home), Cameron started on his return. We stopped, on our way up the creek, at the spot where we had erected our landmark by which to find the balloon. We struck back for the place, and in about twenty minutes found her, impaled on the tops of four smallish spruce trees, and very much torn. LaMountain concluded to abandon her. He took the valve as a memento, and I cut out the letters "TIC," which had formed part of her name, and brought the strip of silk home with me. We reached what is known as the "New Farm" on Friday night, and there ended our sleeping on the ground. Up by early dawn, and on again, through the drenching rain, reaching Desert on Saturday evening.

At Desert we were a good deal troubled to obtain Indians to take us further on. La-Mah McDougal had told his wife about the baloon, and she, being superstitous and ignorant, had gossipped with the other squaws, and told them the balloon was a "flying devil." As we had traveled in this flying devil, it did not require much of a stretch of Indian credulity to believe that if we were not the Devil's children we must at least be closely related. In this extremity we appealed to Mr. Backus*, a kind-hearted American

* Something quite curious grew out of my naming Mr. Henry Backus as having assisted us at the mouth of the Desert river. My account was generally published throughout the country, and some ten days after our return I received a letter from a lady in Massachusetts asking me to describe to her the man Backus, as that was the name of her long-absent son, who, twenty years before, had disappeared from home, and had never afterwards been

trader, who agreed to procure us a complement of redskins, who would take us to Alexis le Beau's place (sixty miles down the river), where it was thought we could obtain horses. Sunday morning (our eleventh day from home), we started from Desert, and reached Alexis le Beau's just at night. The scenery upon this part of the route was sublime and imposing. The primeval forest stood as grand and silent as when created. Our Indians, too, surpassed anything I ever beheld, in physical vigor and endurance. In the day's run of sixty miles, there were sixteen portages to be made. On reaching one of these places, they would seize the canoe as quick as we stepped out of it, jerk it out of the water and on to their shoulders in half a minute, and start upon a dog trot as unconcernedly as though bearing no burthen. Arriving at the foot of the portage, they would toss the canoe into the stream, steady it until we were seated, then spring in and paddle away, gliding down the stream like an arrow. In the morning we traveled fifteen miles and made seven portages in one hour and forty minutes.

At Alexis le Beau we first beheld a vehicle denominated a "buckboard"—a wide, thick plank reaching from one bolster of the wagon to the other, and upon the middle of which plank the seat was placed. This sort of conveyance is often used in new countries, being very cheap, and within the reach of ordinary mechanical skill. Starting off as soon as we could get something to eat, we travelled all night through the forest, over one of the worst roads ever left unfinished, and reached Brooks' farm, a sort of frontier tavern, in the early morning, where we slept a couple of hours, and after breakfast pressed on by the rough frontier stage towards Ottawa.

While the stage was stopping to-day to change horses, I picked up a newspaper at Her Britannic Majesty's colonial frontier post-office, and in it read an account of our ascension and positive loss, with a rather flattering obituary notice of myself. And then, for the first time, I began to comprehend the degree of concern our protracted absence had aroused in the public mind. And if the public felt this concern, what would be the degree of pain experienced by wife, children, parents, friends? These reflections spurred us forward — or rather, our money induced the drivers to hurry up their horses — and at last, on the twelfth day of our absence, at about five o'clock in the afternoon, we jumped off the stage in front of the telegraph office in the good city of Ottawa, whence, in less than five minutes, the swift lightning was speeding a message to home and friends. That was a happy moment—the happiest of all my life—when I knew that within thirty minutes my family would know of my safety.

I do not know how the people of Ottawa so soon found out who we were—but suppose the telegraph operator perhaps told some one; and that "some one" must have told the whole town, for in less than half an hour there was a tearing, excited, happy, inquisitive mass of people in front of the grand hotel there—the clerk of which, when he looked at our ragged clothes and bearded faces, at first thought he "hadn't a single room left," but who, when he found out that we were the lost balloon men, wanted us to have the whole hotel, free and above board, and had tea and supper and lunch, and "just a little private supper, you know!" following each other in rapid, yet most acceptable succession. The happy crowd in the hotel and upon the street were determined to shake hands with us every one, and nearly all wanted to give or loan us money. Pretty soon the newspaper men and some personal acquaintances began to press through the crowd, and some cried while others laughed and huzzahed. Indeed, every one acted as if

---

heard from. I answered the letter immediately, and soon after learned that the man proved to be her son, and that he had promised to come home. What had driven him away from civilization to live among the Indians, was best known to himself. But a man of his generous impulses might have been an ornament to society, and a blessing to his friends. [This note was written the next week after we escaped from the wilderness. The article following this treats of Backus' experience quite exhaustively.]

they had just "found something!" And such is human nature always, when its noble sympathies are aroused for the suffering or distressed.

Although the president of the Ottawa and Prescott Railroad (Robert Bell, Esq.), volunteered to send us on by a special engine that night, we thought it best (inasmuch as our friends had been informed of our safety), to stay at Ottawa until morning. It did seem as though the generous people of that city could not do enough for us, and their kind attention and disinterested enthusiasm will never be forgotten.

hibit unmistakable evidence of the deep interest felt in our fate. At Watertown, which had been my home from boyhood, the enthusiasm had reached fever heat, and the whole town was out to greet the returning æronauts. They had out the old cannon on the Public Square, and it belched forth the loudest kind of a welcome. My family had, of course, suffered deeply by my absence. Everybody had given us up for dead, except my wife. I felt very cheap about the whole thing, and was quite certain that I had done a very foolish

BAY IN LA RUE ISLAND, CANADIAN CHANNEL.

Well, the next morning we left Ottawa, and were quickly carried to Prescott; thence across the St. Lawrence river to Ogdensburg. Here a repetition of the same friendly greetings took place; and at last, after a hearty dinner, we left for home, now distant only seventy-five miles by rail. All along the line of the road we found enthusiastic crowds awaiting our coming, and all seemed to exact. Not so the people — they thought it a big thing to have gone through with so much, and yet come out alive.

Several general conclusions and remarks shall terminate this narrative, already too long. "Why did you permit yourselves to go so far?" will naturally be asked. To this inquiry I reply: that the wind was exceedingly light when we ascended; that we were very soon among the clouds, and consequently unable to take cognizance of our course, or to judge how fast we were travelling. It should be distinctly understood that when you are sailing in a balloon, you are unconscious of motion and progress, unless you can see the earth. Even when you first leave the earth, you seem to be stationary, while the earth appears to drop away from you. Nor can you, when out of sight of the earth, although you may have a compass, judge of the direction you are travelling, if travelling at all. In a few words, *unless you can see the earth, you cannot tell how fast nor in what direction you are travelling*. This, perhaps, better than anything else will explain why we unconsciously drifted off to latitudes so remote. When we arose above the thick mass of clouds, before sundown, we undoubtedly struck a rapid current that carried us north-east, and after we had travelled in this current about an hour, we probably struck another current, from the variation of our altitude, which bore us off to the north-west, for the place where we landed is about thirty miles west of due north from where we ascended.

When we first desended near the earth, and saw lights and heard dogs barking, we should have landed. But we were unwilling to land at night in a deep wood, even though we knew that inhabitants were near by, and we thought it best to pick out a better place. This was our error; and it came near being a fatal one to us — it was certainly so to the balloon. In trying to find our "better place" to land, we were up longer than we supposed, and as we were travelling in a current that bore us off to the northward at the rate of 100 miles an hour, we soon reached a point beyond the confines of civilization.

THE AWAKENING OF HENRY BACKUS.

A ROMANCE OF THE BALLOON JOURNEY OF HADDOCK AND LA MOUNTAIN.

IN the preceding account of the balloon voyage made by LaMountain and Haddock into the Bos-ke-tong wilderness of Canada in September, 1859, allusion was made by the writer to one Henry Backus. The early history of this man and the peculiar manner in which he was restored to civilized society and to his mother, from whom he had foolishly separated himself twenty years before, forms a story which would be called a "romance" were it not founded upon actual facts.

LaMountain and myself made our balloon ascension from Watertown, N. Y., and were carried by a swift northerly current far beyond the bounds of civilization, landing in that immense forest in Canada, which is larger than the great States of New York, Pennsylvania and Ohio combined, and limited on the north only by Labrador and the Arctic circle. Having been rescued from starvation and probable death by the brave Cameron and his Indian guides, whom we providentially encountered, we had reached, on our way "out of the wilderness," that frontier post of the Hudson Bay Company, known as Desert, where we were detained by inability to procure Indians for the further prosecution of our journey, because one of Cameron's Indians, who lived at Desert had circulated a story among his associates that we had come into that wilderness in a "flying devil," which had fallen from the sky. Naturally superstitious and densely ignorant, these boatmen readily concluded that we were really children of the Devil himself, and undesirable people to work for, even if well paid. We were very impatient at the detention, and Cameron, who could take us no farther towards Ottawa, advised us to consult one Henry Backus, the local trader, who might be able to help us, for he sold "fire-water" to the Indians and had great influence with them. To Backus' little store, then, we went, and found him somewhat hard to approach, as if he were suspicious of any attempt at intimacy; but when we told him our trouble and urgently solicited his good offices, he appeared anxious and willing to aid us. He struck me as being too intelligent and well educated for the position he was filling, as a small trader in so remote a place, but we were too much concerned with our own plans for reaching civilization to scrutinize him very closely. He knew just how to deal with the ignorant river men, and soon had a crew selected who promised to depart with us at early daybreak, so that we might reach Alexis-le-Beau before nightfall. The promise was redeemed, and in the morning we departed, and Backus saw us no more, but from one of us he was yet to hear.

Who was Henry Backus? To answer this inquiry I must take the reader back more than fifty years, to 1837, when there lived in Western Massachusetts a family named Hancock, consisting of the parents and two daughters, sixteen and eighteen years of age, the elder named Mabel, the youngest Harriet. It is with Mabel we have more particularly to deal. She was above the average in beauty of person, bright and engaging, and, like most of her sex, well aware of her good points, and not by any means unmindful of the admiration she elicited from the young men of her neighborhood. As a result, she was often invited to the merry-makings of that section, accompanied sometimes by one, sometimes by another young gentleman — but for a long time she gave none of her admirers any special preference. In her twentieth year, when the heart is said to be the most susceptible, she had two admirers who had distanced her hitherto numerous gallants, and whenever she went to church or to the country parties, one or the other of these was always her attendant. Henry Backus, one of these young men, was rather a silent and reserved, but really handsome young man of twenty-two, well-educated in the country schools, active and enterprising, the comfort of his mother, who was a widow and the owner of a good farm, left her by her husband. Henry was somewhat in appearance like an Indian, tall and dark-skinned, and there was a tradition that the Backus family, a hundred years before, had been crossed by Narraganset blood.

Be that as it may, Henry was observant but silent, seldom gay and never frivolous, but he was popular among his companions, who gave him their full confidence, for they knew he meant all he said, and that his word was as good as most other men's bond. His competitor in Mabel's good graces was equally regarded, but in a different way. Witty, agreeable, full of vivacity and animal spirits, James Atwell was the life of every social gathering, greatly admired by the girls, and welcome in every circle. Although a year older than Henry Backus, he had not yet settled down to any serious pursuit, which, in his case, was thought to be a necessity, as his father had never accumulated more than a mere subsistence. James had twice left home, and had spent a whole year in a dry goods store at Worcester, Mass., but he had given up that business as too confining. He had also taught the district school one winter, but was thought deficient in discipline, and was not asked to teach a second time. While nothing could be said against him, the older people rated him much below Backus in prospective usefulness and position. The girls considered him as "just too nice for anything," but thought, and some of them said, that Henry Backus was "an old cross-patch." They unanimously predicted that James Atwell would have a "walk-over" in the contest for supremacy in Mabel's affections. But this prediction did not have any speedy fulfilment, as both the young men were equally well received at the Hancock mansion, and so a whole year wore away without any material change in the relation of these young people to one another, but close observers saw that Backus was wonderfully smitten with Mabel, a fact which he did not try to conceal. Yet it gave his mother considerable concern, for she well knew the intensity of his nature, and how restless he became under even slight disappointments.

A change, however, was soon to come. While returning from a dancing party in the winter of 1838, Henry proposed, and was at least partially accepted by Mabel as her future husband. At her request the partial agreement was to be kept a secret, much against Henry's wish, but he loved the girl too much to deny her anything. While this understanding was being faithfully observed between them, invitations came for the grand winter wind up dancing party, to be held at the county town, and Henry was duly accepted as Mabel's escort thither. When the evening of the party drew on, he started in his sleigh for his companion, but the snow was deep, and in trying to turn out for a loaded team his cutter was upset, himself thrown out, and the horse ran away. It took fully two hours to recover the horse and reach the Hancock mansion, and then only to find that Mabel had become tired of the delay, and, in a moment of pique, had accepted James Atwell's proffered escort and gone to the dance with him. Backus was thunderstruck, and finally burst into a passion of tears, due as much, probably, to the excitement he had just passed through, as to the unexpected departure of Mabel with his rival. His jealousy was terribly aroused, and he at once reached the conclusion that his delay had been gladly taken advantage of by her in order to accept the company of one whom she loved more than himself. He did not go to the dance, nor would he make much reply to Mrs. Hancock's trembling efforts to put Mable's action in a favorable light, but went straight home and made such explanations as he could to his tearful mother. Talk as she might, she could not move him from a sullen fit of depression, which the night did not wear away, and in the morning he harnessed his horse and drove away, with a determination to have a final understanding with Mabel. He demanded that their betrothment should be made public, and be sanctioned by her parents. That young lady bore herself during the interview with considerable independence, declaring herself as satisfied with what she had done, and captiously declined to ask her parents to ratify their engagement, which she declared was not considered as final, but rather as a matter subject to further contingencies, in all of which she developed a feminine spirit of contention so characteristic of that sex. After much talk and expostulation they parted in anger, utterly estranged — she most likely believing that it would result in a lover's reconciliation, and never dreaming that she would not soon see Henry Backus again. But with him the case was closed. He felt that he had loved and lost, and that, in the eyes of his acquaintances, he had been made a fool of by a heartless woman. His fine sleigh was not used again that winter. The social parties missed him, and as the trouble between the lovers gradually came out (but though never a word from him), the country people took two sides in discussing the matter, nearly all the women upholding Henry; and the men, more gallant, taking the part of Mabel. But she, too, went no more abroad, refusing even to see James Atwell, though he both called and wrote. Doubtless, like many another, she felt a secret desire to repossess what she had recklessly thrown away, and felt too proud to make any effort towards a reconciliation.

Try as he would, young Backus failed to take his former interest in life. His mother's tearful face would at times force him to active exertion on their farm, but it was plain to be seen that his spirit was broken, and that a sullen despondency had taken possession of his mind. Having struggled along through the summer's work and the harvesting, he besought his mother to let him hire a steady young man to do the farm work, and then be allowed to go away for a while. His mother, thinking a change of scene would help her son, reluctantly gave her consent, and late in November, Henry left his home to become a wanderer. But travel as long and as far as he could, he found it impossible to get rid of himself. His burden would not be cast off. For a month he remained at Albany, and then went north to Watertown, Prescott and Ogdensburg, N. Y., and finally to Ottawa, in Canada. The Indian strain of blood, which it was said he had inherited, began definitely to assert itself, more vigorously, perhaps, at the sight of the adjacent forests, and he resolved to leave civilization behind him and forget that busy world where he had been so sadly deceived, and with which he now had so little affiliation.

Those who have visited Ottawa will remember the dense forest which environs that delightful city beyond the rapid river towards the north. Within a few miles of this Canadian capital you can readily lose yourself in the dense growth of trees; and into this then almost unbroken wilderness Henry Backus launched himself, fully resolved never again to live among civilized men. Farther and farther he journeyed, until the stage route dwindled to mere "buckboard" travel, then to solitary paths marked by blazed trees, until Alexis-le-Beau, upon the Upper Gatineau, was reached, and then up that rapid stream he pressed a hundred miles to Desert, which was a mere fringe of clearing in that almost unbroken primeval forest. There Backus passed the late spring and summer. Gradually the need of employment for his mind and strength asserted itself, and he built a small log cabin with store-room in front, and began to trade with the Indians for their furs. When winter came on he made a journey out from the woods to Ottawa, where he perfected an arrangement for the annual sale of his peltry and for a regular consignment to him of such goods as his trade at Desert demanded. He was gone a month, and on his return took up his daily life as before, a solitary, independent, silent man. I leave the imagination of the reader to depict his feelings, his yearnings for his mother, his moments of frantic love for Mabel Hancock, his resolve to break the spell that was upon him and return to his old home and friends, and for the reader to comprehend the depth of a nature that could endure in silence a disappointment so bitter.

For a long time Mrs. Backus expected to see Henry walk into the house almost any day. She managed her farm much better than she had expected, saving something every year. After five years had passed, she lost faith in Henry's return, and almost gave him up as dead. She fell sick, and was in bed for a long time; then it was that Mabel Hancock developed the good that was in her. Humbly she went to the sick woman's bedside, confessed her undying love for Henry, took all the blame upon herself for his departure and long absence, and volunteered to nurse Mrs. Backus through her sickness. At first she was not at all drawn towards the girl, but her remorse and self-condemnation so plainly attested her sincerity that she was permitted to remain. She soon became a permanent fixture at Henry's old home, and so won the mother's heart that they never separated. Jointly they managed the farm, and became so knit together by mutual regard that strangers looked upon them as mother and daughter. James Atwell had married Harriet and they had moved away, but Mabel did not attend her sister's wedding. Woman-like, she cast upon Atwell most of the blame for the unfortunate separation from her lover, when, in fact, she was the one mainly at fault, though there were those who thought Henry Backus himself not without grave responsibility for the turn affairs had taken. And so the years wore on until Mabel was nearly 40 years of age — comely in figure, but with a sad face, seldom lit by a smile. Her constant prayer was that she might be able to pay back to Henry's mother that fealty and support which had been lost when an unwise and needless quarrel had driven away her son.

The coming of the balloon men made an abiding impression upon Backus. He felt a return of that longing for home which he thought he had entirely conquered. He even found himself full of self-accusation, because he had not volunteered to personally accompany them to Ottawa, for from there he could have telegraphed or written to his mother. He found it difficult to put aside the influence these two eager, pushing men had exerted upon him. They were resolutely bent upon returning to that civilization he had been so willing to leave, and he began to feel a conviction that they were right in their course and that he had been wrong in his. For three weeks this struggle went on in his heart until he began to realize the selfishness and folly of his course. He felt like loathing his surroundings as wholly unworthy one who had in his youth given such ample promise of usefulness and honor. Hard as was the struggle, however, and much as he felt the value of what he had too ruthlessly cast away 20 years before, it might have been doubtful what course he would ultimately have taken had not Providence unmistakably warned him that he was trifling with his own best interests, to say nothing of his disregard of filial duty.

About the middle of October, 1859, a party of river men, on their way up from Alexis-le-Beau, the nearest postoffice, brought him a letter, which may have read as follows:

AT HOME, *October* 10, 1859.

MY DEAR SON, if indeed you are my son: I read last week in the Springfield *Republican* an account of the adventures of the lost balloon men, who gave credit to one Henry Backus, a trader at Desert, on the Gatineau river, in Canada, for having aided them in their efforts to return to their homes. My heart prompted me to write to Mr. Haddock, at Watertown, N. Y., for a description of this Henry Backus, and Mr. H. immediately answered my letter. Making full allowance for the changes 20 years may have made, I feel quite hopeful that you are my long lost and deeply mourned son. If so, do not delay an hour, but come home before it is too late to see your poor mother, now past her 60th year, but whose prayer has ever been for her absent son.

Mabel Hancock has lived with me for the past 15 years. She is my stay and greatest comfort, and she desires me to enclose a word from her. For we are more and more convinced that you are my lost son. My heart is too full to write more, but if you are my son hasten to my arms, for a fresh disappointment or long delay may prove too much for my poor strength. Affectionately, your mother,

RACHEL BACKUS.

The note enclosed was from Mabel; it read:

DEAREST FRIEND — If you are that Henry Backus to whom I was once betrothed in marriage, I feel that I owe much in the way of apology for the treatment you received at my hands when I was a young and inexperienced girl. My past life I offer as an evidence of my feelings towards you then and now ; yet that life for many years has been a burden, which I could only have borne for your dear mother's sake. If you are the lost one you cannot be too quick in hastening to your true home, for your mother is not long for this world.

Your attached friend,
MABEL HANCOCK.

If Backus had been tardy in carrying out the plans which the coming of the lost balloon men appeared to prompt, he was on fire now with impatience, and counted every hour as lost that kept him from the telegraph. Placing a trusted clerk in charge of his business, he packed up his important papers, and, on the morning of the fourth day, was in Ottawa, sending a message to distant Berkshire that he was indeed the lost son, who had come to himself and would soon be there.

———

Having thus far dealt in facts, I will invite the reader himself to imagine that meeting, when Backus found under the same roof his beloved mother and that Mabel Hancock who was thenceforth to reign as the undisputed idol of his heart. The natural inclination of a newspaper editor to follow out any incident of more than passing interest with which he had become interested, impelled me to make inquiry of Backus' subsequent career, as well as of all that might shed any light upon his history before we met him at Desert. On the 1st of January following his return, he and Mabel Hancock were married, and the whole neighborhood shared in the merry-making. He soon sold his possession at Desert, and settled down in a prosperous career, becoming a leading citizen of his native county. Himself and wife were noted for their hospitality and open-handed charity, and it was especially remarked that they were exceedingly lenient in their treatment of any one who had lapsed from duty or against whom society held its doors askance. The poor and the outcast found ready sympathy with them, and no hungry wayfarer was ever sent away unfilled.

The casual reader may not be much impressed with the extraordinary means through which Henry Backus came to be fully "awakened" to his true condition, but those who take a broader view of these incidents can, perhaps, discover in them the workings of that Supreme Omniscience which notes even the fall of a sparrow.

THE WAR OF 1755.

WITH AN ALLUSION TO THE "LOST CHANNEL."

THE most formidable military display which ever swept over the waters of the St. Lawrence, was that of 1760, commanded by Gen. Jeffrey Lord Amherst. It consisted, according to Knox, of the 1st and 2d battalions of the Royal Highlanders, the 44th, 46th, and 55th regiments of the line, the 4th battalion of the 60th, eight companies of the 77th, five companies of the 80th, 579 Grenadiers, 597 Light Infantry, three battalions of the New York regiment, four battalions of the Connecticut regiment, a regiment from New Jersey, 146 Rangers, 157 of the Royal Artillery, and a force of Indians under Sir William Johnson, the whole amounting to an effective force of 10,142 men. The transportation for this army, consisted of two armed vessels, the Onondaga and the Mohawk; the first, under the immediate command of Capt. John Loring, who was also admiral of the fleet, was armed with four nine-pounders, and fourteen sixes, with a crew of 100 men. The second carried sixteen sixes, and a crew of ninety men; and in addition to these, there were seventy-two whaleboats, and 177 batteaux. Several of the whaleboats were armed with a gun each, and some of the batteaux carried howitzers. Besides these, there were staff, hospital and sutler's boats, the whole to quote from a writer of that time, who was an eye witness, "making a most imposing array."

The primary object of the expedition, was the capture of Montreal, it being one of three set on foot for that purpose; but its immediate destination was Fort Levis, a strong French fortification the ruins of which are yet to be seen, on what is now called "Chimney Island," in the St. Lawrence river, a few miles below Ogdensburg, which was known to the French as "La Presentation." At that time, Fort Levis, was the only French stronghold above Montreal, and its reduction was a military necessity. The fort, according to the historian Manté, was begun early in 1759, by Chevalier de Levis, who was afterward a Marshal of France, and completed by Captain Pouchot, by whom it was so ably defended. This officer arrived at the fort in March, and proceeded to put it in as complete a condition for defense as was possible with the means at hand. On taking command, he found it garrisoned by 150 militia, six Canadian officers, some colonial cadets, and M'Bertrand an officer of artillery. A reinforcement of 100 men was sent him from below, but of these, twenty soon deserted, carrying away with them the batteaux belonging to the fort. One of these deserters was a lad named Pierre Rigand. A few days later his father brought him back, feeling deeply the disgrace consequent upon having a son who was a deserter.

It would be a pleasure to find that Capt. Pouchot's Memoirs, in which this incident is related, has been able to add that the young man fought bravely, wiped out the disgrace of desertion and returned to the arms of his father, who not only forgave him but received him with open arms and affectionate pride; but they do not. They only state that: "In the battle which followed, Pierre Rigand was killed."

As it is no part of our intention to enter into a minute description of the investment and capture of the fort, we shall content ourselves with a description of the expedition as related by its historian, in its progress down the St. Lawrence river. On the 7th of August, 1760, Capt. Loring with his two vessels sailed from Oswego for Grenadier Island, at the foot of Lake Ontario. Following in boats were the Royal Highlanders and Grenadiers, commanded by Lieut. Col. Massey; the light infantry under Lieut. Col. Amherst, with two companies of Rangers, the whole under the command of Colonel Haldimand, who afterward succeeded Sir Guy Carleton, as Governor-General and Commander-in-Chief in Canada. On the 10th, Gen. Amherst himself embarked with the remainder of the troops, being joined the next day by Gen. Gage with the Provincial troops, among which was a Connecticut regiment under the command of Lieut.-Col., afterward Brigadier-Gen. Israel Putnam. On the 13th of August, 1760, the whole army was encamped on Grenadier Island, and their boats safely moored in Basin Harbor.

By noon of the 14th, everything was in readiness to move, and the troops were ordered to get their dinners and then embark at once. At two o'clock they were sweeping down the south channel of the St. Lawrence in two lines of boats which reached almost from shore to shore. It was an inspiring sight. The long lines of boats, decorated with flags and streamers and guidons, the rowers keeping time with their oars to the music of the military bands, relieved at times by the bugles of the Grenadiers and the pipes of the Scotch Highlanders, while the two vessels, the Onondaga and Mohawk, led the advance.

But the French were not asleep. For some time a squad of soldiers, under the command of a lieutenant, had been stationed on Isle aux Chevreuils, now Carlton Island, from the high grounds of which a splendid view of the lake is to be had, as a corps of observation. With this squad was a small body of Indian scouts, one or two of whom, in swift canoes, were detached at intervals to the fort below to warn its commander of the approach of the English army. Waiting until the entire fleet had entered the river, so that there was no longer any doubt as to its destination, the lieutenant and his men went on board a batteau, and rowed away down the river. It was this batteau which led Capt. Loring of the Onondaga into trouble. But we will let an extract from the journal, kept by the gallant captain, tell the tale:

"Aug. 14th.—This afternoon the entire fleet set sail, and at three of the clock was well within the south channel of the St. Lawrence river, near the island called, by the French, Isle aux Chevreuil, and by us Buck Island, from the foot of which the lookout at the masthead discovered a batteau loaded with French soldiers put off, when I knew at once that the enemy had knowledge of the expedition, and though the wind was light, I signalled the Mohawk and gave chase, hoping to get the batteau within range of my bow guns, but which I failed to do. The Onondaga was now nearly a league ahead of the Mohawk, and the flotilla was yet another league in the rear, the entire fleet being fully eight leagues from where it set sail. At a point where three hills project into the river, the batteau veered away and ran down through a long narrow channel between what seemed to be a large island and some smaller ones, and out into a large bay, beyond which stretched another broad channel, easily seen from the masthead. Having sounded and found deep water, I decided to follow; but owing to light winds our progress was slow, though in running through the narrow channel we gained somewhat on the batteau, which we soon lost sight of among the islands in the north channel, which are very numerous, with narrow swift channels in every direction between them, very difficult to sail among unless favored with a strong breeze, which, unfortunately for us, was now very light, and to add to our difficulties, night was at hand. Had we not been able to distinguish the islands from the lookout at the masthead, we might have thought that the main land lay ahead of us, but with what we could see from that point, and finding that the current set strongly in that direction, and knowing from some previous experience among the islands above that the channels between the islands were likely to be deep. I determined to hold on to our course, not doubting that we should run safely through the archipelago, if it be proper to so call a cluster of islands that are not in the sea. So the Fates would have it, however, we were no sooner fairly within what seemed to be the largest channel than the vessel was attacked on every side from the summits of the islands, which were covered with trees and thickets, and our deck was fairly swept with arrows and musketry, while at the same time we seemed about to strike 'bows on' to a precipice directly ahead. I immediately ordered Coxswain Terry and his crew to lower away one of the quarter boats, with a message to the Mohawk to turn back to the other channel, and then sent the men to the guns quickly, driving the enemy from the summits of the islands and into their canoes, when they soon escaped into the numerous channels on either hand.

Ordering another boat lowered, a suitable channel was soon found, through which we passed safely, and anchored about a league below the thickest of the group of islands, and waited for Coxswain Terry and his crew to return. After some time, I ordered Ensign Barry to take the cutter and search for the coxswain and his crew. After some hours Ensign Barry returned. He had been bewildered among the numerous channels, not being able to even distinguish the channels through which the vessel had come, nor the one by which she entered the group of islands, nor had he discovered the first boat lowered. Ensign Barry called it "The River of the Lost Channel," and in that way was it ever after spoken of among the men. Thinking that Coxswain Terry and his crew had boarded the Mohawk, and that they would return to us when we joined the fleet, I determined to sail as soon as the wind freshened.

"Aug. 15th. All this day there was a strong head wind, and after sounding and finding shallow water in several places, I did not think it best to tack for fear of running aground."

"Aug. 16th. The lookout discovered a vessel this morning at a distance of about four leagues coming up the river, but we could not make her out. Presuming that it was a French vessel, as we knew that they had an armed brig below, we got springs on our cables in order to veer if attacked, but she did not come nearer to us than three leagues."

"Aug. 17th Wind still contrary. There has been heavy cannonading down the river to-day about four leagues distant but hid from us by islands. It cannot be at the French Fort, which cannot be less than fifteen leagues distant."

"Aug. 18th. Got under weigh this afternoon, and will soon be with the army."

"Aug. 19th. Reached the army to-day, and reported to Gen. Amherst. Coxswain Terry and his crew are undoubtedly lost, as they did not board the Mohawk, but started to return to the Onondaga. The firing on the day before yesterday, was the attack on the French brig by our armed gallies under the command of Col. Williamson, who captured her after a severe engagement lasting four hours. It was a most gallant affair. The brig has been named the Williamson, after the gallant colonel. The fort is to be invested to-morrow."

In speaking of this very affair the historian Mantè says:

"All this while, one of the enemy's vessels kept hovering about the army, and as Captain Loring had not yet got into the right channel, it became necessary for the safety of the army, either to compel this vessel to retire or to take her. The general was therefore obliged to order Colonel Williamson with the row gallies well manned, to do one or the other."

Then follows an account of the battle and of the ill luck which seemed to have followed Captain Loring during the attack on the fort, at which time his vessel ran aground and was very nearly taken possession of by the enemy. But as any further description of the capture of Fort Levis is not germane to our history, because it took place beyond the limits of the Thousand Islands, we bring the article to a close, having shown the reader that the name "Lost Channel" is by no means a modern invention.

THE CASTORLAND COLONY.

INTIMATELY related to the St. Lawrence, though not bounded by its very shores, was Castorland. It is described most graphically in "Haddock's History of Jefferson County," pp. 113 to 118. It is intensely interesting, as showing the futility of any plan which takes artisans and mechanics from a large city and plants them upon the soil of a primitive wilderness, has a stop-cock in it, such as you see in kitchen wash-sinks, to prevent the too great rush of the fluid — so that when a bucketful had been drawn the cock could be turned so as to lose no sap while the attendant was emptying the bucket! Those who know the way in which sap runs, a single drop at a time, will find something here to laugh over.

FISHING OFF THE HEAD OF "LITTLE GRENADIER," CANADIAN CHANNEL.

derness, where a knowledge both of woodcraft and of husbandry is every day required. In the illustration of their seal, shown on another page, the reader will notice the "Goddess of Agriculture" standing by a maple tree, from which sap is flowing into a bucket. Please to observe the faucet. It But it was not a matter of laughter for these poor people, whose sufferings, like those of the United Empire Loyalists (driven out of this country into Canada, because they would not ignore their oaths to King George) were severe and in some cases fatal. But we will let Major Haddock tell the story in his own way.

CASTORLAND AND THE FRENCH SETTLEMENT THERE.

TO the excellent article by Hon. Mr. Ingalls, upon the "Waterways of Jefferson County" (see pages 9–12 of Haddock's History), we wish to add a few general remarks. It is a peculiar characteristic, marking all the rivers that flow in and around Northern New York, that, excepting only the Mohawk, all of them flow from and through larger or smaller chains of lakes. The noble St. Lawrence itself, which forms the natural and intensely picturesque northwestern boundary of Jefferson county, seems to be the vast prototype and pattern for all the others, as it flows from its own great continental system of lakes. The Hudson, flowing eastward like the Mohawk, is fed by a system of forest branches which spread over the entire mountain belt of the Adirondack wilderness, the head waters of some of its tributaries being over 5,000 feet above the level of the sea. But, however interesting it may be to follow out this train of thought, our space constrains us to confine our remarks to the streams which flow into and through Jefferson county, or relate to waterways touching that county. Their influence upon the early settlements of the northern wilderness of 1793, in drawing to the Black River country those in pursuit of water power to drive factories, can never be prized too highly, nor too patiently described. These waters attracted to this locality those whose minds were profoundly stirred by that intense activity which always precedes great discoveries and great movements of populations.

The Black River bounds the Great Wilderness plateau of Laurentian rocks on the west, and its valley bounds the Lesser Wildnerness on the east. The principal confluents that enter the Black River from the Great Wilderness, are the Moose, Otter Creek, the Independence, and the Beaver.

The Moose River rises near the Raquette Lake in the center of the wilderness, and winds through and forms the celebrated Eight Lakes of the Fulton chain. The Moose passes in its course the hunting station known to all frequenters of the woods as Arnold's, or the Old Forge, on Brown's Tract. This secluded spot has long been famous in forest story as the scene of John Brown's[*] fruitless attempt at settlement, of the failure and tragic death of his son-in-law Herreshoff, of the exploits of the hunter Foster and his victim, the Indian Drid, and of the life-long home of Otis Arnold, the hunter and guide.

The Independence River rises near the Eight Lakes of the Fulton chain and runs into Black River in the town of Watson, Lewis county, between the Moose River and the Beaver River. In its course, this river crosses the tract of wild land known to land speculators as Watson's West Triangle. The Independence River was so named in honor of our national holiday by Pierre Pharoux, the engineer and surveyor of Castorland. Near the south bank of the Independence, not far from the old Watson house, is Chase's lake. This lake has long been a favorite resort, and is one of the most accessible in the Wilderness for the invalid or pleasure seeker. The Beaver River rises in the heart of the Wilderness to the north of Raquette Lake, and running in its course through Smith's Lake, Albany Lake, and Beaver Lake, waters the territory of ancient

---

[*] Not the John Brown, of Harper's-Ferry fame, "whose body lies a mouldering in the ground, but whose soul is marching on."

Castorland, the seat of French influence on the Black River. Beaver Lake, an expansion of this river at Number Four, a famous summer resort, is one of the most charming lakes in the wilderness.

Among the problematical places of the olden times in Northern New York, whose names were once familiar in European circles but are seldom heard in modern story, no one was once more famous than La Famine.

Two hundred years ago, La Famine was a well-known stopping-place upon the eastern shore of Lake Ontario for the weary hunter and the bold explorer, and the spot where even armies encamped, and the ambassadors of hostile nations met in solemn council.

of the Lesser Wilderness from the west was the Salmon River. On their way to the hunting ground through Lake Ontario, the western Indians landed at the mouth of this river, and their trail then led up its banks.

La Famine then was the ancient seaport of this famous hunting ground of the Lesser Wilderness, and was situated near what is now the village of Mexico, Oswego county. Hence we find on a map of New France, published by Marco Vincenzo Coronelli, in 1688, this place put down at the mouth of what is now known as the Salmon River, but in his map it is called La Famine River. It bears the following inscription: "La Famine, lieu ou la plus part des Iroquois des barquet pour

MEDAL ISSUED BY THE CHASSNAIS FRANCO-AMERICAN LAND COMPANY.
[Enlarged one half, from an original in possession of the Jefferson County Historical Society.]

To-day its name can only be found on the historic page and in the old maps and musty records, while its locality is often a matter of controversy. The ancient Indian landing-place and camping-ground known to the French as La Famine, was situated on the shore of Famine Bay, now called Mexico Bay, in the southeast corner of Lake Ontario, at the mouth of La Famine River, now known as Salmon River.

The Salmon River, the ancient French La Famine, rises in the central part of the plateau of the Lesser Wilderness in the southwest corner of Lewis county, and runs westerly through the northern part of Oswego county into Lake Ontario. The Lesser Wilderness was one of the beaver-hunting countries of the Iroquois. The key to this hunting ground

aller in traitte du Castor," which may be translated thus: "La Famine, the place where the greater part of the Iroquois embarked to go upon the trail of the beaver."

The Lesser Wilderness of Northern New York is situated upon the long narrow plateau which stretches first westerly and then northerly from the Upper Mohawk valley and the Oneida Lake almost to the village of Carthage. The rocky ground-work of this plateau is composed of level strata of limestone and slate, which rise in a series of terraces of a mile or two in width from its borders into a high level table land, which has an elevation of nearly 2,000 feet above the level of the sea. Upon the central part of this table land are situated the forests, swamps, marshes and wild meadows of the Lesser Wilderness.

Down the more regular terraces of its western slope, locally called Tug Hill, the streams which rise in the swamps of the Lesser Wilderness hurry in a series of falls and cascades into the Black River, wearing deep chasms in the yielding rocks along their courses. Among these streams are the Deer River, the Silvermine, the Martin, the Whetstone and other creeks.

This Lesser Wilderness was one of the most famous hunting grounds of the Indian. Its woods were literally filled with game, and its streams with fish. La Hontan says that there were so many salmon in La Famine River that they often brought up a hundred at one cast of the net.

CASTORLAND.

The summer tourist, on his way from Trenton Falls to the Thousand Islands, may pass through the beautiful and flourishing valley of the Black River, over the Utica and Black River Railroad. As the train draws near to the first station north of the village of Lowville, he will hear the sharp voice of the brakeman crying out "Cas-tor-land." He will look out of the car window and see a wide level clearing of pasture-land and meadow, skirted by forests, one side of which is bounded by the river. In the middle of this clearing he will see only the small station house, and three or four scattered buildings surrounding it, and will doubtless wonder whence comes the high-sounding name for such meagre surroundings.

The story of Castorland is the often repeated tale of frustrated settlements in the old wilderness—the story of an attempt of the exiled nobility and clergy of the old régime in France to found a settlement in the wilds of the New World, where they could find a secure retreat from the horrors of the Revolution in the Old.

This attempt was made at the close of the last century in the valley of the Black River, on the western slope of the Great Wilderness. But, like the settlement of the first Catholics on the Patuxent, the Jacobites with Flora McDonald at Cape Fear, the Huguenots with Jean Ribault at Port Royal; like New Amsterdam on the Hudson, New Sweden on the Delaware; like Acadie in Nova Scotia,—Castorland on the Black River lives now only in poetry and history. Its story is one of brilliant promises all unfulfilled, of hopes deferred, of man's tireless but fruitless endeavor, of woman's tears.

To rescue this name so fraught with historical associations from oblivion, it was applied to the railroad station which is nearest to the site of the largest projected city of ancient Castorland. That city was laid out on the Beaver River, which flows into the Black River from the wilderness nearly opposite this station.

For the purpose of effecting the settlement of Castorland a company was formed in Paris, under the laws of France, in the month of August, 1792, and styled La Compagnie de New York. On the 31st day of the same month the company, by its agent, Pierre Chassanis, bought a large tract of land lying in the valley of the Black River, of William Constable, who was the owner of Macomb's Purchase. This tract lay along both sides of the Black River below the High Falls, and extended westerly through the counties of Lewis and Jefferson to Lake Ontario, and easterly into the heart of the Great Wilderness. The Castorland purchase at first comprised the whole of great lot No. 5 of Macomb's purchase, and contained 610,000 acres. But subsequently all south and west of the Black River, being the part which now constitutes the richest towns of Lewis and Jefferson counties, was given up, and only that lying to the north and east of the river retained. The portion so retained contained only 210,000 acres. This was the Castorland of the olden times.

The name Castorland, that is to say, the Land of Beavers, is doubtless a literal translation of the old Indian word, which means the "Beaver Hunting Country," Castorland being taken out of the western half of this old Indian hunting ground.

During the negotiations between Constable and Chassanis for this tract, the French Revolution, that had been so long smouldering, burst forth in all its savage fury, and the streets of Paris were slippery with human gore. Constable locked the door of the apartment in which they met, with the remark that "if they parted before the purchase was completed they might never meet again." The palace of the Tuilleries was already surrounded by the bloodthirsty mob. The attendants of the royal family were butchered, and the feeble king cast into a dungeon. In comparison with such awful scenes as these in the very heart of the highest civilization the world had ever seen, the savage wilderness of the old American forests was a scene of peaceful rest. To the fugitive noblesse of France, the former possessors of great titles, rank, wealth and culture, the quiet shades of Castorland afforded a secure asylum from the horrors of the Reign of Terror.

SCHEME OF SETTLEMENT.

A romantic scheme was at once conceived and perfected by the company in Paris for the settlement of Castorland. In pursuance of this scheme a pamphlet was printed in Paris and issued by the Company, containing a programme of colonization under its auspices. This pamphlet was entitled "Association for the purchase and settlement of 600,000 acres of land, granted by the State of New York, and situated within that State, between the 43d and 44th degrees of latitude, upon Lake Ontario, and thirty-five leagues from the city and port of Albany, where vessels land from Europe." It set forth, among other things, in glowing colors, the wealth of agriculture presented by its fertile soil, the fine distribution of its waters, its facilities for an extended commerce on account of its location in the vicinity of a dense population, and above all the security afforded to its inhabitants by the laws of a people who were independent and rich with their own capital, thus extending to the immigrant all the benefits of liberty with none of its drawbacks. It was stated that the object of the proprietors was to form of the colony a sort of family, in some way united by common interests and common wants, and that to maintain this union of interests a plan had been devised that rendered each member directly interested in the whole property. It was to be done by and in the name of Sieur Chassanis, in whose name they had purchased the estate, and who alone had power to issue certificates of ownership.

There were 6,000 certificates to be issued, each entitling the holder thereof to ownership in manner following: The whole tract at that time consisted of 630,000 acres. Of this 600,000 were divided into 12,000 lots of fifty acres each, and the price of each share fixed at 800 livres ($152.38). In the beginning, 6,000 lots were set apart for individual properties, and the other 6,000 lots were to belong to a common stock which was to be divided at some future time, after improvements had been made thereon by the company. Each holder of a certificate was to receive at once a deed for a separate lot of fifty acres, to be drawn by lot, and also a lot of fifty acres in the common undivided stock.

Of the 30,000 remaining acres, 2,000 were set apart for a city to be formed on the great river in the interior, and 2,000 more for another city on Lake Ontario, at the mouth of the Black River, which was to form a port and entrepot of commerce. Among artisans 6,000 acres were to be divided and rented to them at twelve sous per acre. The proceeds of the 20,000 acres remaining were to be expended by the Company in the construction of roads, bridges and other improvements.

The two cities were divided into 14,000 lots each. Of these lots, 2,000 were set apart for churches, schools, markets, etc. The remaining 12,000 lots were to be divided among the 6,000 holders of certificates in the same manner as the large tract,— each holding one separate lot and one in common.

The affairs of the company were to be managed by five trustees, three to remain in Paris and two upon the tract.

Such was the scheme matured in the salons of Paris for the settlement of Castorland. Beautiful and promising beyond measure upon aper, as an ideal, but utterly impracticable

and bitterly disappointing as a reality. Yet many shares were eagerly taken.

Organization.

On the 28th of June, 1793, it being the second year of the French Republic, the actual holders of certificates convertible into shares of La Compagnie de New York met in the rooms of Citizen Chassanis, in Paris, to organize their society upon the basis already established, and to regulate the division, survey and settlement of their lands. There were present at that meeting forty-one shareholders in all, who represented 1,880 shares. They perfected and completed their organization; they adopted a long and elaborate constitution; they chose a seal for their corporation, and appointed five commissaries to manage its affairs, three for Paris and two for Castorland. In the meantime the tract had been re-conveyed, and the large part lying west and south of the Black River given up, the part retained being that lying east and north of the river, and containing only 210,000 acres. To accord with this fact the number of shares was reduced from 6,000 to 2,000. It was at this meeting that a silver piece was ordered to be struck, termed a "Jetton de presence," one of which was to be given at every meeting to each commissary as an attendance fee.* [See engraving, p. 184.]

---

* These pieces occur in coin cabinets, and have been erroneously called "Castorland half-dollars." A jetton is a piece of metal struck with a device, and distributed to be kept in commemoration of some event, or to be used as a counter in games of chance. The one here noticed was termed a "jetton de presence," or piece "given in certain societies or companies to each of the members at a session or meeting." It was engraved by one of the Duvivier brothers, eminent coin and metal artists of Paris. The design represents on the obverse the head of Cybele, who personified the earth as inhabited or cultivated, while on the reverse Ceres has just tapped a maple tree, in which will be observed a spout provided with a stop to withhold the sweet sap when it flowed too fast !

The Latin legend on the reverse is a quotation from Virgil, which, with its context, reads :

"*Salva magna parens frugum, Saturnia tellus magna virum.*"

The commissaries appointed for America were Simon Desjardines and Pierre Pharoux, who lost no time in proceeding to America to execute their important trust. Desjardines had been a Chamberlain of Louis XVI. He was of middle age, an accomplished scholar and gentleman, but knew not a word of English when he arrived. He had with him his wife and three children, and his younger brother, Geoffry Desjardines, who shared his labors and trials. He also brought with him his library of 2,000 volumes. Pierre Pharoux, the surveyor, who was afterwards drowned, was a distinguished young architect and engineer of Paris, of high scientific attainments and marked ability. He was earnestly and faithfully devoted to his duties; and his love of science, his honesty, his good sense, and genial and ardent friendship were manifested in all his doings. He left behind him in France an aged father to mourn his untimely death.

They sailed from Havre on the 4th day of July, 1793, in the American ship Liberty, but did not arrive in New York until the 7th of September following. There came over in the same vessel with them a young French refugee named Mark Isambart Brunel, who afterward filled the world with his fame as an engineer in England. Brunel had been in the French navy, and was driven from home on account of his royalistic proclivities. He went with them in all their journeys through the wilderness, and shared in all their hardships during the first year, but does not seem to have been employed by them in Castorland.

Their First Exploration.

Soon after their arrival in this country, Desjardines and Pharoux, with their friend Brunel, set out on a voyage of exploration to their "promised land" in the wild valley of the Black River. To realize the difficulties of the undertaking, the reader must bear in mind that the country they were in quest of lay far from Albany in the depths of a howling wilderness, which had then never been visited by white men, except around its border, or when carried across it as prisoners in savage hands; that the only route to it was up the Mohawk, in batteaux, to Fort Stanwix, now the city of Rome; thence by the way of Wood creek, the Oneida lake, and the Oswego river to Lake Ontario, and from Lake Ontario up the unexplored route of the Black River. It was over the old Indian trail, the savage warpath of the French and Indian and of the Revolutionary wars, and even then there was threatened a general Indian war by all the tribes around our borders. But in the face of all these difficulties our explorers, in the autumn of 1793, set out for Castorland.

In describing their passage over the carrying place from Fort Stanwix to Wood creek, of these trunks, presenting at once the images of life and death."

The fort at Oswego was still held by a British garrison. Jealous of Frenchmen, the commander at first refused to allow them to pass into Lake Ontario, but it was finally arranged that Brunel should remain as a hostage for the good conduct and safe return of the others. Brunel, however, was refused access to the fort, and was ordered to encamp alone in the woods on the opposite side of the river. Considering that such treatment invalidated his parole, he escaped from Oswego disguised as a common sailor, and proceeded with his friends on their expedition. They

TOO BIG FOR THE BOX. A 20 pounder.

near where the four busy tracks of the New York Central Railroad now run, they wrote in their journal, under date of October 10th: "Upon taking a walk into the woods a short distance we saw on every hand it was a fearful solitude. You are stopped sometimes by impassable swamps, and at other times by heaps of trees that have fallen from age or have been overthrown by storms, and among which an infinite number of insects and many squirrels find a retreat. On every hand we see the skeletons of trees overgrown with moss and in every stage of decay. The capillaire and other plants and shrubs spring out proceeded cautiously along the shore of the lake over the route that had become historic by the presence of M. de la Barre and his army in their visit to La Famine in 1684, and of Father Charlevoix in 1720, and which had so often been traversed by their countrymen in the palmy days of the old French occupancy, until their arrival at Niaoure bay, now called Black River bay. Here after a long search they discovered the mouth of the Black River, the great river that watered Castorland. But it was already so late in the season that they only explored the river up to the point some five or six miles above the falls at Watertown, and then returned to Albany to complete their preparations for the next year's journey.

In the autumn of 1855, the Hon. Amelia M. Murray, maid of honor to Queen Victoria, made a tour of the United States and Canada, through the lake belt of the Wilderness, over the route now so much travelled. Her companions were Gov. Horatio Seymour, the Governor's niece and other friends. On their way they stopped, of course, at Arnold's. But I will let the Lady Amelia tell the story in her own words, as written in her diary, under date of September 20, 1855: "Mr. Seymour remained to make arrangements with the guides, while his niece and I walked on to Arnold's farm. There we found Mrs. Arnold and six daughters. These girls, aged from twelve to twenty, were placed in a row against one wall of the shanty, with looks so expressive of astonishment, that I felt puzzled to account for their manner, till their mother informed us they had never before seen any other woman than herself! I could not elicit a word from them, but, at last, when I begged for a little milk, the eldest went and brought me a glass (tin cup). Then I remembered that we had met a single hunter rowing himself on the Moose River, who called out, 'Where on 'arth do them women come from?' And our after experience fully explained why ladies are such rare birds in that locality."

THE SETTLEMENT OF CASTORLAND.

The next spring, being in the year 1794, the Desjardines Brothers and Pharoux, with a large company of men, with their surveyors and assistants, took up their toilsome journey from Schenectady to their forest possessions, being this time fully equipped to begin their settlement. Their route this year was up the Mohawk in batteaux to Fort Schuyler, now Utica, thence overland across the Deerfield hills sixteen miles, to the log house of Baron Steuben, who had then just commenced his improvements upon his tract of 16,000 acres,

granted him by the State. From Steuben's it was twenty-four miles further through the trackless forest to the High Falls on the Black River in Castorland.

The difficulties of the journey then still before them can scarcely be imagined by the reader of to-day. At length they reached

38ᴸᵇ MUSKALLONGE.

their tract on the welcome banks of the Black River, and began their labors. But there is no space in these pages to follow them in their operations, in their sore trials and their bitter disappointments, their final discomfiture and utter failure.

Suffice it to say that they began a little settlement on the banks of the Black River, at the place now called Lyon's Falls. That they surveyed their lands and laid out one of their cities, Castorville, on the Beaver river, at a place now called Beaverton, opposite the little station now called Castorland, in memory of their enterprise. That they laid out their other city, the lake port, which they named "City of Basle," at what is now Dexter, below Watertown, and in 1795 they founded the present village of Carthage. That Pharoux was accidentally drowned in the river at Watertown in the fall of 1795. That Desjardines gave up the agency in despair in 1797 and was succeeded by Rudolphe Tillier, "Member of the Sovereign Council of Berne," who in turn gave place to Gouverneur Morris in 1800, and that the lands finally became the property of James Donatien Le Ray de Chaumont, his associates and grantees.

"After toil and many troubles, self-exiled for many years,
Long delays and sad misfortunes, man's regrets and woman's tears;
Unfulfilled the brilliant outset, broken as a chain of sand,
Were the golden expectations by Grande Rapides' promised land."

DEATH OF PIERRE PHAROUX.

One of the saddest incidents in the story of Castorland is the death of Pharoux, at the falls of Watertown, in 1795. In September of that year, after the river had been swollen by heavy rains, Pharoux set out with Brodhead, Tassart and others, all surveyors, on a journey to Kingston. In passing down the river on a raft, they were drawn over the falls. Mr. Brodhead and three men were saved, but Pharoux was drowned. The survivors made unremitting search for Pharoux's body, but it was not found until the following spring. It was washed ashore upon an island at the mouth of Black River, where it was found by Benjamin Wright, the surveyor, and by him decently buried there. M. LeRay de Chaumont many years afterwards caused a marble tablet to be set in the rock near his grave, bearing this inscription:

TO THE MEMORY OF
PIERRE PHAROUX,
THIS ISLAND IS CONSECRATED.

The reader will remember that the year before his death, Pharoux had discovered and named the river Independence, in Castorland, and had selected a beautiful spot at its mouth on the Black River, near a large flat granite rock, for his residence. This spot, called by the Desjardines Brothers Independence Rock, was ever afterwards regarded by them with melancholy interest. They could not pass it without shedding tears to the memory of their long-tried and trusted friend. Under date of May 28, 1796, Simon Desjardines, the elder brother, recorded in his journal: "Landed at half-past two at Independence Rock, and visited once more this charming spot which had been so beautifully chosen by our friend Pharoux as the site for his house. The azaleas in full bloom loaded the air with their perfume, and the wild birds sang sweetly around their nests, but nature has no longer any pleasant sights, nor fragrance, nor music, for me."

CASTORLAND, ADIEU!

And now ancient Castorland may be added to the long list of names once famous in the cities of Europe, and long celebrated in the forest annals of Northern New York, but now forgotten, and found only in history and song — feebly commemorated by the name of an insignificant railway station.

DESCRIPTIONS OF THE THOUSAND ISLANDS.

By Travellers and by Historical and Statistical Writers.

FATHER CHARLEVOIX—(1721)

PIERRE FRANCOIS XAVIER CHARLEVOIX was born in 1682, became a Jesuit priest, and in 1720-1722 made a voyage to North America under orders from the King of France. Passing up the St. Lawrence and through the lakes, he found his way to the Mississippi, and, after encountering many difficulties, finally reached San Domingo, and returned from thence to France. Besides his Journal of Travels, which was written in epistolary form, he wrote a History of New France, which is regarded as high authority. He closed a life devoted to study and travel, on the 18th of February, 1761.

The Journal of his Travels abounds in historical, ethnological and topographical information, and he was a close observer of Natural History. His description of this region is brief, and is given in a letter dated at Catarocoui (Kingston), May 14, 1721, in which he says:

' Five or six leagues from la Galette is an island called *Toniata*, the soil of which appears tolerably fertile, and which is about half a league long. An Iroquois called '*The Quaker*,' for what reason I know not—a man of excellent good sense, and much devoted to the French—had obtained the right of it from the Count de Frontenac, and he shows his Patent to everybody that desires to see it. He has, however, sold his Lordship for four pots of brandy; but he has reserved the usufruct for his own life, and has got together on it eighteen or twenty families of his own nation. I found him at work in his garden; this is not usual with the Indians, but this person affects to follow all the French manners. He received me very well, and would have regaled me, but the fine weather invited me to pursue my voyage.

I took my leave of him, and went to pass the night two leagues from hence, in a very pleasant spot. I had still thirteen leagues to sail before I could reach Catarocoui; the weather was fine, and the night very clear. This prevailed with us to embark at three in the morning. We passed through the middle of a kind of an archipelago, which they call *Mille Îles* (the Thousand Isles), and I believe there are above five hundred of them. After you have got from among them, you have only a league and a half to sail to reach Catarocoui. The river is open, and is full half a league wide. You then leave upon the right three great bays, pretty deep, and the fort is built in the third."

Fort Catarocoui was described by Charlevoix as a square, with four bastions, built with stone, and the ground it occupies as a quarter of a league in circuit. The situation was very pleasant, and the view upon the river remarkably fine.

An anonymous folio printed for Thomas Jeffreys in 1760, repeats (page 15) the account given by Charlevoix about the Indian living on Toniata Island, and what is said by him concerning the Thousand Islands.

JAMES FENIMORE COOPER'S IDEAL "STATION ISLAND."

(Assumed to be about 1755.)

In the third of his series of "Leather-Stocking Tales," as placed by its author, although not in the order of publication, is "THE PATHFINDER," a romance by some regarded as the most pleasing of the many that were sketched by the pen of this popular writer. In his youth, JAMES COOPER (as he was known until a middle name was inserted by a special act of the Legislature of New

York, in 1826), had been a Midshipman in the American Navy, and in this capacity was stationed for a time at Oswego, where the first beginning was made in the construction of an American naval armament upon Lake Ontario, under Commodore Woolsey, in the summer of 1808. Of this period of his life, the author himself says:

"This was pretty early in the present century, when the navigation was still confined to the employment of a few ships and schooners. Since that day, light may be said to have broken into the wilderness, and the rays of the sun have penetrated to tens of thousands of beautiful valleys and plains, that then lay in 'grateful shade.' Towns have been built along the whole of the extended line of coasts, and the traveller now stops at many places of ten or fifteen, and at one of even fifty thousand inhabitants, where a few huts then marked the sites of future marts."

Amid these familiar scenes, Cooper laid the plan of his romance, and the descriptions of scenery and of natural topography which the book contains, he regards "as nearly accurate as is required by the laws which govern fiction," although these wild solitudes of Lake Ontario as he saw them, are so no longer. The period assigned for the romance, was about the middle of the last century, while the English held a military and trading post at Oswego, and the French the region to the north and west of the lake, extending in a chain of posts from their possessions in Lower Canada to those on the Mississippi. It was not long before the hostilities began that ended in the conquest of the French in Canada, and the full establishment of the English power, and of peace along the whole line of this memorable frontier.

We will not attempt to give an outline of the plot of the tale, leaving that to be known by those who would wish the details from the book itself. It is sufficient for our present use, to copy some of the descriptions of scenery of the Thousand Islands,— among the intricate mazes of which the author has placed THE STATION, upon which depends a part of the plot. It was, indeed, as he represented it, in that day, a place hard to find, the approach being full of difficulties and dangers. The way was known to but a favored few, to whom the secret was in confidence entrusted, and the place is now, like Calypso's favored Isle, an open question for those who choose to explore:

"The Station, as the place was familiarly termed by the soldiers of the 55th, was indeed a spot to raise expectations of enjoyment among those who had been cooped up so long in a vessel of the dimensions of the 'Scud.' None of the islands were high, though all lay at a sufficient elevation above the water to render them perfectly healthy and secure. Each had more or less of wood, and the greater number at that distant day were clothed with the virgin forest. The one selected by the troops for their purpose was small, containing about twenty acres of land, and by some of the accidents of the wilderness, it has been partly stripped of its trees, probably centuries before the period of which we are writing, and a little grassy glade covered nearly half its surface. It was the opinion of the officer who had made the selection of this spot for a military post, that a sparkling spring near by had early caught the attention of the Indians, and that they had long frequented this particular place in their hunts, or when fishing for salmon — a circumstance that had kept down the second-growth, and given time for the natural grasses to take root, and to gain dominion over the soil. Let the cause be what it might, the effect was to render this island far more beautiful than most of those around it, and to lend an air of civilization that was then wanting in so much of that vast region of country.

"The shores of Station Island were completely fringed with bushes, and great care had been taken to preserve them, as they answered as a screen to conceal the persons and things collected within their circle. Favored by this shelter as well as that of several thickets of trees and different coppices, some six or eight low huts had been erected to be used as quarters for the officer and his men, to contain stores, and to serve the purposes of kitchen, hospital, etc. These huts were built of logs, in the usual manner, had been roofed by bark brought from a distance, lest signs of labor should attract attention, and, as they had now been inhabited some months, were as comfortable as dwellings of that description usually ever got to be.

"At the eastern extremity of the island, however, was a small, dense-wooded peninsula, with a thicket of underbrush so thickly matted as nearly to prevent the possibility of seeing across it, so long as the leaves remained on the branches. Near the narrow neck that connected this acre with the rest of the island, a small block house had been erected with some attention to its means of resistance. The logs were bullet proof, squared and joined with a care to leave no defenceless points; the windows were loopholes; the door massive and small; and the roof, like

LOOKING EAST FROM SMOKE ISLAND.

DESCRIPTIONS OF THE THOUSAND ISLANDS. 197

the rest of the structure, was framed of hewn timber, covered properly with bark to exclude the rain. The lower apartment, as usual, contained stores and provisions; here, indeed, the party kept all their supplies; the second story was intended for a dwelling as well as for a citadel, and a low garret was subdivided into two or three rooms, and could hold the pallets of some ten or fifteen persons. All the arrangements were exceedingly simple and cheap, but they were sufficient to protect the soldiers against the effects of a surprise. As the whole building was considerably less than forty feet high, its summit was concealed by the tops of the trees, except from the eyes of those who had reached the interior of the island. On that side the view was open from the upper loops, though bushes, even there, more or less concealed the base of the wooden tower. The object being purely defense, care had been taken to place the block house so near an opening in the limestone rock that formed the base of the island, as to admit of a bucket's being dropped into the water, in order to obtain that great essential, in the event of a siege. In order to facilitate this operation, and to enfilade the base of the building, the upper story projected several feet beyond the lower, in the manner usual to block houses, and pieces of wood filled the apertures cut in the log flooring, which were intended as loops and traps. The communications between the different stories were by means of ladders. If we add that these block houses were intended as citadels, for garrisons or settlements to retreat to in cases of attack, the general reader will obtain a sufficiently correct idea of the arrangements it is our wish to explain.

"But the situation of the island itself formed its principal merit as a military position. Lying in the midst of twenty others, it was not an easy matter to find it, since boats might pass quite near, and, by the glimpses caught through the openings, this particular island would be taken for a part of some other. Indeed, the channels between the islands that lay around the one we have been describing were so narrow, that it was even difficult to say which portions of the land were connected, or which separated, even as one stood in their centre, with the express desire of ascertaining the truth. The little bay in particular, that Jasper used as a harbor, was so embowered with bushes and shut in with islands, that the sails of the cutter being lowered, her own people, on one occasion, had searched for hours before they could find the 'Scud' in their return from a short excursion among the adjacent channels in quest of fish. In short, the place was admirably adapted to its present uses, and its natural advantages had been as ingeniously improved as economy and the limited means of a frontier post would very well allow."—(The Pathfinder, Chap. xix.)

CAPTAIN POUCHOT — (1760).

This writer was a Captain in the Regiment of Bèarn, in the war of 1755-60; was commander of the fort at Niagara when captured by Sir William Johnson in 1758, and again was captured in Fort Lévis, a little below Ogdensburg, where the last resistance was made by the French in the conquest of Canada, in 1760.

His Journal was published in Switzerland after his death, and affords much valuable information concerning the country as it existed in his day. In speaking of the customs of the Canadian voyageurs, he remarks that in ascending the river in their bateaux, they kept as near as possible to the north shore. Of the river above, he says:

"At five leagues from Pointe au Baril [near the present village of Maitland] is the Island of Toniata. The main channel of the river is between this island and the south shore. The north part of the river is filled with rushes, and in summer is a celebrated eel fishery.

"The Island of Toniata is three leagues long by a quarter of a league wide. At the upper end is a little passage with but little water, and full of rushes, which they call the Petit Detroit. This is the route that bateaux always take in going up to avoid the currents.

"We should notice that we ought to pay no attention to the little channels which we meet among the rushes, and which have no outlet and would ground a vessel.

"At the Petit Detroit they perform the ceremony of 'baptizing' those who have never gone up the river before.

"At a league and a half above, begins the Thousand Islands, which continue at least three leagues. There are an infinite number of little rocks covered with trees, with channels quite large in some places. In others, vessels in passing through would almost touch them. They are very safe, almost always have a good depth of water all around them, and there is but a slight current.

"At the end of three leagues we find larger islands. We should take care and not go astray. In following the bateaux channel nearest the north side, we shall notice several inlets ending in marshes, which are near the shore.

"It is necessary to turn very short to enter the Bay of Corbeau, which is large and fine. We pass between the south point, which is very straight, and a little island which we have to pass very near. From thence they coast along the Isle au Citron, which is a good league in length. It is fine and well wooded.

"They make a crossing of three leagues to reach the Isle Cochois, which is three leagues long, and half a league wide, abounding in game and fish.

"The view from the foot of this island, with the neighboring islands and the north shore, forms a prospect most delightful on account of the beauty of the channels. This part appears to be very proper for cultivation, and good for hunting and fishing. From thence to Frontenac is three leagues. We find the bay sufficiently deep and quite good before coming to Montreal Point, which is the south point of the Bay of Catarucoui."

JOHN LONG.

This author, who was a roving Indian trader, appears to have met some adventures worthy of notice, although not immediately relating to the place more particularly under description. He stayed only a day or two in a place, bartered his goods for peltries till there were no more to buy, and then pushed off to a new field of enterprise. He stopped three days at the German Flats on the Mohawk — and on the 14th of September, 1784, arrived at the "Jenesee Lake," probably Seneca Lake of the present day.

A council was called, and he asked permission to stay awhile and trade. They deliberated, and returned the following answer:

"You are the Sugar, for so you are called in our tongue, but you must not have too much sweetness on your lips. All the Oneida Indians say they have heard that you are come only under a pretense to get our lands from us; but this must not be. My young warriors will not suffer any Englishman to settle here. You are like the Great Chief General Johnson, who asked for a spot of ground, or large bed, to lie on; and when Hendrick, the Chief of the Mohawks, had granted his request, he got possession of a great quantity of our hunting grounds; and we have reason to think that you intend to dream us out of our natural rights. We loved Sir William, and, therefore, consented to all his requests; but you are a stranger, and must not take these liberties; therefore, my advice is, that you depart to-morrow, at break of day, or you will be plundered by the young warriors, and it will not be in our power to redress you."

He "departed" for Fort Oswego, which he attempted to pass without permission; but was prevented by a sentinel, and his goods were all seized and confiscated.

In this miserable condition he got across to Cataroqui (Kingston), and put up at Howell's tavern. He afterwards took up 500 acres of land in this region, on the Canada side; but not liking the tame routine of farm life, he obtained another stock of goods, retired up the lake, and established himself at Pimitiscotyan Landing, on Lake Ontario. He had scarcely opened his premises for trade, before an officer took possession of everything he could find, even to the tent that sheltered him from the weather, and carried them down to Montreal, where everything was sold for less than a fourth part of its cost. Again stripped of his all, Mr. Long retired to the "Bay of Kenty," and lived ten months among the friendly United English Loyalists. Early in the spring of 1786, he crossed to Carlton Island, and thence proceeded to Oswego, intending to go into the States by post. Having no pass, he was there stopped, but returning eastward, he resolved to proceed from Salmon River through the woods to Fort Stanwix. Having rested a day, he set out with five pounds of pork, and two loaves of bread, with a companion, and a faithful Indian as a guide — but the old path was obliterated; they suffered great hardships, and were finally thankful at being able to get back to their point of departure alive. From there they made their way to Oswego along the shore, a distance not over twenty miles, but they were six days on the way. Towards the last, they were entirely without food, except wild onions (leeks); but, fortunately, they found on the sand about a hundred and forty birds' eggs, which they boiled and eagerly devoured, notwithstanding the greater part had young birds in them, with small down on their bodies. They were again turned back, and advised to proceed either to Niagara or Montreal, without further attempting to run their blockade. He adopted the latter alternative.

At this period, there were along the north bank of the St. Lawrence, beginning at Point au Baudet, and extending to the head of the Bay of Quinte, about ten thousand inhabitants, mostly Loyalists from the States, who had been driven out by the Revolution, and who were truly faithful subjects of the British Crown.

Cataroqui, or Fort Frontenac, was, in his day, held by a small garrison, and a commanding officer, who examined all boats that passed either to the new settlements or the upper posts. Mr. Long gives some notes upon the military defenses of this frontier, on the south side of the lake, after the close of the Revolution, that have historical interest:

"The first post I shall notice is Oswegatchie, on the River St. Lawrence, about one hundred and fifty miles above Montreal, at the mouth of the Black River, where there are about a hundred savages, who occasionally frequent it, and are called Oswegatchie Indians, although they belong to the tribes of the Five Nations. To this fort the inhabitants from New England may with ease transport goods to supply the Mohawks, Cahnuages, Conneedagas, St Regis, and some straggling Messesawger Indians, who live near the Detroit, at a smaller expense than they can possibly be obtained from the merchants of Quebec and Montreal, but particularly rum — which has now become an essential requisite in every transaction with the savages; for though they used formerly often to complain of the introduction of strong-water by the traders (as appears by the language of their chiefs in Council), to the prejudice of their young men, yet they have not now the resolution to refrain from the use of it. On the contrary, it is become so familiar, and even necessary to them, that a drunken frolic is looked upon as an indispensable requisite in a barter, and anticipated with extreme delight.

"Carleton Island is higher up the river, and has greater conveniences annexed to it than Oswegatchie, having an excellent harbor, with a strong fortification, well garrisoned. It affords excellent accommodation for shipping, and may be considered as the naval storehouse for supplying Niagara and the other posts. There are vessels of considerable bulk constantly sailing from thence to Niagara, Oswego, etc. There is also a Commodore of the Lakes, whose residence is on the Island."

Mr. Long gives some sketches of Indian life as it then existed in this region, that may be read with interest:

"Early one winter a newly married couple arrived, and having given them a little rum, they got very merry; and perceiving the woman was in great humor, I desired her to sing a love song, which she consented to do with cheerfulness.

THE SONG.

"Debwoye, nee zargay ween aighter, payshik oathty, seizee-bockquoit shenarguissey me tarbircoach nepeech cassawicka nepoo, moszack pemartus, seizeebockquoit meteek."

"It is true I love him only whose heart is like the sweet sap that runs from the sugar-tree, and is brother to the aspen-leaf that always lives and shivers"

In one of his descriptions, it would appear that he tarried among the Thousand Islands. The description is too obscure for us now to locate the place — but the account is as follows:

"I was then left with two white men, and two Indians and their wives. We passed our time in hunting and fishing; and as there were a great many small islands near us, we made frequent trips to shoot wild fowl, which enabled us to keep a good table. On one of the islands we discovered two Indian huts, but from their appearance no one had visited them for a length of time. About half a mile from the place we saw a high pole, daubed over with vermillion paint; on the top were placed three human skulls, and bones hung around. The Indians supposed it had been erected many years. About an hour before sunset we returned to our wigwams."

When he was living on the lake shore not far from the eastern end, he had a large dog for protecting himself and property. An Indian one day came in, rather the worse for rum, and attempted to strike the dog; but the animal instantly seized him by the calf of the leg, and wounded him dreadfully. The Indian returned to his hut, and made no complaint till the next day, when, being sober, he called and desired to speak to our trader. He told the master how he had been used by the dog, saying he hoped he would give him a new pair of leggins to supply those which the dog had torn; but that with regard to his leg, he did not trouble himself much about that, as he knew it would soon be well. Wounded flesh would heal — torn leather, never. The request was granted; the Indian retired with a bottle of rum as a present, with which he seemed well pleased, and nothing more was heard of the matter.

P. CAMPBELL—(1791).

This traveller set out from the Highlands of Scotland with an intention of exploring the interior of North America, and with an old and faithful servant, a dog and a gun, he travelled much in the wilderness, in birch-bark canoes, and through regions where comfort and safety were scarcely to be looked for, and often not enjoyed. Thus writing from day to day, in a canoe, or on the stumps of trees, or by the dim fire-light of a settler's cabin, he has given us impressions of the country as he saw it, that make up in vivid description for what he may lack in style. He had learned from a British officer that a lady was living on his way, whom he had known when she was a child, in a poor widow's family that he had befriended in time of need, and he resolved to visit her. She had married Captain Thomas F——, and was living not far from the river, We cannot describe the incident, which gives a pleasant glimpse of domestic life in those days, better than in his own language:

"When I came opposite to Captain F——'s house, which was a little way from the road, my servant said that was the place we had been directed to; but, on my looking about and remarking the good house, but a still larger barn of two stories high, several office houses, barracks or Dutch barns, the sufficiency and regularity of the rails, and extent of the enclosures, — considerable flocks of turkeys, geese, ducks and fowls, I said it could be no Highlander that owned that place, — that the barracks or Dutch barns were foreign to any Scotchman whatever; that I had not hitherto seen any of them that had such a thing; and that he must be a German who lived in that place. Still he affirmed this must be it, agreeable to the directions we had; but I could not be persuaded, and pushed on to the next house which was then in sight. When I came up, I asked for Captain F——'s, and was told I had left it behind; I, therefore, had to return.

"When I came in, they took no sort of notice of me, further than desiring me to sit down. My trowsers being torn with the bushes, and the rest of my dress being in the like situation, they supposed me to be a Yankee come from the States. After sitting awhile in this way, nobody speaking to me, or I to them, as Mrs. F—— happened to sit by me, I looked full in her face; and clearly recognizing her features, I accosted her in Gaelic and asked her if she had ever seen me before. She could not say whether she had or not. This turned the eyes of everybody in the house toward us; but on my asking if she had heard of or known such a person, naming myself, she said she did, and knew him very well, but could not suppose that I was him. On my saying I was, she turned about to her husband : 'My dear,' she said, 'this is the gentleman whom I often told you was so kind to us when he was Forester of Mam Lorn; and whatever disputes we and our neighbors had when our cattle trespassed upon the Forest, he always favored our family.'

"Captain F—— on this instantly welcomed me to his house, and ordered dinner and venison steaks to be got ready immediately. While dinner was getting, Mrs. F—— showed me nine or ten large, fat hogs, then lying dead on the floor of her keeping-house, and said they, every fall, killed twenty such, and two fat oxen, besides other provisions for their winter's store. After dinner Captain F—— treated me with port wine until we could drink no more, and pressed me much to stay that night; but as the boats had passed, I could not wait. When he found that I would be away, he ordered a couple of horses to be saddled immediately. * * * *

The boats arriving, I stepped on board, and the water now becoming smooth and more like a lake than a running stream, the wind favorable, we put up sails and made great way till late at night, when we put up at a poor, lame, ragged man's house, with a numerous family of small children; but the wife was buxom and well dressed. I and my Canadian crew threw ourselves down upon the floor opposite to the fire and slept soundly till four o'clock next morning, when we got up and set off in the usual way. The wind still favored us, and we soon entered the Thousand Islands, which never were, nor do I suppose ever will be counted, by reason of their numbers, and for which reason they were formerly called by the French, and now by the British, the Mille Iles. They are of very little value, and produce nothing but scraggy wood of useless pine. Here are innumerable flocks of water fowl, mostly of the teal kind. Such a diversity of creeks, bays, channels and harbors, I suppose is rarely to be met with in the world ; and if a crew be not well acquainted with the direct course, and if they once miss it, they may chance to be bewildered, and for days may not find it again. After passing these islands, we entered upon the lower end of Lake Ontario, and about night-fall arrived at Frontenac or Cataroqui, now called Kingston, and put up at the Coffee House."

Mr. Campbell describes Kingston as a young but promising town, most beautifully located, and already (within eight years after the beginning) a place of considerable trade. Over 6,000 bushels of wheat had been bought up and stored here the year before, and at least a fourth more would be purchased each succeeding year. He was told that six score of deer had been sold in town the same year, and venison was sold every day in the market. He met old acquaintances and formed new ones, and greatly admired Parson Stuart's farm, and the prospect from Sir John Johnson's house, that commanded a fine view of the harbor and town. Kingston was then looking forward to a time that seemed near, when the governor-general would here fix his abode, and the place would become a great emporium of trade, and the seat of government of Canada.

On the 24th of November, 1791, Mr. Campbell took passage on board the sloop "Colville," Captain Baker, for Niagara. The vessel was armed with two six-pounders and two swivels, and he had as a fellow passenger, Lieut. William McKay, a fellow countryman, whom he had met in Kingston. The day was hazy, and the wind fair, but promised no continuance at this late period in the year, and just on the verge of winter. The early part of his voyage brings us to a point of especial interest:

"We passed several large, woody, uninhabited islands. About night-fall, the wind changed to straight ahead — the captain, quite drunk, went to bed, the crew, little better, went to rest, and indeed, were almost useless when sober, as they seemed to know scarce anything at all of their business. No watch or reckoning was kept, and but an ignorant wretch at the helm. The wind increased, and now became a storm. In this way, beating to the windward, the night dark, and surrounded by land-shoals and islands, our situation could not be very agreeable. None of us knew where we were, and in fear of being aground every moment. A man was ordered to sound, and once sung out of a sudden, 'five fathoms.' I expected the next moment to hear her strike. The ship was put about, and the mistake in the sounding discovered to be owing to the ignorance of the sailor, and the lines having been entangled in the rails, as at the next sounding, no bottom was found. From these circumstances I clearly saw that if we escaped being wrecked, it would be a mere chance, and it appeared that there was at least five to one against us. * * * But drunk as this man was, before he went to bed, he ordered the main-sail to be double-reefed, and the fore-sail to be handled, — a precaution I was very glad to see. About midnight a severe blast or hurricane was heard coming on. The man at the helm sung out, which brought the captain and all the crew on deck, who got all the sails handled, and we now went under bare poles; that done, he again returned to bed, eternally bawling out, 'Oh! my poor family!' and with the next breath, 'Let us all go to —— together!' Thus we continued till day-light. The surge ran very high, but not equal to that I have seen on sea; and as the wind blew very fresh and hard against us, we had nothing for it but to return back and anchor at 2 P. M. at the head of Carlton island, opposite to Kingston; but as several large islands were between us and the town, they could not see us, or know what had become of us. The 25th, 26th and 27th, we lay here without stirring, the wind continually ahead or calm.

"On the 28th I went on shore on Carlton island, where the British had a garrison last war. The barracks, dry-ditch and rampart are still remaining, but in a decayed state. A sergeant and twelve men are kept here, to prevent the barracks from being burnt by the Indians, and the Americans from taking possession of it and the dismounted guns thereon. The cause assigned for our forsaking this post is said to be, because it is doubtful whether these islands be within the British or American lines."

They tried to get off on the 29th, but were soon obliged to return and anchor, and the next day they went hunting on the New York shore. They durst not venture far into the woods, and killed nothing, but afterwards had better luck upon some of the islands. Thus day after day, for ten days, they were detained by adverse winds, and even after getting well on their voyage, they were enveloped in fogs of hoar-frost, and so benumbed with cold, that it seemed almost necessary to turn about for Kingston and winter there. The fog cleared up at last, and they got safely in at Niagara.

It being very cold, the captain invited our traveller into his house to warm him, — and this gave him an occasion to note down the following reflection in the interest of temperance:

"I there found a decent looking young woman, his wife, with five beautiful children, of whom the father seemed uncommonly fond; and though their whole support, and in a manner their existence, depended on his life and industry, yet such is his love of grog that it would seem he would forsake them and every other consideration in the world for its sake; at least, that he would not forsake it for them."

LA ROCHEFOUCAULD-LIANCOURT. — (1795).

François-Alexandre-Frederic La Rochefoucauld-Liancourt, a French Duke, and a distinguished philanthropist, was born in 1747 and died in 1827. A faithful adherent of the unfortunate Louis XVI, he was obliged to emigrate, on the approach of the French Revolution, and was several years in England and America. He returned to France under the Consulate, and resumed the efforts he had formerly made for the improvement of agriculture and the industries. He was one of the chief promoters of vaccination in France, and took an active part in various measures of education, benevolence and reform, holding high positions in public and social life, and scattering seeds of kindness with generous hand. He lived to see the fruits of many salutary measures that he was active in promoting. His son, Frederick G., who died in 1863, was distinguished for his literary publications.

The duke, after passing through the country to Niagara, remained some time in Upper Canada, as the guest of Lieut.-Gov. Simcoe, at Newark, then the seat of government of the Upper Province. From thence he took passage for Kingston, on board the Onondaga, one of the armed vessels belonging to the British naval force on Lake Ontario. This vessel was pierced for twelve six-pounders, but carried only six. It was employed in carrying freight for the merchants, when the public service allowed. The passage was usually performed in thirty-six hours, being sometimes ten or twelve hours, less or more, according to the wind. At Kingston, he hoped to receive from Lord Dorchester, the governor-general, a pass allowing him to proceed to Lower Canada. He was thus detained there several days, and finally received a letter absolutely forbidding him from going down the river. This made it necessary for him to cross over to Oswego, and proceed from thence by water to New York. During his sojourn at Kingston, the duke was able to obtain much information about the country, and his record concerning Carlton Island is particularly explicit. Of Kingston, he says :

"The barracks are built on the site of Fort Frontenac, which was built by the French, and leveled by the English. The latter built these barracks about six years ago. During the American war their troops were constantly in motion; and in later times they were quartered on an Island which the French call Isle aux Chevreaux [Goat Island], and which the English have named Carlton, after Lord Dorchester."

In the conflict of interests for securing the seat of government in Upper Canada, Lord Dorchester preferred Kingston, while Lieutenant-Governor Simcoe insisted upon the advantages offered in the country between Lakes Erie and Ontario. At the period when the Duke visited Upper Canada; the capital was located at Newark; but the treaty of the previous year stipulated for the surrender of the posts still held by the British on the American shore, and York or Toronto was soon after selected.

The trade of Kingston at this period consisted chiefly of peltries from the Upper Lake country, and in supplies brought up the river from Montreal. There were then three merchant ships on the lake, that made eleven voyages in a year. The town contained about one hundred and twenty or thirty houses, none more distinguished than the rest, and the only one conspicuous was the barracks, a stone building surrounded by a palisade. All of the houses stood on the northern bank of the bay, which stretched a mile farther into the country, while on the southern bank were the buildings belonging to the navy, and the dwellings of those connected with that department. There the King's ships lay at anchor, apart from the port where the merchant vessels landed.

The duke speaks kindly of the Rev. John Stuart, curate of Kingston, a native of Harrisburg, Pa., who sided with the Loyalists of the Revolution, and received a grant of 2,000 acres near Kingston, a part of which, about seventy acres, he cultivated himself. Although decidedly loyal, he was still liberal in his politics — a man of much general information — mild, open and affable, and universally respected. There was then but one church in Kingston, lately built, and more resembling a barn than a church.

ISAAC WELD, JR.

Mr. Weld was an Irish gentleman, who was induced by political troubles to leave Ireland in 1795, with the view of observing the op-

IN THE RIFT.—SHOWING CANADA UPON ONE SIDE AND THE UNITED STATES UPON THE OTHER.

portunities for settlement which America afforded. His "Travels Through the States of North America and the Provinces of Upper and Lower Canada, in 1795-96-97," were published in quarto in 1799, and afterwards in other editions in English and French. We find in this work an abundance of economical and statistical facts, an ardent appreciation of the beauties of nature, and a candid picture of social institutions and domestic life, that gave it a permanent value.

Washington Irving — (1803-1853).

In the summer of 1803, Washington Irving, then a youth of twenty years, made a journey to Ogdensburg, by way of the Mohawk and Black River Valleys, in company with the families of some land-proprietors of St. Lawrence county. From the High Falls on Black river [Lyon's Falls], they floated down on a scow to the Long Falls [Carthage], consuming two days on this voyage of forty-two miles, the intervening night being spent in a humble log cabin on the bank of the river, in Lowville. Soon after starting on the second day, they had an exciting chase of a deer swimming the river, and finally secured it.

On reaching the foot of navigation, at the beginning of the Long Falls, they found only one public house, which was kept by a Frenchman, the last survivor of the "Castorland Colony," and of this he says :

"A dirtier house was never seen. We dubbed it 'The Temple of Dirt,' but contrived to have the venison cooked by a servant, and with crackers and gingerbread felt quite independent." Before leaving next morning, Irving wrote with a pencil over the fire-place the following verse:

"Here Sovereign Dirt erects her sable throne,
The house, the host, the hostess all her own."

Some years after, Mr. Hoffman (who was with Irving on this occasion) put up at the same house, in company with Judge William Cooper (father of J. Fenimore Cooper, the novelist), and their attention being attracted by the legend, the judge, who had seen too much of pioneer life to be over-nice about trifles, wrote underneath :

"Learn hence, young man, and teach it to your sons,
The wisest way's to take it as it comes."

The remaining sixty miles of Irving's journey led through a wilderness along a road newly cut, and in a vehicle drawn by oxen.

Coming by railroad from Lake Champlain to Ogdensburg, Irving says :

"Here we passed part of a day—a very interesting one to me. Fifty years had elapsed since I had visited the place in company with a party of gentlemen-proprietors, with some ladies of their families. It was then a wilderness, and we were quartered in the remains of an old French fort at the confluence of the Oswegatchie and the St. Lawrence. It was all a scene of romance to me, for I was then a mere stripling, and everything was strange and full of poetry. The country was covered with forest; the Indians still inhabited some islands in the river, and prowled about in their canoes. There were two young ladies of the party to sympathize in my romantic feelings, and we passed some happy days here, exploring the forests, or gliding in our canoe on the rivers.

"In my present visit I found, with difficulty, the site of the old French fort, but all traces of it were gone. I looked round on the surrounding country and river. All was changed. A populous city occupied both sides of the Oswegatchie, great steamers ploughed the St. Lawrence, the opposite Canada shore was studded with towns and villages. I sat down on the river bank, where we used to embark in our canoes, and thought on the two lovely girls who used to navigate it with me, and the joyous party who used to cheer us from the shore. All had passed away—all were dead! I was the sole survivor of that happy party: and here I had returned, after a lapse of fifty years, to sit down and meditate on the mutability of all things, and to wonder that I was still alive."

Mr. Irving lived about six years after this journey, and died November 28, 1859.

Johan Georg Kohl. — (1854).

Of the numerous quotations we have made, there is not one more worthy of notice than that of the distinguished traveller and learned geographer, Johan Georg Kohl, Ph. D. His voluminous publications, including travels in every part of Middle and Nothern Europe, and his admirable geographical memoirs (the most valued of which by Americans is his elaborate work on the Early Discoveries upon the Coast of Maine), have been uniformly regarded as productions of high authority, as they evidently were of profound research. Dr. Kohl was born at Bremen in 1808, and was educated at the Universities of Gottingen, Heidelburgh and Munich. He first studied law, but turning his attention to archæological and scientific pursuits, he perhaps rendered the greater service to mankind. His work on the Influence of Climate upon Man, is one of particular merit. This writer returned home from America in 1858, and died October 28, 1876. His sister, Madame Ida Kohl, was the author of several books of European travel.

Dr. Kohl's full and intelligible description of the Islands, is enlivened by a poetic sentiment, and by legendary associations that indicate a mind keenly alive to the beauties of nature, as well as thoroughly trained in the field of historical inquiry. His description of this region is as follows:

"The middle of that portion of the St. Lawrence, which, as I have said, was formerly called Cataraqui, has become, I scarcely know why, the chief centre of traffic for this part of the country. The two most important towns of the district here lie opposite one another, Prescott on the Canadian side, and Ogdensburg on the American. Railroads from the interior terminate at both places, and there is therefore, a great deal of life and bustle on the water. The St. Lawrence is rather narrower at this point, and nowhere can a comparison be made more conveniently between a Canadian and an American town. Prescott exhibits much darker hues than Ogdensburgh, where all looks brighter and pleasanter; the houses of the former are built in solid style of grey stone, and the same building material that has served for Montreal. The Americans have a passion for white and green houses, and plant willows and other elegant trees between them, and the contrast might be continued to many other particulars were it worth while. You have before you at once a picture of the 'old country,' and one of the quite new.

"Ogdensburg is the capital of the tract of land that I have described a chapter or two back; some miles beyond it lies another pretty river port, Brockville, and then again some miles further begins the celebrated 'Lake of a Thousand Islands,' but to have a clear idea of the origin and configuration of this lake, you must begin at Lake Ontario.

"Lake Ontario forms on its western side a regularly drawn oval, with smoothly cut shores, and no considerable islands or appendages. On the north-eastern side, however, where its waters have broken through the obstacles that opposed their progress, its hitherto broad, smooth expanse is broken up among numerous islands and peninsulas.

"First comes the large peninsula of Prince Edward, then Duck Island, and several others, as well as long gulfs, bays and islets, breaking the land right and left. Then near Kingston, you have the Great Wolfe Island, Amherst Island, and others — rugged masses of land that the water could not overcome, or possibly which rose above the surface when the Ontario subsided into its present bed. At length, beyond Wolfe island, the lake contracts to a breadth of six or seven miles, and here begins the 'Lake of the Thousand Islands.' These islands are, as the name indicates, extraordinarily numerous, and the water is split up into a corresponding number of channels, but at length the river develops itself again out of the labyrinth. For a distance of thirty miles, reckoning from Kingston, the waters contract more and more, hollow out a deeper and deeper channel, and wear away more and more of the islands, which gradually become less numerous, and cease entirely about a mile above Brockville. The current now becomes stronger, the two shores appear, the lake disappears, and the river takes its place; but this is for any one coming down the river; we were pursuing an opposite course.

"The name of the locality, 'Thousand Islands,' was probably bestowed by the Jesuits, or the celebrated Canadian traveller, Champlain, who was the first discoverer of Lake Ontario. The number of the islands is, of course, only guessed at. Some make them 1,500, and some as many as 2,000, as there perhaps may be, if they bestow the name of island on each separate bit of rock that sticks out of the water, or every reef or sand bar that lies just under it.

"Half of these islands lie along the American shore, the rest nearer to Canada, and the frontier line has been drawn between the two, and the channel for steamers keeps pretty closely to that line. The whole scene is renowned as interesting and picturesque, both in the United States and Canada, and parties of pleasure, picnics, and sporting excursions are made to it both from Kingston and Brockville. People hire one of the elegant yachts or boats built at Kingston, and sail about with their friends from island to island, dine, camp under the trees, shoot the water-fowl, fish, and am se themselves in many ways. Many remain for days together, for the tours among these countless islands have something of the charm of discovery. One of the party, perhaps, declares he knows of an island that has never been visited; another tells of a deep, wooded bay, in whose clear, calm waters no one has yet tried to anchor.

"We reached the first of the islands, a little above Brockville, and soon found ourselves surrounded by them; sometimes lying in a long string, like a row of beads, sometimes flung pell-mell together in a heap. Some are large and covered with thick woods; all have trees, and there are some so small that they have only just room for one tree or a bush. There is an infinite variety in the grouping of the trees, too, some being gathered into social parties, some living as solitary hermits, so that perpetually new combinations are formed in the scenery. Some of the islands are just barely hidden under a thin covering of moss and other vegetation, and sometimes the crystal water is flowing over a mass of naked rocks that it barely covers.

"The foundation of all these islands I believe to be granite, and in general they are not high, though picturesque pedestals are afforded for the trees by banks of twenty feet deep. The larger have hills and valleys, and arable land enough to be worth cultivating, though hitherto little has been obtained from them besides game, fish and wood. Villages there are none, and only a few scattered dwellings or shanties for sportsmen, wood-cutters, and lumbermen, with a few mechanical contrivances, such as are seen on the Ottawa, for the collecting and transporting of the felled trees. The islands all have owners, but as everywhere in America where land, wood and water remain unsettled, they have been to some extent invaded by squatters, whose huts we saw here and there on the shores, and the owners seldom offer any objection, as they consider that these people help to reclaim the land, and make some steps towards its cultivation.

"The best time to visit the islands is in spring and in the early summer, for then the trees and shrubs are fragrant from every cliff; the woods are full of birds and various animals; and sometimes when the air is very hot, the water is so deliciously cool and fresh, that it is a delight to plunge into it. But in the cold autumn day when I visited the lake, the water is less attractive. Goethe's fisherman could only have been enchanted by the Nixie on a warm summer's evening.

"The autumn is, however, the loveliest time for one of the greatest attractions of the islands, and the green, red, yellow, brown and golden leafage was beautifully mirrored in the clear water beneath. Some of the islands, when the sunbeams fell on them, seemed quite to flame, and, in fact, this does sometimes happen in more than a metaphorical sense, and the burning woods produce, it is said, a most magnificent spectacle. If you chance to be passing in a steamer, you may enjoy the sight nearer and more conveniently than a similar scene elsewhere, as the intervening water renders it safe. The boats there run very close in shore and th passengers can look deeply into the recesses of the blazing woods, and yet remain in security. I was told this by a gentleman who had enjoyed the sight; and another, who noticed the interest I took in these Thousand Islands,

mentioned some further particulars. In his youth, he said, they were inhabited by Indians, remnants of the Iroquois, or Six Nations, to whom the whole north of the State of New York belonged. These islanders were called Mississagua, a name that still occurs in various localities on the St. Lawrence; their chief resided on one of the principal islands, and the rest of the tribe was scattered about on the others, in birch huts or tents. Their canoes were of the same material, and with these they used to glide softly over the water, and, in the numerous little bays, or arms of the river, surprise the fish, which, having never been disturbed by noisy steamers, filled the waters in countless abundance. The birds and other game were equally plentiful in the woods, but now, when greedy squatters and sportsmen, with guns, have exhausted the district, the islands are comparatively devoid of animal life.

"It was the practice among the Mississaguas, at certain times of the year, to leave the islands to their young people, and make great hunting expeditions northward into the interior of Canada, and southward into New York. My informant had visited them once when he was a young man, and being hospitably received, had afterwards repeated his visits, made acquaintances and friends among them, lived with them for weeks, and shared the joys and sorrows of the hunter's life. Once when he had been on a journey to Niagara and the west, and had been a long time absent, he could not desist when he passed the Thousand Islands on his return to his native town, Brockville, from making a call by the way on his Mississagua friends. They recognized him immediately, gave him the warmest reception, and carried him on their shoulders to their chief, who made a great feast in his honor, and canoes full of Indians came gliding in crowds from the islands to see and welcome him. He had to pass the night among them; the squaws prepared his couch, and two of the Indians insisted on serving him as a guard of honor at his tent door, where they camped out and kept the fire. 'I was almost moved to tears myself, sir, on seeing my half-savage friends again. Believe me, it is a race very susceptible to kindness, though at the same time certainly very revengeful for injuries. They never forget their friends, but are very terrible and even treacherous against their enemies. We have very erroneous notions of the Indians. We call them poor and miserable, but they appear quite otherwise to themselves. They are proud of their prowess and animal daring, and of the performances of their forefathers. In fact, they think themselves the first race in creation.'

"'Are there now any remains of these proud people on the islands?'

"'No. They have been scattered like the chaff; their fisheries and their hunting became continually less productive ; the villages and towns of the whites grew up around them ; they began to feel the pressure of want ; their race died away like the fish in their waters, and at last the few who remained, accepted a proposal of the government, that they should exchange these islands for a more remote habitation — I do not myself know exactly where.'"

We are here able to supply some information which our author had not the opportunity to obtain :

Before the year 1826, these Indians were pagans, wandering about in the neighborhood of Belleville, Kingston and Gananoque, and earning a precarious living by hunting and fishing. They claimed the title to a large tract north of the river, and the islands as far down as Prescott. Below that place the St. Regis Indians claimed, and these have never ceded to the government their right to the islands.

In 1826-7, between two and three hundred of these "Mississaguas of the Bay of Quinte," as they were called, or more properly the Eagle band of the Chippewas, were induced to settle on Grape Island in the Bay of Quinte, about six miles from Belleville, where a Wesleyan Methodist Mission was established, schools opened, and the simpler arts of civilized life began to be introduced. Under kind and gentle treatment they made much progress, and began to plant and improve their homes with commendable zeal. After living eleven years on the island, they gave up their improvements, to be sold for their benefit, and removed to Alnwick, in the county of Northumberland, eighteen miles from Coburg, and ten from Hastings, where a location of 2,000 acres was secured to them by Sir John Colburn, and laid out into farms of twenty-five acres each. Nine years after this removal, a report showed that their settlement had thirty-six dwellings, of which twenty-two were framed buildings and the rest of logs. They had from 360 to 400 acres cleared, and had a population of 233.

Many years ago they ceded to the government their lands in Newcastle, Midland and Johnstown districts, and in 1856 they relinquished the management of their property in the islands, reserving whatever rents or profits might result therefrom. This trust is managed by the Indian branch of the Department of the Interior, at Ottawa. The report for the year ending June 30, 1878, gave the capital of their account as $51,408.61 — their revenue as $5,159.08, chiefly from interest, and the expenditures as $1,234.69 chiefly in distribution to those entitled.

Several of the larger islands were granted, or leased for long periods, a century or so since, and some of the smaller ones are held under Indian titles by residents upon them, or the owners of lands opposite.

In the map of the Canadian islands prepared by Mr. Unwin, under date of June 14, 1873, upon a scale of ten chains to the inch, names or numbers are applied to all of them, 348 in number. They are divided among four agencies for supervision. By far the greater number of these islands are still wholly unoccupied, and in a state of nature, except as the timber has been despoiled by unauthorized persons for pleasure or profit, or as destroyed by fires.

We will now resume the narrative of Dr. Kohl, on his voyage among the islands:

"The only living being that appeared very common here now was the bird the English call the loon. It is a water fowl as large as a goose, with a very thick head and long beak; its color black, with white spots on the wings. This large bird was swimming about everywhere among the islands, and it was curious to see how exactly similar was the impulse of instinct in the numerous specimens that we met in the course of thirty miles. As long as our boat continued pretty far off, they swam quietly about on the glassy water, attending only to their own affairs, and busy in catching insects or fish; but as soon as we came within 300 yards, they shot up into the air, with their long necks stretched out, and rolling about their still longer heads, so as to look at us timidly, now with the right, and now with the left, eye. In the second state of their fear, this anxious movement was communicated to their whole body, and they steered alternately right and left, and at last flew straight on before us; but when they noticed that our winged steam monster was soon again within a hundred yards or so, they seemed fairly to give it up, — rolled their heads about a little more, and then threw a somersault, and went down heels over head in the water and disappeared. All these motions were repeated by every individual as exactly as if they had been previously agreed upon.

"These 'loons,' the 'wintergreens,' and the numerous watch-towers among the islands, were the only objects that attracted my attention. This wintergreen, or pyrola, is a low plant or bush, that does not at all, at least in the autumn, correspond with its name, for it looked blood-red, and covered the ground under the trees with a red carpet. Sometimes it ran as a border round the islands, and then the groups of trees seemed to be enclosed in a wreath of red flowers, as I have seen them in an English park. The light-houses, too, tended to convey the impression that we were not upon the mighty St. Lawrence, but on the artificial waters of some pleasure ground, — for they were elegant white buildings, like pavilions, or kiosks, sometimes hidden in a grove, sometimes rising from a little island or promontory. They are numerous, and of course very necessary, as the winding watery channel is continually changing its direction in this labyrinth of islands.

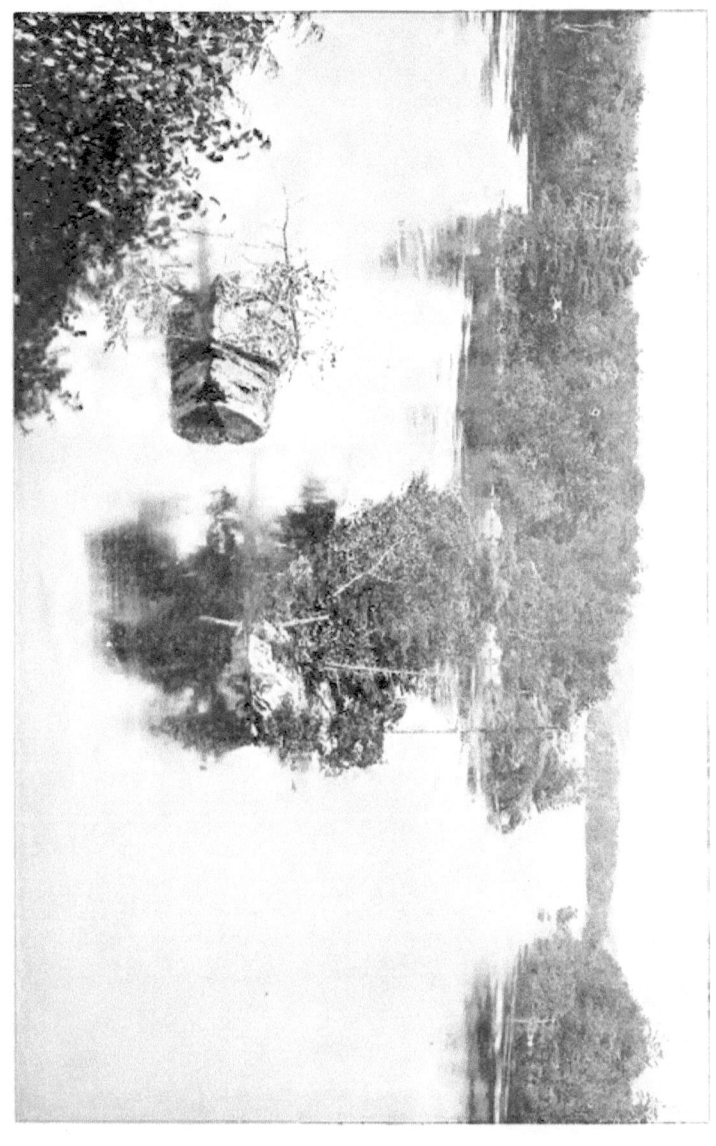

THE LOST CHANNEL, LOOKING NORTH.

"By degrees—after you have breakfasted once, and had one dinner—the garden comes to an end, and you emerge upon the open field—that is to say, the broad water, and the approach of the Ontario and the city of Kingston is announced."

BENSON J. LOSSING.—(1850–1860).

This well-known historical writer has many allusions to the upper St. Lawrence, and the events with which they are associated. While collecting materials for his "Pictorial Field-Book of the Revolution," he passed up the river by steamer, in the summer of 1850, and thus records his impressions of the scenery:

"A calm, sweetly consonant with ideas of Sabbath rest, was upon the main, the Islands, and the river, and all the day long not a breath of air rippled the silent-flowing, but mighty St. Lawrence. We passed the morning in alternately viewing the ever-changing scene as our vessel sped towards Ontario, and in perusing Burke's 'Essay on the Sublime and Beautiful.' I never read that charming production with so much pleasure as then, for illustrative examples were on every side. And when, towards noon, our course was among the Thousand Islands, the propriety of the stars as an example, by their number and confusion, of the cause of the idea of sublimity, was forcibly illustrated. 'The apparent disorder,' he says, 'augments the grandeur, for the appearance of care is highly contrary to our idea of magnificence.' So with these Islands. They fill the St. Lawrence through nearly forty miles of its course, commencing directly opposite the city of Kingston, and varying in size from a few yards to eighteen miles in length. Some are mere syenitic rocks, bearing sufficient alluvium to produce cedar, spruce and pine shrubs, which seldom grow to the dignity of a tree; while others were beautifully fringed with luxuriant grass and shaded by lofty trees. A few of the larger are inhabited and cultivated. There are twelve hundred and twenty seven in number. Viewed separately, they present nothing remarkable, but scattered, as they are, so profusely and in such disorder, over the bosom of the river, their features constantly changing as we made our rapid way among them, an idea of magnificence and sublimity involuntarily possessed the mind, and wooed our attention from the tuition of books to that of Nature."

Again, ten years later, while preparing his "Field-Book of the War of 1812," in referring to the Islands, he says:

"This group of Islands, lying in the St Lawrence, just below the foot of Lake Ontario, fill that river for thirty seven miles along its course, and number more than fifteen hundred. A few of them are large and cultivated, but most of them are mere rocky islets, covered generally with stunted hemlocks and cedar trees, which extend to the water's edge. Some of them contain an area of only a few square yards, while others present many superficial square miles. Canoes and small boats may pass in safety among all of them, and there is a deep channel for steamboats and other large vessels, which never varies in depth and position, the bottom being rocky. The St. Lawrence here varies from two to nine miles in width. The boundary-line between the United States and Canada passes among them. It was determined in 1818. The largest of the Islands are Grand and Howe, belonging to Canada, and Carlton, Grindstone and Wells belonging to the United States. They have been the theatre of many historic scenes and legendary tales during two centuries and a half."

JOURNEY OF THE PRINCE OF WALES.—(1860.)

In 1860, the Prince of Wales (known in the United States as Baron Renfrew), accompanied by His Grace, the Duke of Newcastle, Secretary of State for the Colonies; the Earl of St. Germains, Steward to the Queen's Household; Major-General Bruce, Governor to the Prince; Dr. Ackland, the Prince's Physician; Major Teesdale and Captain Grey, the Prince's Equerries, and Mr. Engleherst, private secretary to the Duke of Newcastle, travelled through portions of the United States and Canada. He was everywhere received by the officials of both countries with the honors due to his rank. Besides those properly belonging to his suite were several correspondents of newspapers, who kept the public informed of the incidents of the journey, and several books were soon after published, giving these in a collected form. We present extracts from two of these works, one by a correspondent of the New York Herald, and the other by the writer representing the London Times. The Prince, after visiting Lower Canada, proceeded to Ottawa, and laid the corner stone of the new Parliament buildings, of what has since become the Dominion Government. From there he proceeded to Brockville, where he took passage on board the steamer Kingston, and passed through this part of the St. Lawrence on the 3d of September, 1860.

At Kingston, the Orangemen had prepared to join in the reception of the Prince, in their regalia, justifying themselves in this by alleging that the Catholics in Lower Canada had been recognized upon similar occasions. The Duke of Newcastle addressed a letter to the city officials, requesting them to prevent these partisan demonstrations, but neither party appeared willing to yield; and, after waiting nearly a day, the steamer proceeded on its way up the bay without landing. At Belleville a similar event happened, and at Toronto a serious misunderstanding arose from like causes.

RECEPTION OF THE PRINCE OF WALES, AS DESCRIBED BY KINAHAN CORNWALLIS, CORRESPONDENT OF THE NEW YORK HERALD.

The letters of this writer were afterwards collected in book form. The party arrived at the railway station by the Grand Trunk Railway, where our extract begins:

"At twenty minutes to eight, the train entered Brockville; there the greatest crowd that Brockville ever gathered was seen at the railway station.

"On stepping on the platform, the cheering prevented anything else being heard for several minutes; but when this burst of joy and welcome had subsided, the Mayor of the town, accompanied by several members of the Common Council, advanced and read an address, to which His Royal Highness replied. The Prince was conducted to his carriage, in which he took his seat beside the Governor-General, with His Grace the Duke of Newcastle on the opposite seat. A torch-light procession of the firemen and others was in waiting, and a general illumination had the effect, in the midst of the triumphal arches and other evergreen and floral decorations, of lending a species of fairy enchantment to the scene, which was one of the prettiest I have ever seen—far more so than that of the great Japanese Ball. The flaming torches in the background, the exploding rockets high above, the brilliant transparencies spanning the streets, the Chinese lanterns swinging from roofs, and windows, and arches, the distant bonfires, the ringing church bells, and the ringing cheers, combined to make a spectacle as brilliant as it was exciting. The procession then moved forward towards the steamer Kingston at the wharf,—the firemen and other torch-bearers following in the rear, and were saluted with fireworks that lent a terribly lurid aspect to the whole, at every point of their progress.

"The display was highly creditable to the townspeople, many of whom, however, went home very much disappointed at having been unable to catch a glimpse of the royal visitor.

"On the next morning, the Prince appeared on the steamer's deck at nine o'clock, and being recognized by those on shore, there was great cheering. The steamer being anchored a short distance midstream, was surrounded by numerous boats filled with those eager to see him. At a quarter to eleven, he gratified a general wish by coming ashore in a small boat, and driving through the principal streets of the town. All the resources of the place were taxed to provide carriages for the party, and with tolerable success, although there was a great want of uniformity in the size, color and shape of the vehicles and horses enlisted in the service. The Prince took his place in an open carriage by the side of the Governor-General, while the Duke of Newcastle and Earl of St. Germains sat opposite. Lord Lyons and the suite followed in separate carriages. The streets were very dusty, owing partly to the crowd that ran alongside and before and behind the Prince's carriage, which was guarded by the policemen, one at either side, armed with batons. The royal party had to keep their eyes shut for a while, but afterward the clouds diminished, both in volume and density. The drive lasted about half an hour.

"At twenty minutes past twelve, the Kingston steamed away, and in a few minutes afterward was pursuing her course among the Thousand Islands.

"The weather was fortunately warm and sunny, and the granite islands were seen to great advantage. There nature appeared to have fancifully prepared a grand proscenium to feast the travellers' eyes, for nothing could have exceeded in singularity the scene that presented itself. The mighty St. Lawrence—the 'Iroquois' of the red man—here, in ages long elapsed, urged its vexed waters, before pent up in the vast inland basin of North America, against that portion of the primitive barrier which visibly extends from the granite mountains of the east over to the dividing ridge between the wild regions of Hudson's Bay and the tributary waters of the Ottawa and St. Lawrence; and, here, by some tremendous effort, which has evidently shaken the whole country from Kingston, at the eastern extremity of Lake Ontario, to the other side of the region through which the granite ridge pursues its northwesterly course, the river has at one time rushed over a sheet of cascades and rapids miles in breadth, but which have long disappeared under the wearing influence of time. Island succeeded Island, group succeeded group, till the eye almost wearied of the succession. Most of these were beautifully wooded, and many of them so low and flat as to suggest to the mind the tranquil prospect of an Italian lagoon. Others again were split and rent into a variety of fantastic forms, forming views of peculiar wildness.

A turn in the channel disclosed a new labyrinth, while we passed under a dark wall of rock, coated with moss and lichens that had likely flourished there for generations, and from whose bare and rugged top the hoary fir lifted its sombre head. Further on, a light-house stood perched on a rock, and further, still another. All was still and lonely — the cerulean vault above, the tranquil tide below — the sunshine over all. Was the poetry of the scene felt by that fair young man gazing so calmly, so thoughtfully upon it from the deck of that steamer, over which the rich tints of a Prince of Wales' standard autumnal sky, and this sheet of water reflected the forms of an assemblage of islets of the most picturesque, diversified and inviting aspect; here a naked crag, there a majestic bouquet yonder a clump of trees, or a perfect island supporting a solitary stem. Such happy confusion, such an indiscriminate sprinkling of all shapes and sizes and varieties of vegetation, was unique in the extreme.

"As we neared Kingston, after leaving Brockville, the channel by which we had advanced, and which was formed by Long Island, on the borders of which were several islets, and by the mainland,

THE JOSEPH BONAPARTE HOUSE, AT NATURAL BRIDGE, N. Y.

flaunted in the sun? If I were a novelist, I would say, 'Yes.'

"Then another fairy picture presented itself in groves, growing, as it were, out of the water, and seeming to bar our further progress, till suddenly the sylvan curtain was withdrawn, and the eye wandered over a wide sweep of water, dotted here and there with a few small rocks, and bounded by the endless forest of the mainland. Towns and villages were meanwhile passed on either shore, and once a lonely fisherman was seen practicing his gentle art in a small row-boat. The islands extended the whole way from Brockville to Kingston, but the most compact cluster was seen in front of Alexandria Bay. Here the view was exquisite. A wide expanse of river reposed, mirror-like, beneath the rich

Pittsburgh and Kingston, gradually widened. These were well wooded, and the larger one disclosed several neat farms."

THE THOUSAND ISLANDS AS DESCRIBED BY N. A. WOODS, CORRESPONDENT OF THE LONDON TIMES.—THE ISLE OF DOGS.

After pleasantly discoursing of the rapids of the lower St. Lawrence which appeared after all to be not very difficult to descend, and no great affair, notwithstanding all that had been said of their awful grandeur, he remarks:

"This language is dreadful guide-book heresy, of course, but the worst is yet to come. Canadians tell you that if there is anything better worth seeing than the rapids, it is the Thousand Islands, which dot the surface of the St. Lawrence just where Lake Ontario and the river commence. Here, you are told the rich grandeur of the Hudson, the luxuriance of the Bosphorus, the wild, stern magnificence of the Saguenay, and, for aught you hear to the contrary the flowing beauty of the Euphrates in spring, may all be met with.

"It is a trying thing to have to contend against such notions; but if an individual opinion is worth anything, I must unhesitatingly give mine, that these Thousand Islands are in their way a delusion and a snare, and will as much bear comparison with the Hudson or the Saguenay, or the Bosphorus, as the Thames below Blackwall. Take slips of the Isle of Dogs of all sizes, from an island as large as a footstool, up to ten or twelve acres; plant the larger ones with stunted firs; strew the little ones over with broken stones as if they were about to be macadamized, put them near the surface of the water in a mechanical disarranging confusion without picturesqueness, and number without variety,— imagine them choking the highway of a noble river, and you can fancy yourself on the St. Lawrence, and in the middle of the far-famed Thousand Isles."

It appears, a few pages further on, that the writer of the above extract, took the railroad from Brockville to Kingston, nor does it anywhere appear that he saw the river at any point between these two places. His recipe for making "Thousand Islands," will, therefore, very probably be classed with the prescriptions of the quack, who might recommend an untried remedy for a patient he had never seen.

To better appreciate his brilliant comparison, we should remember that this Isle of Dogs lies in a bend in the Thames, within five miles of St. Paul's Church, London. It consists of some 600 acres, and a part of it covered with steam-factories, chain-cable works and other establishments incident to the commerce and industries of the great metropolis, while much of the remainder is covered seven feet deep at every high tide. Out of such materials this pleasant writer requests his readers to construct the ideal of the Thousand Islands of the St. Lawrence!

W. D. HOWELLS.—(1872.)

In a pleasant little romance, full of wit and sentiment, called "Their Wedding Journey," this writer describes the ideal incidents of a journey over some of the more fashionable routes of northern travel, with a fidelity that proves his personal familiarity with the localities described. The romantic couple, whose adventures he is describing, had come from Niagara, and had just left the landing at Kingston, where our extract begins:

"Kingston has romantic memories of being Fort Frontenac two hundred years ago; of Count Frontenac's splendid advent among the Indians; of the brave La Salle, who turned its wooden walls to stone; of wars with the savages and then with the New York Colonists, whom the French and their allies harried from this point; of the destruction of La Salle's fort in the old French war; and of final surrender a few years later to the English. It is as picturesque as it is historical. All about the city, the shores are beautifully wooded, and there are many lovely islands — the first, indeed, of those Thousand Islands with which the head of the St. Lawrence is filled, and among which the steamer was presently threading her way. They are as charming, and still almost as wild as when, in 1673, Frontenac's flotilla of canoes passed through their labyrinth, and issued upon the lake. Save for a light-house upon one of them, there is almost nothing to show that the foot of man has ever pressed the thin grass clinging to their rocky surfaces, and keeping its green in the eternal shadow of their pines and cedars. In the warm morning light they gathered or dispersed before the advancing vessel, which some of them almost touched with the plumage of their evergreens; and where none of them were large, some of them were so small that it would not have been too bold to figure them as a vaster race of water-birds assembling and separating in her course. It is curiously affecting to find them so unclaimed yet from the solitude of the vanished wilderness, and scarcely touched even by tradition. But for the interest left them by the French, these tiny islands have scarcely any associations, and must be enjoyed for their beauty alone. There is about them a faint light of legend concerning the Canadian rebellion of 1837, for several 'patriots' are said to have taken refuge amidst their lovely multitude; but this episode of modern history is difficult for the imagination to manage, and somehow one does not take sentimentally even to that daughter of a lurking 'patriot,' who long baffled her father's pursuers by rowing him from one island to another, and supplying him with food by night.

"Either the reluctance is from the natural desire that no recent a heroine should be founded on fact, or it is mere perverseness. Perhaps I ought to say, in justice to her, that it was one of her own sex who

VIEW FROM THE DRAPER'S ELBOW, LOOKING WEST.

refused to be interested in her, and forbade Basil to care for her. When he had read of her exploit from the guide-book, Isabel asked him if he had noticed that handsome girl in the blue and striped Garibaldi and Swiss hat, that had come aboard at Kingston."

VISIT OF THE EDITORS' AND PUBLISHERS' ASSOCIATION OF THE STATE OF NEW YORK.—(1872.)

Perhaps no incident has contributed to bring more widely before the public a knowledge of the beautiful scenery of the Thousand Islands than the occasion of the annual meeting of the association above named, at Watertown, in 1872. This association had been formed as early as 1853, but its annual gatherings had been interrupted by the war. Partaking of a social as well as of a professional character, these meetings had come to be regarded as both pleasant and profitable to the members and their families; and on the second day of the convention at Watertown (June 26, 1872), the whole day was given up to a railroad and steamboat excursion to the Thousand Islands.

The R., W. & O. R. R. Co. had provided a train of eight cars, drawn by the engine "Antwerp," gaily adorned with flags, evergreens and flowers, which took the party (about 200 in number) to Cape Vincent, from which a steamer conveyed them down among the islands — stopping at Clayton for a reception, and dining in the open air on Pullman's Island. The day was beautifully calm, and the islands, in the full verdure of early summer, appeared to best advantage. A cornet band from Watertown accompanied the party, and added much to the enjoyment of the occasion. Among the visitors were a considerable number from the Southern States, and many of the editors were accompanied by their wives. The descriptions published in local papers throughout the State, made the incidents of the excursion well known among their readers, and created with many a desire to view the scenery for themselves. From that time to the present, this interest has been increasing, but more especially since the beginning of summer encampments, partaking of a religious and of a social nature, of which a further notice is elsewhere given.

Mr. Norris Winslow, of Watertown, was one of the few now living and in active life, who participated in this excursion and contributed liberally for its happy completion.

ANOTHER SIDE IS GIVEN BY MONSIEUR JULES LE CLERCQ —(1876).

This writer, a Frenchman, had made an extended tour in the West, and was returning by way of the Lakes. We begin our extract at the moment of his departure from Toronto:

"We found ourselves on board the Spartan, a very large crowd, thanks to a legion of pilgrims on their way to Wells Island, one of the Thousand Islands of the St. Lawrence, for the purpose of assisting at a great religious meeting, or revival, as they say in this country. The 'revival' is an effervescence of devotion, an outburst of fanaticism that generates itself at intervals, and suddenly comes on like a storm. There are spiritual fevers that generate and keep alive the strangest sects in America, and it is seldom that some new and extraordinary sect does not arise from a revival. * *

"Before our pilgrims had landed at Wells Island, the revival spirit had already appeared among them with some intensity, but this was nothing but the prelude.

"Towards evening, as the setting sun was touching the waves of Lake Ontario, they began their songs. To these succeeded exhortations, which might perhaps have made me a new convert, had they not been so entirely grotesque. A personage who seemed to act the part of a president invited any persons who might be moved from Heaven, to give the company their inspirations. A profound silence followed this solemn request, and every one was looking around, when some one more inspired than the rest, arose, and spoke in a solemn and prophetic tone, his countenance lit up as if under the influence of a Divine Spirit. This spectacle interested me very much, from its entire strangeness, but all of these inspired people, who seemed to think themselves holier than the rest of the world, gave me an impression quite repulsive. One or two of them, in their extravagance, implored the Supreme Being to enlighten the minds of every person aboard — first the passengers, one and all, and then from the captain down to the humblest deck-hand. Being unable to endure more of this, I left this saintly assemblage, to retire at the further end of the steamer.

"I know not what passed the next day at the revival on Wells Island; but if we may believe an English writer, worthy of credit, these revivals become the scenes of the gravest disorders.

"As the night came on, the disorder became indescribable; for, including the revivalists, there were not less than four hundred persons aboard, and there were only some fifty state-rooms, with two berths in each, all of which were occupied by the ladies. There were, therefore, three hundred persons without beds, and I found myself among these unfortunates, obliged to sleep on a plank, with a satchel for a pillow. At my age, happily, this does not matter, and although I would not like to renew the experience, I am not ashamed to know how it seems to sleep on a plank. On awaking in the morning, I found to my great astonishment that I had a severe headache, and on raising the plank, found that I had been sleeping just over the boiler.

"They undertook to give breakfast to four hundred passengers — but the tables would accommodate but a hundred guests. They got over this difficulty by setting the table four times. In this setting and serving four tables in succession, it required from six to ten o'clock, and it was marvelous to see how every one rushed forward as soon as the gong sounded. It was a pitched siege, where the strongest had the best chances. Not caring to engage in such a skirmish, I patiently waited for the last edition, and by the time I had finished, those who had breakfasted first, were coming about for their dinners. Such are the little incidents of travels in America, and if my star ever guides me to that country again, I trust it will not be at the time of a revival.

"After passing Kingston, the second largest city in the Province of Ontario, we entered the St. Lawrence, and for two hours were steaming through the midst of the Thousand Islands, concerning which Mr. Xavier Marmier and other travellers have expressed an admiration in which I cannot join.

"I will, therefore, content myself with giving one of those descriptions found in the guide-books. I can only get up a sort of cold enthusiasm, for this is not my trade. I can understand how amateur hunt-

ers and anglers can here find their delights; but, though I am not altogether hostile to the mysteries of shooting and fishing, I cannot truly say that I found much to admire in this River Archipelago.

"They tell me that the number of these islands amounts to eighteen hundred; but if there were a hundred thousand, would they therefore be the more beautiful? For my part, I would not exchange a single pearl in the enchanting group of the Borromeo Islands, in Lake Maggiori, for the whole eighteen hundred islands of the St. Lawrence. At the risk of incurring the reproach of heresy, I will venture to say, that the Thousand Isles have a reputation altogether adorned. They have been honored by so many pompous and emphatic descriptions, that all tourists are obliged to believe them the wonder of wonders. Tourists have an unfortunate way of admiring all that Murray, Joanne, and others, tell them they must admire, and they think they must not return from America without having seen them. If otherwise, the conversation would take some such form as this:

"' You have been in America?'
— "' Yes.'
— "' And have seen the Thousand Islands?'
— "' I did not see them.'

"At the end of the dialogue you would hear — 'Simpleton' don't you know they are cited in prose and verse? You might be pardoned for passing Niagara — that is superannuated — but the Thousand Islands! What, then, did you go to America to see?'

"To finish off: 'I know some part of Sweden, and upon that part of Lake Maclar, that extends from Stockholm to Upsal, is an archipelago infinitely more picturesque than that of the St. Lawrence; yet the Swedes have not the tact to boast of their Thousand Islands like the Americans.'"

A HOUSE-BOAT.

POETIC ASSOCIATIONS OF THE THOUSAND ISLANDS.

CANADIAN BOAT SONGS.

MOST early travellers speak of the songs with which the Canadian voyageurs were accustomed to beguile their labors at the oar, and of the impressions they left upon the memory. These are now entirely unknown upon this part of the St. Lawrence, but are still heard upon the upper waters of the Ottawa, and in the regions not yet invaded by the power of steam.

These souvenirs of travel belong to a period in society that appears to be passing away, and like the popular songs of all countries, that perpetuate their historical legends and the traditions of ancestors, they are unknown in cities, and are found only in rural life. In this instance, they may be often traced back to an European origin, and are of the kind that tend to keep alive the poetic associations of a gay and happy peasantry, rather than the historical memories of a great and powerful people. In fact there appear to be very little sense, much less a connection of narrative, in any of these popular songs of these people, and the most that can be said of many of them is, that they were a jolly string of words without rhyme or sense, with frequent repetitions, and a joyous refrain.

In their incoherent stanzas and their repetitions, they resembled in some respects the slave-songs of the south before the late war, although wholly devoid of that religious sentiment which formed a feature in many of the social songs of the slaves.

Some years since, Mr. Ernst Gagnon, of Quebec, prepared a collection of these Canadian songs. It contains only those most commonly known, for according to this author, "ten large volumes would scarcely contain them." He further remarks, that as a general thing there is nothing indelicate or wanton in these popular melodies, and that even in some of this description that can be traced back to French origin, the objectionable features have been dropped. In other cases, the change in these airs has been so great that their origin can scarcely be traced back beyond the period of emigration, and in others they are unmistakably and entirely Canadian.

We will limit our notice of these songs to two or three of the most popular and well-known, and of these the one first given is altogether the most important:

"A LA CLAIRE FONTAINE."

Says Mr. Gagnon:—"From the little seven-year-old child to the gray-haired old man, every body in Canada knows this song. There is no French Canadian song that in this respect will compare with it, although the melody is very primitive, and it has little to interest the musician, beyond its great popularity."

It is often sung to a dancing tune, and is even brought into the fantasies of a concert. It is known in France, and is said to be of Norman origin, although M. Marmier thinks it came from La Franche Comtè, and M. Rathery thinks it was brought from Bretagne, under the reign of Louis XIV. In France it has nearly the same words, but with this difference — that the French song expresses the sorrow of a young girl at the loss of her friend Pierre, while the Canadian lad wastes his regrets upon the rose that his mistress rejected. The air as sung in France is altogether different. Some years since this song in its Canadian dress was brought out in all the principal theatres of Paris with immense success. This led to a distressing burlesque of "La Claire Fontaine, as they sing it in Paris."

On the occasion of the visit of the Prince of Wales to America in 1860, a little incident occurred on board the "Hero," on the last evening before the landing at Quebec, that brought this song and its air into notice upon a much wider field than before. Several prominent Canadians had come on board, and as the evening wore away, Mr. Cartier, a high official in the Colonial government, stepped forward, and began to sing this song in a clear and melodious voice.

The chorus was easily picked up by the listeners, and after once hearing it, a few voices joined in — at first in subdued and gentle murmur, but at each return more clear and strong, until at the end, the whole party were in full accord, and singing with enthusiasm the oft-repeated declaration —

"Il y a longtepas que je t'aime,
Jamais je ne t' oublerai."

From this time onward till the end of his journey in America, this simple melody became the favorite piece, or was brought in as an accompaniment to other music, at receptions and parties, and in short, upon all occasions wherever music was in order, and for this reason it is now better known outside of Canada than all the rest of French-Canadian songs put together.

The following not-very-literal English translation of this chanson, has in one sense more poetic merit than the original, inasmuch as it has a rhyme, to which the French does not pretend.

As by the crystal fount I strayed,
On which the dancing moonbeams played,
The water seemed so clear and bright,
I bathed myself in its delight;
 I loved thee from the hour we met,
 And never can that love forget.

The water seemed so clear and bright,
I bathed myself in its delight;
The nightingale above my head,
As sweet a stream of music shed,
 I loved thee, etc.

The nightingale above my head,
As sweet a stream of music shed,
Sing, nightingale, thy heart is glad,
But I could weep, for mine is sad;
 I loved thee, etc.

Sing, nightingale, thy heart is glad,
But I could weep, for mine is sad;
For I have lost my lady fair,
And she has left me to despair!
 I loved thee, etc.

For I have lost my lady fair,
And she has left me to despair,
For that I gave not, when she spoke,
The rose that from its tree I broke.
 I loved thee, etc.

For that I gave not, when she spoke,
The rose that from its tree I broke,
I wish the rose were on its tree,
And my beloved again with me.
 I loved thee, etc.

I wish the rose were on its tree,
And my beloved again with me,
Or that the tree itself were cast
Into the sea, before this passed.
 I loved thee, etc

Of the above chanson, Marmier observes: "As you notice, there is neither verse nor rhyme, nor anything else besides an outlandish measure of syllables ; * * * Yet these rude couplets, sung in the rudest of melodies, have in them an indescribable melancholy that penetrates the soul."

An English writer who published his observations in 1864, gives one of these songs, prefaced with the following descriptive account of its execution:

"The French Canadian boatmen seem to be a happy devil-may-care sort of fellows, who did not allow the thought for to-morrow to interfere in any way with the enjoyment of to-day. They sing in concert very plaintively; and some of their favorite ballads are highly pathetic. One day I was prevailed upon by a friend to take an excursion in a canoe, manned by half a dozen of these thoughtless people. Upon sailing up the St. Lawrence, as they warmed to their work, they commenced singing the following chanson, and so prettily was it executed, that the effect was most extraordinary:

POSING FOR A PICTURE.

The following rather free translation has been furnished us:

> With hearts as wild
> As joyous child,
> Lived Rhoda of the mountain ;
> Her only wish
> To seek the fish
> In the waters of the fountain.
> Oh, the violet, white and blue !
>
> The stream is deep,
> The banks are steep,
> Down in the flood fell she,
> When there rode by
> Right gallantly,
> Three barons of high degree.
> Oh, the violets, white and blue !
>
> "Oh, tell us, fair maid,"
> They each one said,
> "Your reward to the venturing knight
> Who shall save your life
> From the water's strife
> By his arm's unflinching might."
> Oh, the violet, white and blue !
>
> "Oh ! haste to my side,"
> The maiden replied,
> "Nor ask of a recompense now !
> When safe on land
> Again we stand
> For such matters is time enow."
> Oh, the violet, white and blue !
>
> But when all free
> Upon the lea
> She found herself once more,
> She would not stay,
> And sped away
> Till she reached her cottage door.
> Oh, the violets, white and blue !
>
> Her casement by,
> That maiden shy
> Began so sweet to sing ;
> Her lute and voice,
> Did e'en rejoice,
> The early flowers of spring.
> Oh, the violet, white and blue !
>
> But the barons proud
> Then spoke aloud :
> "This is not the boon we desire ;
> Your heart and love,
> My pretty dove,
> Is the free gift we require."
> Oh, the violets, white and blue !
>
> "Oh, my heart so true,
> Is not for you,
> Nor for any of high degree ;
> I have pledged my truth
> To an honest youth,
> With a beard so comely to see."
> Oh, the violet, white and blue !

TOM MOORE'S BOAT SONG.—(1804).

In the years 1803-4, the social favorite and graceful writer, Thomas Moore, made a hasty tour through the Middle and Northern States and Canada. It would appear from his writings, and it has been strongly intimated, that this visit to America was designed to afford capital for satire and song in the interest of British prejudice, and under the political agitations of the day there can be no doubt but that this result was in some degree realized.

But whatever may have been the animus or the effect of his writings, we may well afford, after this lapse of time, to forgive him, since he has left us some verses that throw a charm over the places he described, and impart an interest, due to the smoothness of their measure and the poetic sentiments which they embody. His lyrics, entitled "The Lake of the Dismal Swamp," and "The Canadian Boat Song," are of this number. Moore was born in 1779, and when he passed this way, in 1804, was therefore about twenty-five years of age. He had already gained popular notoriety by his writings ; and the extraordinary attentions paid to him, especially among English officials in Canada and elsewhere, gave a prominence to his presence wherever he travelled. In a letter to his mother, written soon after his passage down the St. Lawrence from Niagara in a sailing vessel, in August, 1804, he shows how exceedingly flattering to his vanity these attentions were, making him at once satisfied with himself and with all the rest of mankind. He says :

"In my passage across Lake Ontario, I met with the same politeness which has been so gratifying, and, indeed, convenient to me, all along my route. The captain refused to take what I know is always given, and begged me to consider all my friends as included in the compliment, which a line from me would at any time entitle them to. Even a poor watch-maker at Niagara, who did a very necessary and difficult job for me, insisted I should not think of paying him, but accept it as the only mark of respect he could pay one he had heard so much of, but never expected to meet with. This is the very nectar of life, and I hope, I trust, it is not vanity to which the cordial owes all its sweetness. No; it gives me a feeling towards all mankind, which I am convinced is not unamiable; the impulse which begins with self, spreads a circle instantaneously round it, which includes all the sociabilities and benevolences of the heart."

As to the circumstances under which the Boat Song was written, these can best be learned from his own pen. In a note appended to the full edition of his writings, we find the following account :

"I wrote these words to an air which our boatmen sung to us frequently. The wind was so unfavorable that they were obliged to row all the way, and we were five days in descending the river from Kingston to Montreal, exposed to an intense sun during the day, and at night forced to take shelter from the dews in any miserable huts upon the banks that would receive us. But the magnificent scenery of the St. Lawrence repays all those difficulties. Our voyageurs had good voices, and sang perfectly in tune together. The original words of the air, to which I adapted these stanzas, appeared to be a long, incoherent story, of which I could understand but little from the barbarous pronunciation of the Canadians.

"The stanzas are supposed to be sung by those voyageurs who go to the Grand Portage by the Utawas river."

ET REGIMEN CANTUS HORTATUR. — QUINTILIAN.

Faintly, as tolls the evening chime,
Our voices keep tune, and our oars keep time;
Soon as the woods on shore look dim,
We'll sing at St. Ann's our parting hymn.
    Row, brothers, row, the stream runs fast,
    The rapids are near, and the daylight's past.

Why should we yet our sail unfurl?
There is not a breath the blue wave to curl!
But when the wind blows off the shore,
Oh! sweetly we'll rest on our weary oar.
    Blow, breezes, blow, the stream runs fast,
    The rapids are near, and the daylight's past.

Utawa's tide! this trembling moon
Shall see us float over the surges soon.
Saint of this green isle! hear our prayer,
Oh! grant us cool heavens and favoring air.
    Blow, breezes, blow, the stream runs fast,
    The rapids are near, and the daylight's past.

We have met with two translations of Moore's Boat Song into French, but neither of them are of much merit.

Besides these Boat Songs, the islands present many poetic associations that give to them peculiar interest. The late Caleb Lyon, of Lyonsdale, many years since, published a poem somewhat after the style of Byron's "Isles of Greece," that has been so often reproduced that we deem it proper not to include it in this volume.

The religious meetings that have been held upon Wellesley Island have given rise to some poetic reminiscences of peculiar interest, especially those relating to Mr. Philip B. Bliss, whose participation in the Sunday-School Parliament, in 1876, was brought sadly to mind by the railroad casualty that, before the next year, ended his life at Ashtabula, Ohio. This event has been made the subject of memorial verses by Miss Winslow, of Brooklyn. The following are the opening stanzas of this poem:

    Last year he stood amongst us all,
      Acknowledged King of Song.
    Last year we heard his deep tones fall
      The river side along;
    We saw his reverend mien, we knew
      His spirit true and bold,
    But of our singer's inner life
      The half was never told.

    We heard the story, as it flew
      On the western wires along,
    With bated breath we heard it true,
      God took our King of Song :
    We read of fiery chariot wheels,
      Of wintry waters cold,
    But angels saw the agony-
      The half was never told.

THE "MILLE ILES" OF CRÉMIZIE, THE CANADIAN POET.[*]

This poem extends through more than fifty stanzas, in which the author lets his fancy

---

[*] Joseph Octave Crémazie, a native of Lower Canada, was gifted with a fine poetic talent, and produced several pieces that have been greatly admired for the elegance of their style, and the highly poetic sentiments which they express.

M. Crémazie was a merchant at Quebec, but proving unsuccessful in business, he went from Canada dwell upon what he would do, were he a swallow. He would fly to where the snowflocks fall, and make the wildest places echo to his song. He would visit Spain, where the almond blooms; the gilded dome of Alcazar, and the Royal Palace where the Caliph Omar reigned; Cordova, and Old Castile; Leon, with its brazen gates, and Seville; the Escurial and the Alhambra, and river banks fragrant with opening flowers. He would view the city of Venice, and the Lions of St. Mark; listen to the serenades of an Italian summer evening, and, in short, explore on light and rapid wing whatever region or place the wild world offers — in Europe, in India, or in the land of the Nile, that awakens poetic sentiments, displays pictures of beauty, or recalls the memory of great events.

Having thus touched, as it were, a thousand islands of interest throughout the world, he says:

"But when with floods of light, the balmy springtime comes, with its melodies, its mantle of green and its perfumes—its vernal songs with the morning sun, and all the freshness of awakening life, I would return to my native skies.

"When Eve plucked death from the Tree of Life, and brought tears and sorrow upon earth, Adam was driven out into the world to mourn with her, and taste from the bitter spring that we drink to-day.

"Then angels on their wings, bore the silent eden to the eternal spheres on high, and placed it in the heavens — but in passing through space, they dropped along the way, to mark their course, some flowers from the Garden Divine. These flowers of

---

to Brazil, and from thence to France, and died at Havre, January 17. 1879.

Mr. Lareau, in his Histoire de la Litterature Canadienne, in speaking of the style of this poet, says:

"There is something in Crémazie's talent that is found only in those of native genius — it is inspiration. By sudden and passionate flights, he carries you into the highest spheres of poetry and thought. He adorns his style with coloring the most brilliant, and in his hand everything is transformed and animated. He invests the most common of events with features that elevate and magnify, yet in this exuberance of coloring, and this wealth of words and ideas, he in no degree impairs the simplicity of his subject. The poetic thought of his writings is clear and refined, and his verse is natural, and flows from an abundant source."

changing hues, falling into the great river, became the Thousand Isles — the paradise of the St. Lawrence.

"The Thousand Isles; magnificent necklace of diamond and sapphire that those of the ancient world would have preferred to the bright gold of Ophir! Sublime and beautiful crown that rests upon the ample brow of the St. Lawrence, on her throne of the vast lakes that display the tinted rainbow, and return the echoes of thundering Niagara! The Thousand Isles — charming wonder — oasis on the sleeping waves — that which might be thought a flower-basket borne by a lover's hand! In my picturesque retreats I find naught but peace and happiness, and spend the tranquil days in singing the lays of a heart content!

"Not proud Andalusia—nor the banks of Cadiz— nor the kingdom of the Moors sparkling like rubies — nor the poetic scenes of Florence and Milan — nor Rome with its ancient splendors — nor Naples with its volcano — nor that charmed sea where Stamboul lifts its towers — nor the vales of sorrow where the fierce Giaours dwell — nor India in its native wealth, where Para-Brahma shines, or the seas of verdure that Kalidasa celebrate — nor the land of the pyramids — nor all the treasures of Memphis — nor the rapids of the Nile, where we seek and admire Osiris— shall ever thy echoes repeat from the notes of this lyre which is tuned amid these charming scenes."

GEOLOGY OF THE THOUSAND ISLANDS.

There is much geological interest in the rock formations of this part of the St. Lawrence, and in the evidences that they present as to the changes that the earth's surface has undergone since the beginning. For the most part, the islands consist of gneiss rock, belonging to the Laurentian period, which here form a connecting link between the vast Primary Region, so called, of Upper Canada, and an extensive district of the same in Northern New York. This gneiss is generally obscurely stratified, but with much confusion in the lines of original deposit, as if they had been softened by heat and distorted by pressure, and the stratification, such as it is, is often highly inclined. The rock is composed largely of a reddish feldspar, with variable proportions of quartz and hornblende, and occasional particles of magnetic iron ore. In some places on the New York side it is found to contain dykes of trap and greenstone, that ramify into thin veins, as if injected under great pressure, and in a perfectly liquid form. It also contains, in Jefferson and St. Lawrence counties, most interesting crystalline mineral forms, in great variety and in Rossie, lead was formerly mined in this rock to a large amount.

Upon one of the Thousand Islands opposite Gananoque, the gneiss rock is quarried for cemetery monuments, which are sent to Montreal for polishing, and are thought by many to be as beautiful as the red Scotch granite for this use. The rock is there also quarried for paving blocks, and other uses.

At Gananoque, and at various places among the islands, the Potsdam sandstone occurs in thick masses, rising into cliffs fifty feet or more above the river, and affording a fine material for building, being easily worked when freshly quarried, and hardening upon exposure to the air. A little back from that town, gneiss forms the principal rock, rising in naked ridges, with intervening plains that indicate the presence of level strata of limestone or sandstone beneath. In this region, white crystalline limestone, steatite and various other minerals occur.

Before reaching Brockville, and for a long distance below, calciferous sandstone and the older limestones constitute the only rock in situ, and afford excellent quarries of building stone. These strata are for the most part level, and the very flat region in Jefferson county, lying a little back from the river, and extending several miles inland, is underlaid by this rock. It contains, in many places, the organic remains of lower forms of animal and vegetable life, that sometimes stand out in fine relief upon weathered surfaces of the rock.

At Kingston, and at various points upon both shores, and upon Carlton, Wolfe, Howe, Grindstone and other islands, the Birds'-eye and Black River limestones occur in nearly horizontal strata, and in some places are seen resting directly upon the gneiss, which comes to the surface, here and there, and often rises to a greater elevation than the adjacent limestone. It would appear that at these places an island existed at the time when the sandstones, elsewhere so abundant, were being deposited, and that the limestones were formed directly over the gneiss. This limestone is largely used for building purposes, at Kingston and elsewhere, and it makes excellent lime. From the lower and impure strata of this rock, water-lime, or hydraulic cement, was formerly made in Jefferson county. These limestones at various places contain fossil corals, sponges, shells, and other organic remains peculiar to the older Silurian period. The Black River limestone, in Watertown, Brownville, and other places, has extensive caves, worn by currents of water in former times. These have been explored to considerable distances, and appear to have been formed by the widening of natural fissures in the rock. Their section is more or less oval in form, sometimes wider than high, and nearly uniting along the line of the fissure, above and below.

The broken region, of which the Thousand Islands are a part, affords on either side of the river, in various places, a number of picturesque lakes, and within a distance of twenty miles in Jefferson county, there are extensive mines of red hematite, that have been wrought for more than fifty years, supplying several iron furnaces in their vicinity, and a large amount of ore for exportation to other points. Geologically, these iron ores occur in thick beds along the junction of the gneiss and the older fossiliferous formations, and they seem to extend downward to an unlimited extent.

In speaking of the Thousand Islands as a field for geological study, a writer, who has taken a great interest in this subject, says:

"One of the finest River Archipelagoes on the globe, is this of the St. Lawrence. Indeed, it is almost the only one that has such a vast number of islets, all of rocky formation; high, healthy, wooded, without muddy or marshy shores, small enough for inexhaustible variety deep, navigable channels everywhere, and above all, the very crown and glory of the picturesque. * * * The location is one of the very best for geological study. The Laurentian system is reckoned the oldest exposure, or among the oldest, on the globe. The granite is largely composed of feldspar, and so differs widely from the

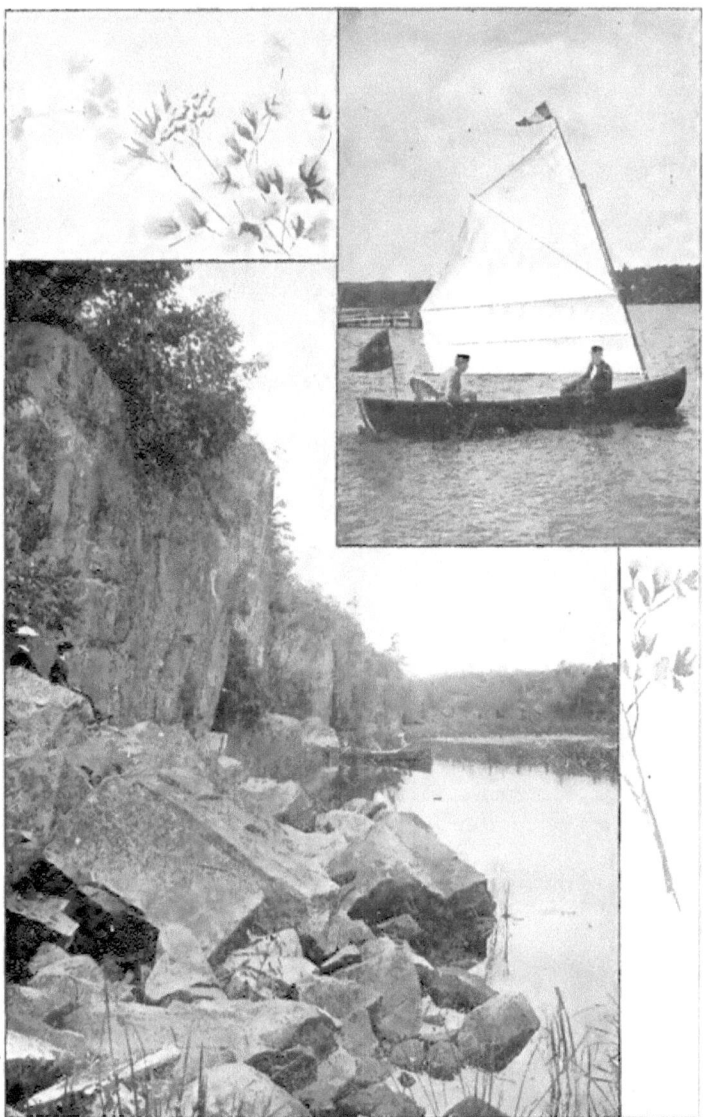

A HUGE PILE OF GRANITE.   BAT-WING SAILING SKIFF.

famous granites of New England, in which hornblende forms so large an element, and which are nearly a true syenite. The Potsdam sandstone here lies directly upon the granite. Both show wonderfully the erosion of waves by which the great inland sea, of ancient geological ages, wore down this partial outlet to the sea. Both show, also, the grinding and planing action of the glacial drift, which here wrought with enormous power. There are drift strise or grooves here, cut into this hard granite, some of them showing for several rods in length, straight as a line, and as wide and deep as half a hogshead divided lengthwise of the staves.

"A block of granite, as large as a small house, held fast in the under surface of a moving sheet of ice, as a glazier's diamond in its steel handle; another sheet of ice, hundreds of feet thick and thousands of miles wide, and creeping onward with a slow but irresistible movement — what a glass-cutter that! And when that whole sheet of ice is thickly studded on its under side with such blocks, great and small, we can get a conception of what an enormous rasp the hand of Omnipotence wielded in planing and polishing all the upper surfaces, especially the northern, western, and north-western exposures of these mighty rocks. The tooth-marks of this rasp are the glacial striæ of geologists, and this is an excellent place to study them.

"For half a mile, fronting on Eel bay, there is an almost continuous frontage of the glacier-planed rocks. At its western end, this rocky ridge breaks down abruptly in lofty precipices called the 'Palisades,' with a deep, navigable strait of the river, called the 'Narrows.' Here is an admirable place to study the cleavage and fracture of these rocks, and the whole is one of the finest scenic views of the Great River."

An anonymous writer, in a book of Travels "dedicated to the Wanderer by one of his class,"— but known to be John F. Campbell, of Islay, had his attention much attracted by geological phenomena, and in noticing glacial agencies, remarks as follows concerning this part of the St. Lawrence :

"At the foot of Lake Ontario, at Brockville, a rock of gray quartz in the town is so finely polished that lines on it were invisible, and almost imperceptible, till a heel-ball rubbing brought them out. Their main direction is N. 45° East (magnetic), and large polished grooves, in which sand-lines occur, are ten feet wide. At other spots on the same rock, lines point north and have other bearings, but the whole shape of the country bears N. E. and S. W.

"Beyond Brockville, the Thousand Islands of Lake Ontario closely resemble groups of low rocks off Gottenburgh. The solid rock foundation of Canada, up to the level of Lake Ontario, is glaciated. It is striated in various directions, but the main lines observed aimed from Belleisle towards Niagara. Upon or near the rock are beds of sand, shells, gravel, and clay, with large and well scratched bowlders of foreign origin. Higher than these beds of drift are more beds of sand, shells, gravel, clay and bowlders as high up as the top of Montreal Mountain, and the top of Niagara Falls."

In noticing these phenomena of glacial action, it may be remarked that the whole surface of the country north and south, and to a great distance, is found strewn here and there with bowlders, some of them of immense size, and in other places are moraines or ridges in great abundance. Drift-hills composed of sand, gravel and bowlders, sometimes cemented by clay into "hard-pan," are a common occurrence.

LAKE RIDGES.

We may in this connection notice the "Lake Ridges," so-called, that occur on both sides of the lake, and various elevations above its present level. These particularly engaged the attention of Prof. Charles Lyell, the English geologist, who, in his journey in 1842, stopped at Toronto to examine them as they occur northward from that city. The first of the ridges was a mile inland — and 108 feet above the present level of the lake. It arose from thirty to forty feet above the level land at its base, and could be traced by the eye running a long distance east and west, being marked by a narrow belt of fir-wood, while above and below, the soil was clayey, and bore other kinds of timber.

The second ridge, a mile and a half further inland, was 208 feet above the lake at its base, as determined by canal and railroad surveys, and arose fifty to seventy feet high, the ground being flat both above and below, and at the foot lay a great number of bowlders, which, from their composition, showed that they came from the north. Some of these bowlders lay on the top of the ridge, but there were but few erratic rocks on the soil between these ridges.

Another ride of two miles and a half, in a northerly direction, brought him to a third ridge, five miles from the lake — less conspicuous than either of the former, being little more than a steep slope of ten feet by which the higher terrace was reached, only eighty feet above the base of the second ridge. Thus he went on, passing one ridge after another, sometimes deviating several miles from the direct course, to fix the continuity of level, and observing their general character. He saw no less than eleven of these ridges in all, some of which might be called cliffs, or the abrupt terminations of terraces of clay, which cover the silurian rocks of that region to a great depth, and belonging to the drift or bowlder formation.

The highest ridge was about 680 feet above the lake, the water-shed between Lakes Ontario and Simcoe being 762 feet. From the summit the slope toward Lake Simcoe descends 282 feet, and along down this, several ridges were found, showing that water had formerly flowed to a higher level than the present.

Mr. Lyell remarks that he had never before observed so striking an example of banks, terraces, and accumulations of stratified gravel, sand and clay, maintaining over wide areas so perfect a horizontality as in this district north of Toronto. He remarks that the hypothesis of the successive breaking down of barriers of an ancient lake or fresh-water ocean has now been generally abandoned, from the impossibility of conceiving here, as in the west of Scotland, as to where lands capable of damming up the waters to such height could have been situated, or how, if they have existed, they could have disappeared, while the levels of the ancient beaches remained undisturbed. He, therefore, inclines to the belief that they were the margin of the ancient sea, which has changed level from the upheavals of the continent. This must have been intermittent; so that pauses occurred, during which the coast-line remained stationary for centuries, and in which the waves would have time to cut cliffs, or throw up beaches, or throw down littoral deposits and sand-banks near the shore.

In support of this theory, he cites the example of Scandinavia, which has been slowly, yet perceptibly rising from the sea within the historic period, at the rate of two or three feet a century. We know too little of the laws that govern these subterranean movements, to deny the possibility of such intermittent changes in the level of the sea.

While the cliff margins might have been the abrupt shore in an extremely ancient period, the bars of sand on the highest levels may have been formed on the inland margin of shallow waters, at some distance from deep waters, as may be seen in course of formation in some places at the present time.

DEPTH OF THE ST. LAWRENCE.—TIDES IN THE LAKES.

The soundings in the river, among the islands, indicate a great irregularity of depth, the bottom being generally rocky, and quite as diversified as the parts that rise above the surface. The greatest depth is 120 feet, but the usual soundings are from thirty to sixty feet. As a general rule, the navigation among the islands is entirely safe to vessels of the size usually employed upon these waters, and all the dangerous rocks and reefs have their positions marked.

The level of the river differs one year with another, the extreme range being about seven feet. These changes are not the immediate effects of the excessive rains, such as cause floods in other rivers, but appear to be occasioned by the different quantities of rain falling, in some years more than in others, and which finds its way down months afterward. A series of several years of high water, and others of low water, are known to occur. The level of the river is also affected by strong prevailing winds, blowing up or down the lake, and several instances of rapid fall, followed by a returning wave of extraordinary height, have been reported. Some have supposed these sudden changes of level to be caused by earthquake-shocks, but a more probable theory appears to be that they are occasioned by the passage of a water-spout, or a tornado at a distant point. There is also found to be a slight, but well-marked tide in the lakes, depending upon lunar changes, like those upon the ocean, capable of the same prediction, and governed by the same laws. This fact has been proved by long-continued, self-recording observations. It may often be disguised by oscillation in the level occasioned by the winds. It was observed by Charlevoix, in 1721, that the level of the lake changed several times in a day, as may be seen anywhere along the shore, especially upon a gently-sloping beach. This is probably due chiefly to the action of the winds.

BOUNDARY LINES BETWEEN THE TWO GOVERNMENTS.

In French colonial times, there was no boundary acknowledged by both governments, as existing between the French and English settlements. Each party claimed far beyond the point allowed by the other, and the encroachments of the former upon Lake Champlain and in the west are well known to have led to the war that ended in 1760, in the establishment of English authority over the whole.

The province of Quebec, as created by royal proclamation, was bounded on the south, from the Connecticut to the St. Lawrence rivers, by the line of 45° north latitude, and south-westward by a line running from the point where this line intersected the St. Lawrence to the south end of Lake Nipissing. A survey of the line of 45° was begun in 1772 by John Collins, on the part of Quebec, and Thomas Vallentine, on the part of New York, but the latter having died, Claude Joseph Sauthier was appointed in his place, and the work was completed October 20, 1774.

In the treaty of 1783, the line of the river and lakes was adopted as the boundary westward from St. Regis, but no surveys of this part were undertaken until about thirty-five years afterwards. The military posts on the American side of the boundary were held by the British for the purpose of protecting the claims of British subjects until definitely relinquished under the Jay treaty, signed November 19, 1794, under which it was agreed that they should be given up on or before June 1, 1796. In the meantime, the discussion as to boundaries continued, and Lieutenant-Governor J. G. Simcoe, of Upper Canada, was particularly strenuous in insisting upon an aggressive advance of the frontier, that should secure to British interests in the interior the magnificent empire which the French had endeavored to establish. He would have had Niagara the seat of government of this English America, and had his first concessions been allowed, the western boundary of the United States would have been the Genesee river, and a line extending from its headwaters to the sources of the Ohio, and thence southward, along the Alleghenies to the Gulf coast.

When this could not be secured, he proposed a line from Presque Isle [Erie, Pa.] to Pittsburgh; then the Cuyahoga, and, as a last extremity, the Miami river. Early in 1792, in a long letter to the home government, he pointed out the great advantages that would result to Canada from the adoption of a line that should run from Lake Ontario across the country to the southern end of Lake Champlain, including the disputed boundaries upon that lake. Until the last moment, he had clung to the hope of attaching Vermont to Canada, and the correspondence of that period shows that an expectation of this result had been encouraged by the turbulent leaders in that State as an alternative preferred to submission to the authority of either of the claiming States. He adds:

"I should think Oswego, and I question whether Niagara would not be a cheap sacrifice for such a limit, which would be strictly defensive on our part, and calculated to prevent future disagreements. I have heard that Carlton Island, the most important post on Lake Ontario, is on the British side of the line, as the better channel is between that and the southern shore."

Again, in writing to the Rt. Hon. Henry Dundas, November 4, 1792, he says: "I beg to send a map of the river St. Lawrence, that in case of a treaty being entered into with the United States, it may plainly appear of what consequence it is to render it effectual and permanent, that the British boundary should enclose the islands of the St. Lawrence."

Under the treaty of Ghent, which ended the war of 1812-15, Peter B. Porter was appointed on the part of the United States, and Andrew Barclay on the part of Great Britain, as commissioners to run and mark the line. The survey was begun in 1817, and their report was signed June 18, 1822, subject to ratification by their respective governments. Their operations were conducted with much precision, and the details were reduced to maps that have never been published. Copies of these are preserved in the offices of record of the countries concerned.

While the boundary survey was in progress, Col. Samuel Hawkins, the agent of the American commission, gave a fête champêtré upon one of the lower islands, to which the members of the commission on both sides were invited. The incident is described by Mr. Darby, who says:

"The day was even on the St. Lawrence uncommonly fine, and amid the groves of aspen, wildcherry, and linden trees, the scene seemed more than earthly. Mrs. Hawkins presided, and in the bowers of the St. Lawrence recalled the most polished manners of civilized society in the crowded city. At the close of evening Major Joseph Delafield and myself walked over the island, and in full view of the objects which excited our feelings, concluded that no spot on the globe could unite in so small a space more to please, to amuse, and gratify the fancy."

The earlier surveys between the St. Lawrence and Connecticut rivers being made without precision, were found in 1818 to be almost everywhere upon a line too far north. At St. Regis the departure from the true latitude of 45° was found to be 1,375 feet; at the French Mills [Fort Covington] it was 154 feet; at Chateauguy river, 975 feet, and at Rouse's Point, 4,576 feet.

The government of the United States had begun to erect a fort on Lake Champlain, near what was the supposed boundary, soon after the war of 1812-15, and this was wholly carried over into Canada, by the survey of 1818. It had been christened "Fort Montgomery," but now in common parlance was called "Fort Blunder." The Americans being unable, and the Canadians unwilling to protect the property, it became the prey of whoever chose to plunder it of materials, as needed for building purposes. Finally by the surveys of 1842, the old line of 1774 was taken as a compromise, and the site being thus restored to the possession of the United States, work was resumed and carried, we believe, to completion under the original name.

In the surveys made under the Webster-Ashburton treaty of 1842, J. B. Bucknall Estcourt, lieutenant-colonel, was appointed by the government of Great Britain, and Albert Smith by that of the United States. They confirmed the line in the river, as it had been located under the treaty of Ghent, and the old line marked by Vallentine and Collins between the St. Lawrence and Lake Champlain. They were able to follow this line by the marks on the trees, still visible, or found by cutting into them; but where these could not be found, or where clearings had been made, straight lines were run between these old landmarks, and iron monuments were set at every angle of deflection, and at the crossing of rivers, lakes and roads. The boundary line is, therefore, not on the true parallel of 45°, nor in the middle of the channel, but it is a conventional line, agreed upon by both governments, and accurately defined by monuments and records.

The larger islands in the St. Lawrence, below Ogdensburg, had long been settled under St. Regis Indian titles, and were occupied at the time of the survey by settlers, who, up to that time, had been regarded as British subjects.

Some forty years afterwards, the persons who had sustained losses by this transfer applied to the State of New York for compensation, and their claims became the subject of investigation and of legislative action for their relief.

HYDROGRAPHICAL AND TOPOGRAPHICAL SURVEYS.

BRITISH SURVEYS.

The first surveys of Lakes Ontario and Erie were made in the summer of 1789, under the direction of Mr. Niff, an engineer. They only embraced the south shore of Lake Ontario, from Carleton Island to Niagara, and the south shore of Lake Erie, from its eastern end to Detroit.

The engineer's instructions required him, in addition to the soundings, to note the locations proper for ship-building, the quality of land for settlement, and the kind of timber along the shores. It will be remembered that the whole of this region, now within the States, was then still held by the British military authorities, and it may be inferred from the above instructions that they were looking forward to a time when it should be permanently under their control.

Soon after the war of 1812-15, a survey of the eastern end of Lake Ontario and of the river St. Lawrence, as far down as the Gallop Rapids, was made by Capt. W. F. W. Owen, of the Royal Navy, with soundings, a definite delineation of the shores and islands, and some topographical details concerning the adjacent parts. This survey was completed in 1818, and published by the Hydrographical Office of the Admiralty in 1828, forming a series of five charts. These were re-engraved, with corrections, in 1861, and are found in the collections known as the "Bayfield Charts," which in all embrace an extensive series of lake surveys.

An elaborate survey of the region around Kingston, including the adjacent islands, upon a large scale, and showing the contour of surface and details of topography, with special reference to its military defences, was prepared a few years since, and a limited edition printed.

UNITED STATES LAKE SURVEYS.

For many years, the survey of the northern and northwestern lakes has been in course of execution by the corps of engineers of the war department. These trigometrical and hydrographical surveys were begun upon Lake Ontario and the river St. Lawrence about ten years since, and during the years 1871 to 1875, were extended along the river from St. Regis to the lake, under the direction of Brig.-Gen. C. B. Comstock. In 1876, the results were published in six charts, which represent the part of the river from St. Regis to the foot of Wolfe Island, upon a scale of 1 to 30,000 or a little more than two miles to an inch. They embrace the whole of the river, and the topography of both shores, but do not indicate the boundary line. A map of the eastern end of Lake Ontario, being No. 1 of a separate series, on a scale of 1 to 80,000, or about four-fifths of an inch to a mile, has also been published under the same direction. These charts all have a great number of soundings, with indications of the nature of the bottom, the contour and cultivation of the land on the islands and adjacent shores, the place of buildings, the lines of roads, and of streets in villages, and the character and extent of woodlands, with an accuracy of detail that proves the excellence of the work.

LIGHT-HOUSES.

A few facts concerning the light-houses along the St. Lawrence, may not be without interest:

The AMERICAN LIGHT-HOUSES are under the care of a "light-house board," in the Treasury Department, and the coasts and rivers of the country are divided into fifteen districts. Of these, the tenth district extends from St. Regis to Detroit, with the headquarters of the inspector and engineer at Buffalo. Within this district, there are sixty-seven light-houses, and about 150 buoys (spars and cans), anchored so as to show the course of the channel, or the position of dangerous places. These spars, etc., are taken up at the close of navigation, and replaced after the ice has disappeared in the spring. By their color and numbers, they give information that all navigators must understand. There are six American lights from Ogdensburg to Tibbett's Point, inclusive. They have all fixed white lights, with lens apparatus of the fourth or sixth order. Their names and position are as follows:

Ogdensburgh, on a rocky islet, 190 yards from south shore; built in 1834; refitted in 1870; a square tower, 42 feet high, with keeper's dwelling.

Cross-over Island, 20 miles above Ogdensburg; a tower 37 feet high, on keeper's brick dwelling; lantern black; built in 1837; refitted in 1870.

Sister Island, 6¼ miles further up; a tower on keeper's stone dwelling; lantern black, with red dome; built in 1870; height, 43 feet.

Sunken Rock, 6 miles further up, on Bush Island, about a quarter of a mile north of Alexandria Bay; an octagonal brick tower, sheathed with boards; white; height, 31 feet; built in 1847; refitted in 1855.

Rock Island, 7 miles further up; keeper's dwelling of brick, white, with a low tower on top; dome black; height, 39 feet; built in 1847; refitted in 1855. [Shown hereafter.]

Tibbett's Point, 23 miles above, at the outlet of the lake; a stone building connected by covered way with a round brick tower 67 feet high; white; built in 1827; refitted in 1854.

The oldest light-house on the lake is that near Fort Niagara, built in 1813; the next oldest is the one on Gallo Island, built in 1820. All the lights on the St. Lawrence and the Great Lakes are discontinued from January 1st until the opening of navigation, unless otherwise specially directed.

The DOMINION LIGHT-HOUSE SYSTEM is under the charge of the Minister of Marine and Fisheries, and at the beginning of 1880 embraced 482 lights, of which Labrador had 4; Newfoundland 3; Gulf and River of St. Lawrence 140 to Montreal — 19 from thence to Windmill Point near Prescott, and 10 from thence to the lake; Saguenay River 6; Richlieu River 5; Lake Memphramagog 6; Ottawa River 16; Lake Ontario 29; Lake Simcoe 1; Lake Erie 15; Detroit River 2; Lake St. Clair 1; Lake Huron 32; Lake Superior 9; Prince Edward Island 29; Cape Breton Island 23; Nova Scotia (Atlantic Coast) 63; Bay of Fundy 48; St. John's River 13; Winnipeg 1, and British Columbia 7.

The Canadian lights from Prescott to Lake Ontario are as follows:

Cole Shoal, on a pier five miles west of Brockville.

Grenadier Island (S. W. point), two miles below Rockport.

Lindoe Island, five miles west of Rockport.

Gananoque Narrows, five miles below Gananoque, on Little Stave Island.

Jack Straw Shoal, on a pier, north side of channel, three miles below Gananoque.

Spectacle Shoal, on a pier, north side, one and a quarter miles west of Gananoque.

Red Horse Rock, on pier, S. E. side of channel, one mile above Spectacle Shoals.

Burnt Island, at S. E. point of island, north side of channel, half mile from Red Horse Rock.

Wolfe Island, on Quebec, or east point of island — and Brown's or Knapp's Point, on Wolfe Island.

These are all fixed single lights, with metallic reflectors, on white square wooden towers, and were all built in 1856, except Wolfe Island Light in 1861, and that on Brown's Point in 1874.

STEAM NAVIGATION UPON LAKE ONTARIO AND THE ST. LAWRENCE.

The first steamboat that appeared upon this lake was the Oneida, in 1817. The boat was 110 feet long, twenty-four feet wide, and eight deep, and measured 237 tons, and had a low-pressure cross-head engine, and a thirty-four-inch cylinder with four-feet stroke. She had two masts, and used sails when the wind favored. It was indeed a new era in navigation, and from this time Durham boats, bateaux, and all the pleasant associations which boat songs recall were doomed to disappear. The new steamboat was indeed a wonder in this part of the world, and at every landing crowds assembled from far and wide, to catch a view of the first wreath of smoke from her stack, and to watch and wonder as she slowly and majestically came up, and as she independently departed on her appointed course. Every village that could muster a cannon, and every steeple that had a bell, announced the event, and joined in the welcome. Bonfires and illuminations, the congratulations of friends and interchange of hospitalities, signalized the event along the whole of the route, and the occasion was jotted down as one to be long remembered. The round trip

SPORT ISLAND—THE PROPERTY OF F. P. WEHUR, MAUCH CHUNK, PA.

from Ogdensburgh to Lewiston required ten days. Fare, $16 in the cabin, and $8 on deck. Master, Captain Mallaby. The Oneida ran till 1832, seldom making more than five miles an hour. The Frontenac came out from Kingston not long after. From this time down, the number has been legion; but since the completion of the Grand Trunk Railway, the importance of steam navigation has greatly declined, and several fine steamers were taken down the rapids never to return.*

But whatever the future may determine, as regards the lines of business travel, the St. Lawrence will always, in its islands and its rapids, present an attractive route for tourists in the summer season. We may never again witness a fleet of steamers as magnificent as those of the " Ontario and St. Lawrence Steamboat Co.," which in its best days had eleven such in daily us,—while the Canadians at the same time had numerous elegant steamers fully employed; but under the law universally true in business, that the supply will be regulated by the demand, we may confidently look for abundant comfort and elegance in these steamers upon the St. Lawrence. The history of steam navigation scarcely presents a more remarkable freedom from accidents than does that upon this lake and river — a circumstance due as well to the intelligence of those entrusted with their navigation, as to the sagacity of owners, who saw their true interest to consist in the certainty of their engagements, rather than in a reputation for extraordinary achievements in amount of business, or high rate of speed.

The fine boats of the Folger Brothers, as well as of the Richelieu and Ontario Navigation Company, have certainly reduced precision to perfection, and accidents to a minimum.

Life-saving stations were first established by the Government of the United States upon Lake Ontario, in the summer of 1854, consisting originally of Francis's Metallic Life-Boats, with fixtures, but without buildings to shelter, or crews to manage them. The system has since been perfected as the wants of the service required.

The present lines through the Thousand Islands are quite numerous, by far the larger part being owned and run by the Folger Bros., of Kingston. Their boats are in every way superior, and really leave nothing to be desired.

LUMBERING UPON THE RIVER ST. LAWRENCE.

In several of the descriptions given in the preceding pages, allusion is made to woodland scenes and woodmen's labor. One of the earliest and most extensive operators in this line was William Wells, eldest son of Thos. Wells, from Sandown, N. H., who came to Canada in 1787, and began lumbering operations about 1790, on the island to which his name is now often applied. He would establish a shanty at a convenient point, and with the aid of hired men, work up into staves all the timber suitable to his use within convenient reach, and when this was exhausted he would remove to another place. He thus went over the whole of this island and other islands in the river, until the business became no longer profitable. His market was England, by way of Quebec, to which place his stock was sent upon rafts. At a later period, Carlton Island for a short time became an important lumber station, and later still, Clayton, where for many years immense quantities of timber, brought down from the upper lakes in vessels, were made up into rafts in French Creek, and sent down to Quebec. It was there again loaded into vessels, for the European markets. In recent years, the foot of Wolfe Island, and Garden Island, opposite to Kingston, have been the principal lumbering

---

* A large amount of information concerning steamboats upon the lake will be found in Hough's History of St. Lawrence and Franklin Counties (1853), and in Haddock's History of Jefferson County (1895).

For many years Clayton was a noted place for steamboat building. Some of the finest steamers that ever appeared on these waters came from the shipyard of Mr. John Oades, of that place. Of these the New York and the Bay State,—truly magnificent in their appointments, were afterwards employed on government service in the South. Other lake steamers were used during our late war as blockade runners on the Southern coast.

stations on the river. The business has for a long time depended upon supplies brought down from distant points in the West, and is now greatly reduced from the exhaustion of supplies.

AUTUMNAL SCENERY OF THE NORTHERN STATES AND OF CANADA.

We have noticed in the descriptions of several travellers in the preceding pages an allusion to the coloring of the forests of this region towards the close of autumn, forming, indeed, one of the attractions most likely to fix itself in the memory in the declining season of the year. This was most fully given by the German traveller, Dr. Kohl, whose account of the islands will be found on preceding pages. We will commence the description with his arrival at Kingston, late on a warm, bright, richly-colored autumnal afternoon, when the setting sun presented a most imposing appearance. There was still enough of daylight left to get a fine view of the city and its suburbs, and he departed by steamer for Toronto the same evening. He describes the passage as one of exquisite beauty, the last glow of twilight shedding a glory over the apparently boundless water, which seemed, like the sea, without limit. As it grew dark, the waters presented the novel spectacle of moving lights near the shore, where the fishermen were following their business by torchlight; and, later in the night, the heavens were lit up by the aurora borealis with unusual splendor.

It may almost be questioned as to whether, amid these shifting scenes of novelty, our worthy traveller got time for a moment's repose, for his description of the midnight aurora, with its gleaming pencils of light, its corona, and its dazzling arch, passes directly into the picture of a morning on the lake, that follows:

"But its splendors were far exceeded in beauty by the tender tints of the aurora orientalis that afterwards showed themselves on the eastern horizon, and then filled the whole atmosphere with their light. A delicate mist had risen toward sunrise, and the sun had made use of this gauzy veil to paint it with the loveliest pale tints. I do not wonder that the taste for coloring should develop itself in such a land of mist, where the palette of nature is provided with such a variety of finely graduated hues. The eye is sharpened to their differences, while in tropical regions, where the chief colors appear most strikingly, the senses are dazzled. As the sun rose, I remarked to my surprise that the redness of the morning dawn had not passed from the horizon, as it commonly does, but remained hanging as a very decided red segment of a circle, and the higher the sun rose, the further it stretched, till towards eleven o'clock it occupied one-half of the horizon, while the opposite side, which was of a light grayish tint, lost ground more and more, and at length the sun appeared as a radiant focus in the center of an atmosphere of light, which, with few variations, passed into red all round the horizon. I saw this remarkable phenomenon here for the first time, but afterwards frequently, and learned that it especially belonged to the 'Indian Summer,' and was known under the name of 'the pink mist.'"

A short time after, our traveller, in passing northward from Toronto, on the route to Lake Simcoe, had occasion to again revert to the glories of the autumnal forest, which he had already noticed in passing amid the Thousand Islands. His description has no local application, but will faithfully represent the impressions of an intelligent observer in the deciduous forests of any part of the Northern States, and of Canada, in the fading season of the year:

"The trees here still gloried in the rich coloring of their leafage, although in Quebec, a fortnight before, the vegetation had assumed a bare and wintry aspect. The elegant and much-prized maple was conspicuous among them, as it mostly is in Canada, and its leaves exhibited more shades and gradations of golden-yellow and crimson than can be found in the best furnished color-box. Even when you walk on dark cloudy days in the forest, the trees shed around you such gorgeous colors that you might imagine it was bright sunlight. You seem to be walking in the midst of some magic sunset of the declining year. The leaves of the maple are, too, as elegantly cut as they are richly adorned with color, and the Canadians pay them the same homage as the Irish do their green immortal shamrock. They are collected, pressed and preserved; ladies select the most beautiful to form natural garlands for their ball-dresses. You see in Canada tables and other furniture inlaid with bouquets and wreaths of varnished maple leaves, and you see an elegant steamer with the name Maple Leaf painted in large letters on the side. Sometimes the Canadians would ask me, in their glorious woods, whether I had ever seen anything like them in Europe; and if I answered that, though their woods were especially beautiful, I had elsewhere observed red and yellow autumn leaves, they would smile and shake their heads, as if they meant to say that a stranger could never appreciate the beauties of a Canadian forest thus dying in golden flame. I have seen a Swiss, born and bred among the Alps, smile just as pityingly at the enthusiasm of strangers for their mountains, evidently regarding it as a mere momentary flare, and that they only could know how to value the charms of a land of mountains.

"The magnificent coloring of these trees strikes you most, I think, when the gilding has only just begun, and the green, yellow and scarlet tints are mingled with the most delicate transitions. Sometimes it seems as if Nature were amusing herself with these graceful playthings, for you see green trees twisted about with garlands of rich red leaves, like wreaths of roses, and then again red trees, where the wreaths are green. I followed with delight, too, the series of changes, from the most brilliant crimson to the darkest claret color, then to a rich brown, which passed into the cold pale grey of the winter. It seems to me evident that the sun of this climate has some quite peculiar power in its beams, and that the faintest tint of the autumn foliage has a pure intensity of color that you do not see in Europe. Possibly you see the climate and character of Canada mirrored in these autumn leaves, and it is the rapid and violent transitions of heat and cold that produce these vivid contrasts.

"The frost that sometimes sets in suddenly after a very hot day, is said to be one of the chief painters of these American woods. When he does but touch the trees they immediately blush rosy red. I was warned, therefore, not to regard what I saw this year as the ne plus ultra of his artistic efforts, since the frost had come this time very gradually. The summer heat had lasted unusually long, and the drouth had been extraordinary, so that the leaves had become gradually dry and withered, instead of being suddenly struck by the frost while their sap was still abundant, a necessary condition, it appears, for this brilliant coloring."

As if quite unable to tear himself from a subject that had so thoroughly awakened his attention, our keenly observant traveller, after describing many other scenes of Indian and Pioneer life, presented in his northern journey, again recurs to his favorite impressions. He had been so often interrupted by impertinent inquiries, as to who he was, where he was going, on what business, where he intended to buy land, and where he meant to settle, that he had devised a ready means of getting rid of these annoyances — for when he saw one of these inquisitors approaching, he at once began a short biographical recitation, stating where born, his origin, what he had come for and what not, and so forth, ending with the declaration that he did not intend to settle in the country, nor to buy land. As soon as everybody knew who and what he was, they cared little more about him, and having thus cheaply purchased a truce from further inquiry, he could settle down to the calm enjoyment of the scenery before him. He says:

"I would gladly give some idea of its beauty, but it is often difficult to convey impressions of this kind, without falling into repetitions, which, though often far from unwelcome in nature, where there are always shades of difference, are very apt to be so in books. To me, there was a never-ending enjoyment in gazing on the coloring of a Canadian forest in its autumnal glory, and observing the modifications of their colors produced by a greater or less distance. From the immediate foreground to the remotest point there was a scale of a hundred degrees. The trees near at hand were of a full rose or orange hue, and every leaf a piece of glittering gold, and yet every tree had something that distinguished it from all the rest, and although there were only leaves, the colors equaled those of a tropical forest in spring, when it is covered with blossoms. Farther on, the colors were melted together into one general tint of bright pink, then a little blue mingled with it, and there arose several softest tones of lilac; sometimes according to the conditions of the atmosphere, the distant woods appeared of a deep indigo, and then, perhaps, would interpose a little island of glowing red-gold upon an azure ground, but if your eye followed the line of forest to the east, the colors as well as the trees shrank together, and a great wood of leafy oak, elm and maple would look like a low patch of reddish heath."

The poet Whittier, in describing an autumnal scene, strikingly applicable to this region, although intended for another, says:

Beneath the westward-turning eye
A thousand wooded islands lie —
Gems of the waters! — with each hue
Of brightness set in ocean's blue.
Each bears aloft its tuft of trees
Touched by the pencil of the frost,
And, with the motion of each breeze,

A moment seen — a moment lost —
Changing and blent, confused and tossed,
The brighter with the darker crossed.
Their thousand tints of beauty glow

Down in the restless waves below,
And tremble in the sunny skies,
As if from waving bough to bough
Flitted the birds of paradise.

THE ST. LAWRENCE REAL ESTATE ASSOCIATION.

THIS is the name of an association lately organized at Alexandria Bay, duly incorporated under the Laws of the State of New York.

The following are the officers for 1895:

President,
WILLIAM C. BROWNING.

Vice-President,
E. R. HOLDEN.

Secretary and Treasurer,
EDWARD W. DEWEY.

Directors,
WILLIAM C. BROWNING. CHARLES I. HUDSON.
CHARLES G. EMERY. JAMES C. SPENCER.
EDWARD W. DEWEY. GEORGE C. BOLDT.
E. R. HOLDEN. JAMES H. OLIPHANT.
GEORGE M. PULLMAN.

Executive Committee,
WILLIAM C. BROWNING
E. R. HOLDEN.
EDWARD W. DEWEY.

The objects for which this Association was formed are as follows:

First. To purchase and to hold and occupy, and to buy and sell and mortgage, or to lease, lands and real estate on the shore or on the islands of the St. Lawrence river, and to that portion of said river known as "The Thousand Islands."

Second. To lay out, improve and beautify said lands and real estate by the erection and construction thereon, or upon portions thereof, a club-house or casino, and cottages and other buildings, and piers and wharves, terraces and pleasure grounds, for the use and occupation of this association or other persons, or of clubs or societies organized for the promotion and cultivation of social enjoyment and recreation as summer residents of the St. Lawrence river, among said Thousand Islands, to whom this association may sell or lease said lands or real estate.

Third. Especial reference is hereby made to "The Thousand Island Club," an incorporated association under the Laws of the State of New York, of which the undersigned are members, to whom the said lands and real estate purchased and improved, or portions thereof, may be leased or sold by this association.

The amount of the capital stock of this association shall be twenty thousand dollars ($20,000), divided into two hundred (200) shares, of the par value of one hundred dollars ($100) each, all of which shall be common stock.

The location of its principal office or place of business is in the village of Alexandria Bay, where the stockholders, directors and officers of this association may meet and transact their business, as may be provided and stated in the by-laws of this association, or ordered by the directors from time to time.

The duration of this Association shall be fifty years.

The number of the directors of The St. Lawrence River Real Estate Association shall be nine, each of whom shall be a stockholder, having at least five shares of stock.

THE ST. LAWRENCE CLUB'S DOMICILE, ALEXANDRIA BAY.

MEMBERSHIP OF THE THOUSAND ISLAND CLUB.

Active Members.

Name.	Residence.	Property owned.
Richard A. Anthony	New York	Point Marguerite, Alexandria Bay, N. Y.
George C. Boldt	New York	Waldorf Hotel.
Wm. C. Browning	New York	Hopewell Hall, Alexandria Bay, N. Y.
Henry S. Chandler	Brooklyn	Florence Island, "
Michael Chauncey	Brooklyn	Cuba Island, "
Alson E. Clark	Chicago	Comfort Island, "
Royal E. Deane	New York	Island Royal, "
Edward W. Dewey	New York	Dewey Isle. "
Charles Donohue	New York	St. John Island, "
Charles Donohue, Jr.	New York	St. John Island, "
Francis Donohue	New York	St. John Island, "
Richard H. Eggleston	New York	Idlewild, "
Charles G. Emory	New York	Calumet Island, Clayton, N. Y.
Charles W. Hachett	Utica	St. Lawrence Park.
John L. Hasbrouck	New York	Manhattan Island, Alexandria Bay, N. Y.
Charles H. Hayden	Columbus, O.	Hayden Island, "
William B. Hayden	New York	Hayden Island, "
Henry R. Heath	Brooklyn	Nobby Island, "
C. E. Hill	Chicago	Wanwinet. "
E. R. Holden	New York	Thousand Island Park.
Charles I. Hudson	New York	The Ledges, Alexandria Bay, N. Y.
Nathaniel W. Hunt	Brooklyn	St. Elmo Island, "
James W. Jackson	Plainfield, N. J.	Kewayden, "
Fred'k L. King	New York	Hotel Westminster, "
Egbert LeFevre	New York	Manhattan Island, "
Mortimer G. Lewis	New York	Hotel Westminster, "
D. C. McEwen	Brooklyn	Wildwood, "
C. A. Meyers	New York	The Frontenac, Round Island.
James H. Oliphant	Brooklyn	Nemah-Bin, Alexandria Bay, N. Y.
S. T. Pope	Ogdensburg	Welcome Island, "
Geo. M. Pullman	Chicago	Castle Rest, "
Gilbert S. Rafferty	Pittsburg	Isle Imperial, "
James C. Spencer	New York	Manhattan Island, "
Frank H. Taylor	Philadelphia	Shady Ledge, Round Island.
W. J. Townsend	New York	Sunny Side, Alexandria Bay, N. Y.
Royal C. Vilas	New York	Resort Island, "
E. P. Wilbur	South Bethlehem	Sport Island, "
Rollins H. Wilbur	South Bethlehem	Sport Island, "
W. A. Wilbur	South Bethlehem	Sport Island, "

Associate Members.

H. W. Berlin	New York	Hotel Westminster, Alexandria Bay, N. Y.
Louis Hasbrouck	Ogdensburg	Huguenot Island, "

ISLAND DIRECTORY.

The following is a late revised list of islands and points, with their owners' names, from Clayton to Goose Bay, on the American side:

Cement Point, head of Grindstone Island, owned by W. F. Ford and others.

Goose Island, two acres, owned by E. S. Brooks, Brooklyn.

Hen Island, one-half acre, owned by W. F. Morgan, New York.

Davitts' Island, one-quarter acre, owned by H. G. Davitts, New York.

Carroll Island, two acres, owned by James A. Cheney, Syracuse.

Boscobel Island, one-half acre, owned by G. S. Hopkins, Kansas.

Bluff Island, twenty acres, owned by E. H. Washburn, New York.

Clinton Island, No. 1, fifteen acres, owned by N. S. Seely, New York.

Clinton Island, No. 2, three acres owned by N. S. Seely, New York.

Governor's Island, owned by Charles G. Emery, New York.

Calumet, owned by Charles G. Emory, New York.

Etheridge, head of Round Island, owned by Dr. Geo. D. Whalen, Syracuse.

Shady Ledge, near foot of Round Island, owned by Frank R. Taylor, Philadelphia, Pa.

Brooklyn Heights, foot of Round Island, owned by C. S. Johnson, Brooklyn.

Long Rock, one acre, owned by W. F. Wilson, Watertown.

Hemlock Island, twenty acres, owned by W. F. Porter and W. F. Wilson, Watertown.

Stewart, or Jeffers Island, ten acres, owned by E. P. Gardiner and twelve others, Syracuse, and other places.

Two in Eel Bay, two acres, owned by Dr. E. L. Sargent, Watertown.

Twin Islands, one acre, owned by I. L. Huntington, Theresa.

Watch Island, one acre, owned by S. F. Skinner, New York.

Occident and Orient, three acres, owned by E. N. Robinson, New York.

Isle of Pines, two acres, owned by Mrs. E. N. Robinson, New York.

Frederick Island, two acres, owned by C. L. Frederick, Carthage.

Bay Side, one acre, owned by H. F. Mosher, Watertown.

Riverside, mainland, one acre, owned by J. C. Lee, Gouverneur.

Killain Point, mainland, one acre, owned by Mr. Killain, Lockport, N. Y.

Holloway Point, mainland, one acre, owned by N. Holloway, Omar, N. Y.

Fisher's Landing, mainland, two acres, owned by Mrs. R. Gunn, Omar, N. Y.

Island Home, one acre, owned by Mrs. S. D. Hungerford, Adams, N. Y.

Harmony, one-quarter acre, owned by Mrs. Burger, Syracuse.

Waving Branches, on Wells' Island, owned by D. C. Graham and nine others.

Bonnie Eyrie, on Wells' Island, owned by Mrs. Peck, Boonville, N. Y.

Throop's Dock, on Wells' Island, owned by Drs. C. E. and D. S. J. Latimer, N. Y.

Jolly Oaks, on Wells' Island, twenty acres, owned by John L. Norton and others from Carthage.

Blanch Island, ten acres, owned by Mrs. A. M. Kenyon, Watertown.

Josephine, twenty acres, owned by Mrs. A. M. Kenyon, Watertown.

Craig-Side, Wells' Island, owned by H. A. Laughlin, Pittsburg, Pa.

Covert Point, Wells' Island, owned by B. J. Maycock, Buffalo.

Calumet Island, one-half acre, owned by Oliver H. Green, Boston.

Van Patten, one acre, owned by Gen. J. H. Van Patten, Claverack, N. Y.

Point Vivian, mainland, ten acres, owned by R. Toyer and ten others.

Lindress, one acre, owned by John Lindress, Jersey City.

Cedar Island, one acre, owned by J. M. Curtis, Cleveland, O.

Wild Rose, one acre, owned by Hon. W. G. Rose, Cleveland, O.

Alleghany Point, mainland, one acre, owned by J. S. Laney, Pa.

Plato, two acres, owned by H. R. Heath, Brooklyn.

Seven Isles, five acres, owned by Gen. Bradley Winslow, Watertown.

Louisiana Point, Wells' Island, three acres, owned by Hon. D. C. Labatt, New Orleans.

On this point the Lambie Brothers have erected (1894) a fine cottage.

Bella Vista Lodge, mainland, three acres, Wm. Chisholm, Cleveland, O.

Neh Mahbin Island, two acres, owned by James H. Oliphant, Brooklyn.

Comfort Island, two acres, owned by A. E. Clark, Chicago.

Warner's Island, one acre, owned by Mrs. H. H. Warner, Rochester.
Wanwinet Island, one-half acre, owned by C. E. Hill, Chicago.
Kewaydin, owned by J. W. Jackson, Plainfield, N. J.
Cuba, one acre, owned by M. Chauncey, Brooklyn.
Devil's Oven, one acre, owned by H. R. Heath, Brooklyn.
Sunnyside, Cherry Island, five acres, Rev. George Rockwell, Tarrytown.
Melrose Lodge, Cherry Island, owned by A. B. Pullman estate, Chicago.
Ingleside, Cherry Island, owned by Mrs. G. B. Marsh, Chicago.
Stuyvesant Lodge, Cherry Island, owned by J. T. Easton, Brooklyn.
Safe Point, Wells' Island, four acres, Rev. R. H. Pullman, Baltimore.
Pullman Island, three acres, owned by Geo. M. Pullman, Chicago.
Nobby Island, three acres, owned by H. R. Heath, Brooklyn.
Little Angel, one-quarter acre, owned by W. A. Angell, Chicago.
Edgewood Park, thirty acres, owned by S. W. Sessions, Cleveland, O.
Edgewood Point, one acre, owned by G. C. Martin, Watertown.
West View, one acre, owned by S. G. Pope, Ogdensburg.
Welcome, one acre, owned by S. G. Pope, Ogdensburg.
Friendly Island, three acres, owned by E. W. Dewey, New York.
Linlithgow, one-half acre, owned by Mrs. R. A. Livingston, New York.
Florence, two acres, owned by H. S. Chandler, New York.
St. Elmo, three acres, owned by N. W. Hunt, Brooklyn.
Felesneck, owned by Prof. A. G. Hopkins, Clinton, N. Y.
Point Lookout, one acre, owned by Miss S. J. Bullock, Adams.
Vilula Point, one-half acre, owned by Capt. F. Dana.
Isle Imperial, one acre, owned by G. T. Rafferty, Pittsburg.
Fern Island, one acre, owned by J. Winslow, Watertown.
Hart's Island, five acres, owned by E. K. Hart's estate, Albion, N. Y.
Deshler, fifteen acres, owned by W. G. Deshler, Columbus O.
Netts, one acre, owned by Wm. B. Hayden, Columbus, O.
Bonny Castle, fifteen acres, owned by Mrs. J. G. Holland, New York.

Crescent Cottage, ten acres, owned by B Van Wagoner, New York.
Point Marguerite, thirty acres, owned by Mrs. E. Anthony, New York.
The Ledges, owned by Mrs. C. J. Hudson, New York.
Long Branch, ten acres, owned by Mrs. C. E. Clark, Watertown.
Manhattan Island, five acres, owned by Hon. J. C. Spencer, New York.
Maple Island, six acres, owned by John L. Hasbrouck, New York.
St. John Island, six acres, owned by Hon. Charles O. Donohue, New York.
Fairyland Island, twenty acres, owned by Charles and William B. Hayden, Columbus, O.
Little Fraud Island, one-half acre, owned by R. H. Pease, New York.
Huguenot Island, two acres, owned by L. Hasbrouck, Ogdensburg.
Resort Island, three acres, owned by W. J. Lewis, Pittsburg.
Deer Island, twenty acres, owned by Geo. D. Miller, New York.
Island Mary, two acres, owned by Mrs. L. Palmer, Carthage, Dakota.
Walton Island, seven acres, owned N. J. Robinson, New York.
Idlewild, four acres, owned by Mrs. R. H. Eggleston, New York.
Sport Island, four acres, owned by E. P. Wilbur, Mauch Chunk, Pa.
Little Lehigh, one acre, owned by R. H. Wilbur, Bethlehem, Pa.
Summerside, two acres, owned by W. Stevenson, Sayre, Pa.
Summerland, ten acres, owned by Summerland Association, Rochester.
Arcadia and Ina Islands, five acres, owned by S. A. Briggs, New York.
Spuyten Duyvel, one acre, owned by Alice P. Sargent, New York.
Douglass, five acres, owned by Douglas Miller, New York.
Kit Grafton, one-half acre, owned by Mrs. S. L. George, Watertown.
Lookout, two acres, owned by Thos. H. Bordin, New York.
Ella, one-half acre, owned by R. E. Hungerford, Watertown.
Little Charm, one-quarter acre, owned by Mrs. F. W. Barker, Alexandria Bay.
Frost, two acres, owned by Mrs. S. L. Frost, Watertown.
Excelsior Group, five acres, owned by C. S. Goodwin, New York.
Sylvan and Moss Islands, three acres, owned by S. T. Woolworth, Watertown.

Elephant Rock, one-quarter acre, owned by T. C. Chittenden, Watertown.

Sunbeam Group, one acre, owned by H. F. Phelan, Watertown.

Alice, two acres, owned by Col. A. J. Casse, New York.

Schooner, six acres, owned by J. N. Whitehouse, New York.

List of Post-offices among the Thousand Islands, during the Season.

Thurso-Grindstone Island.
Clayton.
Round Island (summer only).
Grinnell's (summer only).
Thousand Island Park.
Fisher's Landing.
St. Lawrence Park (summer only).
Point Vivian (summer only).
Westminster Park (summer only).
Alexandria Bay.
Grand View Park (summer only).

Table of Distances from Alexandria Bay.

To Montreal	148 miles
To Ogdensburg	36 "
To Morristown	24 "
To Brockville	24 "
To Chippewa Bay	12 "
To Point Vivian	2 "
To St. Lawrence Park	3 "
To Fine View	6 "
To T. I. Park	7 "
To Fishers' Landing	7 "
To Pullman House	7½ "
To Grand View Park	12 "
To Round Island	10 "
To Clayton	12 "
To Prospect Park	12 "
To Riverview	20 "
To Carleton Island	23 "
To Cape Vincent	28 "
To Gananoque	19 "
To Kingston	34 "
To New York	356 "
To Boston	339 "
To Philadelphia	447 miles
To Saratoga	239 "
To Chicago	812 "
To Niagara Falls	298 "
To Toronto	185 "
To Syracuse	122 "
To Utica	119 "
To Rochester	213 "

A Few "Don'ts" for Excursionists.

Don't be in too great a hurry, you will get along easier.

Don't rush to get on board the steamer until the passengers are off, and then you can get on board without rushing.

Don't push, and jam, and crowd, either in going ashore or aboard; you only hinder and delay.

Don't stop to gossip on the gang-plank, it blocks the passage and delays others.

Don't act as though you thought that other people had no rights which you were bound to respect.

Don't act as though you belong to the genus Sus, lest people believe it.

Don't crowd to the forward part of the boat; the after part passes the same objects of interest.

Don't stand up, so that those back of you can see nothing — it is extremely ill mannered.

Don't try to gather in all the easy chairs just for your party — it looks selfish.

Don't be continually grumbling, you annoy others and do yourself no good.

Don't be too critical about the running of the boat; in all probability, those who have charge of it are as well informed in regard to their business as you are.

Don't berate an employe because of some fault you think the company has committed — it is inconsistent.

Don't fail to treat others with that consideration with which you would like to have them treat you, and then all will go well.

You have often heard it said that such a one "could be a gentleman, if he chose;" you may rest assured that if any one can be a gentleman (or lady) he or she is pretty certain to be one; so when on an excursion don't be anything else, lest people thinking that you can be but will not, attribute your action to pure and unadulterated "cussedness," and treat you accordingly.

EARLY RECOLLECTIONS OF ALEXANDRIA BAY.

BY WILLIAM FAYEL, ESQ., OF ST. LOUIS, MO.

ALEXANDRIA BAY, when I first knew it, just before the existence of railroads in the United States, was a place of small importance. It was a depôt for the back-country merchants and new settlers who sent lumber, staves and potash, principally for shipment to the Quebec market, and returned with dry goods, salt, etc, for the village stores. Except river transportation, the place was side-tracked on the landward side by the most abominable roads, almost impassable in the spring and fall, so that for years butter and cheese and other country produce were under the control of contractors, forwarded to Watertown and Sackets Harbor. it is true, over better roads, but a much longer route. Owing to its isolated situation, the Bay, which within a few years has attained a magical growth and become the central attraction of the most popular summer resort in America, was, at the time mentioned, unfrequented by the tide of pleasure seekers, except perhaps a few local fishermen. The mode of transportation was then by stage-coach and canal. The world of fashion resorted to Saratoga Springs, the Catskill Mountain House, Niagara Falls, and some favorite sea-side resorts now seldom heard of. The most famous resorts and watering places were brought into journalistic notoriety by letter writers, some wielding graceful pens, as N. P. Willis in the New York Mirror, and Willis Gaylord Clark, the "Ollapod" of the Knickerbocker Magazine. Some of these descriptions were extensively copied, and showed the advantages, as one mode of judicious advertising, in turning the tide of travel and posting the public on the charms and striking beauties of the places described.

I first saw Alexandria Bay in 1832, the cholera of that year having struck Quebec, the earliest outbreak of the dread pestilence on the continent, and then following up the St. Lawrence, it visited Kingston and the large cities, leaving the Bay entirely untouched. The village contained about a dozen frame dwellings and shops, scattered promiscuously among the granite knolls and level grounds, wherever a favorable site offered. The only store, a red frame structure, owned by John W. Fuller, was at the steamboat landing on the lower point jutting into the Bay. The only tavern, a weather-worn frame structure, at the end of the main street, leading to the right on entering the village, was kept by Smith. The front was marked by a flight of wooden stairs that led to the bar-room. This important feature, like all country bar-rooms, had the upper portion of the bar shielded from outside intrusion by a grating of round wooden rods, through which could be seen a row of flint-glass decanters, surmounted by heavy stoppers of the same material. The upper shelf had round glass jars, containing sticks of ribbon-colored candy and Jackson balls.

The edibles consisted of small crackers (two for a cent), then in universal use, and "cookies," a second cousin of the popular ginger-cake. A box of dried herrings was also temptingly displayed to satiate the pangs of appetite, especially when irrigated by draughts of strong liquor. On wooden pegs in the proper place were hung yellow slippers for the retiring guests at bed-time. Tavern customs and the empire of fashion have very materially changed since those pristine days. The open tavern shed, with a loft for hay and oats over head, was located on the Bay at the extreme end of the street. Between the tavern and the store on the water front, was a large wooden warehouse in which the goods, shipped to country merchants were stored until called for. In the open spaces near the warehouse immense piles of staves and lumber were corded up, awaiting shipment, and constituted quite a feature in the river commerce of the place.

In my early recollections of the scenery I recall with curious interest the intensely sea-green color of the waters of the Bay, and the beautiful displays of graphic granite sometimes seen in the rounded granite knobs.

The arrival of a steamer at the wharf in rear of Fuller's store was always an event that enlivened the drowsy quietude of the village. A few passengers would usually step on shore to ease their sea-legs, but the most important personage was the faultlessly-dressed clerk of the steamer who stood on the wharf, with a lot of invoices in his hand noting down or checking the discharge and shipment of freight. To the boyish fancy he was an envied individual, a stupendous official character, through whose deft fingers all business transactions between the shore and steamer had to be transmitted before the boat could leave the wharf. Sometimes a glimpse was obtained of singular people and outré characters, emigrants from foreign lands, making their way towards the illimitable West. At a period somewhat later I saw twenty or thirty young French Canadians land from an up-bound steamer. They were a lusty looking set of youths in robust health, hardy visage, well developed, athletes in strength and physical symmetry of form. They were dressed in fine new suits, rather flashy, and wore their boot-legs outside up to the knees, bound on top with red morocco, with fluttering tassels dangling therefrom. These adventurous young men had left their homes at Chambly, St. Johns and Montreal, and were bound for Green Bay, thence to the fur-trading town of St. Louis. Some thirty years afterwards, while accompanying the Indian Peace Commissioner among the Sioux of the Upper Missouri, I encountered an Indian interpreter, who, as near as time and place could be indentified, was one of the party seen at Alexandria Bay at the period mentioned. This man, like all the French Canadian traders and interpreters, had an Indian wife and a numerous progeny. Our interpreter abandoned his Indian wife and married a respectable white girl at North Platte — General Sherman and the other commissioners being invited to attend the wedding. The relatives of the old squaw came to kill the interpreter's horses in revenge for his desertion of the once attractive and dusky maiden of his youthful days.

Alexandria Bay was slow in coming to the front as a fishing resort, owing to the adverse causes mentioned. In this respect, for several years, Theresa, in the same township, rather took the lead. The stream at that then remote village abounded in the spring with mullet, and throughout the season that king of the piscatory tribe, the muscalonge, came up the Indian River, to the falls at Theresa, and was taken with the spear or trolling spoon. The Sixberries had long beaten up the ground, and the Indian River with its tributary lakes, became the paradise of the hunter, trapper and fisherman. Theresa, as the headquarters for the outfit of boats and fishing tackle, came into note, and was made popular by the annual excursions down the river from that point, of Mr. Norris M. Woodruff, of Watertown, and his friends, who brought with them Loren Soper, an old fisherman acquainted with the ground, and then the keeper of the United States Arsenal at Watertown. There was a fascination amid the scene and haunts of nature, in the wild scenery and freedom from the public gaze in a jaunt of this kind, that a large river, open to all the world, did not possess. No man enjoys reading his newspaper in the thronged thoroughfares.

In spite of these little rivalries of neighboring fishing resorts, Alexandria Bay, in no spirit of jealousy, abided its time. The fame of its waters in yielding abundance of pickerel and muscalonge to the sportive fishermen, became extended far and wide. Of the last named fish it was reported that a big one, the real sockdoger, had been captured by an amateur sportsman from Syracuse, and that in his

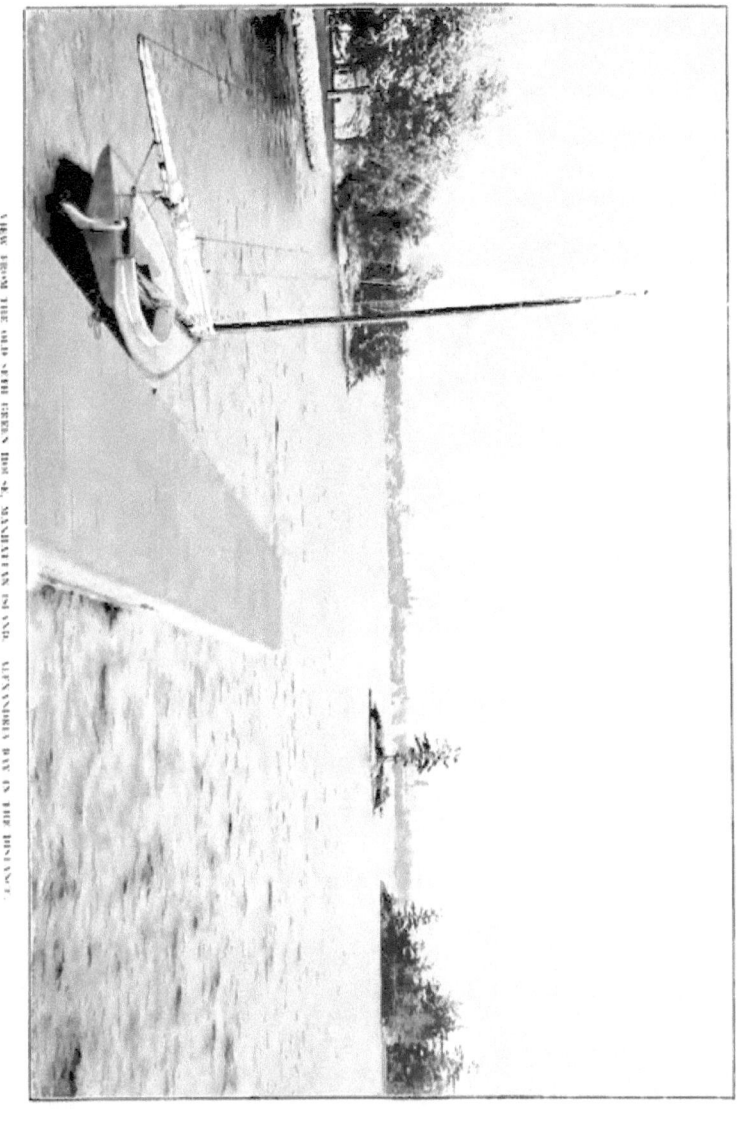

VIEW FROM THE OLD "FRED GRAY'S HOUSE," MANHATTAN ISLAND, ALEXANDRIA BAY, ON THE ST. LAWRENCE.

vain glory he had a full-length picture of himself taken by an artist, with the big fish, held up by the gills, painted by his side.

In due time the Bay became the resort of some famous men, and it is but repeating a twice-told tale to state that among these noted characters were Silas Wright and Martin Van Buren. Of these two distinguished men, I may, in passing, be permitted to mention a phase of their personal traits. Old fishermen tell of the generosity of Silas Wright, in quietly slipping into their hands, on returning from a trip, a liberal "tip," while Mr. Van Buren, less thoughtful, to put it mildly, never exceeded the exact sum stipulated in the contract by dispensing the expected douceur to his boatmen.

It is probable that political friendship, as well as the genial hospitality of the host, rather than the fish, drew these great men to the Bay. The Waltons stood high in social distinction throughout that section. I am speaking from boyhood impressions. They were the first in a small town, and in the neighboring villages were regarded as superior beings. Their arrival at Theresa on a transient visit produced a sensation, among the younger people especially. The head of this family, Mr. Azariah Walton, I regarded as a grand old man, by whom I was always treated with kindness and courtesy. At his store, I frequently saw his massive figure seated behind the counter employed in thumping some refractory substance into use for trolling spoons.

The shelves in the rear were garnished with lines, hooks, bright brass spoons and other fishing tackle. In one corner was seen a forest of fishing poles, some of these being suspended by wooden supports overhead, like the old-time rifle on hooks, in the hunter's cabin. In the winter section, skates were suspended, showing that a demand for these articles could be supplied at all seasons.

Mr. Walton was collector of customs for the port. He never disparaged the duties of the office, and spoke with pride of his success in checking and finally putting an end to smuggling, that formerly prevailed to the detriment of the government. He once told me that the revenue collected from customs in the Cape Vincent district, to which he was attached, exceeded in amount that collected in any other port of the United States, as the official figures would verify. He was withal a warm political partisan, the leading Democrat in that section, and though his mercantile partner, John W. Fuller, was a pronounced Whig, no disputes on that score seeming to disturb their business relations. But to his outside political opponents he was not sparing in his jibes and sarcastic hits at their expense. With what unction would the words "Whig" and "Whiggery" roll from his tongue, in contemptuous tones and in utter depreciation of the claims of that young and growing party.

In those anti-Masonic and early Whig days, the election was held on three successive days in separate precincts. Theresa was then attached to the town of Alexandria, and when the election was held in that precinct, Mr. Walton always came up in full force, a dreaded opponent, in his withering gibes, to the leading Whigs, Squire Nathan M. Flower, Anson Ranney and Benjamin Still. The division of the town at length gave these good men a rest. Amid his multifarous business and official duties, Squire Walton found leisure to court the poetical muse. He composed campaign songs, which were never written out or read; one of these he recited to me, the burden of which extolled in the popular rhymes of that day, "The Favorite Son of Kinderhook."

In closing this imperfect sketch of a notable man, I desire to add, that although a violent partisan, he was a patriotic lover of his country. When the Mexican war broke out, he everywhere, in and out of season, denounced the opposition to President Polk and the war, declaring that it was unpatriotic in private individuals and bar-room ranters, to question the right or wrong of the war, when the honor of the country was at stake.

His eldest son, George Walton, followed in the footsteps of his father, as a politician, and as his active life, too early cut off by the fell destroyer, comes within the period under consideration, a word may be added. Much might be said in praise of this gentleman who bore "the mould of beauty and of form," but one incident only will be given, illustrative of the times, in his connection with "general training day," that great event of mustering battalions and parody on grim war, always looked forward to by wondering youths and gingerbread-vendors as a gala day, now gone into desuetude, and is only a memory of the past. George Walton was the colonel of a militia regiment; and his brother-in-law, General Archibald Fisher, commander of the brigade, transferred the general muster, from Antwerp, where it assembled from time immemorial, to Theresa. Col. Walton, as the ranking officer, superintended the customary evolutions, and towards evening he headed the perspiring troops in their march from the Cooper farm, where the muster was held, to the village. The militia companies were halted, and on being massed in regulation order for dismissal, the gallant colonel in a grandiose speech, not unmixed with a quiet undercurrent of humor, wished the men a safe return to their homes, their waiting wives and children, and capped the climax of dismissal by designating the brigade as "soldiers of the great American Army."

As if to add to the ludicrous character of the scene, an auctioneer from the Quaker settlement, named Kirkbright, who had been vending gingerbread during the day, brought forward for sale a menagerie of wild and tame sugar animals. Having disposed of the elephants at a fair valuation, he then held up between his thumb and finger a two-cent rooster, with red comb and gills, about the size of a small ball of yarn. The bids started at one cent, with no raise for some time, when the auctioneer shouted forth indignantly, "Soldiers of the American Army! How can you stand idly by, with arms in your hands, and see property thus sacrificed in the market place?"

Recurring to matters at the Bay, I once, on a visit there, met with an enjoyable incident, characteristic of the chronic characters that one frequently meets with. I was attracted by two gentlemen in front of the hotel, who appeared hotly engaged in a religious discussion,— the one a skeptic; the other, whom I took to be a religious enthusiast by the warmth with which he supported his side of the argument. Gifted in speech, he overwhelmed his antagonist with a torrent of excellent advice, as well as sound argument.

The reverend gentleman proved to be the Rev. P. C. Headley, the author of a popular "Life of the Empress Josephine." He was then quite a young-looking man. He informed me that he was settled in the ministry at Adams, Jefferson county, and was on the way to join his brother, Rev. J. T. Headley, also a widely-known author on war heroes, for a trip through the great Northern woods, then, as may be remembered, unvexed by the Rev. Adirondack Murray and his fellow tourists. Mr. Headley turned out to be a most genial companion, full of animal spirits, and ready to indulge in boat excursions and other pastimes, except playing billiards, then a favorite amusement among the frequenters of the place.

A boat party was made up to sail among the islands, with Mr. Ed. Tanner, collector of the port, in charge. We trolled up the streams, and encountering a squall, landed on a nameless island. While there, a large sail boat, it might be called a yacht, also landed on the island, driven in by stress of weather. An elderly, sturdy-looking man came on shore and looked anxiously around. The newcomer proved to be the famous Bill Johnston, whose name became linked with the Thousand Islands.

He wore a blouse, a plain-looking old gentleman, with strong features and an expression of determination about the mouth. Otherwise he would be taken for a very ordinary farmer, in general appearance. He was rather reticent and conversed in a low tone of voice, as is usual in men supposed to have some great secrets locked up in the breast. He was a man just to Mr. Headley's hand, who pumped the old gentleman as to the history of the islands and his connection with them during

RESIDENCE OF W. C. BROWNING.

the late troubles. Johnston, meantime, had a far-away look, his mind reverting to his boat and the condition of the weather. After the detention of a couple of hours we parted, on a lull in the gale.

Before the extension of telegraph lines, and with limited postal connections inland, the people of the Bay were behind their neighbors in getting the news. But this was not always the case, very important news reaching there by river in advance of the neighboring villages. An instance may be given. About the 12th of July, 1850, going with a party to the Bay, when arrived within three miles of the place, we met old Ezra Cornwall, father of George W. Cornwall of Theresa, coming up the road on foot, who imparted the intelligence that General Taylor, President of the United States, was dead. The news was received at the Bay by steamer from Oswego, and was unknown at Theresa until obtained from this source.

My last visit to Alexandria Bay was in 1867, when, after the absence of some years, great changes in the aspect of the town were visible. Two hotels, the renowned Crossmon House, widely known, and the St. Lawrence Hotel, kept by Edward Fayel, assisted by his sister, Mrs. Sophia Spalsbury, were in operation. Since then a greater change, amounting to a perfect "transformation scene," has supervened, supplementing the wonders of natural beauty with the improvements suggested by unsparing wealth, art and taste. But despite all these enchanting improvements, effected by man, the great natural features of rocky islands and glorious river will stand unaltered till the end of time.

JONATHAN THOMPSON.

Among the earliest to forsee and urge the advantages of the Thousand Islands as a resort for pleasure seekers, and the establishment of a hotel to entertain them, was doubtless Jonathan Thompson, of Theresa. Thompson was a genial character, quaint in speech, or rather of cute sayings, a harmless romancer with a brain fertile in projects. He was a man past middle age, buoyant in hope as a grown-up boy, had seen something of the world, and, in fact, among his early experiences, had "gone out" with the Green Mountain Boys in September, 1814. In working up his scheme he had visited the islands, selected one of the group to erect a fishermen's resort upon. But the time had not come for the realization of such an enterprise. Other more favorable and fortuitous circumstances had to arise before the scheme could become practicable. Thompson would have made a good second to a man of financial ability; a good chief of a restaurant, and a capital entertainer of guests.

A few years before this time, Thompson had pitched upon one of the most romantic little lakes, situated between the Indian and St. Lawrence rivers, much nearer the first named stream, as a home, which he intended to improve. It was an expanse of clear, limpid water, nestled among wood-crowned shores, six miles from any settlement. It had lost its Indian name, the lake being on the main water route followed by the Canadian Indians during the French and Indian War, and up to the War of the Revolution, in their predatory incursions to the Dutch settlements on the Mohawk. In recent times the hulks of their abandoned boats could be seen lying deep through the clear water on the lake bottom. It was known as Lake of the Woods, latterly as Thompson's Lake, from the new proprietor, and was three miles in length north and south, and from one mile and a half to half a mile in breadth.

In a spirit of enterprise and unbounded hopes that inspired visionary schemes, Thompson pre-empted a few acres, near the western cove, which a squatter had cleared up and abandoned, leaving his deserted log cabin among the assets of the place. On obtaining possession, his original design was to stock the ranch with geese, as his flocks would have the unlimited privilege, like himself, of the lake. But, owing to a change in domestic economy (except among the blanket Indians, who still adhered to skins for bed clothing), feather beds began to be discarded, and a demand for feathers consequently ceased. He, therefore, was compelled "to feather his nest" in some other more profitable product. Whereupon, like Thoreau, the hermit of Waldon Pond, he determined to cultivated a bean patch, finally adding to his agricultural operations crops of potatoes, cabbage and cucumbers. On an adjoining little islet, that rose like a wart above the bosom of the lake, the only excrescence of the kind that fretted the ripples into complaining murmurs, he erected a house of primitive accommodation. In its construction, he was ably assisted by a Watertown journalist (JOHN FAYEL), who, seeking recuperation for broken health, found pleasant recreation in the exercise of his constructive talents upon very scant materials. Poles were ferried across from the opposite beach, and the deserted log-cabin of the squatter was dismantled of its boards, shingles, nails and window sash, to supply the needed material. That house was a "daisy," and ranked with the common shanty in architectural adornment, having a door swung on hinges, and a window to admit the light. It was a large single barrack-like room, and for years became also the sleeping apartment of tired pleasure-seekers, who, rolled up in their blankets on the board floor, were lulled to sleep by the monotonous chafing of the ripples on the beach.

Meantime, chance visitors to the lake returned with enchanting descriptions of its varied beauties. Mr. Thompson, on his return to the village, exhausted the vocabulary of adjectives in extolling its wonders. It was "the land of promise" spoken of in the Scriptures, the original "Fountain of Youth," sought after by De Soto, "the loveliest spot under the canopy," to use his favorite expression. In truth, his representations could not well exaggerate the admitted beauties of the lake and wild surroundings.

Curiosity was worked up to a high pitch, and to gratify it by actual realization, an expedition was fitted out, composed of some twenty or thirty citizens, who descended the river in boats. Mr. Thompson took the lead alone in his little canoe, ballasted with a few sacks of provisions. As commodore of the fleet, he issued instructions, and paddled ahead, a happy man, not unmindful of his glory. From long experience he became a marvel in handling a paddle, which he did as deftly as an Indian. He protested against a useless waste of power and misapplied movements of the arm in paddling. "Never," said he, "dip the paddle too far ahead, as the force would then be expended in lifting up the keel of the boat, but when the paddle falls in a perpendicular line with the rower's body, then the back-push against the resisting medium gave the only impulse forward to the boat." In his progress, to show off his dexterity and knowledge of the river, he sometimes cut across a bend, through rushes and over lilly-pads, thereby avoiding a long detour in keeping to the currents. About seven miles down the river a landing was made for a march of three miles over the carrying place to the foot of the lake. The landing place was designated by a beacon seen from a long distance above, consisting of the stub of a big tree on the bluff, which had been splintered by a thunderbolt. From the landing place to the lake, the labors of the traverse commenced, sometimes through thickets and underbrush, over fallen logs, and across swails and quagmires; but a portion of the route was unobstructed. The men started cheerily forward, lugging paddles, fishing poles, and sacks of flour, salt pork and other supplies of the commissary department. Thompson took the lead as generalissimo of the expedition overland, limping briskly forward, shouting words of encouragement, and ready to diverge from the route to show up some remarkable scenery; in one of these, for instance, from the brink of a precipice, was seen, spread out beneath, a vast marsh, carpeted with moss, extending for miles towards the river.

Arriving at the foot of the lake, a halt was called, when the generalissimo expatiated on the wonders of the scene soon to open on the astonished gaze. To many minds, striking images, thus presented to the imagination, through the ear, even when conveyed through the medium of gushing, bloviating rhetoric, leave a stronger impression than when conveyed to the eye by careless observation.

At the place of embarkation on the lake there was but one canoe and two leaky skiffs to take the party to the Island House, the terminus of their toils. When tired and hungry, curiosity lags, and the most romantic scenery loses its charm. The party divided, some passing up one side and others on the opposite side, to the nearest point, until Mr. Thompson, having landed the first installment from the boats, could cross over and take them to the island. The shouts of the men in their slow progress along the heavily wooded shores, the Sabbath day, hundreds of visitors flocked to the lake, some to fish, but mostly others to gather huckle (whortle) berries, blue-berries and raspberries, which abounded in their proper season on the bluffs and in the swamps; but Mr. Thompson received little or no revenue from these people, who accepted his hospitality rather as friends than as paying guests.

The lake abounded in black bass, a most edible fish. He had a favorite spot, a headland, for catching them, and having captured a lot of small frogs for bait in the damp grass

AN ICE-BOAT, WINTER OF 1894-95.

and the responsive shouts from the opposite side, kept up continuously for several hours, startled the three loons seen sailing on the lake, causing the bewildered birds to tack from one point to the other, for no such yells had stirred up the wild varmints in that region since the ancient war-whoop was sounded by the Indian warriors that passed through on their scalping expeditions.

In the course of time boating facilities were increased, and some days, more particularly on the evening before, at dawn would paddle out in his canoe, that could be seen courtseying in the distance like a dark bubble, and returning with "the beauties," as he called them, had them served up for breakfast. On rainy days he rowed to the east side of the lake, where the deep water was filled with the branches of dead cedar trees that had fallen in, and rowing slowly along, in perhaps two hours' time, he would return with the bottom of his boat covered by the flopping beauties.

He had an intimate knowledge of the habits of fish — those shrinking creatures best studied when out of their native element. Of birds and beasts, he also possessed an intimate knowledge of their habits and instincts. Regarding the loons, to which reference has been made, he believed with old hunters that they could not be killed by a rifle while on the water, though he would not permit the experiment to be tried upon the loons that frequented his lake. The tradition concerning these wary birds is that they can dodge a bullet after seeing the flash, for instantly diving down, they remain for some time under water, and emerge to the surface a long distance from the spot where they went under. Thompson said he could predict a change of weather from the movements of his loons. It was observed that owing to their heavy conformation they could not rise in a calm much above the surface of the lake, and when inclined to change their present habitat, they flew against the wind, which lifted them above the woods, thus affording an exit beyond their old prison limits.

He declared that his loons, before a storm, would sail to the head of the lake, and when the south wind blew they would rise, and, flapping their wings, seem to walk on the water, but rising gradually, the wind buoying them upward higher and higher, until they reached the lower end of the lake, three miles distant from the place of starting, they would attain such an elevation as to clear the highest trees, and, thus regaining their freedom, seek "fresh fields and pastures new." He remarked the curious fact that though they could dodge a bullet on the wave, they could not dodge a tree in a calm.

Talking about the instincts of animals, he once remarked on a curious habit of the bears. On a heavily wooded ridge along the west side of the lake, there was a certain tree that on one side was deeply gashed, as if made by some huge gnawing animal. It would heal over for a time, like the scar made on a maple tree by the sugar-tapper's axe, and then it would exhibit a freshened appearance, like the re-opening of an old wound.

This peculiar phenomenon, old hunters declare, was the work of bears. It was a guide-post to them in their journeys, the same as blazed trees were to any backwoodsman. The bears, in traversing the woods from Canada to the great northern wilderness, thus left their mark as a guide to the other bears which followed them on the same path. Each bear in passing would stand on his plantigrade feet, gnaw out a fresh chunk, to be freshened up by his successors, and thus the great bear-route, a genuine international line, was kept open.

I once asked Prof. Ebenezer Emmons, the geologist of our district, his opinion as to the truth of the statement. The eminent naturalist rather doubted the explanation, and attributed gnawing of the tree to the cutting season of those animals.

As the novelty of Mr. Thompson's kind of life wore away he turned his eye to the Thousand Islands with the outcome as before stated.

LITTLE LEHIGH, FROM SPORT ISLAND.—PROPERTY OF F. H. WILBUR, BETHLEHEM, PA.

ALONG THE ST. LAWRENCE IN THE WAR DAYS OF 1861-5.

BY COL. ALBERT D. SHAW

NOT all the stirring events of the days of the Great Rebellion took place along Mason's and Dixon's Line. The northern border of our country had its experiences of more of less interest during these perilous and stirring times, between 1861-5, and especially was this true along the noble river Saint Lawrence. No battles were fought, it is true, but many a line of retreat marked the passage of myriads of men from Uncle Sam's possessions, seeking an asylum where they might be safe from dreaded "drafts" and the dangers before the enemy in the field. These men loved life more than they loved their country, and rather than serve in the ranks, they chose to bear the ills of a skulker's existence in Canada, in preference to flying to others they knew not of, amid the shriek of shells and the whizz of bullets. Some incidents connected with deserters during this period will not be without interest, it is believed, inasmuch as this river marks the last stage of the entrance or exit of deserters; for, strange as it may appear, English soldiers deserted to the United States to enter the Union army, while Americans deserted to Canada to get out of the service! Most of the deserters from our army, it should be explained, were soldiers who had been wounded and allowed to come home on furloughs, and, from brooding over physical sufferings, became unnerved, and so found it easier to cross the St. Lawrence into Canada than it was to return to their regiments at the front. The life of a "skedaddler" in Canada was far from agreeable. Thousands of Canadians served in the Union army, as brave men as ever carried a gun, and the presence of Americans who were known to have "skipped" there — either as deserters or to avoid being drafted — called down upon their defenseless heads no end of ridicule and contempt. A case in point will illustrate this fact. A deserter from the then Twentieth Congressional district, comprising the counties of Jefferson, Lewis and Herkimer, wrote to Hon. Addison H. Laflin, who then represented it in Congress, saying that if he could be assured that he might serve out his time without arrest or punishment, he would at once come back and be a good soldier. Mr. Laflin took this letter to the President, explained the circumstances, and urged that the deserter be given the chance he sought. "Certainly," replied President Lincoln; "when a poor fellow has made a mistake, by all means give him a chance to live it down. There is good stuff in that man, for no coward would make such a plea." The President took a large blank card which lay on his desk and wrote upon it:

"Private —— is herewith allowed to come to me, wherever he may be, and on his promising to be a good soldier and serve out his time faithfully, I will pardon him.

"A. LINCOLN."

It happened that there was not room enough on the front of the card to write the above, so it was turned over, and the sentence completed. As he did so, a blot of ink fell on the card, and after using the blotter, the President scratched off a part of the ink-stain with his thumb nail! This card was sent to the deserter by Mr. Laflin, and in quick time the soldier made his way to Washington. Mr.

Laflin accompanied him to the White House, and introduced him to the President. The card was handed Mr. Lincoln, who said: "My dear fellow, I am glad you have returned. I know you repented of your weakness in going to Canada, and that you will be a brave Uncle Sam's boy now. Are there many more like you over there who would come back, if they could know they would be pardoned?" "Yes," replied the weeping deserter, "lots." "Then I will give them all a chance," was the reply, and the famous proclamation of amnesty to deserters who would return to their regiments was immediately issued.

The enamelled card, with the plain thumb-nail marks upon it, which this deserter brought back, he gave to Mr. Laflin, who had it

COL. SHAW.

mounted between plate glass, with a gold band about it, and it is now a precious souvenir of President Lincoln's largeness of heart, in the late member's family. It is interesting to know that a great many deserters returned to their regiments under this offer, and — so far as known — not one of the number ever went to Canada again during the war! This incident is worthy of record, as it shows how keenly President Lincoln grasped every question affecting the trials and hardships of the private soldiers. He divined, in an instant, how men home on furlough, near the Canadian border, while half sick, and importuned by glib-tongued false advisers, might, in a moment of weakness, desert; and he saw, in the appeal which was brought to his notice, that there was an opening to get many of these deluded and repentant soldiers back into the ranks again. The result proved how wisely he took in the true situation.

Deserters from Canada.

During the American war a good many deserters from the English troops stationed in Canada, from Halifax to Toronto, enlisted in our army. The garrison at Kingston furnished quite a contingent. A well-known Canadian became somewhat famous for his prophetic forecast of coming visitors to the provost-marshal's office, who wore the scarlet uniform of British soldiers. His horoscope of the stars was so faultless that he frequently foretold to an hour when a squad of deserters would make their appearance. Death having removed any necessity for silence concerning actions which were later condoned by Canadian officials with the full facts before them, it is fit and proper that the name of this brave recruit-furnisher should be given in this connection. George Briggs, the party in question, was a stalwart six-footer, very muscular, and weighed about two hundred pounds. Born on Long Island, just opposite Kingston, Ontario, he knew every inch of the islands and river. He was famous for his personal courage, and few cared to test the size of his clenched fist. He was a jolly, good-hearted fellow, about twenty-five years of age, and possessed of rare coolness and resources under trying conditions. As a general, he would have rivalled some of the most capable cavalry officers of the war. When three hundred dollars bounty was offered for volunteers, Briggs saw his opportunity. He put himself in touch with the British soldiers at Fort Henry, and soon found a way to direct them how to reach the American side. The deserters were always treated according to agreement by this fearless director on the underground road to the United States. Captain Emerson, the provost-marshal at Watertown, always made it a rule, before enlisting a man, to explain to him the amount of bounty he was entitled to receive, and insisted that the money due him should be paid to the recruit in his presence. In no instance did these deserters, brought over by Briggs, refuse to promptly pay over to him such sum as they had arranged to give him, after receiving their bounty. These men made fine soldiers. The writer served with one of them — Charles Flemming, a member of Co. A, 35th N. Y. Vols. At the battle of Fredericksburg he lost both legs by a cannon shot, and died the next day in hospital. He had served in India and the Crimea, and often declared that he never had seen hotter fighting than he experienced in our regiment. He lies in an unmarked grave within sight of the bloody field on which he received his death wound. How many thousands — foreigners to our soil — died like Flemming, on the battle-fields of our struggle, in helping tread out the heresy of secession amid the horrid havoc of contending armies!

Some of the incidents attending the escape of British deserters from the 47th Regiment of the line, at Kingston, are worthy of record. The distance between the American shore and Kingston is only some twelve miles, but to most of the soldiers it was an unknown route. Long Island intervened, and guards were thickly stationed on its southern shore to intercept any deserters who might be caught making their way to the American side. For many months, during 1863-64, the 9 o'clock evening gun at Kingston was eagerly listened for, as one gun each was fired at that hour for all deserters, in order that the guards might keep a keen watch for them. A party of six deserters from the 47th Regiment seized a boat at Kingston, late one evening, and rowed away around the head of Long

Island, intending to land at the light-house on Tibbett's Point, near Cape Vincent. By some mistake, being strangers to the route, they kept too far to the westward, and after an exhausting tug at the oars, an exercise few of the soldiers were used to, they made land on Grenadier Island, near its eastern point. Seeing a light in the early morning, one of their number cautiously approached it, and this proved to be in the house of Abram Cooper, a wealthy farmer, and owner of most of the island. The deserter nervously inquired, "What place is this; is it in Canada or the United States?" "The United States, and you are all right," was Cooper's cordial greeting, as he took in the situation at a glance. Turning to his comrades, who were anxiously awaiting his report, he shouted, "Come on, boys, we are all safe." Their delight was unbounded, and happier men never sat down to an ample breakfast than were those weary and hand-blistered deserters. The next day Mr. Cooper accompanied them to Cape Vincent, where quite an excitement was created by their appearance in bright scarlet uniforms. Cooper, who was quite a character in his way, pompously led the three files of splendid young fellows as they marched up to the hotel, and many a joke was bandied over the excited civilian chieftain who was dauntlessly leading his column to an attack on—glass-fortified bottles in the hotel bar! Soon after their arrival in the village, several officers of their regiment came over to try and induce them to return to their regiment. The citizens of Cape Vincent made it somewhat uncomfortable for these officers, and the soldiers would not go into any private room for consultation, but making the interview very public, with any amount of advice freely interspersed by the excited bystanders. The change in the relations between these soldiers and the young martinets, who a few hours before were formal and indifferent to them, was striking. The deserters appreciated it keenly, and curtly refused all the persuasive appeals made to them on the part of the officers. They all at once enlisted in our army. Tourist who pass to or from Kingston from Cape Vincent, around the head of Long Island, can easily take in the route of these deserters in their unknown way to the freedom they sought. Another party of ten deserters crossed over on the ice, following the line of the Long Island Canal. All went well until they came to Big Bay, which somehow puzzled them, and two of the party became exhausted through heavy walking in the deep snow, and had to be left behind. The others pressed forward, and seeing a light on Carlton Island made for this point. The walk was a long and tiresome one, and they soon found that they had several miles to tramp before they would reach Cape Vincent. Few can realize how bitter cold a walk in the night on the ice in the river St. Lawrence rarely is, who have had no experience; and when the night is cold, and the distance long, the situation is far from being an agreeable one. On finally reaching the "Cape," they struck the shore near the engine-house, at the railway, and seeing a light, just at the dawn of day, one of them peeped in, much to the surprise of the night watchman. "Is this in the United States?" was his pathetic query. On being assured that he was on Uncle Sam's free soil he called to his half frozen companions to "Come on," and a grateful coal fire never seemed friendlier to these deserters than on this occasion. The following day they enlisted at Watertown. Briggs was at the Cape to go with them to headquarters; and he could not understand how ten men could possibly make any mistake in crossing direct to Cape Vincent after all the object lessons he had taught them, and all the descriptions he had given them, a day or so before they unceremoniously left their quarters in Kingston. They had made a sharp detour out of a direct course from the canal to Cape Vincent, by turning to the eastward so as to touch at Carlton Island.

Briggs was fertile in his expedients in getting deserters across the river, in summer as well as in winter. In the winter of 1863 he put four deserters in an open sleigh, covered them with blankets and bags of bran, and

ENTRANCE TO HARBOUR BAY.

drove through the city and across Long Island, passing two lookout posts on the route without trouble, and reached Cape Vincent in safety. Two days later he repeated the same action, but somehow suspicion had fallen on his plans, and, as he drove out upon the ice in Kingston harbor, detectives made chase with a fleet horse. Briggs scented the danger at once, and, forcing his fine span of fleet horses into a run, made hot time to the island and swept across in great shape, until he reached "Tom Horn's," a noted hotel opposite Cape Vincent. Here the British patrol was quartered, and as he drove up, his horses covered with foam, a guard asked, "What have you got, and why have you run your horses so?" "Come and see," was Briggs' reply, and, as the guard approached him, he seized the soldier's musket, pushed him into the snow, and, putting his horses to their best pace, was soon out of the reach of the shouts and bullets of the irate and dumbfounded guards! He knew that he could get away before another guard and gun could put in an appearance, and in this he made no mistake. He sent the gun back the next day, with his regrets that he found it necessary to borrow it, and hoping that his slipping down in the snow did not inconvenience him in the least! This bold adventure was rather a serious one, as it finally turned out. Briggs could not return, the team was under the ban of Canadian law, and so team and man found quarters at Cape Vincent for a time. Duty was paid on the animals, and this naturalized them, while the hero of the incident made merry over the success of his action. But it was too hot in Kingston for him for some time. Great excitement prevailed there. The long suspicion was at last moulded into certainty. Briggs had been the mysterious agency through which so many deserters had been piloted to "the States," and a price was set on his head.

Captain Kidd and Claude Duval of earlier times had a rival in George Briggs for many months. Daring to return to Canadian soil, after the excitement had largely subsided, he was arrested and placed in prison, without bail. It looked dark for the dauntless "George," behind unfeeling bolts and bars, in strong walls confined, and the end of his career as a "deserter's pilot" was supposed to have been reached. But not so with Briggs. He had no idea of languishing long in prison, and living on the plain fare of criminals. One day his father was allowed to visit him, and while he was there Briggs suddenly but gently disarmed the guard, and strode unconcernedly past the sentinels and regained his liberty! A little later the guard sounded an alarm, and when the room was visited, old Mr. Briggs was calmly looking out of the grated window! There was revelry by day for a few minutes, and when the facts of the situation were ascertained, there was great commotion. Father Briggs was the only cool man in the room. He was greatly surprised at seeing so many officials of the prison come in. "Where is my son?" asked the father, with much feigned feeling. "Where is he!" was the reply. "What did you do to help him escape?" "Do!" said the apparently surprised father; "what do you mean? Where is my son? I came in to see George half an hour ago, and after a little, he said he wanted to speak with the guard a minute, and I looked out of this window. It appeared kind of natural, and so I enjoyed it for a few moments, and then I heard a rumpus and, looking round, saw the guards rushing in here. That's all I know about it. Really, has George gone for good?" And, as there was no proof that he had done anything to abet his son's escape, he was finally released. The grim humor of the escapade — to those who knew the cool calculations for the event — was fully appreciated by all who knew father and son intimately. Old Mr. Briggs was a counterpart of his son in features and in burly form, and it was this close resemblance, when similarly clothed, that made his passing of the guards possible and easy. They supposed that the father was on his way home, and so had not the least suspicion of the real facts of the case. As may well be imagined, the city of Kingston and surrounding country were profoundly stirred by this second adventure of the redoubtable and inextinguishable Briggs. For a time, he kept out of the British dominions; but at length he returned to his old home, the friend of everybody, and a general favorite. Years afterwards he set his wits to work in smuggling oil from the States into Canada, and so expert was he that the Canadian authorities actually appointed him an inspector of customs, thus bringing to the support of the laws one of the keenest offenders against them. This move put an end to this sort of smuggling, practically. Few dared to take the chances of falling under Briggs' veteran eye; and to the end of his life he did his duty faithfully and well. He was a noble-hearted friend, as brave a man as ever lived, and tender, as few are, to the sufferings of the poor and afflicted. The writer knew him well, and greatly admired the rugged side of his manly character. Again and again has he listened to the graphic and yet modest recitals of the adventures of this jolly and fearless man during the war period, which were told in a manner profoundly impressive. Briggs was the Rob Roy of Canada,— clever, of boundless resources, and yet gentle as a child in the presence of sorrow and distress. His career was a unique and remarkable one, as it opened by his piloting many British soldiers out of Canada to enlist in the Union army. It was continued by smuggling large quantities of oil from the States into Canada, and it closed by his admirable services as an excise officer in the service of the Crown! His name and fame will long abide as that of a man famous in his day in the circles where he lived; and few public characters of his time, along the St. Lawrence river, created a deeper interest, or was more popular, than the daring, erratic and chivalrous George Briggs,— outlaw, smuggler, and admirable public officer.

DESERTERS, "BOUNTY JUMPERS," AND "SKEDADLERS."

There were two classes of deserters who became well known along the northern frontier, bordering on Canada, during the war days of 1862-5. First there was the "bounty jumper," who came over from Canada to enlist, with the sole purpose of securing a large bounty and then making his escape back to Canada, only to re-appear at some distant point in the States to repeat the operation. "Jumping the bounty" and "bounty jumpers," describe this precious class of rascals in the popular speech of the time. Second, then came the much smaller class who deserted from the front, or while home on furlough, and made their way to Canada, or, as was frequently the case, hired out to farmers on the American side near the border, so as to easily cross into the Dominion, in case of danger. The first class named were, as a rule, a bad lot, without patriotism or character, and mere robbers of the bounty paid for the purpose of securing recruits for our army; while many of the second class, returning to their homes along the Canadian borders, on sick-leave, in a moment of weakness and fear, weary of the dangers and hardships of active service, and not infrequently suffering from wounds and ill-health, were tempted to make their way across the St. Lawrence River into the Queen's Dominions. A third element of safety seekers during this period was the "skedadler," who ran away to Canada for fear of the dreaded "draft." This was comparatively a large class — and a pitiable one also. Every young man who left for Canada was a marked object for keen ridicule by all who knew him. To admitted cowardice there was added the sharp tooth of criticism, of a kind that made sure wreck of any future promise in the land of his birth. Every such "skedadler" dug his own grave when he made Canada a shelter from duty's manly service. If a record of the arrests and attempted arrests of deserters along the St. Lawrence River could be given, it would furnish interesting matter, but only a few cases can be mentioned here.

The writer of this chapter was a special agent of the War Department during the period of which this treats, and it fell in the line of his duty to become the principal actor in several exciting scenes in this connection, along the historic river St. Lawrence.

Word reached the Provost-Marshal at Watertown, that a number of deserters were in the habit of returning to this side of the river, just below Millen's Bay, and the writer was ordered to try and arrest them. Taking a soldier with him, he went to a point on the St. Lawrence, just opposite Grinnell's Island. On the Canadian shore, opposite this point, quite a little colony of deserters had found work at small pay on farms about the section, and several were in the habit of crossing over the river to pay visits to relatives and friends who met them at the shore. Taking up quarters with a family named Carter, living just opposite Grinnell's Island, on the Union shore, the detectives had not long to wait before the wife of a deserter came down and waved a signal to her husband to come across. The detectives were concealed in the house, and soon saw a small boat put out from the other side. It came over, and, just as it struck the beach, the officer, pistol in hand, stepped forward and ordered the deserter to surrender.

He was sitting in his skiff, talking to his wife, so as to be ready for any surprise, as was his custom ; and the moment he was confronted by the officer he sprang up, and with an oar quickly pushed his boat out beyond reach. Pointing his large Colt's revolver at the deserter, the officer commanded him to come ashore, or he would fire. His wife jumped up and down in a half frantic manner, and shouted shrilly, "Don't you do it; don't you do it; let him shoot you first!" She, at least, was no coward; her ringing words and dramatic acts had a strange effect upon the now pale-faced deserter, giving him courage — the blind courage of despair ; and his wife's stirring words, shrieked into his ears, spurred him on in his desperate effort for freedom. The officer shoved off his boat, and, being a good oarsman, soon gained upon the retreating deserter. The wife kept up her encouraging appeals, while the lady residents of the solitary house on the shore were eager spectators of the comical and yet serious race before them. The deserter had a small sail to his skiff, and this began to aid him as he pulled out from under the shore into the breeze, which happened to be from the south, thus strongly aiding him in his efforts to escape. The officer found that the race, under the conditions of oars and sail, was an uneven one, and in hastily glancing at the fleeing fugitive over his shoulder, to see how things were working, an oar slipped up on the iron thole-pin, which bent down, and over went the officer on his back, in the bottom of the boat, with his heels in the air ! A shout went up from the jubilant wife on shore, which did not add to the officer's good feelings; and, regaining his feet in the tottling boat, he called to the deserter that he would shoot if he did not instantly surrender. No heed was paid to the summons, and fire was opened upon him in brisk fashion, at less than 100 yards distance.

Bullet after bullet, from the heavy Colt's revolver, was sent point blank at the desperate man, who was rowing for dear life to get across the river. Each shot went close to the mark, as could be seen as they splashed into the river just beyond him. Six shots were fired, when the chase had to be abandoned, and the officer returned to the shore a greatly disgusted and beaten man. The deserter's wife was still on the shore and greeted him with stinging jeers, but an ungallant and yet forcible threat that her own arrest might follow, silenced her nimble tongue — which was, perhaps, not unnatural under the peculiar circumstances. Later in the day a drum and fife were heard across the river, and by the aid of a good glass a gathering of men could be seen there. Early in the evening a neighbor, who had been on the other side, came and told the officer that an attack was contemplated from the deserters, who had sworn vengeance for the attempt to arrest one of their number. The officer and guard prepared to give them a warm reception in case they should come. Their situation, however, was not at all desirable, in view of the fact that a dozen desperate deserters were in easy reach, and only two men were present to meet any attack. Mrs. Carter was a widow, with two daughters, living at the landing alone, and yet these young ladies had the real pluck and courage of true heroines. They volunteered to go out on picket, but this was not permitted. Bullets were cut up into slugs so as to make a scattering charge, doors and windows were barricaded, and all was made ready for a stubborn defense. The drum and fife could be plainly heard for more than an hour, and when darkness came on a sharp outlook was kept for the threatened attack. But none came. Discretion was held to be better than indiscretion, by the irate deserters, and while many counseled "war to the knife," the majority finally concluded not to make an attack on Uncle Sam's soldiers. The night passed with no alarm, and the next day the forces of the United States silently and somewhat sullenly withdrew—beaten but not disgraced.

This deserter, after the war, said that one bullet passed through his hair, and that several of them whistled so near to him that he felt the swish of the air, and feared he had been hit. He declared that he was too "scared to surrender," and that he mechanically took the oars, rowing away in vigorous fashion, in sheer desperation from the first impulse that came over him. This adventure had a marked effect, however, upon the actions of the deserters living across the river. They at first made a great deal of noise and loudly threatened great things because of this attempt to arrest one of their miserable clan, but they thereafter took good care to keep themselves safely on the Canadian side of the river. The officer on returning to Watertown was unmercifully hectored over this failure to arrest the deserter. This was one instance where the force of the United States was baffled by the escape of the enemy, on the Saint Lawrence, during the days of the southern rebellion. One cause of great gratitude on the part of the officer failing to make the arrest was that none of his shots hit the unfortunate deserter, during his desperate exertions to reach the Canadian shore. Years afterwards the writer visited this spot, and mused over the exciting scene enacted there many years before. It is a lovely view from the shore where the deserter landed his boat Grinnell's Island, covered with fine foliage, looked like a large Emerald gem in the clear, sweet river, while on the right, looking Canadaward, a well-wooded plot lined the far shore of the little bay. The heroic ladies were gone—the mother dead, and the daughters married—and all changed about the spot except the charming scenery along the noble river. Cows stood in the shallows near the shore, gently whisking the flies from their bodies as they drank the sweet water, and cooled their feet in its grateful current. Small in importance as the incident was, of the escape of the deserter, it brought back memories of the war days of more than passing interest to one of the chief actors in the serio-comic little drama of years before.

Another very interesting event happened not far from Clayton in the fall 1862. Captain John A. Haddock, while home from the 35th N. Y. Vols., on recruiting service, was informed that deserters from our army living in Canada, were constantly coming over and stealing poultry, pigs and other things, greatly to the annoyance of our farmers along the St. Lawrence. This was more than the energetic Haddock could bear, and so, with a detail of five soldiers, he went to the scene of these depredations. He ascertained that several deserters were stopping at a point near the American shore, and he laid his plans to cross over in the night, capture them and bring them back with him. The scheme was a bold one—for it simply meant an invasion of foreign territory, and the high-handed arrest of men on foreign soil. But the fiery captain paid small attention to these trivial considerations, in view of the dastardly actions of deserters he loathed. A little before midnight Captain Haddock had his command embark in a boat with him, and, owing to the ice in the river between the main land and the island, some difficulty was experienced in reaching the foot of Long Island. Once safely landed, a careful disposition of the force was made, so as to be sure that the deserters known to be in the house could not escape, and a loud demand was made for these men

A HAPPY MURRAY BAY.

to come out and surrender. The Canadian light-house keeper, at whose home the deserters were stopping, rushed out, ax in hand, and loudly declared that he would kill any Yankee mother's son who attempted to invade the sacred soil of Canada, in an unlawful effort to arrest any one under his roof. He stormed and raved, and proved his right to be called brave as well as valuable by the stalwart way he defended his own by act and speech. But the undaunted Haddock finally got his ear, and plainly told him he was there to arrest the two deserters; that he was backed by the army of the United States; and, finally, that he was there to take them — without bloodshed, if possible — in "gore," if necessary. This resolute stand caused the overpowered Canadian to yield, his threatening ax was laid down, the two American deserters were seized, and the American forces made an orderly return to the main shore in triumph, bringing their prisoners with them! Captain Haddock's bold and rash adventure created a profound impression among the American deserters, along the river especially. They "climbed to the rear lively" immediately afterwards, as one described it, because they were dreaming dreams and seeing visions of approaching officers in search of Uncle Sam's delinquents. The hue and cry that followed made no end of talk along the border on both sides of the river. Pig and chicken stealing on the American shore ceased at once, and one of the scarcest specimens seen for a long time of the genus homo was an American deserter in these parts.

Haddock was for a time a typical dare-devil hero — greatly admired by the small boy, and gratefully appreciated by all haters of deserters and the "blarsted Britishers" — as the phrase went in these exciting and turbulent days. Not long after this much discussed "invasion," Captain Haddock returned to his regiment in Virginia, then in winter quarters. But a cloud suddenly fell upon his short-lived glory. The Canadian Government had made haste to lay before the British foreign office the facts about the unwarranted arrest of the two deserters on British soil, and angrily demanded satisfaction. The British Government immediately notified the British Minister at Washington to secure prompt redress from Secretary Seward for the indignity which Captain Haddock and his merry soldiers had inflicted on the soil of Long Island. Secretary Seward sent this demand to the Secretary of War, and Secretary Stanton forwarded it, in due course, to Captain Haddock for a reply. The Captain had thought the matter over, and the case of the Steamer Caroline which was captured many years before at Schlosser's Landing, in the Niagara River, by British subjects — one man being killed, and the steamer set on fire and sent over the Falls — seemed to him a fair set off, inasmuch as the act was highly applauded by the British Government at the time. What was sauce for the goose he thought might be sauce for the gander — internationally considered. But this defence and explanation were deemed insufficient, and a general order was read to the regiment dismissing Captain John A. Haddock from the service, for his midnight raid into British territory on the St. Lawrence River, at the head of five brave American soldiers. His official head was off — but he still lived. He made haste to Washington, and at once called upon Secretary Stanton. "Oh," said the Secretary, "you are Captain Haddock, who invaded Canada with a force of five men and captured two American deserters, and whom we have just dismissed from the service because the British Minister demanded this thing done." Pausing a moment, he added: "No matter, Captain, we had to dismiss you for your act, under all the circumstances, but I will give you a better position right away," and he had a commission as Major in the Reserve Corps issued and signed by President Lincoln the same afternoon. It remains one of the most precious souvenirs of the gallant Major to this day. It is evidence of the both laughable and serious performance which took place in the pale moonlight, on an island in the St. Lawrence, where a blow was struck that, literally, later on, "echoed round the world." True, its tones did not create much of a commotion, but they helped make the diapason of history, and the event is believed to be fittingly worthy of a place in this Souvenir history of the majestic river this same Major Haddock is preparing for the public.

BIOGRAPHICAL SKETCH.

The following notice, taken from the *Watertown Daily Times* of April 3, 1895, contains a brief but clear biographical notice of the author of the deeply interesting chapter of historic reminiscences which are printed on the preceding pages. It is inserted here because it tersely describes in part, Col. SHAW's services to the country in war and peace.—[THE EDITOR.

AN EVENING WITH THE GREAT.—A LARGE AUDIENCE HEARS ELOQUENT PORTRAYALS OF SOME OF THE WORLD'S FAMOUS MEN.

"The closing lecture of the course at the Baptist church last evening was a charming event. The audience was large and appreciative, and their attention never flagged for a moment. Major J. A. Haddock presided, and Mr. Seymour Knowlton sang a solo with great feeling, and gave a delightful encore, charming the audience by his remarkable voice. The chairman in introducing the distinguished speaker, said:

"When I joined the 35th regiment, it was in the field. At Falls Church, during our first winter's cantonment, I made the acquaintance of a young man in Company "A." The company contained probably more capable young men than any other that went from Jefferson county, perhaps from any other section. Upon its rolls were the names of Gen. Bradley Winslow, Col. Enos, Col, D. M. Evans, Capt. Henry Chittenden, Lieut. Morgan, Capt. Beckwith, Capt. Little, Lieut. Greenleaf, and others equally as bright, a wonderfully capable lot of young men. This young man, who was destined to prove himself the peer of the best of these, had a face like an interrogation point, one eternal question—always wanting to find out something. His pursuit of knowledge was phenomenal, an honorable and marked characteristic to possess. He tramped and fought with us all through the habitable parts of Virginia, ever present, ever hopeful, the raconteur, the charming story-teller. He was in the thickest of the fight at Falmouth, at Fredericksburg, at Cedar Mountain, at White Sulphur Springs, at Groveton, at Second Bull Run, at Chantilly, at South Mountain, at Antietam — he was in every place where the regiment was, for it never went into camp unless this young man with the inquiring face was there, up in time with a clean gun, and with a fine lot of ammunition. He shared in our inglorious provost duty for the best part of a long year. Through the Watertown papers I kept track of him, and after he was honorably discharged I saw that his name was in every good work. At last I heard of him as the representative of this great nation in one of the greatest commercial cities of the world, a city celebrated even in a whole kingdom of greatness. There he 'justified the honors he had gained,' and his associates in Manchester thought it right to shower upon him many marks of well-earned distinction. In this model soldier, this good citizen, this pattern husband and parent, this Christian gentleman, with that same inquisitive face turned towards knowledge, you will recognize my beloved comrade, COL. SHAW, whom I have the honor to present to this large audience in intelligent and discriminating Watertown. The colonel will talk to you of the men he has met in his long and varied service as a public officer of the American government, not only in Canada, but in the British Islands."

FRANK H. TAYLOR.

AMONG the favored residents at the pleasant summer colony of Round Island there are none better known or more enthusiastic regarding the charms of the Thousand Islands than Mr. FRANK H. TAYLOR, one of the few Philadelphians who spend their summer in this region. After much and varied travel as an illustrator and writer, Mr. Taylor came to the St. Lawrence upon a mission for Harper's Weekly in 1881, and at once recognizing the certainty of its supremacy as a summer resort, he built the pretty cottage at the foot of Round Island, which he calls "Shady Ledge." Mr. Taylor, with his wife and only son, who is also an artist, return here each season with great regularity in June, and devote the summer to the congenial work of the water colorist. Mr. Taylor's illustrations of island life, accompanied by vivid descriptions, have appeared in many publications, and have done much to popularize the beautiful islands throughout the country. The writer is indebted for several picturesque chapters in this work to Mr. Taylor's facile pen. He has done more to popularize the St. Lawrence Archipelago than any other man. This he has been enabled to do from the fact that he is not only a fine writer, but an artist as well, and can both describe and delineate anything he desires to present. This is a most happy combination of talent, as valuable as it is rare. Mr. Taylor's delineations have been delicate but most expressive. He is one who brings the love of nature into his work, fully believing that honest delineation of scenery much above any attempt to introduce fancy effects.

GRAND VIEW PARK.

ON the north-western point, at the head of Wellesley Island, is located GRAND VIEW PARK. A more appropriate name for this charming spot it would be difficult to conceive. Nature has been kind in its endowment of qualities valuable in a summer resort; jutting far out into the waters, with the Canadian main channel on one side and Eel Bay on the other, it receives the prevailing west wind fresh and pure full in its face — yet because of the thrifty growth of young forest trees, almost covering its surface, visitors at this Park may find shelter when desirable from the winds, blow whence they may.

The prominitory lies high and dry, and from the head, on which stands the comfortable Grand View House, with its broad piazzas, may be seen both main shores and many of the mazy islands lying between, Grand View being about four miles from the American and three from the Canadian shore. A fine sandy bathing beach, extending gradually into deep water, renders bathing safe even for women and children. It is acknowledged to be the finest beach among the islands, and many yachting parties from Alexandria Bay, Round Island, Thousand Island Park and other resorts spend the afternoon pleasantly at this point. Fishermen who sojourn at Grand View Park say they are "right in it."

Among the very desirable qualities of the place is, that being in the center of the river, it is just off the great thoroughfares of travel, and hence affords its guests and cottagers the much sought-for rest, comfort and quietude which they leave their town homes to find.

In connection with the hotel are several annex cottages where many of the guests find just the quarters they most prefer, and fishing and boating parties on the river from other

FRANK H. TAYLOR, THE ARTIST.

points come to the hotel in great numbers for dinner.

The private cottages as well as hotels are served with water from the reservoir tanks, which are frequently flooded from the waters of the river pumped from beyond the head of the park.

The post-office, established three years ago, receives and dispatches mails twice daily, and at the dock Uncle Sam's customs officer will attend to the imposts and other duties of his office. The docks are ample for the landing of any of the Folger boats, and on her ramble and search lights trips the "St. Lawrence" makes landing here after leaving Clayton, on all occasions desired, while the Park's own ferryboat makes from four to eight round trips daily to Thousand Island Park, where connection is made with other line steamers for points up or down the river.

The founding of Grand View Park was due to the efforts of the well known book publisher, Mr. Hamilton Child, of Syracuse, N. Y., a gentleman who had for many years spent portions of his summers on the water, and in more recent years at the Thousand Islands.

Fond of fishing and rowing, he had often noticed in his wanderings the beautiful location of this sightly point and the magnificent views obtained from its surface. Finally, in 1885, he purchased the site, embracing twenty-five acres of land, and with the aid of Mr. E. A. Bond, then chief engineer of the Utica and Black River Railroad, he surveyed the park into blocks and lots, divided by about

GLIMPSE OF THE DOCK, GRAND VIEW PARK.

two and one-quarter miles of avenues and rambles — new buildings appeared — improvements which are still going on each year. Fifty-nine buildings lots are now in private hands, while nearly one hundred and seventy are yet in the market for purchasers.

The vistas from "The Head," "Bayside," "Prospect Point," and "Overlook," are varied and charming, — from the latter point and vicinity the views command nearly the entire Canadian town of Gananoque — its electric lights in the evening, glaring like so many

A RACE WITH CANOES.

glittering stars. Every lot on this park, we are informed, is suitable for building upon.

Mr. Child, while recounting his own efforts in upbuilding this comfortable and delightful resort for those who make it their abiding place in vacation time, reverts

ON THE LAWN. GRAND VIEW HOUSE.

also with commendable pride to the labors of his grandfather and of his father in connection with the two principal villages of the island region, Alexandria Bay and Clayton, and a brief account of which may not be uninteresting to the general reader. Cadwallader Child, the grandfather of Hamilton, fourth in descent from Henry, one of the original settlers under William Penn, then living near Philadelphia, Pa., came to Brownville in 1804 by direction of James D. LeRay de Chaumont, to confer with his agent, Jacob Brown, afterward General of the American forces on the northern frontier in the war of 1812-14, relative to projected roads Mr. Child was to survey. One of his first roads was that from the site of Friends' settlement (Philadelphia) to the St. Lawrence, since known as the "Alexandria road," and it was in

PIAZZA GRAND VIEW HOUSE, THOUSAND ISLANDS.

that same summer he selected the site of Alexandria Bay for a port and village, and by his recommendation a mile square was set apart by Mr. LeRay for that purpose.

On that survey he also selected and recommended the site of Theresa for a village. He afterward went back to Pennsylvania, organized a company of Friends, who with their families returned and settled in Philadelphia. Cadwallader Child made the first clearing, and his son Oliver, father of Hamilton, was the second child born in that town. He, too, became a prominent surveyor for Mr. LeRay, and in 1833 he resurveyed the village of Clayton.

WHAT CAUSED THE GREAT ST. LAWRENCE RIVER, AND WHY DOES IT FLOW WHERE IT DOES?

PREPARED BY F. A. HINDS, C. E., OF WATERTOWN.

THESE are questions that will ever present themselves as the majesty and immensity of this noble river impresses itself upon us.

Prof. James D. Dana, of Yale College, in his Manual of Geology, declares it is not by chance, or a haphazard circumstance, that there is a great water-course flowing through a valley to the eastward in the middle of the North American continent; but that it is "a law of the system of surface-forms of continents." In his chapter on Physiographic Geology he says:

"First. The continents have in general elevated mountain-borders and a low or basin-like interior.

"Secondly. The highest border faces the larger ocean.

"A survey of the continents in succession with reference to this law will exhibit both the unity of system among them and the peculiarities of each, dependent on their different relations to the oceans.

"The two Americas are alike in lying between the Atlantic and the Pacific; moreover, South America is set so far to the east of North America (being east of the meridian of Niagara Falls), that each has an almost entire ocean-contour. Moreover, each is triangular in outline, with the widest part, or head, to the north.

"North America, in accordance with the law, has on the Pacific side — the side of the great ocean — the Rocky Mountains, on the Atlantic side the low Appalachians, and

CAPTOR AND PRIZE.

VIEW AT PINE VIEW, BELOW TIDE AND ISLAND PARK.

between the two there is the great plain of the interior.

"To the north of North America lies the small Arctic ocean, much encumbered with land; and, correspondingly, there is no distinct mountain-chain facing the ocean.

"The characteristics of the interior plain of the continent are well displayed in its river systems: the great Mississippi system turned to the south, and making its exit into the Gulf of Mexico between the approaching extremities of the eastern and western mountain range; the St. Lawrence sloping off northeastward; the Mackenzie, to the northward; the central area of the plain dividing the three systems being only about 1,700 feet above the ocean, a less elevation than about the headwaters of the Ohio in the State of New York.

"South America, like North America, has its great western range of mountains, and its smaller eastern; and the Brazilian line is closely parallel to that of the Appalachians. As the Andes face the South Pacific, a wider and probably much deeper ocean than the North Pacific, so they are more than twice the height of the Rocky Mountains, and, moreover, they rise more abruptly from the ocean, with narrow shore plains.

"Unlike North America, South America has a broad ocean on the north — the North Atlantic, in its longest diameter; and, accordingly, this northern coast has its mountain chain reaching along through Venezuela and Guiana.

"The drainage of South America, as observed by Professor Guyot, is closely parallel with that of North America. There are first, a southern — the La Plata — reaching the Atlantic towards the south, between the converging east and west chains, like the Mississippi; second, an eastern system — that of the Amazon — corresponding to the St. Lawrence, reaching the same ocean just north of the eastern mountain border; and, third, a northern system — that of the Orinoco — draining the slopes or mountains north of the Amazon system. The two Americas are thus singularly alike in system of structure; they are built on one model."

Thus one of the most noted and most credited geologists of our time, declares it to be as it were a fixed law, in the forming of continents, that there should be a great river system flowing from the middle portion of each continent eastward, or toward the lesser ocean.

Whatever may have been the conditions of this locality in the earlier ages of the world, with regard to subsidences and elevations of the earth's crust, it is quite probable that the relation between the river valley and the adjoining hills and mountains has remained approximately the same; that is, it was always a valley.

There is evidence, however, that there was an age when even this mighty river was turned back upon itself, and the waters were refused an outlet to the sea. This evidence is found in the elevated lake borders and gravel or pebble ridges that are to be seen along the adjoining highlands in New York State and Ohio.

Prof. G. Frederick Wright, of Oberlin College, in his book, "The Ice Age in North America," after discussing the present topography of Ohio, and the evidence that glacial action has changed the course of many ancient streams, says:

"On coming to the region of the Great Lakes, the influence of ice-barriers in maintaining vast bodies of water at a high level is very conspicuous. Around the south shore of Lake Erie there is an ascending series of what are called lake ridges. These are composed of sand and gravel, and consist largely of local material, and seem to maintain throughout their entire length a definite level with reference to the lake, though accurate measurements have not been made over the whole field. The approximation, however, is sufficiently perfect to permit us to speak of them as maintaining a uniform level. These ridges can be traced for scores of miles in a continuous line, and in the early settlement of the country were largely utilized for roads. In Loraine county, Ohio, an ascending series of four ridges can be distinguished at different levels above the lake. The highest is from 200 to 220 feet above it; the next is approximately 150 to 160 feet; the next lower is from 100 to 118 feet, and the next lower less than 100 feet, while some appear on the islands near Sandusky, which are not over 70 feet above the water level. Eastward from Buffalo portions of this series have been traced, according to Gilbert, until they disappear against the highlands, near Alden, on the Erie railroad.

"That the ridges on Lake Erie mark temporary shore-lines of the lakes cannot well be doubted, for they are not related to any great natural lines of drainage, but follow the windings of a definite level, receding from the lake wherever there is a transverse valley, and forming in some cases parallel embankments on either side of such valley, running inland as far as to the general level of the series, and then returning on itself upon the other side, to strike off again parallel with the shore at the same level. Their relation to the lake is also shown by the local character of the material. It is usually such as would wash up on the shore out of the rock in place. In the sandstone region the ridges are largely made up of sand, mingled with fragments from the general glacial deposit. Over the regions of out-cropping shales, the ridges are composed largely of the harder nodules which have successfully resisted the attrition of the waves. Other evidences that they are shore-deposits are their stratification, the relative steepness of their sides toward the lake and the frequent occurrence of the fragments of wood buried at greater or less depths on their outer margin.

It need not be said that there has been much speculation concerning the cause which maintained the waters of the lakes at the levels indicated by these ridges, and permitted them to fall from the level of one to that of another in successive stages, so suddenly as they seem to have done; for, from the absence of intermediate deposits, it is evident that the formation of one ridge had no sooner been completed than the one at the next lower level began to form. In the earlier stages of glacial investigation, before the full power and flexibility of glacial ice were appreciated, and before the exact course of the southern boundary of the ice-sheet was known, the elevation of the water to produce these ridges was supposed to have resulted either from a general subsidence of the whole region to the ocean level, or from the elevation of a rocky barrier across the outlet. Both these theories were attended with insuperable difficulties. In the first place, there is no such amount of collateral evidence to support the theory of general subsidence as there should be if it really had occurred. The subsidence of the lake region to such an extent would have left countless other marks over a wide extent of country; but such marks are not to be found. Especially is there an absence of evidences of marine life. The cause was evidently more local than that of a general subsidence. The theory of the elevation of a rocky barrier would also seem to be ruled out of the field by the fact that no other direct evidence can be found of such recent local disturbances. Such facts as we have point to a subsidence at the east rather than to an elevation.

But a glance at the course of the terminal moraine, and at the relation of the outlets of these lakes to the great ice movements of the glacial period, brings to view a most likely cause for this former enlargement and increase in height of the surface of the lower lakes. It will be noticed that the glacial front near New York city was about 100 miles further south than it was in the vicinity of Buffalo. Hence the natural outlet to the great lakes though the Mohawk Valley would not have been opened until the ice-front over New England and Eastern New York had retreated to the north well-nigh 150 miles. A similar amount of retreat of the ice-front from its farthest extension in Cattarangus county, in New York, would have carried it back thirty miles to the north of Lake Ontario, while a similar amount of retreat from eastern Ohio would have left nearly all the present bed of Lake Erie free from glacial ice. With little doubt, therefore, we have, in the lake ridges of Upper Canada, New York and Ohio, evidence of the existence of an ice barrier which continued to fill the valley of the Mohawk,

THE ST. LAWRENCE ON HER SEARCH-LIGHT EXCURSION. (SEE THE "RAMBLER.")

and choke up the outlet through the St. Lawrence, long after the glacial front farther to the west had withdrawn itself to Canada soil. A study of these ridges may yet shed important light upon the length of time during which this ice barrier continued across the valley of the Mohawk.

By the work of our local civil engineers in and about Jefferson county, it has been found that the gravel deposits and beds of waterworn pebbles found along the first escarpment of the Rutland Hills and the Dry Hills, so called, of Jefferson county, correspond in actual elevation with about 100 feet above the level of Lake Erie, and, therefore, quite probably mark a shore-line of the same lake referred to by Professor Wright, as marked by gravel ridges along the south shore of Lake Erie and as 100 feet above its level, and being caused by the damming up of both the St. Lawrence and the Mohawk River valleys. In this way we can also find a plausible theory for the formation of our own lower gravel ridges, in the fact that after the glacier front had receded farther, and the Mohawk Valley was opened as an outlet, the great inland lake was drawn down to a correspondingly lower level, and its waves and surface motion lashed a new shore-line, and gave us a new line of ridges and water-worn pebbles.

The grooves and lines, and the polishing of the rocks in Jefferson county, show plainly that the general direction of the moving ice of this locality was in parallel lines with the general direction of the St. Lawrence River, only the ice was moving up-stream or to the southeast. The streams and valleys of Jefferson and St. Lawrence counties also in general follow the same trend. The Oswegatchie and the Indian Rivers flow first southwesterly and then, making a sharp turn, each flow back almost parallel with their former course and with the guiding trend of the St. Lawrence. Even the Grass and Raquette Rivers, further east, find themselves swung around into this general course. The same course is followed in the deep valley known as Rutland Hollow, about three miles east of the city of Watertown, and the Sandy Creek and Stony Brook in the southerly part of Jefferson county follow the same general course. The Black River itself, from the Great Bend to Watertown, takes the same course, and a valley now occupied by low, swampy land continues the same direction to the lake, though the river itself, from Watertown city, takes a lower and shorter direction through rocky gorges to its present mouth at Dexter.

During the period of this higher glacial lake the mouth of the Black River must have been near Carthage, and the great sand deposits in the towns of LeRay and Wilna, known as the Pine Plains, were probably the shoal water or sand-bar formation, such as usually occurs at the mouth of a stream where it enters a lake or sea. There was also, probably, a glacier coming down the Black River Valley and joining in, and following along with, the greater St. Lawrence Valley glacier, heretofore described, as moving to the south-west. The above fact is proven by the well-defined medial moraine, extending from near Carthage through near Tylerville and the towns of Rodman and Ellisburg, to the lake just south of Ellis village. This moraine is almost entirely of granitic stones and bowlders, the characteristic rock of the right bank of the Black River Valley, and the moraine itself from Carthage to the lake is exactly parallel with the St. Lawrence river.

A glance at the map of the Thousand Islands shows the general outline of the islands to be long and narrow, and laid lengthwise of the river. An inspection of the rocks and ledges, and hills and valleys of the adjoining shores, and the surface of the islands themselves, develops the fact that all have followed the same law of direction.

The ice age no doubt has wrought great changes in the present surface forms, and to its influence we may properly ascribe the rounded and smoothed surfaces of the hard rocks and ledges, but it is also probable that there was a general direction given when the Azoic and Laurentian rocks were cooled off from the great molten mass, and that the St. Lawrence Valley, with its adjacent uplands, was an early and original form of the surface, and that the direction of the glacier movement here was due to this original configuration.

The parallelism, however, of the streams and valleys of the adjoining country, and the grooving and wearing off of the rocky projections, and the filling up of old channels, and the depositing of long lines of stones and bowlders, foreign to the locality where they are found, and the depositing of large areas of sand-beds — all these, and many other features, are, beyond doubt, the work of a glacial age.

THE TECHNIQUE OF FISHING.

IN GOVERNOR ALVORD'S most interesting and instructive articles upon the Great River, he has much to say about the "men he has met," and he speaks of all of them more as beloved comrades than as mere acquaintances or as the passing visitors of an hour ; but he does not say much about the technique, the appliances, the methods of fishing. Ourself an amateur, we have not failed to seek information upon the points indicated; and, like all amateurs, we try to believe that there is some "royal road to learning," by pursuing which we may exceptionally "get there" without the labor and inconveniences of learning by experience. From the great IZAAK WALTON himself down to our own day, and taking our distinguished GOVERNOR ALVORD as one of the brightest teachers of modern times in all arts piscatorial, the methods, the little incidentals by which the agile waterdenizens are lured into the voracious frying-pan, have been much disputed — this grand "faculty" of becoming an expert fisherman being as elusive, various, and sometimes as intricate as wooing one of the fair sex, whose moods are often as contradictory as are those of the most artful muscalonge or bass, and yet, when captured, are almost "too sweet for anything." From the crookedest tree-limb, with a piece of twine at its end, to the jointed and polished rod, with linen line and silver reel, the margin is wide and expensive. The poorest and the best of these appliances have each won great renown, but generally in the hands of those who know how to use them, the fish being largely democratic, and as willing to take a wriggling worm from a pin-hook as from one of Skinner's best treble-arranged, feather-decorated devices. As in all good things, in fishing there are many methods ; but in all fishing, good bait is an indispensable adjunct. With it you feel as a soldier feels with a good gun in his hand ; it is his guaranty of probable success.

The improvements in fishing tackle have been immense during the past forty years. In 1849, the writer saw the elder Walton, long since dead, at work upon spoons that could not now be given away — yet of those rude attempts he could dispose readily of as many as he could put together. Chapman, at Theresa and Rochester, has made many beautiful and successful fishing appliances. But the most successful man in the business for the past ten years has been Mr. G. M. Skinner, of Clayton, whose goods are now known all over the United States and Canada. He began to study the art piscatorial upon the Great River itself, having been long a resident of Gananoque, Ontario, in his early youth. He finally located at Clayton, a place possessing some advantages not apparent to the superficial observer, among them being a prominent angling resort and the principal gateway for tourists coming to the river over the only avenue on the American side, viz.: the N. Y. C. System, comprising the R., W. & O., and U. & B. R. R. R. It is the distributing point for those desiring to reach, by water, the numerous islands and parks in its immediate vicinity, and, also, the fashionable resort, twelve miles down the river, of Alexandria Bay.

In this romantic and favored vicinity he served his apprenticeship in fishing and experimenting with all sorts, sizes and shapes of

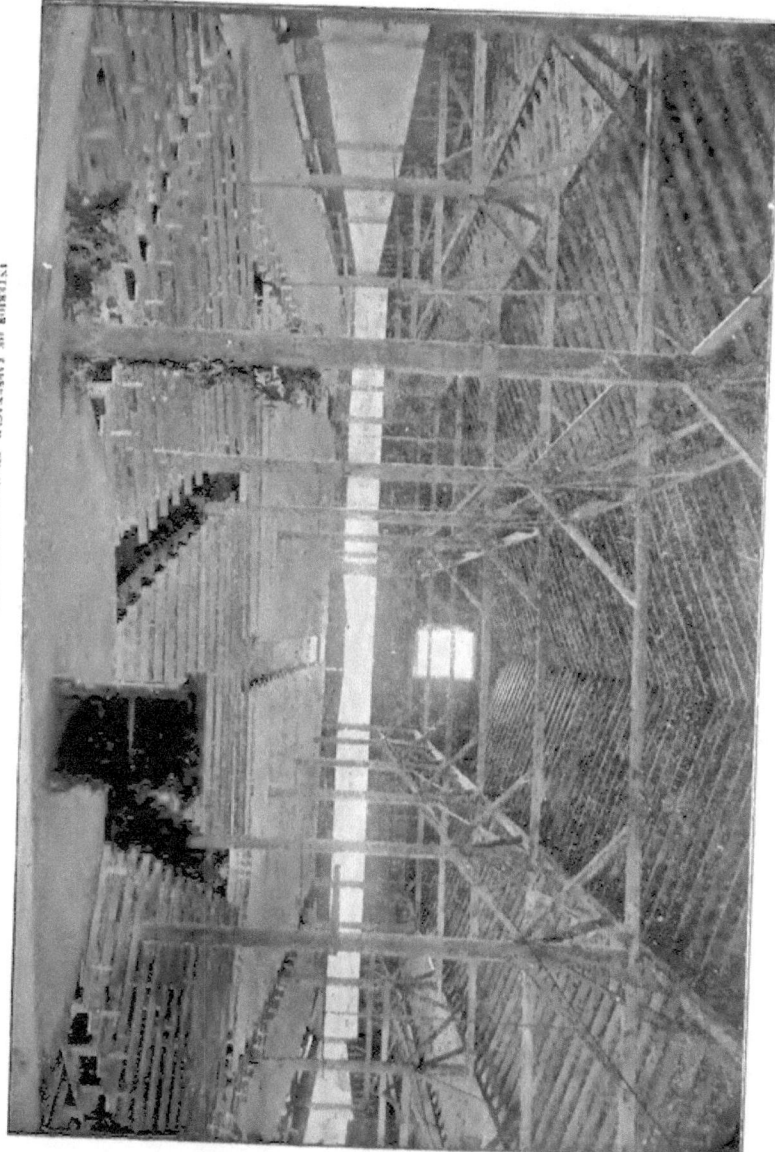

INTERIOR OF TABERNACLE, THOUSAND ISLAND PARK, LOOKING TOWARDS THE AUDIENCE.

artificial baits obtainable. He was not content, but strove to construct a spoon for his own use, which should have decided advantages over any used. As a result of such effort, two corrugated or fluted spoons were made; one being given to a fishing companion, the other he retained for his own use. In numerous practical trials, these two spoons gave satisfactory evidence of having uncommon merit, notably in the capture, by his wife and self, of a muscalonge, measuring four feet eleven inches in length and weighing forty pounds.

Mr. Skinner himself says: "I have been frequently asked, what I considered a spoon to represent, as revolving while fishing, and why are fish attracted by them to such an extent that they will seize them, even when unprovided with any other attraction save the glint of the cold metal. In reply, I offer those of an inquisitive turn my humble opinion that the motion or action of a revolving lure, unquestionably simulates or means, life — prey, to fish, and as a natural sequence, life means food — sustenance."

Mr. Skinner also relates the following: "A party from Clayton went to Hay Bay, Bay of Quinte, to fish for muscalonge. The water in Hay Bay is not very deep where the fish are caught and the weeds come very near the surface. To prevent the trolling-spoon fouling, a gang of naked hooks is attached to the line some distance ahead of the spoon, which breaks off or pulls up the weeds and allows the spoon to go free. Messrs. D. Pratt and Edwin Seymour, of Syracuse, were fishing in one boat. Mr. Seymour, in letting out line, felt a tug when the line was out but a few yards. Turning he saw the water break where the naked hook was and commenced to haul in, finding he had caught a muscalonge upon the naked or weed-guard hook.

"One of the party trolling with two hand lines caught a large pike under somewhat unusual circumstances. The voracious fish had captured one troll and made a race for and secured the other, having both of them securely hooked in his mouth when hauled in.

"A most unusual occurrence I would like to place on record. In August, 1883, Miss Annie Lee, at that time eleven years of age, while trolling near Clayton for bass, with a No. 3 gold fluted spoon, which size is fitted with a No. 2 hook, struck and successfully brought to boat a muscalonge weighing thirty-six pounds, measuring four feet six inches in length. In the effort to secure this large fish the guide's gaff was broken, showing the enormous strength of the fish, yet it was finally secured, brought in and exhibited with those slight hooks still fast in its capacious mouth — an evidence not only of good tackle, but of skillful handling."

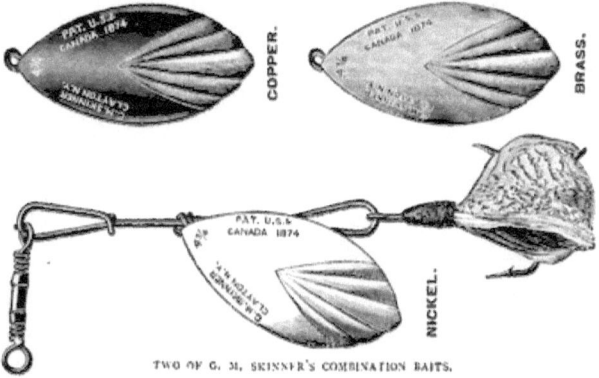

TWO OF G. M. SKINNER'S COMBINATION BAITS.

CARLTON ISLAND IN THE REVOLUTION.

[The following sketch of an historic spot in the St. Lawrence River, furnishes very interesting data, and will be read with pleasure by all tourists. It is from the pen of the Canadian Historian, ERNEST CRUIKSHANK, of Fort Erie, Ontario. This article is in no sense a duplication of a previous article upon the same subject, but contains much that is entirely new.]

THE importance of maintaining a military post on "Isle aux Chevreaux," as it was named by the French, variously translated by English traders as "Buck" or "Deer Island," was recognized by General Haldimand immediately after his arrival at Quebec to assume the office of Governor-General. Traders for some years past had been in the habit of depositing their stores at this place until they could be re-shipped in the "King's vessels" for Niagara, and their batteaux received the peltry on its way from the "Upper Posts" to Montreal. It was the great "entrepot" of the fur trade since the decay and evacuation of Oswego. In this way merchandise valued at $100,000 had been accumulated at this place, where it remained entirely unprotected, and exposed to attack during the winter of 1777-8; meanwhile of forty or fifty traders formerly established at Oswego, but one remained.

In the summer of 1778, he accordingly despatched Capt. Thos. Aubrey with a detachment of the 47th Regiment to occupy the island, accompanied by Lieut. James Glenie of the Royal Engineers, who had instructions to construct a small fortification for the protection of vessels and stores. It was intended as a general depot and base of supplies for all the posts above. He selected a site near the upper end of the island commanding the roadstead used by the vessels, and a small redoubt was traced which he called Fort Haldimand, in honor of the Governor, while the island was re-named "Carlton" after his distinguished predecessor.

The correspondence of Francis Goring, factor for George Forsyth at Niagara, gives stray glimpses of life on the island at this time.

On the 1st June, 1778, Archibald Cunningham writes to him:

"There are upwards of forty canoes of Indians on the ground at present, having come in the other day. Two small parties are now singing the war song, to go on a scouting party to Fort Stanwix, and the remainder wait for their presents."

On the 2d August, Cunningham writes again:

"L. Parlow, sent by our commandant with a party to bring off his family and effects from Oswego, but on his arrival, found that his buildings had, about fourteen days before, been burnt by the rebels, who took most of his effects, even the handkerchief from his lady's neck, and his son prisoner. Yet he had the good fortune to find they had missed his bag of piasters, two milch cows, his wife and two daughters, with which he made his retreat to this place."

Aubrey's letters during September, detail the progress of the works, and some weeks later he reports having received and planted twenty apple trees. In December, the garrison was alarmed by the arrival of Indians from Onondaga with information that a body of Americans from Fort Stanwix was about to attack the island. A second message warned Aubrey that the enemy intended to occupy Oswego, but a scouting party sent to Fort Stanwix, returned with a prisoner who assured him that there was no truth in this report.

In May, Aubrey sailed for Niagara, and was succeeded in command by Capt. George McDougall, who on the 16th, chronicles the arrival of a scouting party with six scalps, having unhappily been obliged to kill two prisoners to enable themselves to evade capture.

A few days later he mentions that Hawton, Johnston and LaMothe, officers of the Indian Department, had marched for Fort Stanwix, at the head of 140 warriors. A gunboat was employed in patroling the coast of the island, and the garrison were engaged in gardening on the "neck of land." A detachment of Sir John Johnson's Royal Regiment of New York had arrived, the works were being strengthened and every precaution taken against surprise which there was all the more reason to fear since several men had recently deserted from the guard.

On the 3d June, the scouts returned with a prisoner from Fort Stanwix.

On the 10th, James Clark writes to Goring: "We are repeatedly alarmed by the enemy's scouts, who a few days ago took away two men from the island not one hundred yards from the fort, and at ten o'clock in the morning. Up the whole of last night by alarms." McDougall blamed the Indians for the negligent watch kept by them, and threatened to hold their chiefs responsible for this misfortune. A party sent in pursuit of the enemy returned without having overtaken them.

About the 1st of July, Captain McDougall was superseded by Major Nairne, who brought a strong reinforcement, having on his way up the river from Montreal, dismantled Oswegatchie and Fort William Augustus, and removed the serviceable cannon.

In September, a considerable body of troops, consisting of detachments of the 34th Regt., Hanau Jägers, and the Royal Regt. of New York, intended for an expedition to the Mohawk River, was assembled here under Sir John Johnson. They were joined by two or three hundred Indians from Canada, commanded by Capt. Alexander Fraser, and proceeded to Oswego about the end of October, but returned almost immediately.

Capt. Fraser succeeded to the command in November, having in the garrison two companies of Hesse-Hanau Jägers under Count Wittgenstein, who had refused to work on the fortifications at Fort Niagara, besides detachments of the 34th and New York regiments.

The winter of 1779-80 was memorable for its severity, but scouts were kept out, and the Indians performed this service cheerfully, "thanks to Tice and the Indian officers," Fraser wrote, "but chiefly to Molly Brant, who has more influence than all the chiefs put together; insatiable in her demands for her own family, but checks the demands of others."

A ship yard was established and a vessel larger than any yet afloat on the lake was built, and named the Ontario.

In the spring, the partisan warfare was resumed with increased activity. On the 20th April, Fraser reported the arrival of Lieut. Crawford from Johnstown with seventeen prisoners, and in a few days he went out again with three other officers and seventy-one Indians. He returned about the 1st of June with sixteen prisoners, taken near Canajoharie. All parties sent out were accompanied by white men, "distinguished loyalists who would be hung if caught." Thirty soldiers deserted in a body from Fort Stanwix. They were pursued and overtaken by a party of Oneidas in the American service. Fourteen were killed after a desperate resistance; the remainder escaped and made their way to Carlton Island, where they immediately enlisted in Sir John Johnson's regiment. On the 21st and 29th June, the return of scouts with scalps is recorded, but the commandant is busily engaged in clearing land for farming purposes.

In September, Sir John Johnson touches at the island, when on his way to harry the Mohawk Valley, and Fraser laments that he is not allowed to accompany him on this errand of destruction. Scouts report a deserted land, with wheat unthreshed and Indian corn ungathered.

A detached house had been built near the barracks for Miss Molly (Brant), and upon taking possession of her new home she seemed "better satisfied than ever before."

On the 30th of November, Major John Ross, of the 34th Regiment, arrived with 100 men and assumed the command. The weather continued unusually fine for a month, and the new commander utilized it to strengthen the works until he was able to write "they cannot be stormed, and I hope never to be surprised."

On the 30th of January, 1781, Crawford accompanied by Lieut. Arden, a young subaltern of the 34th, went off on a scout to the Mohawk. After the absence of nearly a month they returned without a prisoner, all the inhabitants having shut themselves up in the forts. Crawford had made his way into one of these, from which all the men had run away, and learned from the women that there was no talk of an expedition against the island.

In May, the same indefatigable partisan was the first to discover that Fort Stanwix had been abandoned, and entered the place while the barracks were still smouldering.

Ross relates that twelve Missassauga Indians led by David Van der Heyden, a soldier of Johnson's regiment, met and routed a party of twenty-five militia, killing Captain Ellsworth and two others and making three prisoners.

In August, Crawford made another incursion to the Mohawk River, where he destroyed a mill and settlement fifteen miles below Fort Herkimer, driving a much superior number of militia into their forts. A spy named Jacob Servos, who succeeded in gaining the confidence of the enemy in the guise of a deserter, returned about the same time with valuable information, having visited every fortified post in the valley with one exception.

Ross then planned a raid upon the settlement of Duanesboro', which he proposed to the Governor to lead in person. Permission having been secured, he sailed for Oswego on the 4th of October with 250 troops and sixty Indians, and was joined there by Captain Butler with 150 rangers and about 100 Indians. Marching from Oswego on the 11th, he made his way to the Mohawk River by a very circuitous route, and destroyed the flourishing settlement of Warrensboro', which had hitherto escaped the ravages of war. Pursued by Col. Willett, he was obliged to fight near Johnstown, and repulsed him. His rear guard was again attacked at the crossing of Canada Creek, where Captain Walter Butler was killed, but otherwise escaped with slight loss, and the force returned to Carlton Island on the 7th November. The winter passed uneventful, the garrison being occupied in building stockades and clearing land for cultivation. On the 15th April, 1782, Ross took possession of Oswego, leaving Captain Anderson of the Thirty-fourth in command of Fort Haldimand, and there the record practically ends.

THE ANGLERS' ASSOCIATION OF THE ST. LAWRENCE RIVER.

OFFICERS.

President—H. H. WARNER, Rochester, N. Y.
First Vice President—W. C. BROWNING, 408 Broome street, New York.
Second Vice-President—H. R. HEATH, 333 Washington avenue, Brooklyn, N. Y.
Secretary—W. H. THOMPSON, Alexandria Bay, N. Y.
Treasurer—R. P. GRANT, Clayton, N. Y.

EXECUTIVE COMMITTEE.

A. C. Cornwall, Alexandria Bay, N. Y.; G. H. Strough, Clayton, N. Y.; R. H. Pullman, Baltimore. Md.; W. T. Haycom, Alexandria Bay, N. Y.; G. T. Raferty, Pittsburg, Pa.; F. J. Amsden, Rochester, N. Y.; R. E. Waterman, Ogdensburg, N. Y.; G. M. Skinner, Clayton, N. Y.; C. G. Emery, New York; O. T. Mackey, New York.

THE MATERIAL BENEFITS OF FISH PROTECTION.

The sole aim of the organizers of the Anglers' Association of the St. Lawrence River in 1883, was the preservation, protection and perpetuation of game fishing in the St.

ROCK ISLAND LIGHT HOUSE, NEAR FISHER'S LANDING.

Lawrence River. Probably no one of the persons active in its organization had any other idea in view; but they builded better than they knew.

At the time, matters on the St. Lawrence River were at a stand-still; there were very few persons going there for the sake of the fishing, for the simple reason that, owing to the activity of the netters, it had been almost destroyed. But a small number of the islands had cottages built upon them. There were a few people who passed down the river on tourists' tickets from Niagara Falls to Montreal, but there were no inducements for them to stop over on the way. Some of the anglers who had resorted to the river for many years for fishing still continued their yearly visits. The organization of the Anglers' Association created a sort of excitement in reference to the possibilities to be accomplished by it, so that its members lived for two or three years upon faith, believing that the efforts of the Association in ridding the river of netters, would very soon have its effect in much better fishing. Its members continued to visit the river year after year, and to induce their friends to do the same. The results of the exertions of the Anglers' Association are now known to every one who is interested, and its efforts have been attended

MUSCALONGE.
CAUGHT BY JAMES H. MANNING, OF ALBANY, N. Y.,
In Holiday's Upper Bay, St. Lawrence River, on Monday, August 31, 1885. Weight, 37 pounds. Length, 4 feet and 6 inches. Girth, 18½ inches. Spread of tail, 1 foot.

with so great success that it is now possible, and has been for the last three years, for any angler to obtain all the game fish he desires. The object of the organization of the Association has thus been effected in part by increasing the supply of game fish in the river, and in part by ridding the river of the fish pirates. Its efforts in preventing net fishing will not be at all slackened, but will, on the contrary, be increased.

The material benefits which have come from the efforts of the Anglers' Association of the St. Lawrence River have been entirely unexpected, but they are, however, no less welcome. As an object lesson which should be carefully read, marked and inwardly digested, the following facts are given, showing the material benefits which have come to Jefferson county from the organization of the Anglers' Association of the St. Lawrence River.

Jefferson county, the county lying along the St. Lawrence River from Cape Vincent to a point fifteen miles below Alexandria Bay, covering a distance of over forty miles, embracing the celebrated Thousand Islands, is naturally one of the most attractive regions in the country for the tourist and sportsman. Its exquisite river scenery, its banks and islands and its delightful air, leave nothing to be desired, if the fishing is good.

There were in 1894 about 600 persons employed as oarsmen on the river; in 1883 there were perhaps a hundred. In 1894 there were about 250 employed in connection with steam and other boats; in 1883 there may have been thirty. There were last summer forty hotels, capable of accommodating 5,000 people. Six years ago the hotels could accommodate scarcely a thousand. Besides these there are now thirty boarding-houses, with a capacity of 500 guests; there are between 600 and 700 cottages used exclusively by summer residents.

From $1,000,000 to $1,250,000 were spent on the river last summer by tourists, exclusive of railroad fares. A large and increasing business has also grown up in building steam yachts and the celebrated St. Lawrence skiffs.

Here, then, is a veritable gold mine lying at the feet of Jefferson county, by which every resident of the county is benefited either by a reduction in his taxes, by being given employment, or in his business. The population of Jefferson county is 66,000, every one of whom is constantly being benefited by the Anglers' Association. That is one side of the question. The other is this: there were during the netting season of 1888 about sixty or seventy persons engaged in illegal net fishing within the limits of the county, and of this number more than one-half were non-residents. When it is borne in mind that these net fishers do not make nearly as much if allowed to carry on their netting as ordinary farm workers, it will at once be apparent that Jefferson county could, as a business speculation, afford to hire and pay them a fair salary to remain perfectly idle, and to pension them in their old age.

The total tax assessed against the town of Alexandria (the central point on the river) was $10,906.97, of which $2,351.28 was paid by summer property holders. In other words, nearly 22 per cent. of the taxes of the town of Alexandria was paid by summer property owners. The assessed value of summer hotels and island property in the town of Alexandria in 1888 was $256,000, the basis of assessment being one-third of the actual value, while the total amount assessed was $1,218,029.

The organization of fish protection associations accomplishes three distinct things, protects the fish, furnishes the people with cheap fish food, and last, but not least, is of enormous material benefit to the surrounding country.

THE PHANTOM MINNOW.

BY J. M. CLARK.

IN order to make bait-casting an independent sport and to place it side by side with the beautiful and thoroughly scientific art of fly-casting, the fisherman should recognize very many artificial allures and improvised baits that can often be effectually used when indulging in the fascinating pastime. The Phantom minnow is a taking allure for the salmon, brook trout and black bass, together with all members of the pike family. Its origin dates back ages and ages before the advent of modern bait casting, and as it has maintained a reputation through all these years, we certainly can look upon it as a successful allure. But in order to make it a desirable bait to use in this sport, the construction should be somewhat modernized. In this sport the fine silk line becomes a very prominent factor, and the great aim of the fisherman should be to keep the line in a perfect condition for casting the bait, and as the great effectiveness of this allure — same as the trolling-spoon — lays in the fact of its perfect spinning qualities, this very important feature in the construction should be most faithfully carried out by supplying it with ample swivel accommodation, that will make it a perfect spinner beyond all manner of doubt, so it will not twist or kink the casting line. The original phantom is provided with three gangs of treble hooks, and many sportsmen who fully recognize the wonderful killing properties of this allure take exceptions to this feature of the construction, and rightfully object to it as a scientific angler's bait, on the ground of its giving the fish no show whatever. However, this again speaks well for the merits of the Phantom, and if we can smooth over this unfavorable feature in the construction, it will be admitted a practical bait has been secured. This can be accomplished by reducing the number of hooks and yet not harm the minnow a particle when used in connection with the scientific methods employed by the modern bait caster.

As a bait for the black bass, and particularly the large-mouth species, the meadow or grass frog is decidedly the par excellence of baits, and if the smaller specimen of this frog be used, the distinction between the large and small-mouth bass cannot be considered when recommending this allure. In fact, some of the largest catches of the small-mouth bass ever made were taken with the small meadow frog when using it as a casting bait. However, it is sometimes difficult to obtain the frog even if the fisherman be convinced it is the best allure for the occasion, and if its prototype can be supplied in the form of the luminous artificial frog, the fisherman and bait-caster has decidedly scored another point in the shape of an independent allure.

One reason why the use of artificial allures and improvised baits are frequently condemned is owing to the fact of their not being properly worked, and the bait-caster should study this important feature very carefully, and aim to infuse a life-like motion to the allure. This being the case, a chapter of interest is added to the sport of angling, as the fisherman who is a skillful manipulator of artificial and improvised baits, and who makes a positive success of their use, will take more pleasure and pastime in the art of modern bait-casting than will the individual who follows out a positive rule of using only the live minnow or the natural frog, as skill is added to skill when inanimate baits are introduced and made successful in this sport.

In further following out our design to shed some slight light upon the methods pursued by experienced fishermen, we insert the following well-written remarks upon "Minnow-Casting for Black Bass," by Dr. James A. Henshall, in "Clark's Anglers' Guide:"

"There are various ways and means of angling, each of which is satisfactory to its particular practitioners according to the light and experience they have had. And these ways and means are as diverse as those in other pursuits or pleasures. But the way to obtain the maximum amount of enjoyment in any method, or way of angling, consists in the use of suitable means to that end.

"Fly fishing cannot be satisfactorily practiced with a bait rod and a multiplying reel, nor can bait fishing be successfully pursued with a fly rod, click reel and enameled line; and while it is true that fish can be captured in either way, it is no less true that they can also be taken with the spear or net.

"Coming at once to the caption of this article, minnow-casting for black bass can only be fully enjoyed by the use of suitable tackle. After years of patient and exhaustive experiments I demonstrated, to my own mind, that the most suitable rod for all the exigencies of minnow-casting should be eight feet three inches in length and eight ounces in weight, and of a degree of flexibility and resiliency that would admit of both casting the minnow and of playing the bass when hooked. This would, in short, mean a rod that in pliancy would come between a trout bait-rod and a trout fly-rod. This idea is now happily expressed in the Henshall rods of the best makers, who conform to the specifications furnished. Some makers, by very careful selection of materials and excellence of construction, can reduce the weight to seven ounces in split bamboo. This naturally increases the cost of the rod, but to those who can afford it, it is money well spent.

"While a stiff rod will, in some hands, cast a minnow as far, or farther, than a more pliable one, it is not so well adapted for playing a fish, or to diminish the strain on line or leader as the latter — and a rod that is too withy or flexible does not cast well nor give the angler much command over the fish. It is between these extremes, then, that one should choose.

"In multiplying reels for minnow-casting the best is the cheapest, as the best is the most suitable; one that runs with the least friction, and is so finely adjusted as to admit of the least amount of lost motion, is the one to use if the angler's purse will justify the expense, for it will cost as much as a good watch. Such a reel, with careful use, is cheap in the end, for it will answer as long as the angler is capable of fishing, and will do good service unto the second and third generation.

"The line should be of silk, firmly and closely braided, not larger than size G, and preferably of size H. It should be neither oiled nor enameled. A line of this character will cling to the reel in uniform coils, will not absorb much water, and will cast almost as well wet as when dry. With a pliable rod the H line is strong enough for any black bass that swims, and is certainly the best for casting, and occupies less space on the reel than one of larger size.

"As to hooks, the Sproat is best with the O'Shaughnessy a good second. As a rule, most anglers use too large hooks in bait fishing for black bass, many employing sizes as large as 3/0. The number 2 Sproat is large enough, and even smaller sizes may be used, and will be found much more satisfactory after a trial by those accustomed to larger hooks. The smaller the hook the less injurious to the live minnow; and so far as strength is concerned a number 4 Sproat will kill a thirty pound salmon. Hooks should be tied to single gut, always, in minnow-casting.

"Usually no sinker is required beyond a small brass swivel, to which is to be affixed the snell at one end and the reel line at the other, no leader being used. If a sinker is found necessary to keep the minnow beneath the surface of the water, only the smallest size should be employed, and should be attached from six to twelve inches above the swivel.

"In so brief an article as this it would be useless to fully describe the method of casting the minnow, and, moreover, the 'modus operandi' is pretty well understood at this day. The whole secret lies in 'thumbing' the spool of the reel in such a manner that just the right pressure is maintained to allow of the free running of the line, and at the same time to prevent its over-running or back-lashing. When this can be done it is only a question of practice as to the length of the cast. The beginner should be satisfied with very short casts, say twenty feet, and use but little force in the effort. The endeavor should be to cast the minnow as delicately as possible, and to produce as little splashing upon its alighting on the water as may be, rather than to make long, noisy casts.

"Whether wading the stream, or fishing from a boat or the bank, the angler should make frequent casts over the likeliest spots, allowing the minnow to sink to mid-water, between the bottom and the surface, and if the minnow is not very lively, to reel the line slowly, in order to keep it in motion. If there is no response within fifteen seconds, a new cast should be made, the minnow being reeled in slowly, and the rod, meanwhile, giving it a zig-zag motion to simulate somewhat the natural motions of a free minnow — it being premised that the bait is hooked through the lips. These directions apply to pools, or rather deep water near and over shoals, rocks, etc.; but when fishing riffles or shallow falls, the minnow should be kept on the surface, no sinker being used.

"In the usual fishing seasons it is useless to fish waters of any great depth, say of more than twelve or fifteen feet. At other times, when the bass are near their winter quarters, or during excessive heats

BIG MUSCALONGE — 45-POUNDER.

of summer, they are found in deeper water — but I imagine that no true angler cares to fish for them under these circumstances.

"The bait should not be too large; minnows from two and a half to three inches in length are about right for light tackle. If one is fishing for pike or pickerel, larger baits may be used, as the tackle will likely be heavier, and the hooks larger and tied to gimp — but this is not black-bass fishing. It should be the aim of every black-bass angler to elevate and advance the art by employing light, elegant and suitable tools, tackle and appliances, and, in fact, to place it upon an equal plane with brook-trout fishing as practiced in Canada, Maine and the Lake Superior region. As to Catskill rods and the tiny trout streams, 'that,' as Kipling says, 'is another story.'"

THE SPORTSMAN'S SONG.

BY MAURICE THOMPSON.

Ho! for the marshes, green with spring,
    Where the bitterns croak and the plovers pipe,
Where the gaunt old heron spreads his wing
    Above the haunt of the rail and snipe;
For my gun is clean and my rod's in trim
    And the old, wild longing is roused in me:
Ho! for the bass-pools cool and dim—
    Ho! for the swales of the Kankakee

Is there other joy like the joy of a man
    Free for a season with rod and gun,
With the sun to tan and the winds to fan,
    And the waters to lull, and never a one
Of the cares of life to follow him,
    Or to shadow his mind while he wanders free?
Ho! for the currents slow and dim!
    Ho! for the fens of the Kankakee!

A hut by the river, a light canoe,
    My rod and my gun, and a sennight fair—
A wind from the south and the wild fowl due —
    He mine! All's well! Comes never a care!
A strain of the savage fires my blood,
    And the zest of freedom is keen in me;
Ho! for the marsh and the lilied flood!
    Ho! for the tarns of the Kankakee!

Give me to stand where the swift currents rush,
    With my rod all astrain and a bass coming in,
Or give me the marsh, with the brown snipe aflush,
    And my gun's sudden flashes and resonant din;
For I'm tired of the desk and tired of the town,
    And I long to be out, and I long to be free.
Ho! for the marsh! with the birds whirling down!
    Ho! for the pools of the Kankakee!

GANANOQUE PAST AND PRESENT.

THE pleasant village of Gananoque, with a population of about four thousand souls, situated on the north shore of the St. Lawrence, opposite Clayton, and at the outlet of Gananoque River, is a place of no small importance as a manufacturing center. It has an excellent water power, aggregating many hundreds of horse-power, much more of which might be utilized for manufacturing purposes.

As a place of summer resort, it possesses exceptional advantages in the way of locality. Its position at the foot of the "Admiralty Group" of islands, in which is "Bostwick Channel," the finest in many respects of any of the island channels in the river (the entire group being made up of islands in themselves exceedingly picturesque), is, in its entirety, one of great beauty and attractiveness. Already cottages are erected on many of the islands, and as the great desirableness of the locality becomes better known, the number of these cannot fail to increase; and still more so, if the present very unjust and inconsistent policy of the Ottawa government should be modified, as, indeed, it should be for the benefit of the village of Gananoque itself.

The name "Gananoque" is evidently of Indian origin; but which of two Indian names as first applied to the locality is to be considered as having given rise to the present name, is a matter of some doubt. The original orthography of the word was "Cadanoryhqua," meaning the "Place of Health," or what was evidently a synonymous phrase "Rocks-Seen-Under-Running-Water," both of which are descriptive of the locality, so far as physical conditions and a natural fact are concerned. On the other hand, the Hurons called the place "Gananoqui," which means "The Place of the Deer." Another tribe translates their term to mean "A meadow rising out of the waters," so that the real source from which the present name is derived is a matter of some doubt. Be that as it may, the Mississauga name "Cadanoryhqua" was for several years retained in official documents, and it was not until after the year 1800 that the name "Gananoque" came into use. At the time of the survey of Leeds, the name of the Gananoque River was changed to "The Thames," but it never was generally used; in fact it only appears in a proclamation of Lord Dorchester (Sir Guy Carlton) while for the second time Governor-General of Canada, in 1788.

From the variety and extent of its manufacturing interests, Gananoque has been, not inaptly, named the Birmingham of Canada, and as a settlement has now entered upon the second century of its existence. A brief sketch of its early settlement may be of some interest to the general reader, and is therefore subjoined. Two men, Sir John Johnson, an officer of the British army during the War of the Revolution, at which time he commanded an organization of loyalists popularly known as "Johnson's Royal Greens," and Colonel Joel Stone, were the first to receive grants of land which covered the entire limits of the village, and more, as it now stands. Of these two, Col. Stone was the first settler, coming up the river from Cornwall in the summer of 1792, taking passage in a batteau which was bound to Kingston. These grants of land were made in 1792, and the patent to Col. Stone was issued December 31, 1798, and

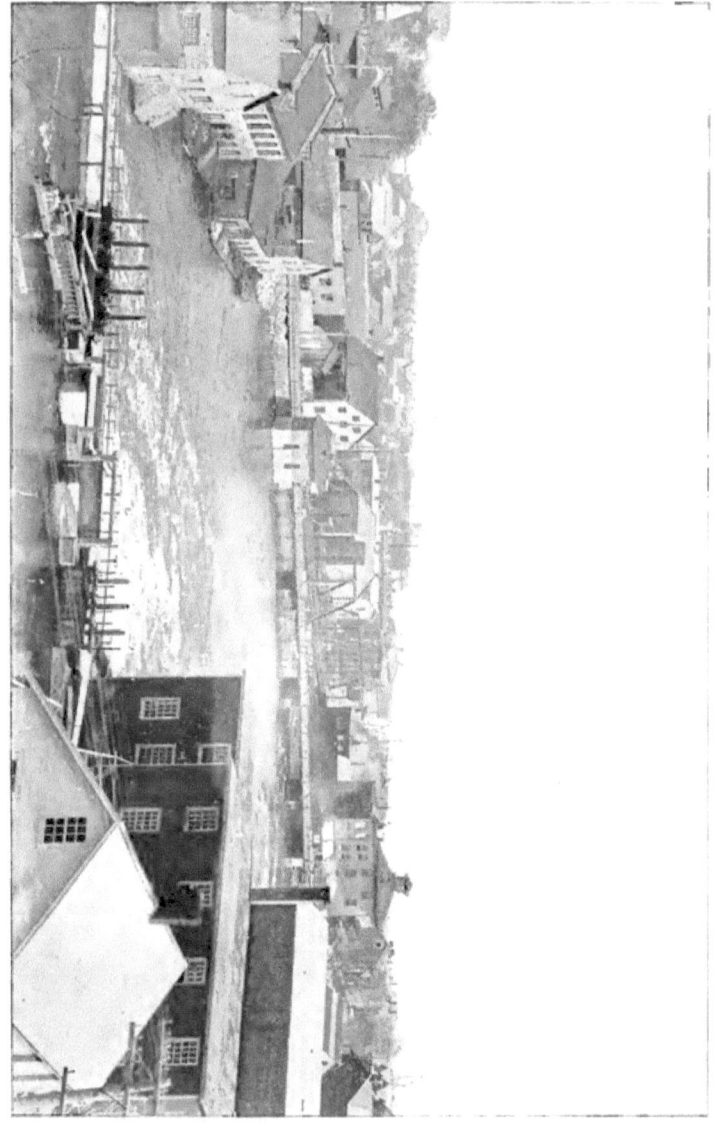

VIEW IN GANANOQUE, SHOWING WATER-POWER.

covers "A certain triangular tract upon the River Cadanoryhqua," etc., which was located on the west side of the river. Sir John Johnson's tract was located on the east side of the river, but his patent was not issued until May 17, 1802. Each grant extended to the center of the Gananoque River, then known by its Indian name as above.

Col. Stone's patent was computed to contain 700 acres of land, to which were added, later, two additional patents of 200 acres each, making in all 1,100 acres; while Col. Johnson's grant covered 1,534 acres. At the time of Col. Stone's arrival, a Frenchman, named Carey, lived on Tidd's Island, now Fremont Park, with whom he formed a temporary partnership, erecting a shanty on the mainland, on the point now occupied by a lumber yard. Having secured a couple of cows, their shanty was opened as a house of entertainment, being the first tavern for many miles along the Canadian shore of the St. Lawrence. During the absence of the proprietors one day, the hotel burned and the partnership ended, each of them entering into business for himself. Mr. Stone proceeded to clear a plot of land on what is know King street, on which he erected a log-house, it being, with the exception of the shanty above spoken of, the first house erected in Gananoque. His next enterprise was the building of a schooner of forty tons measurement, called the "Leeds Trader," which ran on the lake and river for many years. Then he built a saw-mill, which stood on the site of the present Electric Light Company's building; following that with a frame house of two stories in height, fastened with wrought nails brought from England. It was erected in 1796, and for half a century it was known as the "Red House," having been painted that color. This was built on the point near where the upper end of the lumber yard wharf is now. Where the steel and wire shop now is, Mr. Stone built another frame house, known as the "Yellow House," and which became his residence, after his marriage to Mrs. Dayton. Later, he built a long, low frame house with a veranda along its entire front, just west of the "West End Store," which he made his residence as long as he lived. The building was burned only thirteen years ago, and the lot where it stood is yet vacant. In 1852, the late John Bulger tore down the "Red House," and the frame was re-erected on Garden street. It is the house now occupied by Mr. James Beatty. The "Yellow House" was burned in 1850.

Col. Stone was evidently a man of great energy, and was unceasing in his efforts to improve his holdings, keeping all the time an eye to the "main chance," as did his ancestors, and as he himself had been trained to do in the school of actual business. His procedure was in direct contrast with that of Sir

COL. STONE.
(Kindly loaned us by Mr. Benton, editor " Recorder.")

John Johnson, who paid no attention whatever to his estate, only through an agent; in fact, it is a question whether he ever visited his possessions in person, so that to Col. Stone belongs all the honors of a first settler; and hence a brief biographical sketch may prove interesting.

Joel Stone was born in Guilford, Connecticut, August 7, 1749. Before he was two years of age, his father removed to Litchfield, where, "by indefatigable labor and industry, he improved a competency of land of which he was proprietor." During his minority, Joel labored on the "competency," but when he became of age, he adopted a more active mode of life, and became a travelling merchant; or, in the vernacular of those days a "Yankee peddler." Within three years he travelled over very nearly the whole of the then settled portions of the country, returning with a large amount of property. In 1774, he entered into a mercantile partnership with Jabez Bacon, of Woodbury, Conn., their articles of copartnership binding them for six years as copartners in "Merchandizing and all things thereto belonging; and in buying, selling, vending and retailing all sorts of goods, wares and commodities whatsoever." These articles of copartnership are yet in existence. This partnership flourished, and the partners became wealthy; but the breaking out of the Revolutionary War ended the partnership and one of them assumed the hazards and glories of a military life.

Mr. Stone attempted for a time to remain neutral and trade with both parties, though his sympathy was with the Royalists. But he was soon obliged to declare himself for one side or the other. To remain neutral, was to be suspected by both, and in 1776 he was peremptorily ordered by the officials of Congress to declare immediately whether he would take up arms against the British government, or furnish a substitute. He refused to do either; and being warned that he would be called to a strict account, he fled hurriedly to New York, which was then held by the British forces, and which he reached in safety; and on the 20th of June, 1777, he was enrolled in Governor Wentworth's command, by a commission dated April 16, 1778. He recruited fifty-four men or more for two years' service, under command of Sir William Howe. He went on this mission to Huntington, Long Island, where he was surprised while asleep and taken prisoner, May 12, 1778, by a company of whaleboat men, and conveyed to Fairfield, Connecticut. He was held in close custody and charged with high treason. But he managed to escape on the 23d of July, and a week later was back on Long Island.

In the meantime, the selectmen, the constables, bailiffs, and the courts of Connecticut had been attending to the property left there by Mr. Stone when he fled to New York. By due process of law, as it then obtained, his real and personal estate was confiscated, and the proceeds, after deducting costs, were rendered for benefit of the State. Not only did the magistrates and County Court adjudicate in the matter and issue executions, but the Probate Court was also called into operation, as dealing with the effects of one who was described in the inventory as "politically dead." The personal property thus escheated appears by the returns to have amounted to £491: 6: 9, "at the rate of twenty-eight shillings for an English guinea, or six shillings for a Spanish milled dollar." The real estate was appraised under oath at £354: 13: 0. One piece of land, in which Mr. Stone had a one-half interest, in the township of Winchester, was not included, for the reason, probably, that his pursuers had no knowledge of it. According to Mr. Stone's own statement, the firm of Bacon & Stone had a capital of £12,000 sterling in stock; and that in addition to his share of that, his books, bonds and all his personal effects were confiscated.

During his residence in New York, Mr. Stone formed an acquaintance with the family of William Moore, a sea captain, and on the 23d of March, 1780, he was married to Leah Moore, the captain's daughter. The marriage ceremony was celebrated by Rev. Charles Inglis, who was then rector of Trinity church, New York.

In addition to his pension, Mr. Stone, in common with all who had served the King in the Revolutionary War, was entitled to a grant of land. And after his arrival at Quebec, he endeavored by inquiries and personal investigation to ascertain what would be the most suitable locality.

Mr. Stone settled in Cornwall with his family, then consisting of his wife, his son, William Moore Stone, and his daughter, Mary. He purchased some land at Cornwall, and expected to draw 800 or 1,000 acres besides. He erected a dwelling and still house, and otherwise endeavored to provide a permanent home. But he was unable to secure as much land as he wanted. Most of it had been pre-

A CAVE IN A FLY ROCK.

empted before he arrived, and he was, therefore, compelled to come further towards the west in search of unclaimed territory. He went to Quebec and spent some time in an effort to secure all the land along the Gananoque River. But Sir John Johnson brought sufficient influence to bear upon the government to cause a compromise of claims. It was decided that Sir John should be awarded all the land on the east side of the Gananoque River, and Mr. Stone all on the west side, the boundary of each to be the center of the river. Just when this decision was arrived at is not set down. But Mr. Stone took possession of his portion in 1792, and the patent was issued six years later.

In 1791, Col. Stone went to Connecticut with his two children, William and Mary, whom he placed at school in Hartford, having previously placed a son at school in Montreal. Leah, his wife, died at Cornwall, about 1793, but the exact date is not known. In 1798, Mr. Stone, who had then been five years a widower, and had established himself at Gananoque, decided to marry a second time, and made formal proposal to Mrs. Abigail Dayton, widow, who lived in the township of Burford, in Upper Canada.

Suffice it to say, that the wooer prosecuted his suit with vigor, and in time, the fair object of his affections surrendered at discretion, but not in haste. They were married in the summer of 1799, removing to the residence of Col. Stone, at Gananoque.

From that time on, the particulars of Mr. Stone's life are so much a part of the progress and growth of Gananoque as to belong more properly to the history of the town. He filled numerous offices both under the government and by local appointment. He was the first Collector of Customs; a Commissioner, or Justice of the Peace; Chairman of the Court of General Sessions of the Peace for the Johnstown District; Commissioner for administering the oath to half-pay officers; Returning Officer at County election of Member of Parliament in 1812; a member of the Land Board for District of Johnston, established in 1819 for locating settlers; and Road Overseer for the Township of Leeds.

By a commission dated 3d January, 1809, under the hand and seal of Francis Gore, Lieut.-Governor of Upper Canada, he was appointed colonel in the 2d Regiment of Militia for the County of Leeds, and was thereafter known as Colonel Stone. This office he resigned in January, 1822.

Three children were born to Mr. Stone during the life of his first wife. His eldest son William, who is referred to as "Billy" in Mr. Stone's letters, grew to maturity at Gananoque, assisting in the general affairs of his father, and for a time holding the position of Deputy Collector of Customs. He died in 1809, aged twenty-eight years.

In the fall of 1833, the Colonel caught a severe cold, and died on the 20th November, in the eighty-fifth year of his age. Mrs. Stone survived him by nearly ten years, and died August 4, 1843, in her ninety-third year.

The events of his settlement in Gananoque have already been alluded to, but we will add one brief letter, which sets forth the energy and thrift of Col. Stone, better by far than any description could:

MONTREAL, 16th July, 1801.

MY DEAR:—I received your letter dated the next day after I left home, 7th June, about three days past by mere accident. I mark well the contents thereof, approve of what you have done, and must with pleasure submit to your own wisdom to do as you think best until I can get home, which I do not intend shall be long, but I have not yet been able to deliver any of my boards and plank. Andrew, William and David will sett off to-morrow morning with the boat loaded with the following packages and articles agreeable to the enclosed bills: One large cask wine, two trunks, one small trunk, the box or chest, two barrells, two kegs (one best Madeira wine, one cider vinegar), one cask nails, two small bales, one shovel, one spade. Enclosed I send you four keys, one to each of the trunks, and one to the chest. Please to be careful in unpacking the pork barrel. It has a bottle of castor oil and a phial of pickery roped up in the blankets.

In the barrels, and in your chest, you will find a number of articles we had on board the raft, two or three axes, &c., and you will find tobacco and snuff (viz.), 2 lbs. snuff only; also Bohea tea in one of the casks, and Hyson tea in one of the large trunks. The Bohea tea is 6s. per lb. in case you sell any, and the tobacco 3s. Please to put the tobacco in some moist place.

The other articles I have marked the price to sell at in the bills in my own hand writing. I need not caution you to sell for cash only, except where we owe and to pay for what we must buy. The large cask of wine may be very good to drink as wine and water, and you may sell it at 5s per gallon if you can, but I bought it with a view of making vinegar only. I gave 1s per gallon for it. The articles in the large trunk where the Hyson tea is are not marked, nor is the bill sent. You will find Turlington's drops in the trunk where the Hyson tea is, which you may sell at 5s per bottle, but those in the pork barrel, large phials keep for your own use. You will set the people at work as you find most necessary until I get home. I must, if possible, bring down another raft this season. Old Mr. Chaple will be up again as soon as he has done visiting his friends.

I am my dear in great haste, with a very bad pen and ink and my best exertions,

Your most affectionate,

JOEL STONE.

For much of the matter relating to Col. Stone, we are indebted to FREEMAN BRITTON, Esq., editor of the "Gananoque Reporter."

So far as the improvement of his water-power was concerned, Col. Stone did but little towards it, leasing it finally to his son-in-law, Charles McDonald, who, in 1812, began to carry on an extensive business. He built a saw-mill, and a small grist-mill, and engaged largely in the lumber trade, shipping large quantities to Quebec, and also supplying the government with ship timber, several war vessels being on the stocks at Kingston, at that time. In 1817, Chas. McDonald was joined by his brother John, and later by another brother Collin; and in 1826, the firm of "C. & J. McDonald and Brother" erected the largest flouring mill in the Province. To supply this mill, grain was brought in schooners from the West; and owing to its capacity of 250 barrels per day, was for many years enabled to supply one-quarter of all the flour received at Montreal. The flour was sent down in batteaux and Durham boats, a batteau load being from 150 to 200 barrels, while a Durham boat carried 450 barrels. The forwarding business at that time was in the hands of H. & S. Jones. The block houses built at Gananoque, and on Chimney Island, were built for the government by Charles McDonald.

The first store in Gananoque was opened in 1812 by Chas. McDonald, and the McDonalds also built the first church in the place. It was free for all denominations, and was erected in 1832. Some four or five years later, the Methodists erected a small wooden building on the site of the present church. This denomination furnished the first regular services in the village. The first resident minister was Rev. William Carson. Among the first settlers of the village was Ephraim Webster, who was afterward collector of customs at Brockville. In 1831, the steamer William IV was built at Gananoque by a joint stock company. This was the steamer that the noted Bill Johnston and his followers attempted to capture during the so-called Patriot war, by stretching a chain across a narrow channel between two islands. The attempt failed, but was successful as to the Sir Robert Peel, related elsewhere.

The writer's acknowledgments are due to his honor the mayor and several aldermen for many favors in the way of information afforded, but especially to the Hon. C. F. BRITTON, whose interest in the welfare of his town is strong and abiding.

In concluding this brief sketch of the early history of Gananoque, the writer desires to add, that steps are now being taken to build an electric railway from that village to the city of Kingston. In fact there is at this writing a bill before Parliament asking for an act of incorporation, which will no doubt be granted. Its situation, its water power, its commercial opportunities, its manufacturing privileges, entitle Gananoque to a population of fully 15,000 souls; and this it cannot fail to realize, unless its leading citizens, by injudicious acts, shall retard the onward march of improvement, and paralyze progress. A great number of lakes in its rear not only guarantee the perpetuity of its water power, but make the village the gateway to the finest fishing and hunting grounds in America. That Gananoque is destined to become one of the thriving cities of the St. Lawrence region admits of but slight doubt.

A brief biographical sketch of the other

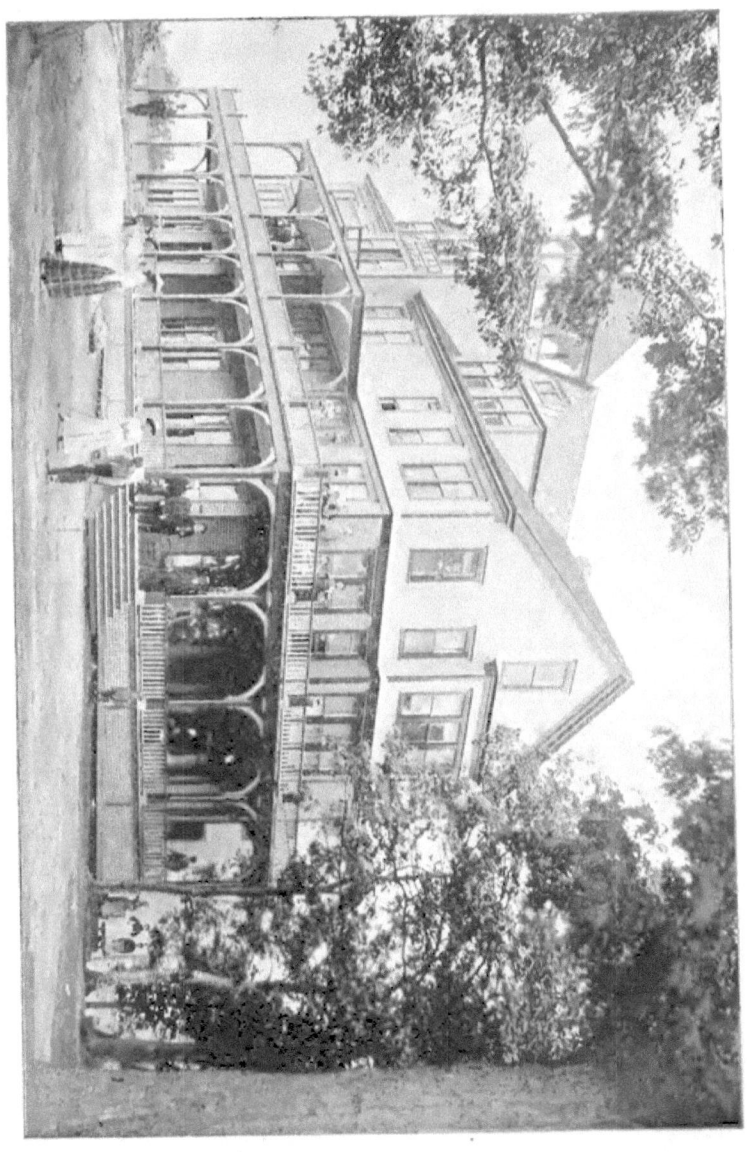

THE PULLMAN HOTEL GEN'L IN LAND.

grantee to the lands which constitute the present site of Gananoque, may prove interesting to the reader. We refer, of course, to Sir John Johnson, Bar't.

This distinguished Loyalist was the only son of Sir William Johnson, by his first wife, Catherine Wisenberg. He was born at his father's residence on the Mohawk River, November 5, 1742. He was educated in England, and while on a visit to the mother country, November 22, 1765, was knighted by George III in his father's lifetime as a mark of favor to the father. He married Mary Watts, daughter of the Hon. John Watts, of His Majesty's Council, June 30, 1773, and on the death of his father he succeeded to Johnson's Hall, and large landed estates on the Mohawk, twenty-four miles from Schenectady, and to his father's rank of major-general in the New York militia.

It was only natural that a family which had received so many favors from the crown, should remain loyal; and hence the distrust with which his every act was viewed, leading to the exaction of pledges for his future conduct, which he, of course, refused to give. Learning that steps had been taken to apprehend him, he summoned a number of his tenants and some of his neighbors who sympathized with him, and together they fled to Canada. On his arrival, he was at once appointed a colonel in the British service, and proceeded to organize a corps of two battalions which was known as the "Royal Regiment of New York," and as the "Queen's Loyal Americans;" but popularly, the corps was known as "Johnson's Royal Greens." This regiment formed a part of the force under the command of Lieut.-Col. Barry St. Leger, in his campaign against Fort Stanwix (now Rome, N. Y.), the defeat of whom did not in the least diminish his intense bitterness against his neighbors in the Mohawk Valley, whose domains he ravaged with fire and sword in 1780, though defeated at Fox's Mills, and forced to make a hasty, if not inglorious retreat.

On the 14th of March, 1782, he was appointed "Commissioner," "Superintendent-General," and "Inspector-General," of the Six Nations and their confederates, and of all the Indian Nations inhabiting the Province of Quebec and the Frontiers, a position which he held for many years. At the close of the war he settled in Canada, where he received grants of land from the crown, and where, in addition to other offices, held by him, he was colonel of the six militia battalions of the eastern townships of Lower Canada, and a member of the Legislative Council.

During his long and busy life, the baronet had no fixed abode, but resided at Montreal, Lachine, Kingston, etc., as his fancy dictated. He had a shooting box at a spot called "Mount Johnson," in the county of Iberville, and a country seat at Twickenham, England. He died at the residence of his daughter, Mrs. Bowers, in the city of Montreal, January 4, 1830, in the eighty-ninth year of his age.

The manufacturers of Gananoque are as follows: The Gananoque Carriage Co., which has a branch at Brockville; the Thousand Island Carriage Co., both of which turn out a large number of handsome vehicles; Mr. George Gillies, manufacturer of bolts and nuts and saddlery hardware; Parmenter & Bullock, manufacturers of rivets, wire nails and a variety of small articles; the Ontario Wheel Company, which turns out an immense number of carriage-wheels annually; the St. Lawrence Steel and Wire Company, manufacturers of corset steels, crinoline steels and articles of that nature. The next is the Electric Light Station, one of the most complete stations of any town its size anywhere. Crossing the railway bridge, you come to to Cowan & Britton, manufacturers of nails, hinges, butts and special articles in iron and steel; O. D. Cowan manufacturer of clothes wringers, harrows and electrical fixtures; Skinner & Co., manufacturers of hames, snaths and wooden goods; Gananoque Spring and Axle Company, manufacturers of carriage springs and carriage axles on a large scale; the D. F. Jones Manufacturing Company, manufacturers of spades and shovels; Gananoque Furniture Company, manufacturers of furniture of

316 A SOUVENIR OF THE ST. LAWRENCE RIVER.

all descriptions; Gananoque Roller Flour Mill; Mitchell & Wilson, planing mills and contractors; O. V. Goulette, turned wooden goods of all descriptions; Thousand Island Railway Company, makes connections with all passenger trains east and west on the G. T. R., and one of the most convenient points for Chicago and the west.

THE "NEW ISLAND WANDERER."
Belongs to the Thousand Island Steamboat Company, making Daily Excursions among the Islands. Steamer "Island Belle," of same line, makes daily trips to Ogdensburg.

RIVER FRONT OF THE CITY OF BRUNSWICK, GA.

BROCKVILLE,

THE GATE-CITY TO THE THOUSAND ISLANDS.

JUST at the foot of the Thousand Islands, 126 miles west of Montreal, and fifty miles east of Kingston, stands the beautiful town of Brockville. Its history is one of interest, as being one of the oldest towns in Ontario, and as one which has not stood still, but has made a steady progress, a solid substantial growth, in step and cadence with modern improvement. The modern "booms," with their consequent reaction, have never been inflicted upon Brockville, and in consequence it has felt none of the enervating influences sequent upon periods of undue inflation.

In 1784, one hundred and eleven years ago, Adam Cole, having left the United States, and being still desirous of remaining under the protection of the British flag, to which he deemed his allegiance due, sailed up the St. Lawrence, and landed on the site of the present city of Brockville; but from the fact that to him the land seemed rough and uninviting, he pushed on to a point six miles above, and finally settled at what is now known as Cole's Ferry. In the following year, another enthusiastic U. E. Loyalist, William Buell, located on the lot where a large part of the western portion of the city now stands. Shortly afterward, Charles Jones, following in the footsteps of his predecessor, took up the adjoining lot on the east. These first settlers were of course subjected to all the inconveniences incident to pioneer life; but in a short time the little settlement became a distributing point for government stores, which were supplied to settlers in the shape of provisions and implements, and quite soon it sprang into some prominence, and began to grow.

The surrounding township was named Elizabethtown, and for a number of years the village was known by that name, and also by the name of Buell's Bay. Finally, the residents began to favor a more dignified title, and then no little difference of opinion arose concerning the name of the place, which, as is almost always the case, resulted in a patronymic bestowed by outsiders, which was far more expressive as to fact, than conducive to dignity. Mr. Buell and his friends were extremely desirous of naming it "Williamstown," in honor of William Buell, the first settler. On the other hand, Mr. Jones and his adherents, insisted that "Charlestown" should be the name, after Mr. Charles Jones; and between the factions such a strife was engendered, and so bitter was this miniature war of the rival roses, that the outlying residents becoming disgusted with the endless bickerings, incontinently bestowed the nickname of "Snarleytown" upon the place, which adhered to it for a long time.

In 1811, however, a new system of grand tactics was introduced into the local war, and Mr. Buell demonstrated his ability as a tactician by having his property surveyed and laid out into town lots, setting aside grounds for a public square, court-house, etc., of which he had a map published on which was duly set forth desirable properties for sale, thus inaugurating for that day and age a veritable approach to the modern "boom," or, at all events, as near to one as Brockville has ever experienced. Desirous of becoming a large landed proprietor, Mr. Jones was averse to disposing of his property in like manner, and therefore practically acknowledged that he was out-generaled, but he was by no means defeated. The factions grew and multiplied in numbers, and the feud in intensity, for a decade, until it seemed a foregone conclusion that "Snarleytown" was likely to become the permanent designation of the locality. Finally, in 1821, Governor-General Sir Isaac Brock, being in the place, the dispute was referred to him, and he immediately settled the difficulty by bestowing his own name upon the place. It was a happy thought, and like pouring oil upon troubled waters, it calmed the storm by satisfying the contending factions, who merged their differences into "Brockville," a name ever since retained, and one to be proud of. As an old resident of the city remarked to the writer: "It was a shrewd exemplification of the fable of the monkey, the cats and the cheese — but it worked well and satisfied all parties."

During the war of 1812-15, Brockville was often the scene of lively operations. On the 29th of July, 1812, the United States armed schooner Julia, and two British vessels, the Earl of Moira and the Duke of Gloucester, had an engagement opposite the town, which lasted for three hours, ceasing by mutual consent when darkness came on, neither party having suffered any material damages; — an emphatic and significant comment upon the skill of both parties in the use of artillery. On the night of the 6th of February, 1813, Capt. Forsyth, of the Rifles, then commandant at Ogdensburg, marched up the river to Morristown, and, crossing on the ice, took possession of the town, capturing several of its prominent citizens, and releasing several prisoners from the jail, most of whom were Americans who had been taken prisoners and confined there. It is related that Capt. Forsyth refused to release a prisoner who was incarcerated on a charge of murder; but in his defense his counsel sought to win a point in his favor by establishing the fact that, while he might have escaped, he would not, thus creating a strong inference of his innocence. He was, nevertheless, convicted and hanged.

LOOKING EAST FROM ARCADE, WATERTOWN, N. Y., SHOWING SNOW OF WINTER 1894-95.

HAILING THE LAZY FERRYMAN.

Fifty-two prisoners, with a large amount of stores and ammunition, was the result of the capture of Brockville, and an equal number of American prisoners was the result of a reprisal which immediately followed, in which Capt. Forsyth was badly beaten at Ogdensburg by the Canadian volunteers under Capt. McDonnell, who, in addition to the prisoners, captured a large amount of military stores, several pieces of artillery, some small arms, besides destroying the barracks. The Americans lost twenty-three in killed and wounded, and were forced to retreat to Black Lake. Since the senseless and uncalled for disturbance of 1837, which culminated in the surrender of the rebels at the Windmill, and the ripple caused by the Fenian Raid, Brockville has enjoyed uninterrupted peace, and has steadily thriven, pursuing the even tenor of its way, until now we have

THE BROCKVILLE OF TO-DAY.

With a population of very nearly, if not quite 10,000, Brockville is fairly on the road toward the dignity and importance of a city. The old methods of navigation on the St. Lawrence, batteaux and Durham boats, have given way to elegant steamers, which have reduced the time from Montreal from weeks to hours. Railways have replaced the uncertain stage coach, and now few towns are more favorably situated than is Brockville, as regards connections both by water and by rail. The main line of the Grand Trunk Railway runs through the town, and has been an important factor in its development. Direct communication with Ottawa, the capital of the Dominion, only seventy-four miles distant, is afforded by the Canadian Pacific Railway, which absorbed into its gigantic system the old Brockville and Ottawa Railway. Already the Brockville, Westport and Sault St. Marie Railway has been completed to Westport, and in addition to making a large section of country tributary to Brockville, when completed to the "Soo," and connecting there with the American railways, this will become one of the great trunk lines, connecting the Atlantic

THE SNOW IN STREETS OF WATERTOWN, WINTER OF 1894-95.

seaboard with the Great West. Besides, there is now projected an electric railway to run between Brockville and Ottawa, which will open the Rideau country, and be of great benefit to that entire section. By steam-ferry to Morristown, connection is had with the Rome, Watertown and Ogdensburg Railway, which forms a part of the great Central system of New York; the largest on the American continent — and now it is proposed to build a bridge across the St. Lawrence at this point, to connect the Canadian and American systems, the preliminary steps to which have already been taken, charters secured in both countries, and it is confidently expected that active steps in the way of construction will be taken within a few months at the farthest.

During the season of navigation, the steamer service is excellent. The steamers of the Richelieu and Ontario Navigation Company call daily on their trips between Toronto and Montreal and various American ports among the Thousand Islands. Besides these, the Ocean, Alexandria, Cuba, etc., do a large freight and passenger business, so that water facilities are of the best quality, and readily available at the minimum of delay. The steamer service to the Thousand Islands has of late years been supplied by the John Haggart, a commodious vessel, well adapted to the purpose.

As a summer resort, Brockville offers exceptional advantages. The great American resorts among the islands are within easy reach, being only from twenty-five to thirty miles away, and easily reached by any one of the daily line of steamers which ply during the watering season. Besides these, the Empire State, America and St. Lawrence, all splendid steamers, make almost daily excursions. These steamers belong to the Thousand Island Steamboat Company line, a company that is sparing no pains nor expense to furnish a river service on the St. Lawrence which cannot be excelled. During the past decade some elegant resorts have sprung up on the Canadian side of the river; among which are Fernbank, Hill Crest, and Union Park, while between these nearly every favored spot is taken up, and every year sees new and beautiful summer homes spring into view. Residents of New York, Ottawa and Montreal, recognizing the beauties of these locations, have already erected fine summer residences, or are prepared to do so in the near future.

Between Brockville and Union Park, seven miles above, a steamer makes four round trips daily, so that business men can attend to their duties during the day, returning to their cottage homes in the evening. In addition to its river attractions, Brockville has some beautiful drives, prominent among which, for beauty and picturesqueness, is the drive to Fernbank Park and the village of Lynn, five miles away. The best known and patronized, however, is that to Prescott, a distance of twelve miles along the bank of the river. Brockville is supplied with water through the celebrated " Holly " system, and it has an excellent system of sewerage, so that as a place of excellent sanitation it is unexcelled. The streets are well lighted with both gas and electricity, or rather a combination of the two. They intersect at right angles, and for the most part are beautifully shaded, so that one might aptly name Brockville the " Forest City," and not go far astray.

In religious and educational matters, Brockville stands deservedly high. Some of the church edifices are magnificent and costly triumphs of architectural skill. There are three congregations of the Church of England, two Presbyterian, two Methodist, one Baptist, and one Roman Catholic, besides some smaller sects. Their pastors are men of marked ability. The schools of Brockville are of a high order. The public schools consist of a central High school, known as the Victoria School, and four Ward Schools. The Separate School is a large and commodious structure, provided with all the modern appliances. The Convent de Notre Dame is a superior ladies' school. There is also an excellent Kindergarten in successful operation, together with some first-class private schools. The Collegiate Institute is one of the best higher educational institutions in the Province. Stu-

THE PALISADES.

dents are here prepared for matriculation in the various colleges, and for entering upon any of the professions. Brockville has also a Business College equal to any in the country in its methods and in the thoroughness of its work. Last, but by no means least among the educational institutions of the town, is the Art School. This has attained a provincial reputation from the excellence of the work exhibited by its pupils in competition with other Art schools in Ontario. The Mechanics' Institute, with its library of many thousand volumes, its ample and well-supplied reading-room, filled with all the current reading matter of the day, is surely an educator whose influence upon the masses can hardly be overestimated. In this respect, Brockville is but another demonstration of the well-known fact that, given a good, well-selected library, and a reading-room abundantly supplied with the literature of the day, a community will stand infinitely higher, morally and intellectually, than will one deprived of those privileges. Brockville has two excellent newspapers, the Times and Recorder, both of which are live sheets and fully up to date, not only as regards the news in general, but also fully alive to the interests of their town. There are many enterprising manufacturing firms, but lack of space prevents the insertion of a list.

For the care of the sick and afflicted, Brockville has two excellent hospitals, the Brockville General Hospital and the St. Vincent de Paul Hospital, both being fully equipped and well managed. The crowning institution, however, is the newly erected

BROCKVILLE INSANE ASYLUM.

This is an elegant structure, standing on a commanding site on what was known as the Pickens Point property, at the left of the Prescott road. From it, the view across and down the St. Lawrence is magnificent. The premises contain 207 acres. The main building stands about 350 yards north of the Prescott road. It is built in the form of a cross, being three stories high in the center and two stories in the wings, having a frontage of 400 feet. The front of the central part is surmounted by a tower 128 feet in height. The central part of the main building projects to the rear 200 feet. There are ample basements, storage rooms, coal vaults, laundries, sewing rooms, offices, dining rooms, kitchens, patients' rooms, bath rooms, linen rooms, with ample accommodations in the main building for 240 patients. In short, the building is provided with every appliance that science, skill and experience could suggest as being beneficial in an institution of the kind. Six cottages, each forty by sixty feet, two stories high, with all the appliances to accommodate sixty patients each, are also a part of this institution. Although interesting, space forbids an extended description of this fine public institution, so likely to prove one of the attractions of Brockville.

The Canadian shore of the St. Lawrence river, it will be noticed, is, in the main, bluff and rocky, and in many places exceedingly precipitous, with here and there occasional breaks, where the land slopes gently to the water's edge. It is in one of these breaks that Brockville is situated, with high bluffs above and below and high ground to the rear. From the river the place presents a very fine appearance. The bluff at the east end of the town rises to a height of fully fifty feet, and is commonly known as "High Rocks," which, with its overhanging shelves, clinging vines and wild honeysuckles draped over the entrances many small caves, presents a charming bit of scenery to the eye of the river tourist, but which is scarcely appreciated by the citizens themselves. This beautiful spot is the home of a legend or tale which may be too true in fact, to relegate to the regions of romance or legend. Be that as it may, it is here "set down," the reader to be the judge.

THE LEGEND OF THE CLIFF.

At a point where the face of the cliff is comparatively smooth, may be seen traces of a painting which is now nearly obliterated, but which, until within a few years past, was visited every spring by a band of Indians, who, with weired ceremonies and incantations, brightened the picture with fresh paint and departed. The picture was a rough representation of a canoe, propelled by several Indians, out of which two white men were falling. The legend relates that in the early days of the French occupation of Canada by Count Frontenac, there was a continual struggle between the New France and the New England, as to which should secure the alliance of the Indian tribes; and although nominally France and England were at peace, there is no doubt that English officers stationed in the colonies, did all in their power to forward this much-to-be-desired consummation. The French had succeeded in securing the alliance of the Algonquins and Hurons, but the great confederacy of the Iroquois held aloof from any entangling alliances, the more, it is presumed, because they were deadly foes to both Hurons and Algonquins, the former of which were settled around lakes Huron and Superior, while the Algonquins were the tribes of the east. The Hurons, to reach the great fur markets of Montreal and Quebec, were obliged to pass through the country of the Iroquois, which that confederacy promptly opposed, and so great was the terror inspired by the Iroquois, that Count Frontenac, then Governor of the New France, decided to protect his allies, and administer such a rebuke to their foes that they would long remember it. The Count's expedition, however, was not an unqualified success; and though he brought off many prisoners, he returned with his army badly crippled, a fact of which the Iroquois were well aware.

At all events, among the prisoners captured by the French were a couple of English officers, who belonged, so history informs us, to the garrison at Oswego; for up to this point, dear reader, our relation is but a veritable historical fact, or facts, if you so choose. These officers were placed in care of a party of Indians, who were to take them to Montreal. Embarking in a canoe, they proceeded down the St. Lawrence, and, when at a point just above Brockville, they were struck by a terrible storm, and being heavily loaded they tossed the British officers overboard, not only to lighten the canoe, but to appease the storm-god by a human sacrifice. But the storm-god was not appeased. The gale increased in intensity, and the storm king howled and shrieked in the ears of the now dismayed Indians, who began to regard their actions in throwing the two men overboard as cowardly. They felt that the Great Spirit would punish them for the act, and so the wail of their death songs, mingled with the shrieks of the tempest, and when opposite the High Rocks the canoe went down with all its human freight, among whom was a distinguished chief. The judgment was well deserved. Of course, those savages did not intend to release their prisoners, but just to torture them at the stake. Had they not been so cowardly as to throw them overboard to drown, how much pleasure they might have afforded the whole tribe, and what horrible tortures, so dear to the savage heart, they might have subjected them to. But they drowned their prisoners instead, and were themselves drowned. Served them right. For more than a hundred years a band of Indians has repainted the picture each spring, at the same time performing incantations to the Great Spirit, whose anger, because they drowned the officers instead of burning them at the stake, must be appeased. As it has now been several years since the picture has been renewed, let us hope that the Indian deity is satisfied.

For much information concerning Brockville, the writer is indebted to Mr. R. LAIDLAW, of the Brockville Times, and to Mr. GEO. P. GRAHAM, of the Recorder, genial gentlemen both, and fully alive to the interests of their town.

THE FOLGER BROTHERS, KINGSTON, ONT.

THE FOLGER BROTHERS.

This widely known firm, of Kingston, Ontario, whose portraits precede this sketch, consists of B. W. FOLGER, born in 1838; HENRY FOLGER, in 1842, and F. A. FOLGER, in 1851, all at Cape Vincent, Jefferson county, N. Y. They were sons of FREDERICK A. FOLGER and LAURA FOLGER, the father being a descendant of Captain MATTHEW FOLGER, of Nantucket, Mass. Their mother was a Miss BRECK, a sister of the junior partner in the Canadian firm of Calvin & Breck. Frederick A. Folger emigrated to Cape Vincent just after the War of 1812-15, and cast his lot at that small country village on the St. Lawrence River, near its source. He was a man of fine intellectual girth and grain, and a poetic vein ran through his composition. He was a ready writer, an excellent critic of literary work, and full of appreciative knowledge of the value of good books. He possessed business talents of a high order, and had he settled in a large town, he would have grasped every sound opportunity to lay the solid foundation of a large fortune. His lamented death, at the early age of 43, was a sad closing of a most promising career; and the following tribute from a contemporary newspaper will show in what high esteem he was held by those who knew his worth and mourned his loss: "Died, on the 28th of September, at Cape Vincent, in the 43d year of his age, F. A. Folger, Esq., the idol of his family, the ornament of the social circle, the useful citizen, the benefactor of the poor, the friend of man. Cut off in the midst of his years and his labors for the public good, his death will be universally and deeply deplored." This tribute proves how strong a place he had won in the hearts of the people where he lived and died. As he was the father of a family that is no doubt destined to fill a large place in the history of commercial and general affairs in the section where they were born, it will be in order to refer to the early history of its pioneers. The following is copied from a Nantucket newspaper, and shows the origin and fame of the Folgers, in connection with that historic town: "Nantucket has been wonderfully prolific of great men and women. Among the first families on the island were the Macys. The Folgers are another noteworthy race. The only child of 'Peter Folger,' born after his removal from Martha's Vineyard to Nantucket, was Abiah, who, in her young maidenhood, removed to Boston and married Jonah Franklin, the tallow chandler. The fifteenth child by this marriage was Benjamin Franklin, the philosopher. The mother in talent and worth is said to have been every way worthy of her illustrious son. Another member of this family was Charles J. Folger, the present Secretary of the Treasury, who was born in Nantucket, in a house which stood on the site of the present Sherbourne House, on Orange street." Captain Matthew Folger, the grandfather of the subjects of this biographical notice, was an adventurous spirit of his stirring times, and figured conspicuously in marine matters. The Folger Bros. inherit the love of marine affairs, for the name of Folger has long been prominent in this line. It was a Folger who gave the best theory of the Gulf Stream; it was a Captain Folger who rescued the mutineers of the "Bounty" from Pitcairn Island. Miss Breck, who became the happy and worthy wife of Frederick A. Folger, was largely endowed with gentle and loving qualities of head and heart, and her influence in moulding the character of her boys was pure and commanding. She still lives, in the full possession of all her faculties, to enjoy the well won success of her fatherless sons.

These brothers were led to locate in the Canadian city of Kingston in 1862, and were no doubt influenced to do so through their relationship to Mr. Breck, through the marriage of his sister to their father. He was the junior partner in the famous firm of Calvin & Breck, who were for years lords of the river on the Canadian side, in steamboat and rafting operations. Their headquarters were at Garden Island, and from this point many millions of dollars worth of timber were put in shape to be rafted down the rapids of the St. Lawrence for reshipment to Europe. It may not be generally known that some of the oak which entered into the construction of Nelson's flagship, the immortal "Victory," and on whose deck the great English naval hero received his death wound at Trafalgar, was cut from the southern bank of the St. Lawrence between Cape Vincent and Clayton, and put into rafts at the foot of Long Island for floating to Quebec. Such is the interesting historic fact, and the old piers can still be seen at this point which were used in the rafting operations of that time.

From 1862 to the present day the firm of Folger Bros. has been the best known and most active of any business house in Kingston. Their history has been one continuous growth in many lines of business. With their banking business, first established, they have large interests now in the Electric Street Railway Company of Kingston, the Gas and Electric Light Company, the Kingston Real Estate Company, the Kingston and Pembroke Railway Company, North American Telegraph Company and the St. Lawrence River and Thousand Island Steamboat Companies. These large and important businesses are all in first rate condition, and are proof of the business energy and tact of the Brothers Folger. They are known over a wide section of Canada and the States for their upright and downright business ways, their great enterprise and far-seeing calculations as to commercial affairs. These brothers have always held equal interests in their business concerns, and present a remarkable instance of family concord of the most intimate and cordial character, extending from childhood up to the present time. There are not now, nor have there ever been, the slightest differences in their family or business associations; and the result is shown in great industrial enterprises carried on by them in all the harmony and smoothness of a single master-mind. If they were to express an opinion as to the reasons for their success in life, they would quite likely attribute it to the strong family ties which have made them all work together with the greatest zeal and harmony. Owing no doubt to the trait of character developed so fully in their paternal grandfather, they take a lively interest in the St. Lawrence River and Thousand Island Steamboat Companies. They first developed and consolidated and systematized the large tourist and general traffic on the upper reaches of the noble river. They have carried over 5,000,000 of people on their steamers, and never wet a foot or injured a passenger. This remarkable record is as unique as it is creditable to the safe and wise manner in which this vast human commerce has been carried on for so many years. No expense or pains are spared to safely and suitably equip and man their passenger steamers, and their names are an assurance of thoughtful and competent management from deck hand to captain. Of the three brothers—each with special characteristics in a business way—Henry Folger is perhaps the best known outside of the immediate business management in and about Kingston. He generally represents the firm in all outside matters. He is a gentleman of fine accomplishments, and a great lover of books. His circle of friends includes many of the leading public men of the Dominion and of the United States, and he is highly respected by all. His generous interests in the poor and needy are such as to endear him to those who are familiar with his unostentatious charities. He dislikes notoriety of any sort, and his modest benefactions are in consequence never heralded about.

The following interesting sketch from the Ottawa "Citizen," a leading Canadian journal, published at the capital of the Dominion, in speaking of the rumor that he was to be appointed to an important position, said:

"The Kingston News announces that Mr. Henry Folger, of that ancient city, is to be appointed general manager of the Richelieu & Ontario Navigation Company. Mr. Folger is a member of the firm of Folger Brothers, who control the gas, electric light and street railway companies in Kingston, who own the island ferries there, are principal stockholders in the St. Lawrence River Navigation Company, are

FOLGER BROS. FINE STEAMER EMPIRE STATE.

largely engaged in mining in the county of Frontenac, and manage the Kingston & Pembroke Railway as representatives of the Flower interest. He is a particularly shrewd and capable business man, far-sighted and sagacious, fertile in resources, with tact to win men and talent to govern men; possessed, moreover, with the genuine Yankee spirit of restless enterprise. Should he assume the management of the Richelieu Company, the great opportunities which that organization possesses of attracting travel to the splendid and unequalled water route down the great lakes from Toronto to Quebec will be developed to the utmost, and a new era will open up for the travelling multitudes as well as for the stockholders. Mr. Folger is known in private as a wit and epigrammatist, and in public as one of the most brilliant after-dinner speakers in Canada. He possesses a taste for literature and an acquaintance with the best authors, as well as discriminating insight into their work, which are seldom met with in such a sharp and energetic man of affairs."

This high commendation was merited, and is reproduced in this connection as independent testimony of a valuable kind, as showing the esteem in which he is held by the first authorities in the county where he now resides.

Several years ago, B. W. Folger, the senior member of the firm, distinguished himself by the vigorous manner in which he resented a discourtesy to the American flag in Canada. It is the special aim of this member of the firm to watch every minute detail of the various businesses in which they are interested. Cool in judgment, keen in his knowledge of men and affairs, and of wide resources in a business way, the senior member is a rare helper in all that pertains to their public enterprises. Fred Folger, the youngest of the firm, combines the good qualities of his brothers, is very popular, and has ability of a high order. If he is less-widely known than his brothers, it is only because he is younger, for in all high business equipment he is their peer. He will not fail to bear aloft the firm's banner of untiring zeal and unquestioned integrity, so long as he is spared to do so. This strong trio of brothers have made for themselves, before the climacteric of life has been reached, a good and famous name and history worthy of emulation, and an honor to the environments in which their business lot and lives have been cast. Their example is worthy of the highest praise.

A. D. S.

THE ORIGIN OF PRINTING ON THE SHORES OF THE ST. LAWRENCE.

BY J. L. HUBERT NEILSON, M. D., R. C. A., DEPUTY SURGEON GENERAL.

IN the year 1749 a learned Swede, Peter Kalm, professor in a Swedish University, a disciple of the great Linnaeus, visited the United States and Canada. He informs us, in the interesting volumes of travel which he subsequently published, that there was then no printing press in Canada. He was told, though, that at one time there had been one. This bit of information appears, however, to have been not in accord with fact. Kalm adds: "All books are brought from France, and all the orders made in the country are written, which extends even to the paper currency. They pretend that the press is not yet introduced here, lest it should be the means of propagating libels against the government and religion. But the true reason seems to be in the poorness of the country, as no printer could put off a sufficient number of books for his subsistence; and another reason may be that France may have the profit arising from the exportation of books hither."

Whatever the cause may have been, and all seems to indicate that reasons of state policy were the true cause, a public press was an absolutely unknown quantity in Canada from the foundation of Quebec, in 1609, until after the conquest by the British arms and final cession in 1763. It had been very different over the border in the New England provinces. Within twenty years of the landing of the Pilgrim Fathers a press had been established at Cambridge in 1638, by Steven Daye. At first, and for many years, small works of a

Godly character were its only output. Gradually matters of a more worldly nature were served by it. But it was not until 1704 that such a secular object as a newspaper made its appearance, and met with sufficient public support and appreciation. It is believed that as early as 1545 a printing press was operated in the city of Mexico.

Well, in the year 1763 — it being made known to the world that Canada was to be irrevocably attached to the British Crown — it occurred to one William Brown, a young printer in Philadelphia, that Canada might be a new field worth trying. Canada was still under military rule. After a short correspondence with the then Governor General, James Murray, for the double purpose of making sure that his scheme would not only be permitted but favored by the authorities, he did not hesitate to put his small savings into the venture.

William Brown, like so many other leaders among men, pioneers and benefactors of their race, was a native of Scotland. He was born in Kirkcudbrightshire, province of Galloway, in 1737. His father, John Brown, was laird of Nunton, in the parish of Twynholm, and of Langlands, in Borgue. William, being a younger son, was sent to paternal relatives in Virginia, to make his fortune as best he could. In 1851-2-3 we find him studying the classics and mathematics at William and Mary College, in Williamsburgh. The year following he had entered a counting house as clerk, but soon there came the seven-years' war; the defeat of Braddock at Monongahela was followed by commercial dislocation and a financial crash which brought an end to Brown's incipient career as a bank clerk.

Unemployed, stranded, and with but slender means in hand, young Brown bethought himself of a trade, which possessed greater elements of stability than banking in those tempestuous times. The printing business, moreover, seemed to him congenial. He accordingly directed his steps towards Philadelphia, with a view of there acquiring the art of printing. He first served as apprentice in the celebrated establishment of William Bradford, which then existed at the corner of Black Horse alley. It is traditional, however, that he finished his time with Franklin & Hall, then publishers of the Pennsylvania Gazette.

In 1758 he had transferred his services to William Dunlap, a printer who was also largely interested in bookselling. Dunlap had married a relative of Benjamin Franklin's wife, and through this family connection had recently been appointed postmaster of Philadelphia. In 1760 he was for a short time partner to James Rivington in the book-selling business in New York. Their book store was at the lower end of Wall street. Brown soon withdrew, returned to Philadelphia, and together with a nephew, John Dunlap, became business managers of the elder Dunlap's concern. In that capacity we find him next residing for two years in Bridgetown, Barbadoes, winding up a bookselling and printing enterprise which Dunlap had there. It was on his return from Barbadoes, in 1763, that he formed the project of trying his fortune in Canada. He selected as partner one Thomas Gilmore, a native of the north of Ireland, a relative of Dunlap's, who generously bolstered up the venture of his two young friends to the extent of £450.

On the 6th of August he left Philadelphia for Boston. He informs us, in his "diary," that he met with disappointment in not finding there a vessel bound for Quebec. He had no choice left but to purchase a horse and make his way as best he could towards Quebec, via Albany, Lake Champlain, Montreal and down the St. Lawrence to Quebec. Brown's diary is replete with details of this journey, now of great interest, but space prohibits quotations. While Brown was proceeding overland, Gilmore was sent to London to purchase the press, type and paper for the new Quebec printing office, the whole to be brought out by the first vessel the following spring.

Brown, after adventures which would be well worth repeating, finally reached Quebec on the 30th of September, 1763. The ensuing autumn and winter months he devoted to perfecting himself in the knowledge of French,

EDGEWOOD PARK HOTEL, ALEXANDRIA BAY

canvassing for subscribers, distributing his prospectus, and making things ready for the installation of the press. He had secured a small house " in Parlour street, in the Upper Town, a little above the Bishop's Palace." Gilmore arrived early in June, with a brand-new hand press and excellent type, which he had secured from Kenrick Peck, of London. He was also provided with a sufficient supply of paper, ink and other necessaries. On the 21st of June, 1764, the first number of the Quebec Gazette was offered to the public.

It will thus be seen that to these citizens of old Philadelphia is due the honor and glory of having planted the first press in its sister colony on the shores of the St. Lawrence, in the now vast and prosperous Dominion of Canada. A word of the worthy William Dunlap, Franklin's relative, who was in a way the sponsor and financial backer of Brown and Gilmore's venture, may not be out of place. By trade he had been a job printer, bookseller and paper manufacturer, and, in 1758, successor to William Franklin as postmaster of Philadelphia. Dunlap had also a printing and bookselling establishment in Barbadoes. He was also interested in the Barbadoes Mercury. His agent there was George Esmond, who so neglected his patron's interest that, in 1765, Dunlap had to go there himself, and there he spent two years in vain attempts to obtain a settlement of his affairs. While in Bridgetown, although advanced in years, he decided to devote himself to the ministry of the Church of England, commenced his theological studies, and, in 1767, went to London to be ordained. He then returned to Philadelphia, his wife having, meanwhile, become insane. John Dunlap, his nephew, took charge of the interests which he still retained in the Philadelphia printing and bookselling establishment. This firm continued to furnish supplies of printing paper, stationery, etc., to Brown and Gilmore in Quebec until the outbreak of the Revolutionary war. These goods were usually forwarded to them by sailing vessels via the Gulf of the St. Lawrence. But they looked for more than inert supplies from Philadelphia. I quote from a long half-business, half-affectionate letter written by Brown to the Rev. William Dunlap, on April 29, 1768:

"* * * Having been long embarrassed with Canadian Boys as menial servants about the Printing Office, who will not engage for any considerable time and as soon as they find themselves useful augment their wages and become intolerably insolent, we are at last come to a Resolution of trying to get a Negro Boy, wherefore we beg you will endeavour to purchase one for us, between 15 and 20 years of age fit to put to Press, who has had the Small Pox, is country born and can be recommended for his Honesty; we would not begrudge a pretty good Price for such a likely Negro: or if you should be inclined to part with your Boy Priamus we would be glad to have him and would be glad to give what would be judged a reasonable price for him. We pray you may try and procure us one so that he may reach us here in the fall; and as soon as you shall be certain of him or determined to part with your own we beg you may loose no Time in acquainting us of the Price, which we will immediately remit to you on a Bol on York (sic) as we shall keep the cash ready till we hear from you. Should it be too late for an opportunity from Philadelphia there has always been vessels from York in August and Septbr, and we doubt not that there will be this Year. * * *" In a P. S. he adds: " If you are so lucky as to get us a Negro, before you embark him we beg he may be *insured*."

William Dunlap evidently took the most kindly, even fatherly, interest in his two protégés in Quebec, judging from the many letters he wrote them, several of which are in my possession. A son named Tomy appears to have been at this period with the printers in Quebec, for he more than once refers to him. He always subscribed himself, "I am, dear gentlemen, Your affectionate W. Dunlap." His confidence in them was not misplaced, for that very year they repaid him in full his advance of £450, with interest at six per cent. There being none or few regular banks in existence in the North American provinces, remitting money was both a difficult and costly matter. Opportunities of purchasing a bill of exchange on a good, solvent firm or individual were few and far between. About this time, 1768, W. Dunlap severed his connection with business to become rector of the parish of Stratton in King and Queen's county, Virginia, where, I presume, he ended his varied earthly career.

Brown & Gilmore had calculated on a subscription list of at least 150; when the first number appeared, only 110 had given in their names. General Murray subscribed for ten copies and two other officials five each. Among these 110 names not more than a dozen French names can be found, most of these were priests. The paper was printed on a folio sheet, with four double-column pages, one column being English, the opposite one a translation into French. A cut of the Royal Arms headed the paper, to one side of which was the title, "The Quebec Gazette," while on the other was the French title, "La Gazette de Quebec." At the foot of the fourth page was the colophone, "Quebec, printed by Brown & Gilmore, at the printing office in Parlour street, in the Upper Town, a little above the Bishop's palace, where subscriptions for this paper are taken in; advertisements of a moderate length (in one language) inserted for five shillings Halifax, the first week and one shilling each week after; if in both languages seven shillings and six pence Halifax, the first week and half a dollar each week after; and all kinds of printing done in the neatest manner, with care and expedition." It appeared once a week, on Thursdays.

The two first pages contained foreign European news, seldom less than six weeks or two months old; occasional items relating to the neighboring Provinces and extracts from their newspapers; then followed scanty allusions to matters of local interest; the third and fourth pages were filled with official proclamations, government and private advertisements, many of which convey curious and important information. Brown appears to have been the business head — editor and manager — of the concern; he and Gilmore had evidently been trained at an excellent school; witness the correctness and neatness of their work. Brown was the essence of regularity and precision in all his work; his diary, his letters, his office books, dating from his arrival in Canada until his death, detailing every business transactions of the printing office and every item of his own personal expenses from 1763 to 1789, are written most carefully in rounded hand; they are all preserved among the collections of the writer of this sketch.

Broadsides, pamphlets and small volumes soon followed the appearance of the "Quebec Gazette;" the first was the "Presentment" of the first Canadian grand jury, a small quarto of forty-two pages, an important and unique document; but one copy is known to exist, and that is to be found in the writer's collection. The second volume was "Le Catechisme du Diocese de Sens in 1765;" a unique copy is in the possession of the Honorable Judge Baby of Montreal.

A curious and now excessively rare book, printed by Brown & Gilmore in 1767, is the "Nehiro-Irinui," a small 8vo, of 96 pages, printed with great neatness and fine type, but entirely in the Montagnais language. It is a prayer book, catechism, etc., composed for the Indians of the Saguenay Valley by their celebrated and saintly missionary, Father La Brosse, a Jesuit, whose life-work and death are the subject of more than one legend, repeated with reverence to this day among the Indians and peasants of the lower St. Lawrence. Miss Machar of Kingston and Gananoque, familiar to many readers under the "nom de plume" Fidelis, has recently rendered one of these La Brosse legends in charming verse. J. C. Filling in his "Bibliography of the Algonquian Languages," published by the Smithsonian Institution in 1891, gives a good description of Father La Brosse's writings and works. The labor of composing and revising the proofs of such a book must have taxed the patience and time of the printer to their very utmost, yet he charged but £45 for 2,000 copies of 6 sheets, 8vo.

Enough of the early issues of the Quebec press — more would cease to interest the general reader. Brown & Gilmore remained in partnership for nearly ten years when, in 1773, Thomas Gilmore died. During the two or three years preceding his death he had been unable to withstand the temptations attending prosperity, he had fallen into loose habits, neglected his work, overdrawn his account — in fact, had become a thorn in Brown's side.

THOUSAND ISLAND HOUSE, ALEXANDRIA BAY.

Brown continued the business alone, but in a very careful and conservative manner. At this time much sympathy was felt throughout Canada for the victims of the Boston massacre and their families; subscriptions were collected for the latter. Brown contributed £50 to this fund, a very handsome sum in those days.

Then came the time when the old French province was invaded by the Congressional army, when the citadel city of Quebec remained the last foothold of England in Canada. Brown's sentiments of loyalty to the British crown and institutions were too deep rooted to permit him to sympathise with men whom he considered to be rebels. He shouldered his musket and served devotedly as a militiaman, on the walls of the city, at the battle of the 31st of December, 1775, when Montgomery was killed, and until the end of the siege in May following, when the retreat of the besiegers under General Wooster became a rout. After the beginning of the siege in December, 1775, all affairs were at a stand-still and the "Quebec Gazette" ceased to appear until the August following, when the country had recovered, to some extent, its normal condition.

It was at this time that a second press made its appearance in Canada. The printers were Fleury Mesplet and Charles Berger, both printers originally from old France. They had settled in Philadelphia; there they had been picked up by Franklin who, together with Samuel Chase and John and Charles Carroll of Carrollton, had been deputed to Canada as Commissioners of Congress, for the purpose of inducing the French Canadians to espouse the Revolutionary cause. It was deemed that French printers would be important factors in disseminating the offers and blandishments of Congress, and with that object in view these two men and a press followed on the heels of the Commission. The Commissioners perceiving their mission a failure, wisely recrossed the borders, but left behind their printers, press and materials. These two worthies first opened an office in Quebec, and their first output was a volume of French hymns. Soon after they returned to Montreal, where they printed several small works of a religious character. Meanwhile, Charles Berger disappears from the scene, leaving Fleury Mesplet alone to prosecute his trade. He signalized himself, in 1778, by publishing the first French newspaper in Canada, "La Gazette Littéraire," also a small almanac for 1778 and 1779, both of extreme rarity. At this time his labors were violently interrupted; he was accused of republican sympathies, sedition, etc., and thrown into prison in Quebec. There he remained incarcerated in the Recollet convent until the peace of 1783, when the mother country and her daughter agreed to live apart. Mesplet, set free, lost no time in recriminations, but founded the "Montreal Gazette," which, although still extant, had at first a very fitful and uncertain existence in the hands of several masters, viz.: Mesplet, L. & J. Roy, Edward Edwards, James Brown a nephew of William Brown, and others.

Meanwhile our friend William Brown and his Quebec Gazette continued the even tenor of their ways. The large number of troops stationed in or coming through Canada during the war, and when peace came, the renewal of commercial activity brought subscribers, printing orders, and gold into his strong box. Previous to 1779 annual sheet calendars had been found amply sufficient for the needs of the country. Brown now judged that almanacs would be appreciated by the public, and that year was issued the Quebec Almanack for 1780, the first of that most important series of almanacs which continued to appear year after year until 1841. The older numbers are now exceedingly scarce — they are valued by collectors at from fifteen to twenty dollars apiece — all are rare and much sought after on account of the curious and important records they contain.

William Brown died suddenly on the 22d of March, 1789, aged about fifty-three. He was buried in St. Matthew's Cemetery, John street, Quebec. He had never married. Four years before his death he had prevailed on his widowed sister in Scotland, Mrs. Isabel Brown Neilson, to confide to him the future of her son Samuel. Subsequently John followed his brother. Although but mere boys at the time of their uncle's death, they continued to manage his printing business, the Gazette, his government contracts, in a word, his large estate, in their own behalf and also for the benefit of other heirs in Scotland, for Brown had died intestate. Samuel survived his uncle but four years. He died in January, 1793. His death was a distinct loss to the Province, for few men are endowed with more practical and brilliant qualities than he had. He was a particular favorite at the Chateau Saint Louis and in social circles. H. R. H. Prince Edward (Duke of Kent, father of Queen Victoria) honored him with his friendship — he was then colonel of the 7th Fusileers in garrison at Quebec. It is said that Samuel Neilson contracted the cold which caused his death while enjoying a tandem sleigh drive with the prince. André Michaud, the botanist, mentions him in his memoirs as being a man of surprising scientific attainments.

The young Neilsons showed enterprise and push enough, first, to found the "Quebec Magazine," in 1791, a monthly issue (some numbers illustrated); it died for want of support after its third volume, shortly after the death of Samuel; second, to buy out the stock in trade, press, etc., of a small rival sheet which had been in existence a few years in Quebec. They sent this material and one of their foremen, named Louis Roy, to found a printing office and newspaper at New Ark, on the Niagara River, the new capital of the new province of Upper Canada, in 1793. The "Upper Canada Gazette or American Oracle," April 18, 1793, was the result of their enterprise, the pioneer press of the west. Louis Roy, however, left alone to himself, disappointed his patrons, abandoned his post, and returned to Montreal the year following. G. Tiffany picked up the work where Roy had dropped it, and continued the publication of the U. C. Gazette until its transfer to York (now Toronto) in 1799, where it was printed by W. Waters and T. G. Simons. These printers proved unequal to the task. This, gave John Neilson, of the Quebec Gazette, a second opportunity of opening a branch printing establishment in Upper Canada. He selected for that purpose his trusted foreman, John Bennett, and supplied him with a fair equipment from his office. Bennett started from Quebec in June, 1801. It took him one month and three days to reach York. On the 20th of August he wrote to John Neilson: "* * * I waited on the Governor (Sir Peter Hunter, nick-named Blue Peter), when His Excellency appointed me "King's Printer for Upper Canada," and Sheriff MacDonell sent with me to demand the types from my predecessors, who had not the least wind of the business. Mr. Simons is a young man of some abilities, and much believes in York's future, but it appears his sentiments were rather inimical to government. Waters, whom I have now to assist me, is as honest, good-natured a fellow as I would wish to see, only he likes to take a hearty twist at the bottle, etc. * * * Simons has acquired a genteel property since he has been in government employ, and Waters is also possessed of some."

Bennett took over the publication of the Upper Canada Gazette, and set immediately about printing the first volume of the "Journals of the House of Assembly of Upper Canada," in 1801, a quarto of 74 pages. The "Statutes" followed in 1802; a beautifully printed "Almanack" for 1803, etc., etc.; all of which are of exceeding scarcity. Bennett, unfortunately by contamination, or natural inclination, drifted into habits similar to those of his assistant, Waters. He neglected his business; he became involved in all sorts of trouble; finally, John Neilson, in 1807-8, had to come to York to close in disgust his connection with the printing business in Upper Canada.

At the end of last century, G. and Sylvester Tiffany continued printing at Niagara. Their paper was known as the "Constellation." They issued an almanac in 1802. The other pioneers of the press, on the banks of the St. Lawrence, were: H. Myles, who founded the "Kingston Gazette" in 1810, at Kingston, now represented by the "Daily News." The same printer started the "Prescott Telegraph" in 1823. The "Brockville Recorder" was originated in 1820.

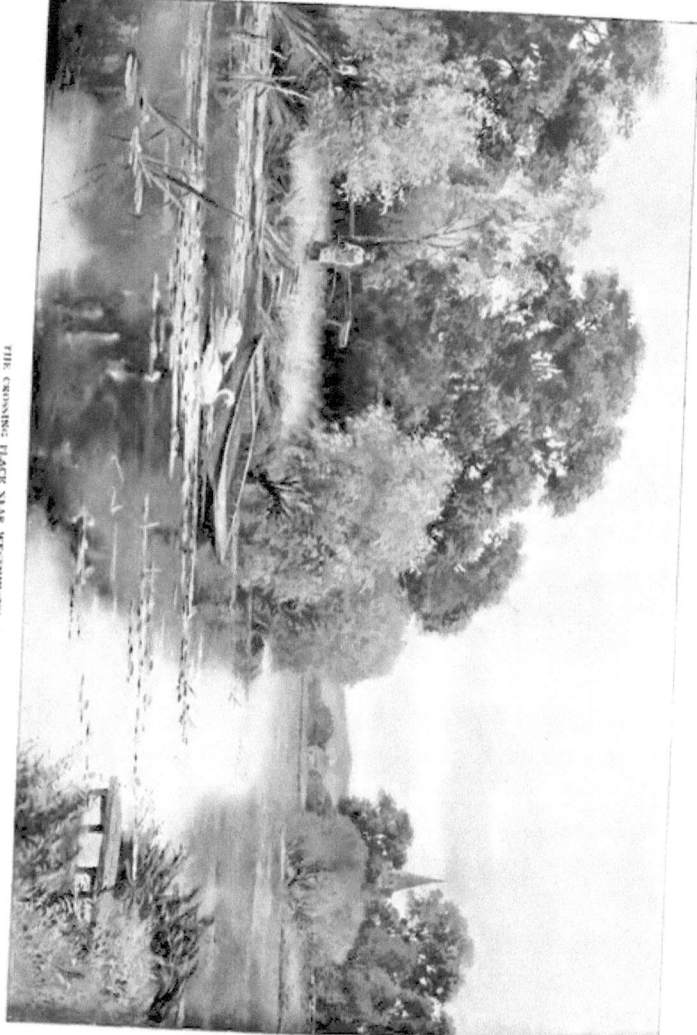

THE CROSSING PLACE NEAR WESTMINSTER PARK.

The population of both Canadas now increased with rapid strides, and with it innumerable presses and periodicals of all sorts—some possessed of vitality; others of the mushroom tribe, and ephemeral in nature, arose, lived and vanished in every new village.

To return to the old Quebec press. After the death of his brother Samuel, in 1793, John Neilson continued the publication of the Quebec Gazette. Under his editorship and management it gained in influence and importance; addressing itself in its French and English columns to both nationalities, with no serious rival in sight, it became a power in the land, while, at the same time, it was the vehicle of government proclamations and mandates. John Neilson was elected to the legislature in 1817, and he occupied a seat in the councils of the nation until his death. His great abilities, his integrity, his devotion to the public weal, his eloquence, his powerful editorials in his paper, soon brought him to the front rank among the public men of his day. Thrice he was deputed to London by his fellow citizens to watch over their interests, and on one occasion to present petitions for redress at the foot of the throne. He died in 1848, aged 73, regretted, loved and revered by all.

The Quebec Gazette celebrated its centennial sixteen years after his death, in 1864. Thirty-one years have since then elapsed, and the Quebec Gazette continues to appear. Its last number, now before me, is dated Wednesday, May 1, 1895, No. 12,371, vol. cxxiv. For some years past it has been practically the weekly edition of the Quebec Chronicle, and owned by the same proprietor. It is twenty-three years older than the London Times, and now one of the oldest newspapers in the world. It may be of interest to the readers of this historical sketch to know that its writer has in his collection a complete file of the Quebec Gazette, from its prospectus and first number, on June 21, 1764, up to 1850, the subsequent years are unfortunately not quite so complete. Such as it is, this long series of files of the same newspaper, covering nearly a century and a half of time, is believed to be unique.

It is safe to state that the preceding pages embody more facts relating to the origin of printing in Canada than has yet been given to the public by any other writer on this subject.

BIOGRAPHICAL SKETCH OF J. L. H. NEILSON,

M. D., R. C. A., DEPUTY SURGEON-GENERAL.

Few, if any, officers at present in the military service of Canada, have experienced such varied war service as the subject of this sketch. Shortly after graduating as M. D., he was appointed assistant surgeon to the Royal Artillery in Canada, in October, 1869. In April, 1870, he was selected to form part of the medical staff of the small army sent under colonel (now Lord Wolseley), to suppress the first Red River rebellion. This proved to be one of the most difficult and arduous expeditions ever undertaken by British troops, but attended with complete success. He remained eighteen months attached to the military service in the north-west, volunteering meanwhile to attend the victims of a frightful small-pox epidemic which raged among the Indians on the plains. In the autumn of 1871, he was recalled to Canada to assist in the organization of A and B Batteries of regular Canadian Artillery, and since that time has remained connected with the artillery service. He accompanied his corps in several bloody encounters with the mobs of the ancient capital during the labor riots from 1872-7. At this time he was attached to the Army Medical School at Netley, in England. During the Russo-Turkish campaign in the Balkans, he volunteered in the Red Cross ambulances. At the close of the campaign, he returned to his former duties in Canada. During the winter of 1879-80, he spent some weeks in Washington, studying the admirable medical organization of the United States Army, then under the able administration of those war veterans, Generals Barnes and Crane.

In 1884, when it was decided to select the Nile route for the Gordon relief expedition, organizing, equipping, disciplining and conducting to the land of the Pharaohs these rough, half-wild backwoodsmen and Indians, previously unaccustomed to restraint or control of any sort; yet, within six weeks of the issue of the first cable order, 480 voyageurs were landed in Alexandria, and ten days later

J. L. HUBERT NEILSON, ESQ., M. D., R. C. A., DEPUTY SURGEON-GENERAL.

Lord Wolseley called to his aid the hardy Canadian voyageurs to assist the troops in overcoming the cataracts and rapids of the Nile. Lord Wolseley specially selected Col. Denison and Dr. Neilson, whom he remembered favorably during the Red River expedition of 1870-71, for the purpose of recruiting, they were at work in the Soudan. After his arrival in Egypt, Dr. Neilson was attached to the first field hospital. He followed the troops in their arduous march across the Bayuda desert, was present at Abu Klea, etc. Then later he was sent to Suakim, on the Red Sea coast. For these services in Egypt, he was specially

THE PASSENGERS OF "UPPER TEN" ON THE "CANADIAN" OCEAN STEAMERS.

mentioned in Lord Wolseley's despatches, as published in the London Official Gazette of August 25, 1885. He was rewarded with the Egyptian war medal with two clasps, the Khedivial bronze star and made Knight of the Royal Order of Milusine, for special services gratuitously given to Christian refugees, who had fled from Khartoum before the siege commenced.

Since that date, Dr. Neilson has served in peace, chiefly as medical officer of the Royal Military College of Kingston, Canada (see page 28 of this volume), and of the garrison of Kingston as Chairman of the Board on Militia Medical Organization, etc., etc.

He has found time between his many professional callings to follow his natural bent towards historical research. His library of books, MSS., maps, portraits and reviews—relating to the history of America, and of Canada in particular — is one of if not the largest possessed by any private individual; in fact, it is quite unique. This famous library was commenced in 1801, when his grandfather, the late Honorable John Neilson, of the Quebec Gazette, purchased the greater part of the rare books and MSS. belonging to the old Jesuit College in Quebec when it was sold by order of the Government. To these beginnings have been added the collections of three lives. We might enumerate a few of the MSS.: One was written by Père Marquette in 1671, the discoverer of the Mississippi, entitled "Præces Illinicæ," written in the dialect of the Illinois Indians; it is thought to be all that remains extant of this language. The Père Sylvie MS. of about 1680, is a dictionary of the Montagnais language, and philologically important, as well as four other old Jesuit MSS. All the Wm. Brown correspondence with Philadelphia, relating to the origin of printing in Canada, his diary, and all his account books from 1764-89, and the office books of the Neilsons and their correspondence until 1850, containing all their printing transactions; an enormous number of correspondence and letters of public men, from the beginning to the middle of the present century, etc., etc., form part of its riches. Among the printed, books are a complete file of the Quebec Gazette from June, 1764, to the present day; fifty-five years of the Quebec Almanacks from 1781 to 1841—by far the most complete series known; the presentment of the grand jury, Quebec, 1765; the Stamp Act, Quebec, 1765; Labrasse's Nehiro-Irenui, 1767; Cugnet's Laws, Quebec, 1775; the Traité des Messieurs, Quebec, 1772; the Mohawk Prayer Book, Quebec, 1780; Règlement de la Confrérie Mesplet, Montreal, 1776 (first book printed in Montreal); the Upper Canada Almanack, York, 1802, together with all of Bennett's and Louis Roy's correspondence relating to the early Upper Canada press; the Quebec Directory, 1790; the Quebec Magazine, three volumes, 1791-2; the British-American Register, Quebec, 1805; the Canadian, 1807-10, etc., etc.; the original Jesuit relations, Champlain, 1619; Lescarbot, 1611; Sagard, 1630; DeLaet, 1640, are represented by choice examples. To these value is added by the binder's best efforts. This collection is also exceptionally rich in early Canadian pamphlets.

Dr. Neilson has supplied the press and magazines with many articles embodying his researches: "The Royal Canadian Volunteers, 1794-1802;" "The Diary of a French Canadian Officer during the war of 1812;" "The Last Days of Fort Frontenac under the Fleur de Lis," are historical sketches of real merit. The article on the "Origin of Printing on the Shores of the St. Lawrence," in this volume, is from his pen. Dr. Neilson has, for years, given much attention and labor to the collection of material for a history of the origin of the press in Canada, and a bibliography of the early Canadia printers up to 1820, and we have reason to believe that his volume may appear before many months.

Dr. Neilson is one of the founders and first vice-president of the Kingston Historical Society and for the second time president of the Mechanics' Institute; he is honorary member of the Numismatic and Historical Society of Montreal; of the Societa Araldicae Historica of Rome; of the Institut de Psychologie of Paris, etc., etc. He is hereditary Seigneur of the

Seigniory of Hubert, in the province of Quebec. His private residence is Glendornal, Neilsonville, P. Q.

His medical sphere of action is strictly limited to the military under his immediate charge. Professional reading engrosses much of his time, being favored with an open, liberal and independent mind — unhampered by the dogmatic teachings of schools — new ideas and new methods enlist his sympathy, and if possessed of merit are adopted by him; he has thus become an adept of the system of medicine known as Burgrasvian or Dosimetric — he has for years investigated the application of Hypnotism to the treatment of certain forms of disease. Under this head he has contributed articles to the "Revue de l'Hypnotism," published in Paris, which have attracted attention abroad.

Dr. Neilson is unassuming, easily approached, a man of many admirable traits of character. As a bibliographer he is probably not excelled in the country. From his library have come the excellent pictures of Count Frontenac and the Chevalier La Salle, which are reproduced in this volume; two pictures that would be difficult to duplicate in Canada. Deputy Surgeon-General Neilson's services in the field have won for him merited promotion, but his real worth is best appreciated by those with whom he has served, and by those who know him best.

MELZAR FOWLER.

MELZAR FOWLER, now only dimly remembered by the older people of Jefferson county, N. Y., was born in Edinburgh, Saratoga county, N. Y., in 1803, and came to Depauville in the early twenties with his parents, Anson Fowler and Maria Esselstyn Fowler. His sister Jane also accompanied them (she subsequently marrying Eldridge G. Merick), and her brother John. The father commenced a mercantile business in Depauville, a new settlement which had just begun to develop its lumbering interest. This settlement was on the rapids of Catfish Creek, which at that time was a stream of fair size, with sufficient water to float timber down to its mouth at Lake Ontario — not at all resembling the greatly diminished stream it now appears, after having its banks, along its whole course, denuded of timber. The care of this business early fell upon Melzar, the eldest son, and when he was about twenty years of age he bore the responsibility of his father's mercantile affairs.

After some years, wishing to extend his operations, Melzar established a store at Brownville, and went there to live, still maintaining the supervision of the store at Depauville. His younger brother, John, also came to Brownville as a clerk, and was given an interest in the business.

At that time one branch of Mr. Fowler's mercantile business was the manufacture of pearl ash from wood ashes. The forests of Jefferson county furnished the only fuel in those days, and the people of the country saved their ashes and sold them to him, and, in a building for the purpose, he converted these ashes into pearl ash, which was an important article of commerce, and found steady market in New York.

Shortly after establishing himself at Brownville, Melzar married Miss Clarissa Spicer, a sister of Mr. Silas Spicer, of Perch River, and during their residence there their two children, Eldridge and Nettie, were born. During these years Melzar enlarged his field of operations at Depauville by engaging with Mr. Merick in the business of getting out oak timber and rafting it to the Quebec market. In the spring of 1835 he moved his family to Depauville, giving up the business in Brownville, in order that he might give his entire attention to the Depauville operations, and be with his aged parents, while John went to Clayton in the interest of Smith & Merick.

At that early day, Watertown was, as it is

ONE DAY'S CATCH OF BASS.
(Not much of a day, either.)

now, the business center for the surrounding country, the only method of travel being by private conveyance. It was while going there on business in August, 1835, soon after the family moved to Depauville, that Mr. Fowler had the great misfortune to have a pair of horses, one of which was vicious and unreliable.

He stopped at a hotel, and when it came time to feed the animal the hostler was afraid to enter the stall, and called Mr. Fowler from the hotel, who at once took the feed-measure in his hand and entered the stall. The vicious horse, not recognizing his master, dealt him a blow with one of his forefeet, which proved fatal in three days. Everything was done for Mr. Fowler that could be known, but the blow had produced an internal rupture.

Thus died, in the flower of his youth, and in the midst of his usefulness, one who had the warm regard of all his business associates, and whose morning of life was full of promise.

It is remembered of Mr. Fowler that many farmers brought their sons to him to educate in mercantile pursuits, so great was their confidence in his possessing all the traits that would bring such youths into an earnest and successful manhood.

His death, so sudden, so tragical, elicited universal regret and sympathy. His wife and her two children remained at Depauville, but the faithful mother never was herself again. A woman of superior mental ability and personal beauty, and with a natural refinement much beyond most of those by whom she was surrounded, her loss wore upon her energies, and she survived her husband only seven years.

The two children, Eldridge and Nettie, thus left orphans at the age of nine and seven years, respectively, were tenderly cared for by their grandmother Fowler and their uncle, Hon. E. G. Merick.

Eldridge went later to live in the family of Mr. Hugh Smith, of Perch River, and afterwards with his uncle John Fowler until coming of age, when he went West, where he has since lived and become indentified with large lumber and land interests in Michigan, Minnesota and Canada.

The daughter grew to womanhood in the home of her grandparents and her uncle and aunt Merick, receiving at their hands the best educational advantages. She married Cyrus H. McCormick, of reaper fame. Both as the right-hand helper of her husband during his life-time, and later in the administration of his estate (with her son Cyrus), she has been called to bear some of the heavier responsibilities of life.

JOHN N. FOWLER.

THE writer of this sketch never had any personal acquaintance with the subject of it. For the facts stated herein he is indebted to several old residents of Clayton, chiefly the following, viz.: Thomas Rees, a partner of Mr. Fowler in some of his business enterprises, who made a written statement of facts; Messrs. D. C. Porter and Perry Caswell, members of the M. E. Church with Mr. Fowler, who was a faithful and substantial member of that church; A. F. Barker, John Johnston and Capt. William Rees.

The father of Mr. Fowler came from the eastern part of this State and settled in Depauville in the early part of this century. There he engaged in mercantile business and reared his family. In time, one of his daughters became the wife of Hon. E. G. Merick, subject of a biographical sketch elsewhere in this volume. One of his sons, Melzar, was father of Nettie Fowler, afterwards the wife, and now the widow of Cyrus H. McCormick, of Chicago. A lady of great wealth, and whose generous heart and bountiful hand have justly earned her a reputation, of which it is no exaggeration to say it is national.

John N. Fowler left Depauville in 1835, and came to Clayton. He purchased the interest of a Mr. Moreton in the old store of Smith & Merick, standing on the bank of the river, where Simon Breslow's store is now located. Stephen Hale, a clerk for Mr. Fowler for a few years, afterwards became his partner in the store. But Mr. Fowler could not confine himself to mere storekeeping. The country was new and rich in both soil and timber. In 1836 or 1837 he purchased several hundred acres of land lying about two miles south of Clayton. In a few years this wild land was converted into a farm, so well improved that the County Agricultural Society bestowed on its owner a first prize for his improvements.

In 1844, Mr. Fowler formed a partnership with Henry Esselstyn under the name of Fowler & Esselstyn. The latter had for years been bookkeeper in the large lumbering business of E. G. Merick, and the business of Fowler & Esselstyn was carried on in conjunction with his. It consisted of rafting and forwarding to the Quebec market a vast amount of timber and staves, brought to Clayton in vessels from the shores of the upper lakes, and in ship building. For many years they built one to four steamers and sailing vessels every year. All the following named, and many more, were built at their yard in Clayton, viz.: Bay State, Cataract and New York. The British Queen and British Empire, designed for use down the river, were built by them at Port Metcalf in Canada.

During much of the time Mr. Fowler was so engaged with Mr. Merick, he dealt largely in real estate on his own separate account. He bought a large tract lying contiguous to Clayton, known as the Lawrence Lands. He disposed of the property to actual settlers, and invested the proceeds in timber-lands in the West; and, as coincidently, the lumbering business of the firm was, year after year, extending farther and farther westward, there was a constantly growing necessity to move the place of business in that direction. At first a branch office was opened in Detroit. But with Clayton as a base of operations, Detroit was found to be an inconvenient outpost with the means of communication then in vogue. And, more than this, Detroit had become a city, rapid in growth, brilliant in prospects, and already taking a prominent position in shipbuilding for the upper lakes. Cut off from that region by the small proportions of the Welland canal, and at great disadvantage in the matter of timber, not to speak of other important items in shipbuilding, little Clayton could no longer hold this great and enterprising firm. In 1856 their Clayton property and business was disposed of to Thomas Rees, and they moved to Detroit. There they opened an immense dry-dock and ship-yard, and continued lumbering operations in the West, under the firm name of Merick, Fowler & Esselstyn.

The old acquaintances of Mr. Fowler still living in Clayton, speak of him as a man of great energy and wonderful endurance, a strict church member, a public spirited citizen, an honorable man and one highly exact in his requirements of others, while holding himself bound by the same rule of conduct. To him may be applied this grand and safe rule of excellence and ability — in every station where he was known, boy or man, and in whatever he undertook, he measured fully up to the requirements of the occasion. That is a test which can be applied to but few men.

G. H. S.

THE SPICER FAMILY.

STANDING well up from the river's edge, on Hemlock Island, one mile west of Thousand Island Park, is the cottage shown above, built in the winter of 1875-6, being one of the earliest upon the river. It is the summer home of Hon. Henry Spicer, for nearly his whole lifetime a resident of Perch River, N. Y.

The Spicer family was one of the early arrivals in Jefferson county, and trace their lineage in an unbroken descent from three brothers, natives of Normandy, who came into

THE CONSTANT READER.

England as "gentlemen volunteers" with William the Conqueror. These brothers settled respectively in Devonshire, Warwick and Kent, England. The two who settled in Devonshire and Warwick still have descendants residing there. In the 36th year of Queen Elizabeth's reign (1594) an account is given of this family, from their first "being officers and magistrates of the honorable city of Exeter, beginning with the first year of England's first Edward (1273) and continuing to the 7th year of Queen Anne (1708); and honorable a city, continuing for so long a course of years, their estate being also equivalent to their antiquity—they having also bestowed a considerable one on the chamber of Exeter, to uphold its guardian." In 1357 it is further related that " the Black Prince (son of Edward III) came out of France bringing with him prisoner, King John of France, whom he had taken a little time before at Poictiers. He landed at Plymouth, and came to Exeter, where John Spicer was mayor, who received the prince and his prisoner with much

"GLEN-COVE" COTTAGE, HEMLOCK ISLAND.

during the whole of these 435 years some one of the Spicer family was mayor of Exeter. Of this illustrious line "John Spicer" was mayor from 1252 to 1359—107 years, though, of course, there were several individual "Johns."

In an accurate account of the ancient family of Spicers, taken from an original manuscript extracted from a description of the County of Devon, A. D., 1714, we learn that "but few families in England can show such a precedent of the office of mayor of so ancient and display." It is further related that the "family of Spicers in the times of the three Edwards were principal officers and magistrates of Exeter, and were then considered for their many and gentlemanly qualities and virtues ; for in those days such men for their virtues and not for their wealth, were magistrates and governors, and in all places of trust."

Members of this distinguished family were in Jamestown, Va., in 1618, and in Rhode Island in 1660. They were also settled in the vicinity of Stonington, Conn., until after the Revolutionary War. They were both officers and privates in the Continental Army, and fought from Bunker Hill to Saratoga. They came into New York in 1792, and into Jefferson county in 1812.

THE ESSELSTYNS.

The author of this volume has had access to papers, well authenticated, which show that the Esselstyn family (commencing with King Clovis in 500 A. D.) were of the same stock as those of that name who came to America, but the date of their arrival in this country is yet uncertain.

THE CHITTENDENS.

Another fact he has discovered, that the Chittenden family are related to the Esselstyns and the Fowlers. Thomas Chittenden, a linen weaver, came with his son Isaac into America in 1635 from Wapping, in Kent, England, settling in Plymouth county, Mass., and his descendants are still found there. William Chittenden was one of the company of twenty-five, gathered chiefly from Kent, Surrey and Sussex in the South of England, who determined to leave their native country and seek a new home in the wilderness of America. Their first recorded acts as a separate community was a covenant which they signed on ship board, while on the passage, binding each other to plant themselves in New England, near Quinnipiack, if possible, and to be helpful to each other in every common work, according to every man's ability,
and as need should require. Besides William Chittenden there were twenty four other signers to this agreement, and, so far as history has been able to indicate, it was solemnly kept.

This William Chittenden had several children born to him in England. His wife was Joanna Sheaffe, whose sister Dorothy was the wife of Rev. Henry Whitfield, the first minister and a leading member of the Guilford Colony. The date of William Chittenden's sixth child's birth is upon the Guilford record, as of November 15, 1649. February 1, 1660, he died. He was undoubtedly the progenitor of the older families of his name in the United States, and the Chittendens of Oneida and Jefferson county undoubtedly sprang from this stock.

Joseph Chittenden, son of Joseph, who was descended in a direct line from the original William, was aged 92 when he died, April 7, 1794. Lucy, his daughter, born at Guilford October 8, 1736, married Melzar Fowler, March 10, 1768. He was the progenitor of the Fowler family in Jefferson county, known so well at Clayton, and represented in this history by the biographical sketch of John Fowler and his brother Melzar, this latter being the father of Mrs. Nettie F. McCormick. This family and the Esselstyns are related through the fact that Anson Chittenden, born December 18, 1768 (son of the above-named Lucy Fowler), married Maria Esselstyn, and in that way the Fowlers, Esselstyns and Chittenden families of Jefferson county are related to one another by marriage.

GEORGE MORTIMER PULLMAN

WAS born upon a farm in Chautauqua county, N. Y., March 3, 1831. His parents were in moderate circumstances, and able to give him only the benefits of the local schools, which were, however, of good quality. His home training was such as to aid him in the formation of fixed habits of industry and firmly-settled principles of morality and integrity. While not of a large frame, he yet possessed an unusual quantity of what we demonstrate "grit" or fibre. On the whole, it may be said that his primary schooling was peculiarly adapted for the life he was to lead, where independent reliance was of more value, coupled with integrity, than any number of college diplomas. At seventeen, he went to Albion, N. Y., where an older brother was already established as a cabinet-maker. Here

he served what was to him a very important apprenticeship, for he learned what could be done usefully as well as ornamentally with wood and wooden fibre, and grew into enlarged ideas as to the varied appliances of upholstering. All this was to be of use to him at a later day; but with his lessons in taste a few dollars of his own to begin business with. About a year later an opportunity was presented to make an addition to his already steadily increasing capital. The widening of the Erie canal necessitated the removal of many buildings of various kinds upon its banks to more desirable locations, and the quick,

GEORGE MORTIMER PULLMAN.

and the like, he acquired much information of another kind. He learned something of engineering and mechanics, and through a series of minor experiences he acquired strong confidence in his own ability for devising mechanical ways and means. He prospered pecuniarily, through constant thrift and industry, so that upon becoming of age he had active brain of this rising young man and future financier suggested a possibility of the task being easily accomplished. He made a success of it financially, and obtained an experience that was a benefit to him in his future career. Other contracts followed, and for a time house-moving was his specialty, but he was also successful in other lines of business.

In 1859 a new idea began to develop in his mind, and a series of experiments followed. The railroad system of the United States was yet in the first stages of its development, and its management had been marked by the most pernicious economy. Improvements began at once, for the first American locomotive, designed and built by Peter Cooper, at Baltimore, was especially adapted to American roads. The primitive "strap-rail," spiked upon a log, had given place to the heavy T rail. The later cars were more comfortable. The process of consolidation had begun; for the seven roads across middle New York had become one corporation, known as the New York Central. Other extensions were going on, and so the days of express companies, through-freight lines and improved passenger cars were approaching. During 1858 Mr Pullman's attention had been especially drawn to the long-distance sleeping-car idea. The sleeping accommodations afforded passengers were but enlarged copies of the bunks on the passenger packets of the Erie canal — three tiers on each side of the car.

The thoughts which began to germinate during one night's ride on one of these primitive coaches did not come into sight until the following year. He began a series of preliminary experiments by remodeling two day-coaches on the Chicago and Alton road, and afterward did the same on the old Galena road. He was a pioneer, and met with little encouragement. The sleeping-cars were invariably the property of the road they ran on, and their trips were limited to their own rails. No attention had been given to the idea of making long-distance railroading enjoyable. Its discomforts were considered unavoidable, and regarded as a matter of course. An entirely different conception of the future of American passenger transportation had now taken possession of Mr. Pullman. With only limited mechanical skill, he had acquired a large fund of varied mechanical knowledge, much of which was in the direct line of his proposed invention.

It was not until 1863 that he was prepared to devote himself entirely to his new enterprise; a shop was hired, and under his personal supervision the details were carried out. It required long months of toil, and the changes were radical, for he was not merely thinking of show. The powerful springs required to secure steadiness to the sleeping-car was an innovation, and the beds and general outfit were to be as good as in a first-class hotel. Only a faint idea of the improvement was expressed by the fact that while one of the old "rattlers" cost $4,000, Car A, the pioneer of the Pullman cars, cost $18,000. This apparent extravagance secured many conveniences and luxuries as well as safety to life and limb. The improvements were readily accepted by the travelling public as a convenience of which it seemed they had so long been deprived, i. e., relief from fatigue, pure air, safety in travelling, cleanliness, refreshments by the way — and, in fact, a moving hotel, rolling over the road, across the continent. This was the result of this man's genius.

We have not adequate space in which to describe the increase in the sleeping-car business which came to Mr. Pullman after his fine cars were put upon the leading lines in the United States. Their construction required the equipment of several shops, but these works could not keep pace with the demand. The result was his founding a new town, in the suburbs of Chicago, and the city of Pullman has been the result of his efforts in that direction. He then became a car-builder, for the public can at any time have freight, passenger or sleeping-cars built at that place. The city of Pullman covers over 3,500 acres of ground, and there are concentrated all the conveniences of a great city.

Considered financially, the business success of Mr. Pullman is hardly exceeded by that of any other living man. Other men are his peers in railway enterprises or exceed him in accumulated wealth, but the distinguishing feature of his own achievement is its originality. He saw a coming demand for the very best sleeping and drawing-room-car that could be built, and he developed it by the very fact of supplying it. During the year

CASTLE REST, GEO. M. PULLMAN'S RESIDENCE.

ending July 1, 1892, the Pullman cars carried 5,279,320 passengers.

The shop town of Pullman and the palace-hotel-car system, taken together, present an exceedingly readable illustration of the great marvel of human life and work ; that is, of the manner in which a mental picture, a mere conception but yet a germinal thought, arising in the mind of a capable man, may be eliminated and practically applied for the lasting benefit of mankind, as well as for the perpetuation of his own name.

COL. O. G. STAPLES,

BUILDER OF THE THOUSAND ISLAND HOUSE.

ONE of the most marvelous enterprises of Northern New York was the conception of building a first-class watering place hotel at Alexandria Bay, and its successful erection and furnishing by Col. O. G. STAPLES, who at that time was not worth a dollar clear of his debts. Certainly nothing short of the highest business genius could have accomplished the feat under such untoward circumstances, and it marked him as a Napoleon of finance.

At the time it was done, in 1872, Alexandria Bay was chiefly known as the home of Azariah Walton, the fisherman story-teller and entertainer of New York celebrities who came to the St. Lawrence River for a week or so of outing, disporting themselves by alter-

COL. O. G. STAPLES.

nate hours of fishing and hearing Uncle Azariah tell stories. The present world-wide celebrity of the Thousand Islands and the sublimely placid scenery of the St. Lawrence archipelago were no more thought of by the people at large then we now think of making a tropical paradise in the Adirondacks. We know of only one man who then read correctly the grand future of the St. Lawrence River and its transcendant charms. That man was O. G. STAPLES, and with the boldness of Napoleon at the bridge of Lodi, he took hold of the enterprise of building and furnishing a hundred thousand dollar hotel without a salted dollar of capital of his own, with only two endorsers of moderate means, and he would have succeeded in paying for it had his creditors been a little more patient and forbearing. But some one got in a hurry and "lit on him," and that caused the whole flock to light down at once. In the litigations that followed he worsted many of his creditors, whom he would gladly have paid had they given more time, and actually saved to himself fully $80,000 of the cost of the hotel structure and furnishings, enabling him to take a lease and furnish Willard Hotel, at Washington, out of which, during the past eighteen years, he has made half a million of dollars—establishing the fact that he "knows how to keep a hotel," said to be one of the highest indications of accomplished wisdom.

The opening of the Thousand Island House was the "open sesame" to the beginning of the present era of the St. Lawrence River visitations from all quarters of the globe. It is unquestionably the most expansive, the most calmly beautiful region, affording the most charming social delights, both day and night,

that the round earth affords. That this should have all been foreseen by this enterprising young man, is of itself evidence of genius of almost prophetic order. Advertising the hotel, necessarily took in the river scenery. The successor to Mr. STAPLES, in running the Thousand Island House, told the writer that it was the best-advertised hotel in the United States. He said everybody knew of it, and whoever came once desired to come again, and the thousands that came the first summer it was opened told their neighbors of the grand delights of the region, and the next year other thousands were added, and so year by year the throng swelled. Associations were organized, islands were purchased for parks and private residences, till now from five to six thousand people migrate hither for temporary summer habitation, and not less than from fifty to a hundred thousand people visit the region for a week or a day's recreation. The land holders of these evergreen islands, worthless for agriculture, have sold hundreds of thousands of dollars' worth, and if the islands have not all changed hands, it was not for the want of an opportunity. The Waltons and Cornwalls, who owned many of them thirty years ago, are under great obligations to the genius, enterprise and daring of O. G. STAPLES in conceiving, building and advertising the Thousand Island House — the first grand step to the consummation of the present renown and glory of the St. Lawrence River region. All Northern New York, our farmers, our railroads, our builders and our furniture dealers have been greatly benefited by the prophetic foresight of the builder of the Thousand Island House, and his face belongs to the history of the section.

PICTURESQUE KINGSTON.

UPON pages 124 to 132 will be found an article relating to the grand historic city of Kingston, and upon pages 28 to 33 will also be found an interesting and ably-written article entitled "Canada's West Point." With these contributions we might have been expected to say no more about Kingston; but a late visit to that "ancient and honorable" town has satisfied us that we had only just entered upon the subject of presenting the city of Kingston in a manner worthy of its ancient history and its present growth and standing. It has been called a "slow" town, a "finished" town, but a ride among its modern improvements, its beautiful private residences and public buildings will demonstrate its proper status as one of the best built and most progressive towns in Canada.

It has one of the finest and best adapted printing offices in America — complete in all its details, a gem in the eye of a practical printer. One of its churches has the finest spire between the two oceans, a real "thing of beauty," and, therefore, a "joy forever." Its public buildings are imposing and upon a grand scale of excellence; its people are hospitable, intelligent, patriotic. Art is not forgotten, for it has one of the ablest photographers (Mr. Henderson) to be found in any country; and its contributions to contemporaneous literature are classical and unusually interesting, as may be seen in the able writings of Dr. Neilson, of the Royal Artillery, a gentleman whose face we are very glad to

F. J. L. JENSE, EDITOR WHIG, KINGSTON.

present in this volume, with one of his latest productions. Thus much we desired to say as a preface for the many illustrations which follow.

THE DRY-DOCK.

Situated as Kingston is, at the actual foot of Lake Ontario, and at the very head of the Great St. Lawrence, a dry-dock became a necessity, for new vessels are

A BUSY LEVEL.

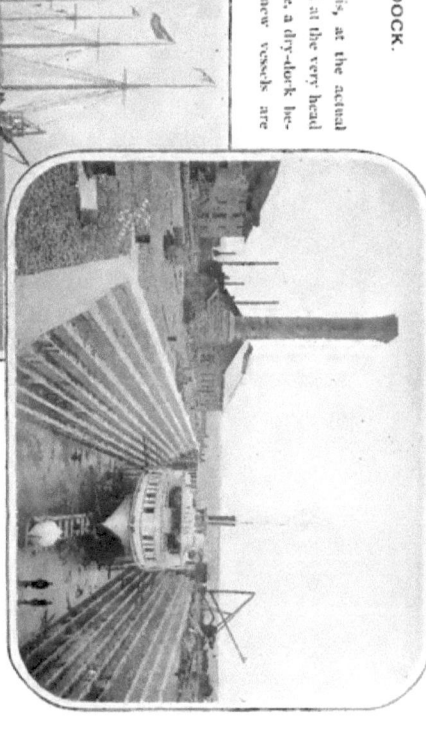

GOVERNMENT DRY-DOCK.

always required, and accidents are inevitable upon so great an extent of water-way. This necessity has been well met by the fine dry-dock shown herewith.

ST. PAUL'S, ANGLICAN, REV. W. B. CAREY, KINGSTON.

ST. GEORGE'S CATHEDRAL, VERY REV. B. B. SMITH, DEAN; REV. G. R. BEAMISH, ASSISTANT, KINGSTON, ONT.

SOME OF THE PUBLIC BUILDINGS, KINGSTON, ONT.

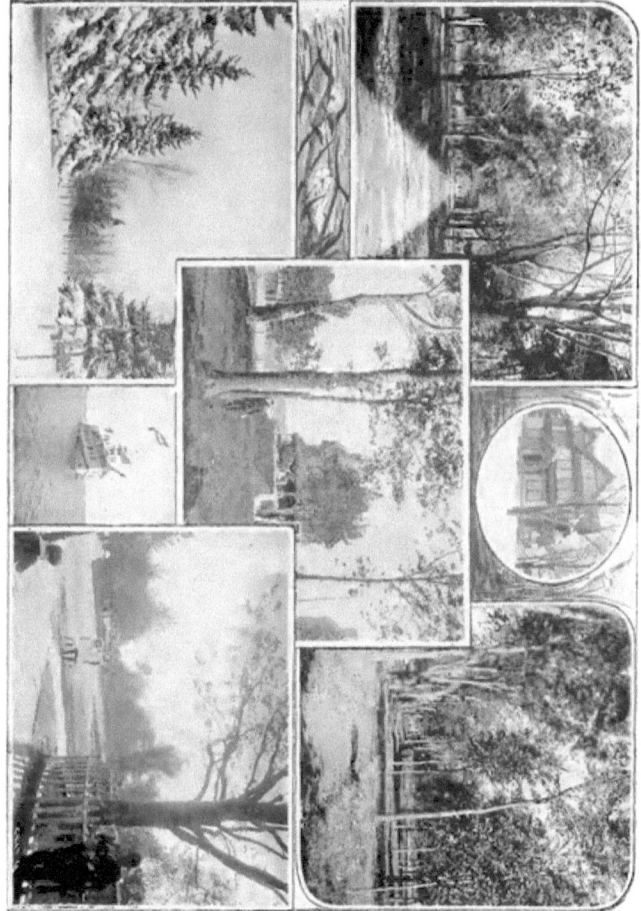

VIEWS IN CITY PARK, KINGSTON.

ST. MARY'S CATHEDRAL, KINGSTON.

RESIDENCE OF DR. LAVELL, WARDEN KINGSTON PENITENTIARY.

CHALMERS' PRESBYTERIAN CHURCH, REV. M. MACGILLIVRAY, KINGSTON, ONT.

COURT HOUSE, KINGSTON, ONT.

LA SALLE—FROM A RARE ENGRAVING.

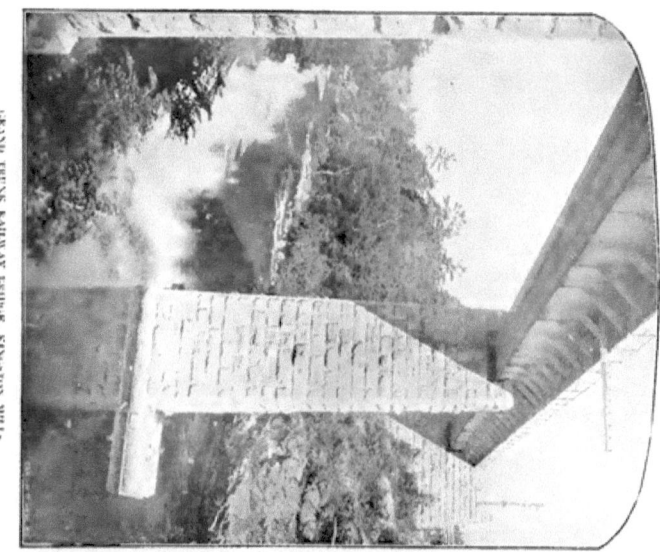

GRAND TRUNK RAILWAY BRIDGE, KINGSTON MILLS.

SYDENHAM ST. METHODIST CHURCH, REV. J. J. STARR, KINGSTON.

OTHER VIEWS IN KINGSTON.

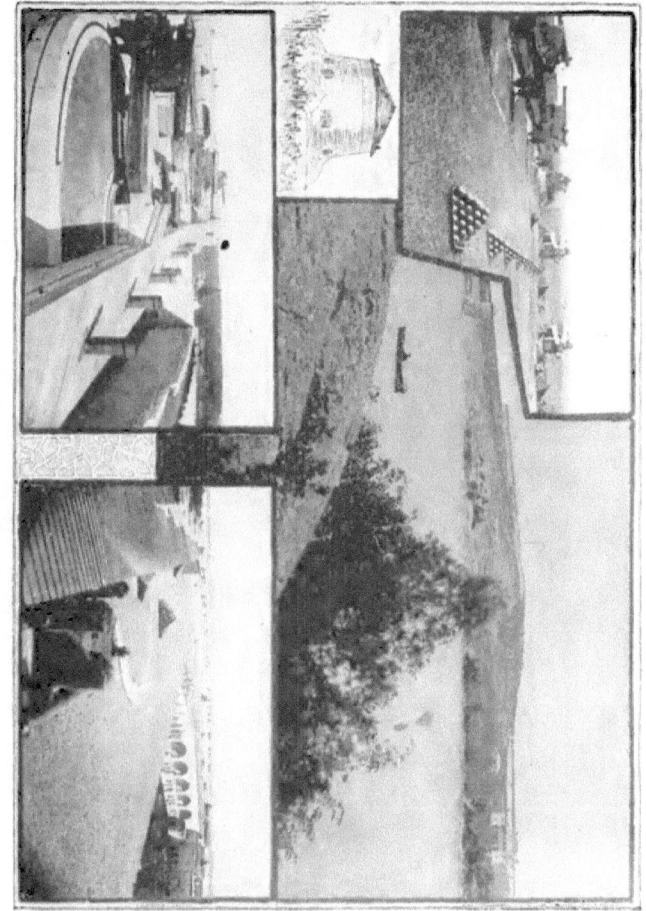

INTERIOR VIEWS IN KINGSTON'S FORT.

MORE ABOUT KINGSTON.

WHEN Major DURHAM prepared his excellent article relating to modern Kingston (see p. 124), we had not then procured the fine illustrations which precede this article, and for which we are indebted to Mr. PENSE, editor of the Whig. We cannot spare the space for a lengthy description of all the individual buildings and views, which appear in this chapter, but we are fortunate in being able to give a somewhat lengthy account of Mr. PENSE'S office-building just completed, and considered the finest in the Provinces — indeed its wonderful adaptation to the wants of a large daily newspaper would make it a fine addition to any city in America.

We copy the following from the Whig's able contemporary, " Pen and Scissors," of Toronto. The writer says:

"At a time when Kingston rested on its garrison and its wealthy men put their money in banks or mortgages, it was said of the city that the penitentiary represented its morality and the newspaper press its enterprise. While this was unduly severe on the fourth estate, which has been fairly representative of the importance of the city, it is nevertheless true that the Kingston papers have made great strides, still it is questionable if any place of 20,000 people, in an isolated locality, can produce journals of equal merit.

"The latest stride has been made by the 'Whig,' which has just entered upon its sixty-second year as lively as in the hey-day of its youth, when it was founded with the distinct purpose of fighting the old Family Compact. Thirty years ago it was taken in hand by its present publisher, Edward J. B. Pense, at a crisis in its history. Opposition had reduced it to almost its last resource, but it was soon built up again to a firm standing and has never since known a difficulty. Under Dr. Barker, its first publisher, it was for thirty-eight years a journal characterized by manly spirit and critical acumen, of which the veteran editor was a master. For the last twenty years as a Liberal paper it has been distinguished as a newspaper in the first place, and secondly, for staunch support of its party, coupled with an independent generous spirit which made it friends on both sides and has led to its uncommon prosperity. The aim of the publisher has been to show that honor and truth can be sustained in a journalistic career, notwithstanding a hundred daily temptations, just as faithfully as in any other private or public career. Therefore, the 'Whig' has retained the respect of all classes.

"The week ending 30th March, 1895, was the first its staff occupied the new building on King street, Kingston, fronting the public square, an ideal location for a newspaper, close to the city hall and all city departments, to the railway stations, leading hotels, post-office, custom house and express offices. Upon the lot, fifty by one hundred, a handsome building has been erected, the materials of the front being Credit Valley stone and red pressed brick.

"The first floor is a semi-basement, affording room for six cylinder presses in a row, besides half a dozen other machines. The power is supplied by electric motor, with gas motor as reserve and auxiliary power. The furnace room is entirely cut off from the press room, as also is a room for the street carriers. The main floor is reached by a hall-way twelve feet wide with English tile for floor and onyx tile dado with embossed border, on the walls.

The entrance and business offices combined are in line with the handsomest in the country. The furniture of the latter is new in its way; the counters (of original design) and desks are of polished oak with cabinets to match. The publisher's room is well-furnished and has oak mantel and fire place of red Tennessee marble and iron fittings with gas log. The partitions, as indeed all the work of the building, are in light woods oiled. The glass, both in windows and partitions, is in the latest style and used without stint, still there is not a dark corner in the building. At the back of the public office is the stock room, with sufficient space for all the stationery that could possibly be required. The rear of that floor is occupied by the job printing department, and its brightness makes it a very pleasant work room. In this department are to be seen not only a very large stock of type, but the latest ideas in wood cabinets and other conveniences.

"The third floor is occupied by the newspaper department chiefly. The three editorial rooms are roomy, bright and attractive, probably the pleasantest offices in the city. The composing room affords conveniences for sixteen men and for three publications, daily,

THE KINGSTON "WHIG'S" NEW HOME.

WYBSVILLE, RESIDENCE OF DR. DOWELL, IN THE CANARIAN CHANNEL.

semi-weekly and weekly. On this floor there is also a large room for bindery, as well as a bindery stock room.

"On the fourth floor there is a lodge hall, 50 x 32, with ante-rooms. Every one of the working departments is independent of the other, all opening into the main hall, so that they are reached with the greatest facility. This facility is increased by modern systems. Warehouse telephones throughout the building, and basket carriers convey copy from front to rear of the building on both floors. The system of heating is direct and indirect, by steam; ventilation is effected by a fan worked by electric motor, which draws the air down to the basement and expels it. The lighting is by combination gas and electricity. An elevator carries type-forms and other heavy materials from floor to floor.

"The interior construction is of iron, the first of the class in Kingston. The ceilings are all of stamped iron, in handsome panels and designs. The floors are double, with hard wood polished for upper surface. The plumbing is exposed, and like the rest of the equipment and plans — up to date. A standpipe furnishes water for fire hose on each flat in the halls.

"The Whig's large circulation (for a local paper) has enabled it to prosper and thus secure comfortable quarters, and few of those who know the industry of the staff, as well as the energy they apply to business, will envy them the distinction and comfort that the building affords. The 'Whig' may not unreasonably claim the handsomest and most complete newspaper building in Canada. Its description may be interesting to other publishers, as showing some new ideas as the result of study and practical test.

"The present publisher began as city reporter at the age of fifteen, and eight years later, after managing the paper for several years, purchased it for $7,500, entirely upon credit, without a dollar of capital or financial backing. His success has been steady and substantial. He saw the necessity of new departures, and the paper underwent a complete change. Its identity in journalism became more marked, its opinions more aggressive, its political influence more potent and direct. As the exponent of Liberal principles it is credited with being largely instrumental in educating the people, so that parties became more evenly balanced than ever before. Mr. Pense, in short, is a born journalist, and he has, in the exercise of a reasonable ambition and by a persistency of purpose, made The Whig one of the best papers in Canada. Its circulation and its usefulness have been increased tenfold; with every department of the business he is familiar. In editorial as well as practical work he is expert. Every advantage he has gained is the legitimate result of energy and ability. In some sense, therefore, he is a representative Canadian in the fourth estate.

"Withal, none has led a more active public life. For five years he served as an alderman, and when elected mayor was the youngest man who had filled the position. He sat for six years on the public school board, and was twice given the chairmanship. He has served thirteen years on the Collegiate Institute Board, and for two years as chairman. He has been president of the Young Men's Liberal Club for seven years; is the president of the Kingston Reform Association and of St. George's Society, being recalled for the third time since 1878; was president of the Kingston Lacrosse Club for many active seasons, as well as of several other clubs; is now president of the Kingston Athletic Association; was master of Minden Masonic Lodge in 1878 and 1879; has been warden of St. James' Church, and lay delegate to the Synod of Ontario for over fifteen years, and has been prominent in church building and in creating parochial improvements; conducted the negotiations which led to the settlement of the medical co-education difficulties, and was president of the Kingston Women's Medical College, the first of the order in Canada; is a life governor of the Kingston General Hospital, and while chairman in 1892 and 1893, promoted several new buildings and general improvements; was president of the Canadian Press Association in 1881-2, when the enjoyable excursion into Manitoba occurred, and Pense Station was named in memory of the visit. He has had a working part in establishing the new dairy and veterinary schools, as chairman of the committee; he is part proprietor and president of Carnovsky Wood Working Co.; is a vice-president of the Kingston Infants' Home; and yet withal he has never canvassed personally for an office, save inevitably for the City Council."

He has appeared to the writer as a man of great earnestness of purpose. Steadily approaching the end he has in view, governed always by the strictest integrity, and entertaining high ideals as to what a newspaper as well as its editor ought to be. These traits have brought him as an active co-worker into all the best growth and life of modern Kingston. No movement there which appeals to the humanitarian, the advancement of the city's interests along the lines of Christian endeavors, or of high public improvement, has failed to command the support of his newspaper and the best personal efforts of himself. Evidently he is worthy of all the success and the high honors bestowed upon him, for he has proven himself a safe and honorable and talented man — entirely devoted to his newspaper, his family, and to Kingston. Such a man should be treasured — we feel quite sure he is appreciated in the city of his nativity and of his best ambitions.

CARLETON VILLA.

AN IDEAL SUMMER HOME.

STANDING on the peninsula-like head of Carleton Island, so named in honor of Sir Guy Carleton,— afterward Lord Dorchester, on what was known in 1778 as "Government Point," is the summer residence of Mr. W. O. WYCKOFF, President of the Wyckoff, Seamans & Benedict Company, of New York, better known, perhaps, from their connection with the manufacture of the celebrated Remington Typewriter. To this residence he has given the very appropriate name of Carleton Villa. Its situation, for many reasons, would be difficult to improve. In its immediate front the broad expanse of the American branch of the St. Lawrence divides into two channels of more than a mile each in width, flowing away on either hand, forming two beautiful bays which afford ample security for the pleasure-craft moored therein, natural harbors whose picturesque shores add much to the beauty of the scene, lying on either side of the old isthmus which connects the old "Government Point" with the mainland of the island itself. To these are given the names, respectively, of "North" and "South" Bays. In front of the villa, the view stretches out on the vast expanse of Lake Ontario. To the left, one gets a pleasant view of the village of Cape Vincent, almost hidden in a forest of maples, and a view of the mainland of the American shore for miles down the river, while on the right stretches away the broad expanse of Wolfe Island, beyond which, in the distance, are plainly seen the spires and towers of the city of Kingston, once the capital of Canada.

Just back of us rises a steep bluff to a height of some sixty feet, on which are the ruins of Fort Haldimand, built by the British in 1778; and which was captured by the Americans in 1812. One hundred and fifteen years ago this was a busy place. It was the most important point above Montreal. It was the great naval and military station of the lake and river. So great was its importance that Fort Frontenac, now Kingston, hitherto the most noted of any point above Montreal, was for years entirely neglected, while Fort Haldimand and the navy yard which it protected was an object of the greatest interest. The history of Carleton Island would form a most interesting bit of old-time reminiscence, if written by itself; but it must be omitted for the present. Aside from the interesting his-

RESIDENCE OF MR. W. O. WYCKOFF, HEAD OF CARLETON ISLAND.

tory it affords, the locality is one to be chosen because of its healthfulness. There is no malaria. The air is pure and bracing even in the midst of the heated term. The death rate of Cape Vincent, according to the statistics found in the report of the State Board of Health, averages only eight per 1,000 per annum. There are no insect pests. Mosquitos are unknown, and to add to the attractiveness of the location, it is in the midst of the finest fishing in the world. Muscalonge, black bass, pike and pickerel abound in every direction. It is an ideal home for a sportsman. Numbering down the river, Carleton Villa is the first of the Thousand Island cottages, and in point of elegance of design and completeness of finish, it is easily first among all the summer palaces on the river. All others, including the celebrated "Castle Rest" and "Greystone Villa," must take second place. In a brief article, as this must necessarily be, it is by no means easy to convey a very clear conception of this elegant structure, and hence an outline must suffice.

The Villa.

Imagine a building 102.7 in length by 73.8 feet wide, and four stories in height, with huge bay windows on each side, giving a cruciform effect to the general plan. Great crypts of cellars extend underneath the entire structure. Here is a gas-room, fitted with one of Terrill's equalizers, which supplies illuminating gas to every part of the house; an extensive laundry with all its appurtenances; a huge refrigerator, with room for a ton or more of ice. Then comes the furnace room, fitted with two heaters furnished by the American Boiler Company; then there is an iron shop, a carpenter shop, a coal room, a canned-goods storeroom, and a vegetable cellar. All this in the basement. In the rear of the next or first floor is the servants' dining-room, connected at this point with the tower by one of the "bridge rooms," of which there are two. Then comes an ample kitchen, 16 x 20 feet in size, completely furnished, as are also the roomy pantries adjoining. These would win the heart of any good housekeeper at sight.

The Main Hall

is elegance itself. It is a room sixty by eighteen, extending to a height of two stories. It is surrounded by a gallery resting on beautiful Doric columns below, while the ceiling is supported by forty Corinthian columns disposed in pairs, connected by a tasteful balustrade. All these columns, as well as the entire woodwork of the house excepting the floors, are of whitewood, elegantly finished and polished. The great fireplace in the hall is a marvel of simplicity and beauty. The tiling is plain, of light cream color, with gilt molding; engaged columns on each side support a heavy entablature, above which the great chimney is enclosed with panel work; the whole, exquisitely finished, as it is, produces a fine effect. On the south side of the hall is the library, or, as it is familiarly called, the "den," a spacious room, elegantly fitted up and supplied with well-filled book cases, writing tables, and in fact every thing that adds to the comfort and convenience of such a room. The library looks out on the broad porch, and commands a delightful view of river and lake.

Across the hall is the spacious dining-room, oval in shape and eighteen by thirty feet in size. A parlor eighteen by eighteen, is also on this side of the hall. There are grates in both parlor and dining-room. Extending across the entire front of the building and on its south side as far as the library, is the grand porch, about twenty feet in width, supported, as is the whole building, on a massive wall of Gouverneur marble. Four heavy granite pillars support the roof in front, while the main entrance is from a double flight of marble steps beneath an archway of the same material, fifteen feet in width, flanked on each side by a marble column of the Corinthian order. The whole front is peculiarly grand and imposing. The lower floors are of oak laid in cement, while all the upper floors are maple, deadened with the same material. The walls of the building above the Gouverneur marble are of Portland cement, and the entire structure is practically fire-proof.

The second floor contains the family rooms, all of which are en suite. From the second floor up, oriel windows grace the corners of the main building, and from every room there is a beautiful view. Each room has that one thing dearest to a woman's heart — an ample closet. Elegant bath-rooms abound everywhere. The furniture throughout corresponds with the finish of the building; birds'-eye maple being predominant. Nothing dark, dull, nor gloomy. The servants' sleeping apartments are on this floor, in the rear of the building. Their rooms are equally pleasant; there is not a forbidding room in the whole villa. The gallery already mentioned is on this floor, and from it and the vestibule every chamber, except the servants' rooms, is reached. The third floor is occupied by the guest chambers, all finished and furnished in the elaborate style which characterizes every other part of the house. In the fourth story are great store-rooms, though its crowning glory is a splendid billiard-room with all its appurtenances, available for either a game of French caroms or of pool. Beginning in rear of the great hall below, a broad oaken staircase winds its way to the floors above by easy stages and roomy landings. Chandeliers and gas fixtures abound everywhere. Once lighted, the building will seem as if illuminated.

Separate from the main building is a tower 111 feet in height, and 16x16 feet at its base. The basement room of the tower contains the pumping engine which sends the water into the great tanks above, whence it reaches every part of the building. Above this is a work-room, and then come the great water-tanks stored with more than two hundred barrels of water. The tower is connected with the main building by two bridges, on each of which is an elegant room familiarly designated as the "bridge-room."

During the entire season brilliant gas-lights will burn in the observatory of the tower every night, and it will not be long ere they will become a well-known signal to the lake navigator. From this observatory at the summit of the tower one of the most delightful views of lake, river and shore is obtainable. The village of Cape Vincent, three miles away, seems to be close at hand, while the spires and towers of Kingston, ten miles away as the crow flies, stand clearly in view. It is, indeed, a charming prospect.

Throughout the entire building the windows are of heavy plate glass, and, indeed, there is nothing lacking in any spot or place that can be in any way conducive to the comfort of either the family or its guests, that has not been thought of and supplied. The term "palatial" has become very common, as applied to everything among the Thousand Islands, from a steam yacht up to a summer residence, but to "Carleton Villa" the term applies with all that it signifies.

Mr. WYCKOFF may well be proud of his summer home, not only because of its quiet and substantial elegance, but because it affords delight to others, in that it appeals to their truest artistic instincts because of its harmony of proportion and of color, demonstrating the fact that strength, solidity and massiveness may be also graceful.

As a setting to the great farm which lies back of it, and the steading near at hand, it harmonizes well. It is not the farm house, of course, but it is a fitting farm residence for an American gentleman of means whose broad domain lies around him, and who delights in passing at least a portion of his time thereon in rural pleasures.

LA SALLE.

IN 1643, at Rouen, in France, was born Robert Cavalier, better known by the designation of La Salle. His name in full was Réné-Robert Cavalier, Sieur de la Salle — the latter affix being the name of an estate near Rouen, belonging to the Cavaliers. His education was liberal, and he early manifested the traits which afterwards made him so illustrious.

FERRY ISLAND, RESIDENCE OF W. F. DOWTY, ESQ., OPPOSITE ALEXANDRIA BAY.

He was a Catholic in faith, and a member of the order of Jesuits. He had an elder brother in Canada, and this fact doubtless shaped his destinies, for in the spring of 1666, in his 23d year, we find him in Canada, where the Seminary of St. Sulpice, a corporation of French priests, had already made a settlement under

ern New York, who had already, notwithstanding their other vast possessions in America, began to feel a desire to possess Canada, and thus extend their sway—as it is seen to day—from Newfoundland to the Northern Pacific and Arctic Oceans. In La Salle they perceived a young man of fine appearance, eager

THE CHEVALIER LA SALLE.

very extensive landed and proprietary grants from the French king. These priests were in great terror continually from the Iroquois Indians, who had lately been severely chastised by Coursell, the Governor of Canada, and their hate was unbounded against the French, stimulated, doubtless, by the English in East-

for just such an engagement as these priests desired to make, which was to procure a man of energy and military capacity who would lead any body of armed men they could raise to defend Montreal, and the settlements thereabouts, from the dreaded Iroquois. They give La Salle a large tract of land nine miles above Montreal, their actual outpost of civilization, which is now known as La Chine, above the great rapids of that name. La Salle entered upon the improvement of his large domain, and began to sell his acres to such as he could induce to join him.

That this young man had come to Canada with a settled purpose in view, now began to be apparent. He began to study the Indian dialects. Hemmed in as he was by the great and apparently interminable forests which surrounded the palisade he had erected for defense against an Indian attack, his fertile mind went beyond his narrow environment, beyond even the great river which roared and fretted upon one side of his domain, and soared westward and southward towards an easier way to China and Japan than had as yet been attained. So imperfect at that time were even educated people's ideas as of the earth's geography, that La Salle did not understand that the countries his enterprising mind would reach were upon the other side of the globe, thousands of miles away. On one occasion he was visited by a band of the Seneca Iroquois, who told him of a river called the Ohio, rising in their country, which flowed southward into the sea. La Salle at once conceived the idea that this great river must needs flow into the Gulf of California, and thus he could find what his soul was on fire to obtain — a western passage to China. His resolution was soon formed. Obtaining, first, the consent of the governors of the seminary to the enterprise he had in hand, he sold to them his lands near La Chine, in order to raise needed money for his enterprise, the whole expense of which was to be borne by himself. He purchased four large canoes, and engaged fourteen men. On the 6th of July, 1670, he set out upon his double expedition for exploration and the purchase of furs from the Indians. We cannot follow his footsteps with the pertinacity of Parkman, whose excellent history is before us, and can, at the best, only generalize the subsequent career of this great explorer.

Thirty-five days after leaving La Chine, they reached Irondequoit Bay, on the south side of Lake Ontario. Here they remained a month or more, and on the 24th of September were at an Indian village only a few miles north of the present city of Hamilton. These Indians proved more friendly than those upon the south shore of the lake, and promised to show La Salle a more direct road to the Ohio. It was here he met Louis Joliet, a young man of about his own age, and also an explorer. He had come from the southwest, the very region La Salle was striving to reach. Paion had sent Joliet to explore the copper mines of Lake Superior. This meeting caused a change of La Salle's plans, for Joliet showed him a map of the region he himself had traversed, including Lake Superior and the Grand River. Step by step La Salle moved westward, spending much time with the Indians, and in 1870-71 he had embarked on Lake Erie, descended the Detroit to Lake Huron, coasted the shores of Lake Michigan, passed the straits of Mackinaw, afterwards reaching a river with a southwestern flow (the Illinois), which took him into the Mississippi, and he may be said to have been the first white man upon that mighty affluent in its upper region. It is claimed by some that he also discovered the Ohio; but if so, he never descended it as far as its junction with the Mississippi. He undoubtedly preceded Joliet, but both La Salle and Frontenac, his ardent supporter, believed, as late as 1672, that the Mississippi flowed directly south into the Gulf of California, and that it thus afforded in reality a direct connecting link to the Pacific Ocean, across which they well knew were China and Japan.

Circumscribed as our limits are, we are unable to follow La Salle much further. Parkman represents him as a man of extraordinary determination, full of virile vigor, with a stalwart frame, and with so enlarged an intelligence that the Jesuit Fathers were afraid of him. They called him visionary, and unstable, and such they have always designated those who were not loyal to their teachings or brought fully under their influence.

In Frontenac, however, the Cavalier de la Salle had an uncompromising and devoted friend. Thus far his dream had been of a short route to China; but when he saw the

THE LEDGES, RESIDENCE OF MRS. SARAH E. K. HUDSON, HALF-A-MILE BELOW ALEXANDRIA BAY.

grand possibilities of the great valley of the Mississippi, with the illimitable prairies which we now see mapped out into Illinois, Wisconsin and Iowa, with the immense forests that line both sides of the river below Cairo, where the Ohio joins the Mississippi, he relinquished as somewhat chimerical, or perhaps postponed for a time, his idea of a short route to China. Then it was that he resolved to leave frozen Canada behind him forever, and lead a French civilization into the great country he had discovered. It was for him to call into light the latent riches of the great West. Frontenac, with whom he kept himself well allied, favored him in all his efforts. They were both great men, and both deserve the highest commendation in history. They were both faithful to their king and France, and their discoveries were of such a character as to make every human being in America their debtor.

In April, 1682, after many adventures and much opposition from the Jesuit Fathers, much struggling with Indian tribes and passing through great dangers and heavy toil, at the mouth of the Mississippi, he had at last the satisfaction of proclaiming " Louis Le Grand," king of all that country we now call Louisiana, and which the English never conquered, but came peaceably into the possession of the United States by friendly negotiation and purchase.

In 1683, somewhat broken in health, he descended to Quebec and sailed for France. Arrived at court, this student and recluse in his youth, but backwoodsman in his matured manhood, had to encounter the risks of a presentation to Royalty and to make headway against the intrigues and jealousies which always surround a king. Louis XIV, however, appreciated him, but the best that could be done for him was to give him a divided command in America, which he was to share with Beaujen, the jealous and incompetent. On July 18th, 1684, he wrote to "his most honored mother" that he was about to sail with four vessels and four hundred men. This voyage to America was principally passed in disputations with Beaujen, and when they landed at St. Domingo, more than half of the people on the vessel were prostrated with fever, among them being La Salle. He soon recovered, however. Proceeding upon their journey they disembarked at Matagorda Bay, thinking it one of the mouths of the Mississippi. Here the Amaible, the ship which contained nearly all their provisions, was wrecked. As we have only imperfectly followed him thus far, and have only but slightly sketched the character of this great man, we must make short work of the matters that led up to his death. While upon a journey of exploration, anxiously desiring to better the condition of the party whom he was trying to lead out of trouble, as Parkman graphically expresses it, "a shot was fired from the grass instantly followed by another, which pierced through his brain, and La Salle dropped dead." Doubtless he was killed by a wretch who had become disobedient and insolent, and whom La Salle had been compelled to rebuke. Thus died at the early age of forty-three, Robert Cavelier de la Salle, one of the greatest men of his age, and one of the most remarkable of the explorers whose names live in history.

His firmness and his courage would have left a more marked impression upon his time, and he would have been better able to completely carry out his grand plans of creating in America a New France, had he been less imperious and haughty in his manner, and less harsh to those under his command, which at last drew upon him an implacable hatred, and caused his death.   J. A. H.

COUNT FRONTENAC

Was perhaps the most remarkable man ever representing the court of France in the new world. From very unpromising beginnings, he rose equal to every emergency that confronted him. His whole career was one of conflict, sometimes petty and personal, sometimes involving the greatest consequences. Under Frontenac occurred the first serious collision between England and France in America, which may be said to have been the opening of a grand scheme of military occupation, designed to hold in check the industrial efforts of the English colonies. All his later energies were directed to making that scheme possible. The contemporaneous history of those times, so ably prepared by Parkman, shows how valiantly New France battled against a fate which her own lack of organizing capacity made inevitable. The drama was a great and significant one, enacted amidst untamed forests, largely by men who had been reared in France, and some of them favorite courtiers of the French king. The wife of Count Frontenac was Anne de la Grange-Trianon. She was born at Versailles, and grew up a favorite companion of Mademoiselle de Montpensier, the favorite granddaughter of Henry IV. She was married to Frontenac in 1648. The happiness of the newly-wedded pair was short. The wife's love soon changed to aversion, which continued even after the birth of her son.

Count Frontenac came of an ancient and noble race, said to have been of Basque origin. At the age of fifteen the young Louis showed a decided passion for the life of a soldier. He served in Holland under the Prince of Orange. He was at the siege of Hesdin. He was at Arras and at Aire, as well as at Callioure and Perpignan. At twenty-three he

COUNT FRONTENAC.

was Colonel of the Normandy regiment, and commanded it in the Italian campaign.

In 1673 he received the appointment of Governor and Lieutenant-General for the king in all New France. Notwithstanding all his ability as a soldier, it was court gossip that he was sent to America to relieve him from the unhappy relations he was known to maintain with his wife, whose temper was outrageous, carrying herself with such a high head that her best friend, Mademoiselle de Montpensier, was obliged to dispense with her ser-

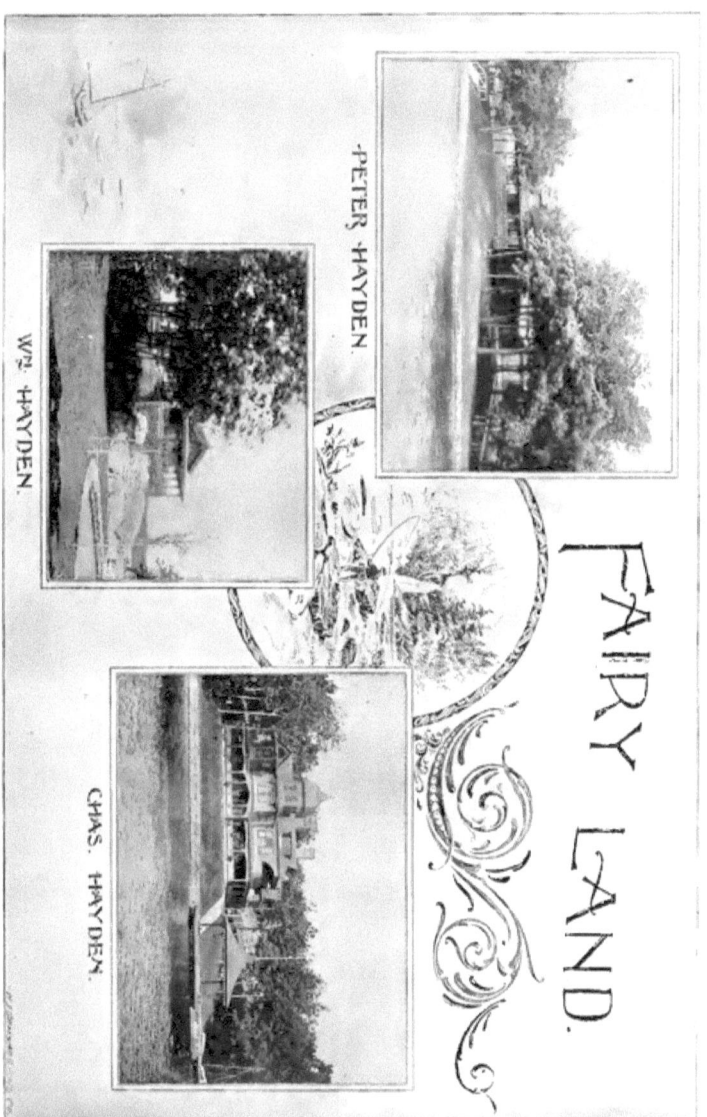

vices as one of her maids of honor. Madam Frontenac declined to accompany her husband across the sea.

Frontenac was fifty-two years of age when he landed at Quebec. Parkman says that "had nature disposed him to melancholy, there was much in his position to awaken it. A man of courts and camps, he was banished to the ends of the earth, among savage hordes and half-reclaimed forests. He exchanged the splendors of St. Jermain and Versailles for a stern gray rock, haunted by somber priests, rugged merchants and traders, blanketed Indians and wild bush-rangers." It was his to see that Quebec should be made the capital of a great empire, which should be tributary to distant France. He took an active interest in all the duties of his new position. It was a strange freak of his that he should administer the oath of allegiance to every person in Quebec. On the 23d of October, 1672, what was known as the "Three Estates of Canada" were convoked with considerable pomp. To these he administered the oath, and then the assembly was dissolved. This very act, is, in brief, a striking illustration of the French colonial rule in Canada. It was a government of excellent intentions, but of the most arbitrary methods. Frontenac unwisely set himself against the prevailing democratic current. The arbitrary government of a land like France, where the Bourbons who "learned nothing and forgot nothing" had held sway so long, was not adapted to a new country where people from all sections had come to accumulate wealth, and (as in all new countries) were possessed of very radical ideas of personal freedom.

The name of Frontenac is one of the most interesting in connection with our own Great River. Courselle, his predecessor in the Governorship of Canada, had begun at what we now call Kingston, a fortification large enough to receive into its stockade such refugees as might desire to fly to a place of comparative safety in the event of any Iroquois invasion, which had then but lately devastated Quebec, and caused the loss of hundreds of innocent lives. Frontenac's attention was soon directed to this beginning of a fort, and he was fortunate in making the acquaintance of a young man who had been in the employ of the French priests at Quebec, and had reached Kingston on his way westward to trade in furs and make the explorations which were yet to make him famous. By direction of Frontenac, La Salle had previously gone to Onondaga, the political center of the Iroquois, and invited the great men of that nation to a council on the Bay of Quinte. Before setting out, La Salle had sent the new Governor a map recommending as a site for the proposed fort the point at the mouth of the Cataraqui, now occupied by the present grand old historic city of Kingston. Frontenac ascended the St. Lawrence quite leisurely, with one hundred and twenty canoes and four hundred men. Parkman says: "Soon they reached the Thousand Islands, and their light flotilla glided in long line among those watery labyrinths, by rocky islets, where perhaps some lonely pine towered like a mast against the sky; by sun-scorched crags, where the brown lichens crisped in the parching glare; by deep dells, shady and cool, rich in rank ferns, and sponges, dark green mosses; by still cove, where the water-lilies lay like snow-flakes on their broad, flat leaves, till at length they neared their goal, and the glistening bosom of Lake Ontario opened on their sight."

This grand flotilla, piloted by Indians in their birch canoes, entered the broad water, passing along the shores so familiar now as the site of Port Henry on one side, and the "West Point of Canada," upon the other, reaching at last the point of land where the artillery barracks now stand, at the western end of Cataraqui bridge. Here they all disembarked, and here were subsequently laid, broad and massive, the foundation of what was subsequently named Fort Frontenac — not so named by the Governor himself, but by the engineer in charge of the work. [See pp. 28, 124.]

It is at this point that La Salle comes prominently into public notice, especially as the friend of Frontenac, whose cause he had espoused at Quebec during the famous quarrels between the new Governor and the priests, whom we describe elsewhere as meddlesome and querulous.

It is a curious historical fact that the old stone fort Frontenac was built by La Salle with his own money, he having been sent to France by Frontenac with letters of the highest recommendation, and the King had made to him a grant of the then fort (a mere stockade) a tract of land of four leagues in front and half a league in depth, including the neighboring islands. In consideration of this rich grant, La Salle completed the fort, armed it at his own expense, and maintained it until near the time of his death, when it reverted to the King, as did all his great tract of land, if we are correctly informed.

Count Frontenac was too independent and able a man to submit quietly to the opposition of the priests, who claimed by both their rights of seigneurage and of their holy office, to interfere with his authority. The most violent of these he arrested and confined in prison, and was in the end sustained by his King, the quarrel having been referred to France for final settlement. Our space, as in the case of La Salle, does not permit us to more than glance at some of the more leading traits and performances of Frontenac, whose abilities were marked and actively developed in the new field he had entered upon. But there was jealousy between Quebec and Montreal, promoted by rival fur dealers and shared in more or less by the meddling priests, whose fingers were in everybody's pie, and the result was that in the end Frontenac was recalled by his king. For seven years he was idling around the French court. But he had powerful friends, and his wife, who seems to have been more affectionate when he was under a cloud than when his word was law and his success apparently assured, became his most powerful intrigante at the French court.

At last the King perceived that he had made a mistake in recalling Frontenac, matters in Canada having gone from bad to worse, until at last his patience was exhausted, and he asked Frontenac to again accept the governorship. The Count was then seventy years of age, but he was tired of inaction and of the petty jealousies of the court of France, and finally accepted the appointment.

We have not space to follow him further in his adventurous career. He returned to Quebec, but Louis XIV had already entered upon his decline from being the first monarch of Europe. William of Orange was coming to the front in England, and before his judicious plans and energetic management, France was soon to be relegated to an inferior position, to lose her possessions in Canada, and, save her ever-faithful Louisiana, to give up, one by one, all she held in America. But the contest was not an uneventful one, though the end was inevitable from the first.

In November, 1698, Frontenac, worn down by many arduous labors, and in his seventy-eighth year, was taken violently ill. On the 28th of that month he died, in full possession of all his faculties.

As will be seen, the portrait of this distinguished man, whose name must forever be inseparably connected with our Great River, was copied from a drawing made as he lay in his coffin. It is undoubtedly a faithful portraiture, and we are indebted for it, as well as for that of La Salle, to Dr. Neilson, Deputy Surgeon-General of Canada, a ripe scholar, a gallant officer, an accomplished historian and archæologist, and a true gentleman. [See his biographical sketch, p. 347.] J. A. H.

VIEW IN THOUSAND ISLAND PARK.

CENTRAL PARK HOTEL,

"THOUSAND ISLANDS," ST. LAWRENCE RIVER. (P. O. ST. LAWRENCE PARK.)

OPEN FROM JUNE 5TH TO SEPTEMBER 15TH.

VIEW IN CENTRAL PARK, SHOWING HOTEL AND BOAT-HOUSES.

THIS fine hotel is one of the most attractive and home-like hotels on the St. Lawrence River. The sanitary arrangements are perfect; the house is supplied with an abundance of water, and there are hot and cold baths on each floor for ladies and gentlemen.

The park has a fine roadway to the main land, giving opportunity for pleasant drives in the country. This house, location, and grounds, are unsurpassed on the St. Lawrence. The hotel is only two and a half stories high, and with the cottages in connection therewith, affords safe accommodations, free from any danger of fire.

It stands in the midst of its own charming grounds, surrounded by a large and beautiful park, shaded by large forest trees of beech, maple, oak, pine and hemlock, and is immediately on the bank of the river.

The hotel and park are situated midway between Thousand Island Park and Alexandria Bay, on the south side of the channel, and are reached by all the local steamers on the river, and is especially noted for its beautiful shady groves, quiet walks, interesting surroundings, and freedom from noisy interruptions.

No resort on the river, or among the matchless Thousand Islands, affords safer boating, better fishing, or more charming views.

WM. B. SOUTHWORTH, Manager.

VIEWS IN CENTRAL PARK.

INDEX.

INDEX

I

	PAGE
Ice Boat, Winter of 1894-95	257
Indian Race, a Legend of	11
Records on the River	11
Independence Rock	192
Ingalls, Hon. L.	185
Introductory and Descriptive	5
Invasion of the Iroquois	41
In the Rift, illust	203
Irving, Washington	76
Island Kate, illust	45
Islander, the steamer, illust	75
Isle of Dogs	271

J

Jayville Mines	112
Jeffreys, Thomas	193
Johnston, Sir William	197
William	137
Kate	137
James	77
Stephen Decatur	19
Judson, Gen. R. W.	144
Judge Spencer's residence, illust	28

K

Kennedy, Geo. N.	78
Keyes, Hon. Perley	150
Gardner	153
Kingston City Hall, illust	125
Electric railway	131
Picturesque	260
Dry-dock	371
Churches	373
Views in	378-380
King, Hon. Preston	160
Kirk, William B	84
Knott, Proctor	74
Kohl, Johan Georg	203

L

La Famine	184
La Rue Island, illust	200
La Salle	127, 208
Lake Bridges	326
Lake of the Isles, illust	105
La Montain, John	164
Lawton, Sylvester	164
Le Ray, Count James D	86
Vincent	89
Lewis, Lyman H	164
Light houses, illust	223
Lincoln's Amnesty to Deserters	364
President Abraham	98
Assassination of	99
"Little Fraud," illust	325
Lo high, illust	204
Lloyd, John	110
Looking East from Smoke Island	195
Long, John	198
Loring, Capt. John	170, 180
Lost Channel, illust	209
Lessing, Benson J	211

M

Manhattan Island and Judge Spencer	26
Martello Towers at Kingston	129
Mason, Charles	88
Massey, Lieut.-Colonel	180
Maple Island and Its Hermit	94
McCormick, Mrs. Nettie F.	21
Medal of Chassanus Co	184
Men I Have Met on the Great River	72
Merick, Hon. E. G., illust	28
M. de la Barre	180
Merick, Fowler & Esselstyn	21
McLennan, Peter B	78
McClellan, Gen George B	144
McKenzie, Wm Lyon	136, 157
McNair, Sir Allan	158
Middleton, Sir Frederick	159
Miller, Hon Warner	77
Mills-Isles of Cromizie	224
Moore, Tom, Boat Song	223
Morris, Robert	80
Gouverneur	80

	PAGE
Morton, Gov. Oliver P	105, 141
Moses, Lucius	84
Mississagna Indians	207
Mudd, Dr.	113
Murray, Mrs Amelia M	191
Musealonge, illust	191, 302

N

Naphtha Launch, Picture of	80
Nelson, Homer A.	78
Neilson, Dr. J. L. H., illust	347

O

Oliver, Col. of the Royal Artillery	31
Oswegatchie, Indian Mission at	44
Under the English	49
Oswego, Capture of	47
O'Bierne, Major	114
Old Fort Frontenac and Modern Kingston	121
O'Neal, William	163
Old North Green House, illust	17
Old Fort Carlton	51
Origin of Printing in Canada	335

P

Pahud, Hon. Joseph	142
Palisades, view in the	325
Park, E. Kirk	77
Parker, Hon. A. X	77
Patterson, Commodore Ned	57
Patriot War	156, 162
Payne, John A.	108, 116, 123
Peel, Sir Robert	157
Peeler, Joel	164
Pense, E. J. B., editor Kingston Whig	309
Pharoux, Pierre	183, 192
Phelps, Russell	164
Pilgrim, the	9
Piazza of Judge Spencer's House	23
Poetic Associations of the Islands	219
Popcorn man, illust	169
Post offices among the islands	346
Pot-holes near the Palisades	147
Ponchot, Captain	197
Pratt, Daniel	78
Calvin E.	78
Prince of Wales	211
Pullman, Geo. M	360
Portrait of	363
Residence of	365
Family of	364

Q

Quinby, John H	85
Queen's University, Kingston, Ont., illust	132
Quinte, Bay of	198

R

Rainy Day at the Islands	15
Rest, Value of	10
Reindeer Vessels, the Fleet of	20
Reeve, Rev. Dr.	79
Real, Count Pierre François	90
Ruins of Fort Haldimand	81

S

Savage, Annette	143
Search light Excursions	285
Sentinels, The, illust	95
Seward, Hon. W H	99, 140, 160
Frederick	99
Seven Isles, illust	7, 11
Seth Green House Rebuilt	17
Settlement of Casterland	191
Scusoma, Gov. Horatio	191
Sherman, Gen. W T	116
Shaw, Col. A. D.	202
Short sketch of	204
Signaling the North King	161
Skinner, Hon. C. R.	77
W J	74

	PAGE
Smith, Judge	78
Jesse	19
Snow in Watertown Streets	323
Sniper, Gen. Gustavus	80
Sons of Liberty	99
Initiation into	40
Sport Island	235
Spincer, Hon. Henry	77
Family	356
Spencer, Hon. Judge, piazza of his house, illust	23
Biographical sketch of	26
Portrait of	27
Residence of	29
Staples, O. G.	367
Staten Island	184
Stone, Colonel, portrait of	307
Story, James	187
St. Lawrence Real Estate Assoc'n	240
Officers of	240
St. Lawrence Club-house	241
Sturgeon Caught in the River	119
Summer Camp, illust	87
Summer Day, A Happy, illust	273
Surrattsville	108
Surratt, John H	108, 109, 113
Mrs	108
Sweet, Sylvanus	164

T

Tabernacle at Thousand Island Park, illust	289
Taylor, Frank H	274
Portrait of	275
Thayendanagea, Indian Chief	53
Thousand Island Park	83
In Autumn	166
Description of	193
Club, Members of	243
Club House	241
Thompson, Jonathan	235
Thomson, Hon. Wm, M	77
Tides in the Lakes	235
Title, Chain of	13
Topographical Surveys	237
Too Big for the Box, illust	129

V

Van Horn	77
Van Valkenburgh	77
Van Vorst	78
Vanderbilt, William H	83, 136
Cornelius	136
Van Rensselaer, Gen	156, 157
Van Slyke, Martin	164
View of Seven Isles, illust	11
View from Judge Spencer's tower, illust	35
Victoria, Queen	191

W

Wagner, Webster	83
Walrath of Oneida	74
Waltons, The Family of	251
War of 1755	170
Webb, H. Walter	132
Seward	135
Weld, Isaac	202
Wells, Butterfield & Co	139
Whittier, the poet	230
Whittlesey Affair	156
Williams, Hon. Pardon C	78
Winslow, Hon. Norris	217
Woolsey, Commodore	194
Woodruff, Jonah	160
Wolf, Chris	87
Wright, Benjamin	192
W. W.	74
Wyderville, Residence of Dr. Howell	99

Y

Yost, Hon. George E	77
Yachting on the St. Lawrence, illust	81

www.ingramcontent.com/pod-product-compliance
Lightning Source LLC
Chambersburg PA
CBHW022146300426
44115CB00006B/375